VOTING AND POLITICAL ATTITUDES
IN DENMARK

Ole Borre
Jørgen Goul Andersen

VOTING AND POLITICAL ATTITUDES IN DENMARK

A Study of the 1994 Election

AARHUS UNIVERSITY PRESS

AARHUS UNIVERSITY PRESS
University of Aarhus
DK-8000 Aarhus C
Fax (+ 45) 8619 8433

73 Lime Walk
Headington, Oxford OX3 7AD
Fax (+ 44) 1865 750 079

Box 511
Oakville, Conn. 06779
Fax (+ 1) 860 945 9468

ANSI/NISO
Z39.48-1992

PREFACE AND ACKNOWLEDGEMENT

Danish political attitudes and voting behaviour have been the topic of many journal articles but no systematic presentation in English. We have felt that there is a need for such a presentation; the field is becoming more comparative and international, less local and national in scope, and Danish political development is becoming of interest to a public that cannot be expected to read the Scandinavian languages.

The authors wish to thank Anne-Grethe Gammelgaard and Helle Jørgensen for their conscientious work in typing and arranging this volume. Professor Jim Sharpe and his wife Pat Sharpe, who were visiting the Aarhus Department at the time the manuscript was being finished, deserve our thanks for their very thorough job cleaning our English. The Danish Social Research Council provided a generous grant covering the interviewing and publishing cost as well as three months leave during which the first critical parts of the manuscript were written.

The authors divided the work such that Ole Borre wrote chapters 1-4, 7, and 10-11, while Jørgen Goul Andersen wrote chapters 5-6, and 8-9; however, we stand jointly responsible for the volume.

Aarhus, March 1997

Ole Borre
Department of Political Science
Aarhus University

Jørgen Goul Andersen
Department of Economics, Politics,
and Public Administration
Aalborg University

CONTENTS

INTRODUCTION

This book contains a study of the Danish 1994 election based on an interview survey of 2,000 voters. As it draws on surveys of previous elections as well, the study deals with Danish political attitudes and their relation to the voting choice during the past ten to twenty years. The Danish election survey programme began in 1971 and by now includes eleven parliamentary elections. The 1994 survey is particularly rich in questions and constitutes an invaluable source of data for anyone interested in the development of the Danish electorate and in Danish politics generally. Furthermore, it includes to a large extent questions that are identical or parallel with those found in surveys of a number of other western countries. Thereby it will be useful for comparative studies of voters in advanced industrial democracies, a type of study that is rapidly developing. In order to facilitate such research we have chosen to publish in English, and to direct attention to previous studies of Danish voting behaviour in English.

The book therefore has a dual purpose. On one hand it describes the political development, seen from the perspective of the voter, of a country which has attracted international attention several times. Denmark presented an early version of protest against taxes and the growth of the welfare state, the issue which split the Danish party system in 1973. At about the same time Denmark joined the European Community in a referendum and quickly became known as a particularly reluctant member of that association. During the 1980s Denmark's position in the NATO organisation was more or less permanently under attack because of the number of reservations ('footnotes') it gave rise to in NATO documents. With respect to economic policy, the bourgeois four-party government during the 1980s followed the neo-liberal line of Thatcher's Britain, the Reagan administration of USA, and Chancellor Kohl's West Germany; but at the same it preserved its welfare society, attempting a policy of integrating rather than excluding the victims of competition from society. Being one of the richest societies in the world, and at the same time a society with a tradition of a high level of public service and of economic equality, Denmark has initiated reforms in labour market and welfare policy strategies which have proved relatively successful. At the same time the Danish public has opted for postmaterial and 'green' policies, although it has not avoided the problems of immigration and the harsh climate of violence of the 1990s. Finally, in 1992 Denmark was noticed for its scepticism towards the Maastricht Treaty moving the EC members towards a European Union; the treaty was narrowly rejected in the summer of 1992 but, after some reservations had been added, accepted a year later.

On one hand, therefore, the peculiar character and development of the Danish electorate come to the fore in our chapters. On the other hand, however, the purpose is to test out various hypotheses about voting behaviour which have been developed over the years in other countries, above all in the United States. Hence we seek to contribute to theory development in various directions. In different chapters we shall therefore present analyses of voting behaviour that respond to contemporary issues in electoral behaviour: For example the issue of declining class voting and the emergence of new classes, the issue of value change and generational change, and of new versus old politics, and the issue of the effect of government performance and leadership on the vote.

Our theoretical approach may be described as an orientation towards policy positions and policy distances as variables explaining the partisan choice. We show that Danish voters indeed have opinions corresponding to policy positions in a number of policy areas, and that these positions are consistently related to their evaluations and choice of parties and alternative governments. Their policy orientations may in part be traced backward to values, interest, and social experiences, but in part they should also be regarded as responses to policies pursued by present and past governments. Furthermore, we show that policy positions, along with other political beliefs, typically are arranged in the individual voter's mind along a few dimensions that reflect ideological structures or schemas, thereby predisposing them to accept or reject specific policy proposals and political symbols coming from the parties. Such an approach may be described as semi-rational or value-rational as distinguished from, on one side, formal public choice theories prescribing what the voter should do, and, on the other hand, 'discourse theory' and similar post-modern conceptualisations which tend towards a top-down view of voting behaviour as determined by a struggle among elites. On several occasions the Danish electorate has turned out to be a breeding ground for opinions and actions running counter to the political establishment, yet containing a logic of their own, and we believe our approach to be the more fruitful in accounting for this type of behaviour.

The book is divided into twelve chapters following this introduction. Chapter 1 traces the origin and history of the Danish party system and then discusses two types of secular change in it. First, the fragmentation that occurred in the 1973 election, doubling the number of parties represented in the Danish *Folketing* from five to ten, did not permanently jeopardise the dominance of the large parties; in contrast to most other western nations, the balance of support between large and small parties has gradually shifted in favour of the oldest and largest parties over the last twenty years. This fact is related to a comparatively high and sustained level of party identification. Second, the balance between socialist and non-socialist parties has been highly constant ever since 1929, giving the socialist side between

45 and 50 per cent of the vote. Nonetheless, underlying cyclical tendencies in left-right attitudes can be discerned, and over the past four elections (1987-94) a rightward drift of attitudes is noticeable.

The following three chapters discuss the policy voting model that represents our approach to the partisan choice. Chapter 2 starts out by analysing the cleavage dimensions that are emerging in the Danish electorate. It is suggested that a new set of issues, less economic in kind, are supplementing the older class issues and changing the character of the left/right division. The 'new politics' issues focus on human relations and the quality of life in the family, in work organisations, and in the society at large. The 'new left' was the first to emerge during the 1970s, and it has been opposed by a mobilisation of a 'new right' during the 1980s. Based on education rather than traditional social class, the new political dimension is gradually changing the voter base of the parties and generating a potential for unanticipated voter flows.

In chapter 3 we therefore introduce a more formal model of issue voting based on the concepts of issue position and policy distance. Issue voting along the economic 'old politics' cleavage probably culminated in the mid-1980s; prior surveys of the Danish electorate are less complete than the 1994 survey for the purpose of studying issue voting. However, based on a new and detailed set of questions on where the parties are perceived to stand on a number of issues, we find a distinct tendency to value and select parties that represent the voter's position. The voter chooses either the 'nearest' party or one with a somewhat 'clearer' stand than the voter. Though the economic issues still dominate the political scene, the impact of new issues such as immigration and the environment upon the vote is noticeable.

Issue positions tend to express political goals rather than past performance on these goals. In chapter 4 we therefore supplement the model of chapters 2-3 by a study, across a variety of policy areas, of the perceived differences between social democratic and bourgeois government; this should be especially close to the electorate since a change from the latter to the former took place in the middle of the election period 1990-1994. We find that indeed performance ratings and ratings of the leaders of the two governments exert a net influence on the vote. As a premise for this conclusion we find the public image of the two governments to differ: The bourgeois government is associated with success in economic policies whereas the social-democratic government is credited with attending to social justice.

Chapters 5-6 deal with the social bases of party support. Denmark has taken part in the general tendency towards declining class voting, but the picture needs to be shaded in several respects. In the first place the numerical change from the old to the new middle class accounts for most of the partisan change, as the old middle class is more solidly bourgeois than ever. Second, the decline of socialist voting among workers is not a result of their 'embourgeoisement' since it applies at least as much to the low-paid workers as to the well-paid. Third, new class divisions, especially between the public and private employees, have replaced more traditional class cleavages. And fourth, the issues of new politics are generating new partisan cleavages in the working class as well as among the salaried employees.

Thus it is only an apparent irony that the classes of industrial society have been eroded whereas the parties that represented these classes have been strengthened. Chapter 6 traces this development by studying the generational and gender differences in voting. A leftist surge characterised the generations who entered the electorate between the 1968 and 1984 elections. This period largely coincides with the expansion of public employment and mass education and the entry of women into the labour market. During the last ten years this development has been halted and a more differentiated 'post-industrial' society is emerging in which professional organisations are beginning to span the cleavage between the public and private sectors.

Chapters 7-10 are less concerned than the foregoing chapters with accounting for the partisan choice as a dependent variable. Instead they embark on a study of public attitudes towards policies in some critical areas. Chapter 7 outlines the structure in these policy attitudes, using respondents' suggestions of which areas should be public responsibility, and which items should be raised or cut on the public budgets. In the case of public spending, a three-way structure emerges in which the respondents divide into a majority advocating welfare expenditures ('welfare-seekers'), a group advocating expenditures on culture and environment ('beauty-seekers'), and a minority advocating more to be spent on police and military forces ('order-seekers').

Chapter 8 is a study of Danish attitudes to the welfare state. It shows that the mass support for the Danish welfare system is largely undiminished in spite of the trend towards market liberalism that has characterised the recent decade. Danish welfare arrangements, unlike those in many other countries, contribute to integrating its clients into society rather than alienating them. However, the support for these programmes varies according to how the client groups are perceived to deserve such integration and to have other options.

Chapter 9 compares a number of different strategies against unemployment with respect to their popular appeal. A schism is shown to exist between on the one side the economists and the political establishment, and on the other side the opinion and reasoning of the mass electorate. The public scepticism about expert solutions seems well founded, however, since these solutions have not been successful through the two decades of permanent mass unemployment.

Chapter 10 brings to the fore another area of widespread scepticism, namely, the well-known Euro-scepticism of the Danish electorate. While a minority of Danes are in favour of extending European economic and military cooperation, and another minority are opposed to the very idea of European integration, the majority make their accept of the EU contingent upon the problems of mass unemployment and environmental pollution being moved to the top of the EU agenda. Support for (Danish membership of) the EU depends primarily on the proximity of the respondent to what appears to be the most likely EU policy; thus the policy distance model of chapter 3 applies also here. Secondarily, a 'European identity';counts positively whereas the respondent's self-image of being politically powerless counts negatively in generating a supportive attitude.

As we have confined the present volume to the form of an election study, it will be outside its scope to comment in depth on what might be termed the Danish political culture. Perhaps that subject is best covered by reference to other western nations in comparative studies such as the Beliefs in Government series[1] and the Scandinavian Citizenship study.[2] However, in view of the central role allotted to the concept of policy space throughout most of the volume, it will be plausible to conclude the analysis by exploring the wider effects of policy distance on support for the political system at large. This is done in chapter 11. There we show that the feeling of trust in government is to a considerable degree dependent on the voter's agreement with official Danish government policy. This is the case for a number of issues but particularly for the immigration issue and the EU issue: Those who want a stricter immigration policy and those who opt against Danish membership of the EU are much more distrustful than other respondents.

Together, chapters 8 to 11 sound a rising note of caution. Economically, Denmark has largely overcome the storms of the 1970s and 1980s. Though marred by a high level of unemployment and uneasiness about the future of the welfare system, the Danish voters are generally prepared to share their wealth fairly evenly so as to avoid deep rifts in their society. The party system exhibits stability with the large parties clearly in the dominating role, something that few would have predicted twenty years ago. The ordinary voters appear to be in a more powerful position than in many other western countries, and continuously employ their power to give policy leads to the politicians. Nonetheless the common voter is very limited in his/her views of the international world, in understanding the way it is moving and the problems it raises. Shocks coming from the outside — in the form of organised crime, a war in Yugoslavia, a wave of immigration from the Levant, a decision in NATO, or an unpopular directive from the EU Commission — tend

---

1. Published in five volumes by Oxford University Press, 1995.
2. Goul Andersen and Hoff, forthcoming 1997.

to upset the Danish bottom-up democracy and cause it to collide with experts, bureaucrats, and the political elite.

Chapter 12 collects the various threads in our analyses concerning the causes of the 1994 election, and from this we may draw some implications for voting research. The main message of our volume is that Danish voting behaviour can be understood as plausible (if not always wise) responses to actual and proposed policies, to outcomes and political events. Hence, we find empirical support for a policy voting model which is open to the input from the electorate — that is, a model which does not rely on rigidly rational assumptions in regard to the utility associated with different policies or parties. As we shall see in several of the following chapters, such a conceptual model has an additional advantage. It permits a fairly simple analytic approach in which the importance of various issues for the vote can be weighted against one another, or in which the supporters of a particular policy can be singled out for analysis. Bearing in mind that our study is a first exploration of comprehensive survey material, we have been more concerned with demonstrating some interesting relationships than with determining the precise forms of these relationships; actually we have applied linear algebra in some cases that would not satisfy a statistician. As the 1994 data base is available to other researchers, they are welcome to apply more refined methods and thereby improve on our findings.

FROM THE SEVENTIES TO THE NINETIES:
OPINION CHANGE AND PARTISAN CHANGE

1.1. Continuity and Change in the Danish Party System

The classical Danish party system took shape in the last decades of the nineteenth century and the early decades of the twentieth. Between 1870 and 1900 it featured a contest for power between the Conservative party, or Right (*Højre*), representing the urban middle class and the Liberal party, or Left (*Venstre*), representing the farmers. Although the Liberals gradually attained a large majority in the lower house, favoured by the system of single member constituencies, the governments were recruited from the Conservatives until 1901, the year in which lower house parliamentarism became the accepted norm.

However, at that time the two party system was already being eroded by the Social Democratic party which gained its first parliamentary seats in 1884 and by 1903 surpassed the Conservative party in voting strength (Elklit 1984, p. 35). By the turn of the century when the first wave of industrialisation was over, the three main social classes of peasants, bourgeoisie and workers had divided the parliament among them almost in the fashion of the diet of an estate society. But politically the middle position of the Liberal party was unstable. Between 1892 and 1909 its right wing formed a separate group, and in 1905 its left wing broke away and formed the Radical Liberal party. With a voter base among intellectuals as well as rural smallholders, the new party already from its first election in 1906 obtained a firm standing in the lower house.

It is to be observed that the formation of the classical Danish four party system took place before the change to proportional representation, initiated with constitutional changes in 1915 that also extended the franchise to new groups, notably women. Thus it seems that proportional representation was a result, rather than a cause, of interests and coalitions in a parliament which under-represented some parties, especially the Conservatives and the Social Democrats (Elklit 1984, p. 36).

Once established, the party system has shown a remarkable capacity for recovering from various crises and challenges, the most serious of which occurred in 1973. The three parties which were represented in the lower house by 1900 are also today the three largest parties, attracting 73 per cent of the voters between them in the 1994 election. In that sense Denmark is a good example of the Rokkan/Lipset thesis about the freezing of the party systems in the early phase of democracy in a form which reflects the class system of that time (Lipset and Rokkan 1967). Furthermore, the four parties composing the party system by 1905 managed to hold a monopoly of supplying the government personnel until 1957, and a monopoly on the position of prime ministers which persists even today. Most often the choice has been one between a Liberal candidate with Conservative support, and a Social Democratic candidate with Radical Liberal support. The Social Democrats first acquired the prime ministership in 1924, when they had grown to become the largest party in the *Folketing*, a position they have had ever since.

Though a number of other parties have had seats in the Danish parliament from time to time, the four party system basically lasted until the Socialist People's party was added as a permanent fifth party in the 1960 election. When in 1966 it doubled its representation in the *Folketing*, this triggered a two-block situation in which the Social Democrats were supported by the Socialist People's party whereas the Radical Liberals made common cause with the Liberals and Conservatives. This was the situation when the party system broke wide open in the December 1973 election (Borre 1974). That election doubled the number of parties in the *Folketing* from five to ten and reduced the combined voting support for the two-block parties from 93 to 64 per cent. Its character of a protest election is reflected in the fact that the left-right orientation of the party system was supplemented by a crosscutting trust-distrust dimension on which the voters of the new anti-tax Progress party scored in the distrust direction (Rusk and Borre 1974; Glans 1984).

The partisan distribution of the vote at the general elections from 1971 onward is reported in Table 1.1. It is evident from the table that the party system which emerged in the 1973 election is still basically in existence twenty years later. To the left of the Social Democratic party a left wing, which has the Socialist People's party as its largest member, obtains between 10 and 20 per cent of the aggregated vote. The Social Democratic party itself is normally expected to get between 29 and 38 per cent; but since the Social Democratic party and the left wing tend to vary against one another, the total socialist vote has varied within the narrow interval between 45 and 50 per cent (except in 1973-75).

Between the Social Democratic party on the left and the Conservative and Liberal parties on the right, three parties constitute the centre in Danish politics: the Radical Liberals, Centre Democrats, and Christian People's party. Together with a fourth centre party, the Single-Tax party, they won 18 per cent of the vote in 1971 and 26 per cent in 1973, but the share of the centrist vote has declined over the years to 9 per cent in the 1994 election, when the Christian People's party fell below the two per cent threshold for parliamentary representation.

	1971	1973	1975	1977	1979	1981	1984	1987	1988	1990	1994
Soc.Peop.party	9.1	6.0	5.0	3.9	5.9	11.3	11.5	14.6	13.0	8.3	7.3
Other left-wing	3.0	5.1	6.3	6.4	6.0	4.0	3.5	5.8	4.7	4.4	3.1
Total left-wing	*12.1*	*11.1*	*11.3*	*10.3*	*11.9*	*15.3*	*15.0*	*20.4*	*17.7*	*12.7*	*10.4*
Soc.Dem.	37.3	25.6	29.9	37.0	38.3	32.9	31.6	29.3	29.8	37.4	34.6
Total Soc.	*49.4*	*36.7*	*41.2*	*47.3*	*50.2*	*48.2*	*46.6*	*49.7*	*47.5*	*50.1*	*45.0*
Rad.Lib.	14.4	11.2	7.1	3.6	5.4	5.1	5.5	6.2	5.6	3.5	4.6
Cen.Dem.	-	7.8	2.2	6.4	3.2	8.3	4.6	4.8	4.7	5.1	2.8
Chr.Peop.	2.0	4.0	5.3	3.4	2.6	2.3	2.7	2.4	2.0	2.3	1.8
Single-Tax	1.7	2.9	1.8	3.3	2.6	1.4	1.5	.5	-	-	-
Total Centre	*18.1*	*25.9*	*16.4*	*16.7*	*13.8*	*17.1*	*14.3*	*13.9*	*12.3*	*10.9*	*9.2*
Conservative	16.7	9.2	5.5	8.5	12.5	14.5	23.4	20.8	19.3	16.0	15.0
Liberal	15.6	12.3	23.3	12.0	12.5	11.3	12.1	10.5	11.8	15.8	23.3
Progress	-	15.9	13.6	14.6	11.0	8.9	3.6	4.8	9.0	6.4	6.4
Total Right	*32.3*	*37.4*	*42.4*	*35.1*	*36.0*	*34.7*	*39.1*	*36.1*	*40.2*	*38.2*	*44.7*
Other Nonsoc.	*.2*	*-*	*-*	*.9*	*-*	*-*	*-*	*.3*	*-*	*.8*	*1.0*
Total	*100*	*100*	*100*	*100*	*100*	*100*	*100*	*100*	*100*	*100*	*100*
Voting t/o	87.2	88.7	88.2	88.7	85.6	83.3	88.4	86.7	85.7	82.2	83.4

Note: Of the small parties, Common Course (obtaining 2.2 per cent in 1987, 1.9 per cent in 1988, and 1.8 per cent in 1990) and the Greens (obtaining 1.3 per cent in 1987, 1.4 per cent in 1988 and .9 per cent in 1990) are included in the left-wing vote.

Of the two large bourgeois parties, the Conservative party was in crisis in the mid-1970s but then showed a remarkable capacity for recovering up to the mid-1980s. Throughout the next four years it has declined somewhat while the Liberal party, normally scoring between 10 and 12 per cent in parliamentary elections, has grown so as to take its place as the leading bourgeois party. Together, the two parties obtained 38 per cent of the vote in the 1994 election, outpolling the Social Democrats. However, as we shall see below, it is still the centre parties which determine the government.

On the right wing, the Progress party which received considerable support as a tax protest party in the 1970s has received less than 10 per cent of the votes since 1981. But thriving on anti-immigration sentiments, it has managed to survive in spite of extreme internal strife leading to the exclusion (1990) of Mogens Glistrup who founded the party. In 1995, his successor as party leader, Pia Kjærsgaard, also left the party alongside with 3 other MP's to form a party of her own, 'The Danish People's party'. At the time of writing (1996), both parties seem to survive, according to opinion polls (Goul Andersen & Bjørklund 1990, 1997).

Table 1.2. Danish governments and prime ministers 1971-97

1971-1973	Social Democratic (Anker Jørgensen)
1973-1975	Liberal (Poul Hartling)
1975-1978	Social Democratic (Anker Jørgensen)
1978-1979	Social Democratic (Anker Jørgensen), Liberal
1979-1982	Social Democratic (Anker Jørgensen)
1982-1988	Conservative (Poul Schlüter), Liberal, Centre Democratic, and Christian People's
1988-1990	Conservative (Poul Schlüter), Liberal, Radical Liberal
1990-1993	Conservative (Poul Schlüter), Liberal
1993-1994	Social Democrats (Poul Nyrup Rasmussen), Radical Liberal, Centre Democratic, and Christian People's
1994-96	Social Democratic (Poul Nyrup Rasmussen), Radical Liberal, and Centre Democratic
1997-?	Social Democratic (Poul Nyrup Rasmussen), Radical Liberal

Table 1.2 indicates the composition of the governments. The recovery of the Social Democratic party had begun already in the January 1975 election which followed upon a brief interlude of Liberal minority government (Borre 1975). From 1975 to 1982 the Social Democratic party under Anker Jørgensen formed single-party minority governments, except that the Liberals took part in the government in one year (1978-1979). Although there was a parliamentary majority to the right of the Social Democrats all the time, the bourgeois parties were unable to exploit it to form a government. In the September 1979 election the Social Democratic vote returned to the level it had before the 1973 cataclysm.

But the triumph was brief. The Danish economy had been riven with growing problems in the balance of trade and in deficits on the public budgets. In that fashion the government had hoped to overcome the unemployment problem which arose in 1974 after the first oil crisis. The second oil crisis in 1979 ruined these hopes permanently and made popular the idea that Denmark was walking toward the edge of an abyss. In the 1981 election the Social Democrats went back from 38.3 to 32.9 per cent while the opposition grew on both sides, the left wing increasing from 11.9 to 15.3 per cent. In August 1982 the government resigned and gave way for a four party government of bourgeois parties headed by the Conservative Poul Schlüter.

The new government, consisting of members of the Conservative, Liberal, Centre Democratic and Christian People's parties, won the January 1984 election easily, and its program of privatisation and market liberalism gained wide credence. The economic tide was upward during 1983-1985, but the government's efforts to stop wage increases in the Spring of 1985 resulted in strikes and a 'red' majority in the polls. By 1986 the economic reins had to be tightened, and in the September 1987 election both the government and the Social Democrats lost while especially the left wing gained strength, coming to over 20 per cent of the vote. The so-called

Voting and Political Attitudes in Denmark

bourgeois 'four-clover government' continued another eight months until May 1988. At that time, a sudden election caused by a foreign policy question (whether ships carrying nuclear rockets could be admitted to Danish territorial waters) meant that the Radical Liberals forced their way into the government, while the members of its two minor parties, the Centre Democrats and the Christian People's parties, were dismissed.

However, the struggle over the budget including the proposed cuts in the welfare state continued to be in the centre of Danish politics. In December 1990 the issue of tax relief led to an election in which the Liberal party represented the forces attacking the welfare state whereas the Social Democrats stood as its main defender. The left wing was handicapped *inter alia* by the fall of socialist regimes in east Europe, and the outcome was a Social Democratic victory which was not large enough to prevent a continuation of bourgeois government, now consisting of Conservatives and Liberals only. When at last Mr Schlüter resigned in January 1993 after more than ten years as prime minister, the cause was an attempt to mislead the *Folketing* as to the treatment of Tamil scandal.

The new government which, like the bourgeois so-called 'four-clover government', came to power between two elections, consisted of Social Democrats together with Radical Liberals, Centre Democrats, and members of the Christian People's party. Thus the three small centre parties had shifted their loyalty from a government right-of-centre to one left-of-centre. The reason was in part their preference for the new Social Democratic leader Poul Nyrup Rasmussen over his predecessor Svend Auken, in part the opportunity for a change caused by the Tamil scandal, and in part their resistance to the ideological liberalism fomented by the Liberal party. What may also have been considered is that the European Union, rejected by the Danish referendum in June 1992, would stand a better chance of getting accepted by Social Democratic voters under a prime minster of their own; in any case the treaty, with its presumed concessions to Danish views, was carried in a new referendum in May 1993.

The Nyrup Rasmussen government had less than two years to go before the ordinary election term would expire by December 1994. It chose to stake its popularity on an attempt to 'crack' the rising curve of unemployment by means of a combination of fiscal and monetary strategies including higher public consumption and investment, abolition of credit restrictions, as well as job leave arrangements. Assisted by a sizeable drop in the interest rate, these efforts succeeded in generating economic growth; consumer expectations improved in the course of 1994, even though the unemployment rate remained high. But even though the voters' expectations as to unemployment were significantly changed (see chapter 9), the government was not rewarded in the election on September 21, 1994. As can be gathered from Table

1.1, the four government parties went back from 48.3 per cent to 43.8 per cent of the votes cast. One of its parties, the Christian People's party, fell below the two per cent threshold for representation, but the remaining three parties were able to continue in government because they could count on support in parliament from two left wing parties, the Socialist People's party and the Unitary List composed of several small leftist groups.

In the remainder of chapter 1 we look at the development from 1973 onward, and particularly from 1979. The parties composing the Danish party system can be classified along two dimensions: size and left-right position. Once a party has proved viable, its location on these dimensions does not seem to vary much. It may enjoy success in one or a few consecutive elections, usually at the cost of neighbouring parties, but order is restored in the longer run. It may move toward the left, right, or centre, but without losing sight of its basic orientation or class base. Yet we shall point to some trends in the support for these groups of parties over the past twenty years. We shall seek to relate these changes to general voter attitudes; then, in chapters 2 and 3, we turn to the issues of the last elections.

1.2. The Recovery of the Big Parties

In most European party systems the period from 1970 onward is characterised by a decline of the large parties. In Denmark this decline came very early and dramatically in the 1973 landslide election. But the general trend since then has been in favour of the old and large parties. Looking at the support for the three old class parties, the Social Democratic, Liberal, and Conservative in Table 1.1, we see that the three parties between them went back from 69.6 per cent of the vote in 1971 to 47.1 per cent in 1973. That seemed to herald an end to the classical party system of the nineteenth century. However, by continuing over the next elections in Table 1.1 one finds that by 1994 the three parties had more than made up for their losses, obtaining 72.9 per cent of the vote between them. Figure 1.1 portrays this development.

In spite of occasional setbacks in 1981 and 1987 the three large parties have steadily gained ground, squeezing the minor parties. In 1973 the Danish party system looked very fragmented. Twenty years later, fragmentation is not its main feature; but we shall postpone until later chapters our judgment as to how it is better described.

The increased concentration of the vote around the large parties since the inception of the new multiparty system in 1973 may be hypothesised to go hand in hand with other long-run changes in the electorate, above all the level of party identification and the forming of habits for vote decisions.

Figure 1.1. Combined voting strength of the three large parties (Social Democrats, Conservatives, and Liberals), 1971-94, per cent

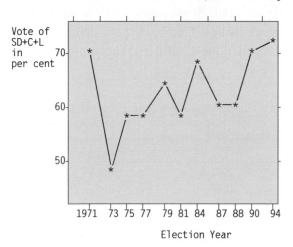

In Denmark the number of party identifiers declined from 55 per cent in 1971 to 50 per cent in 1973, a rather modest decline compared with the dramatic drop in the vote for the old parties; however, judging from the high party membership figures of the 1960s, party identification may well have been on the decline already by 1971. Since 1973 the number of party identifiers has fluctuated around the fifty per cent mark. In contrast to Sweden, where it has declined in a linear fashion since the late 1960s until its present level below 50 per cent, and Norway, where it culminated around 1980 and then began to decline toward 60 per cent, party identification in Denmark shows very modest changes (Goul Andersen and Hoff 1997; Holmberg 1992, p. 24).

Thus it is not possible to account for the recovery of the three large and old parties by means of a rising level of party identification.

However, if we look at the *distribution* of party identifiers over the parties, a different hypothesis may be set forth, namely that the large parties have had the upper hand all the time, even during the turmoil of the nineteen-seventies. It follows from the theory of party identification that those parties which, at a given point in time, have a high proportion of party identifiers, enjoy a competitive advantage over parties whose voters are chiefly non-identifiers. The reason is that party identifiers are more regular voters, less likely to defect to other parties, and more active in promoting and defending the party's ideas in the electorate, than are non-identifying voters of the party. Thus we explain the relative success of the old and large parties in the new party system by their higher proportion of party identifiers.

This evidently does not make them immune against shocks such as the 1973 election; but it does enable them to recover from these shocks.

This explanation presupposes that a higher proportion of party identifiers than non-identifiers vote for the large parties. That is, the non-identifiers tend to choose more evenly among the parties than the identifiers. This is confirmed by the data in Table 1.3.

Table 1.3. Per cent voting for the three large parties among party identifiers and non-identifiers

	1979		1990		1994	
Identify with a party	70	(799)	76	(485)	81	(927)
Don't know, in doubt	65	(84)	72	(67)	74	(70)
Do not identify	53	(517)	59	(258)	64	(773)

Note: Party identification was measured by the question, "Many consider themselves adherents of a particular party. There are also many who don't feel themselves to be adherents of any party. Do you consider yourself as for example a Social Democrat, a Conservative, a Liberal, a People's Socialist or something else, or don't you feel an adherence to any party?" Entries are per cent voting either Social Democratic, Liberal, or Conservative (the remaining voting for other parties).
Figures in parentheses indicate no. of respondents (=100 per cent).

The table breaks down the 1979, 1990 and 1994 samples into party identifiers and non-identifiers with a small group of doubtful in between. It then shows the per cent in each group who voted for one of the three largest parties: the Social Democratic, Liberal, or Conservative party.

It is evident that in all three samples the three large parties obtained a higher proportion of the vote among the identifiers than among the non-identifiers. The difference is seventeen percentage points in all three elections. Therefore, other things being equal the large parties benefit from a tendency to identify with parties generally. Small parties have a better chance in an electorate with loose partisan ties. Of course, small parties with a very narrow base of recruitment in for example an ethnic or regional minority should be excepted from this hypothesis; however, such parties do not exist in the Danish party system with the possible exception of the Christian People's party, which recruits almost exclusively from among the active religious minority.

Table 1.3, furthermore, shows that the three large parties have gained voters both among the identifiers and the non-identifiers between 1979 and 1994: from 70 to 81 per cent among the identifiers, and from 53 to 64 per cent among the non-identifiers. We may attribute this long-term development to the importance of maintaining a resource base of party identifiers.

This reasoning seems inconsistent with the 'dealignment' hypothesis (Dalton, Flanagan and Beck 1984) which states, among other things, that long-term forces are being replaced by short-term forces, and that election outcomes are increasingly determined by media events during the campaign. It has often been claimed that the Danish style of election campaigning, which allots even time on tv and radio to large and small parties (cf. Siune, Svensson and Tonsgaard 1992, p. 158), favours the small parties over the large ones. The tendency may be particularly strong when the campaign is heated and a high proportion of the electorate are stimulated to vote; the mechanism is similar to what Campbell (1960) termed a 'surge election'. In the Danish parliamentary elections there seems to be a long-term decline in voting turnout since the 1970s (Goul Andersen and Hoff 1997); even so, it has remained between 82 and 89 per cent since the 1960s, and the elections may therefore be described as high-stimulus elections. These features of the Danish campaigns should work against the tendency of the old and large parties to recover.

However, if the election campaigns have become steadily more predictable during the new party system, this will attenuate the advantage of the small and new parties. Consequently we need to study how the importance of the election campaign for the vote has developed over time. The most obvious indicator of the effect of the campaign upon the vote is the proportion who report that they made their voting decision during the election campaign. In Figure 1.2 we plot the development of that indicator.

Figure 1.2. Per cent who decided on a party during the election campaign

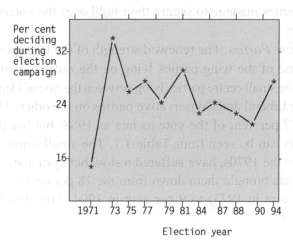

Per cent deciding during election campaign

Election year

We observe in these data that the proportion who decide during the three weeks of campaigning that is typical of Danish general elections, has not risen but rather fallen slightly over the years since 1973 — even though it has never returned to the low point of 14 per cent that characterised 1971, the last election under the old system. In conclusion we can say that election campaigns have not become more decisive, contrary to popular beliefs. Therefore they have not militated against the recovery of the old and large parties. Again, this stands in sharp contrast to Norway and Sweden (see Goul Andersen and Hoff 1997, chapter 5).

In conjunction with this result we see in Table 1.4 that those who make their decision before the campaign overwhelmingly vote for the large parties (74 per cent in 1990, 78 per cent in 1994) whereas those who decide in the course of the campaign divide more evenly between the large and small parties.

Table 1.4. Per cent voting for the three large parties by time of vote decision

	1979		1990		1994	
Decided before campaign	72	(1243)	74	(633)	78	(1232)
Decided during campaign	60	(369)	56	(168)	61	(470)

Note: Time of voting decision was measured by the question, "When did you decide to vote the way you did? Was it in the last days before the election, was it earlier during the campaign, or did you know already before the campaign how you would vote?" The first two categories have been combined in the table. Entries are per cent voting either Social Democratic, Liberal, or Conservative (the remaining voting for other parties). Figures in parentheses indicate no. of respondents (=100 per cent).

Thus it may be true that the election campaign favours the small parties. But since most people continue to make their decision before the campaign, one might as well say that the large parties manage to secure their hold over the voters before the campaign even starts.

The Crisis of the Centre Parties. The renewed strength of the large parties has been partly at the expense of the wing parties lying on the outside of the large parties, and partly that of the small centre parties lying between the Social Democratic party on one side and the Liberal and Conservative parties on the other. The wing parties together polled 27 per cent of the vote as late as 1988, but has declined to 17 per cent in 1994, as can be seen from Table 1.1. The small centre parties, after the rise in support in the 1970s, have suffered a slow but systematic erosion of voting support which has brought them down from the 18 per cent level in the 1970s (and even 26 per cent in 1973) to 9 per cent in 1994. This development is illustrated in Figure 1.3.

Voting and Political Attitudes in Denmark

Figure 1.3.   Decline of voting support for the centre parties 1971-1994

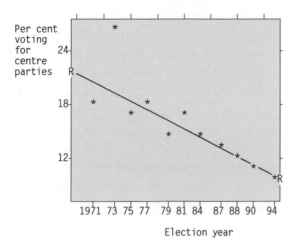

Election year

Note: The centre parties are the Radical Liberal, Centre Democratic, and Christian People's parties, plus the Justice (Single-Tax) party 1973-1987 and the Pensioners' party in 1977.

One may speculate that the source of the increasing large-party dominance, and of the concomitant crisis of the small parties, lies with strategic factors of government formation. The centre parties have played the role of actual or potential supporters of government, either inside or outside the cabinet, giving either permanent or ad hoc support for policies. This role may be necessary for Danish governments to function but it is probably not rewarded by the electors. According to the directional model of party strategy (Rabinowitz, Macdonald and Listhaug 1991), which we shall discuss in chapter 3, the political centre position offers no motivation for policy-oriented voters. About half of the centre parties' voters prefer a Social Democratic government, the other half, some type of bourgeois government. Consequently whatever government comes out of the election, half of the voters of the centre parties are likely to feel disappointed; and as for the other half, some of them may well wonder why they did not vote directly for the Prime Minister's party. In that sense there is some truth in Duverger's doctrine that the centre does not exist in politics (1964, p. 215).

The wing parties, of course, do not have this problem as their voters are agreed on which government to prefer. Instead they have another problem. When the other side is in government, they are located beyond the larger opposition party and therefore without influence. When their own side is in government they may be called upon to rescue the government, a role that leads to an internal conflict between the true believers and the more pragmatically minded among their supporters.

1.3. Waves in Left/Right Support

The decline of the centre vote would seem to make the balance between the left and right more critical than previously for the outcome of Danish parliamentary elections in terms of governments and policies. But there is little evidence that a socialist majority such as occurred in the 1979 and 1990 elections (cf. Table 1.1) results in a socialist government whereas a clear non-socialist majority such as occurred in 1975 and in 1994 results in a bourgeois government. In the first place even a centrist vote of ten per cent has, until now, proved more than enough to make the preferences of the centre parties decisive. In the second place, the Social Democratic party traditionally has a strong centrist and pragmatic faction exerting influence on its policies; thus, Social Democratic support cannot be equated with leftist attitudes, and Social Democratic electoral victories may not lead to socialist policies.

Indeed, if we were to judge from the long-term strength of the socialist vote, Danish politics would seem always to have followed a middle course. As we saw in Table 1.1, the socialist vote has remained steady at between 45 and 50 per cent. But it declined sharply in 1994, and the decline has been reinforced in the polls after the 1994 election.

Figure 1.4.   Social Democratic and Socialist vote in per cent, 1979-1994

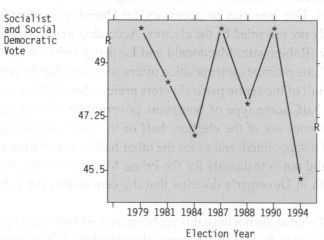

We shall compare these partisan changes with opinion changes in left-right issues of the basic ideological type, shown in Table 1.5. The four items presented in the table were phrased as a choice between two alternative viewpoints held by two persons A and B, of whom one represented the leftist viewpoint and the other, the rightist viewpoint. The table shows the per cent choosing the leftist view minus the per cent choosing the rightist view on each item at every election except the 1981 election, for which we do not have this information.

The items in the table represent our best overall indicators of the ideological trends in the Danish electorate, yet they are not quite free of methodological problems. Notably, the 1987 and 1988 surveys were based on telephone interviews and exhibit a smaller proportion of don't know responses, thus causing the values in the table to deviate more from zero than in the other surveys.

Table 1.5. Mean attitude on four left/right issues 1979-1994. Per cent with left stand minus per cent with right stand

	1969	1974	1979	1984	1987	1988	1990	1994
1. Social reforms	44	–8	24	39	65	53	39	35
2. Economic equality	39	32	18	1	27	25	27	9
3. State control of business	–9	–12	–10	–23	4	–6	–16	–25
4. Nationalise companies	–64	–44	–51	–57	–63	–65	–60	–79
Average	3	–7	–5	–10	8	2	–3	–20

Note: The items were worded as follows. — 1: A says, "Social reforms have gone too far in this country. More than now, people should manage without social security and support from the public" (right stand); B says, "Those social reforms that have been made in our country should be maintained at least to the same expent as now" (left stand). — 2: A says, "The differences in incomes and living standards are still too great in out country, so people with smaller incomes should have a faster improvement in their living standards than those with larger incomes" (left stand); B says, "The levelling of incomes has gone far enough. Those income differences that still remain should largely be maintained" (right stand). — 3: A says, "Businessmen and industrial leaders should be entitled to determine their own business to a greater extent" (right stand); B says, "The state should control and coordinate business life. Public control should at least not be less than it is in Denmark today" (left stand). — 4: A says, "The parliament should decide that the state take over the banks and big industrial enterprises" (left stand); B says, "The banks and big industries should continue to be in private hands" (right stand). — In computing the percentages, 'Don't know' and 'Neither' responses were included in the percentage base.

On the first question, whether social reforms should be maintained or whether they have gone too far, we observe that 1970-1974 was a period with a violent drop in the popularity of the welfare state. Its popularity rose again between 1974 and 1987, only to decline once more between 1987 and 1994. Still, it is important to note that by 1994 the balance of opinion in favour of maintaining the social reforms was almost as positive as around 1970. At least until 1994 we find no downward long-term trend in the popularity of the welfare state.

The second question asked whether income differences are still too large in Danish society or whether existing income differences should be kept up. Here, the 1970-1984 development is clearly in the direction of tolerating more inequality.

During that period the outcome of the biennial wage negotiations was a high level of equality between skilled and unskilled workers, despite the problems of employing the unskilled workers. Since then, the period 1987-1990 witnessed a renewed acceptance of economic equality, which then declined anew between 1990 and 1994, ending almost as low as ten years earlier.

The third question asked if the state should coordinate and control private business or if business owners should be permitted to determine their own affairs. On this item public opinion swung toward market liberalism between 1979 and 1984 and back toward sympathy with state regulation between 1984 and 1987. It is possible that the 1984-87 increase should be seen in connection with a more active industrial policy executed by the bourgeois government. However, since 1987 a consistent trend in favour of economic liberalism can be observed, so that the mood against state regulation is now stronger than ever.

On the fourth question, whether banks and big industry should be nationalised or remain in private hands, the changes are less marked than on the other items and may possibly be due to those changes in survey methodology already mentioned. However, it is safe to conclude that the mood was already strongly against nationalisation by 1970. The tiny minority who favour nationalisation of banks and big industry does not appear to have either increased nor decreased significantly over these 25 years.

A permanent feature of the table is that the level of public support is quite different for the four items. In the table the items are ordered by decreasing sympathy with leftist views, so that the defence of social reforms is the most popular leftist stand whereas nationalisation is by far the least popular. It appears that the public at large wants both social security and free enterprise at the same time, something that would be congenial with the Danish welfare model (cf. chapter 8). The order among the four items has not changed in the entire period.

The bottom line of that table section shows a simple average of the four items. Hence we find that opinions shifted to the right between 1969 and 1974 (exclusively because of the opposition to social reforms), then took a dramatic swing to the left after 1984, and finally shifted toward the right throughout the period 1987 to 1994.

In the following analysis we need an index of issue positions on which respondents can be classified from left to right. For that purpose the four items will be our main indicators. In Table 1.6 the four items were combined into an index ranging from 4 to 12, which was then collapsed into three groups: the left wing (with index values 4-6), the centre (7-9), and the right wing (10-12). So, by means of the four items we divide the respondents into three ideological groups, which can be followed over time because their delimitation rests on the same items in every survey.

Table 1.6. No. of voters with different left/right issue positions 1979-1994. Per cent of respondents

	1979	1984	1987	1988	1990	1994
Left Wing	29	25	38	35	25	20
Centre	33	33	35	34	40	41
Right Wing	38	42	27	31	35	39
Difference, Left-Right	−9	−16	11	4	−10	−19

Note: The left wing is defined as those scoring 4-6, the centre as those scoring 7-9, and the right wing as those scoring 10-12 on an index composed of the responses to the four issues in Table 1.5 in which the left position was scored 1, the intermediate position and don't know responses 2, and the right position 3.

The result shows a change in group sizes that is consistent with the average of the four items in the foregoing table. Opinions moved toward the right between 1979 and 1984, the left decreasing from 29 to 25 per cent in the sample. The pendulum swung back toward the left between 1984 and 1987, the left wing now soaring to 38 per cent. Over the next three election the left wing lost ground, ending on a mere 20 per cent in 1994. The changes in the size of the right wing are almost mirror images. The result is that in 1987, when the leftist mood culminated, the left wing was one and a half time bigger than the right wing. In 1994, when the right mood has so far culminated, the right wing is twice as large as the left wing. The numerical difference between the left wing and the right wing, shown in the bottom row, runs very much in parallel with the 'average' row in Table 1.5.

To further validate these changes, we may look at respondents' self-placement on a left-right scale. Such a scale was introduced in the Danish election surveys in 1979 and has been used in all later surveys except in 1988. Table 1.7 shows the distribution of the samples in five groups.

The extreme left, defined as the positions 1 and 2 on the ten point scale, has consistently been very small, containing three to five per cent of the samples. The moderate left, positions 3 and 4, increased to 26 per cent in 1987 and subsequently has declined to 17 per cent in the last election. Also the centre (positions 5 and 6) is smaller in the last two election than in the previous ones although it is still the largest of the five groups. The moderate right (positions 7 and 8) temporarily went down to 18 per cent in the 1987 election but has since gone up to 30 per cent. The extreme right (positions 9 and 10) has moved in parallel at a lower level, increasing from a low of 3 per cent in 1987 to almost 10 per cent in the last election.

Table 1.7. Left/right self-placement 1979-1994. Per cent of respondents

	1979	1981	1984	1987	1990	1994
Extreme Left (1-2)	5	3	4	4	4	4
Moderate Left (3-4)	17	22	17	26	21	17
Centre (5-6)	48	45	43	49	38	39
Moderate Right (7-8)	23	25	29	18	28	30
Extreme Right (9-10)	7	5	7	3	9	10
Diff. Left-Right	−8	−5	−15	9	−12	−19
N (100 per cent)	1764	854	936	934	930	1854

Except for 1987, the groups on the right have always been larger than the corresponding groups on the left side. Subtracting the former from the latter, as is done in the bottom line, gives an indication of the left-right balance which is strikingly similar to the bottom line of the previous table. The similarity of the two tables suggests that measurement problems are not so serious as to affect our conclusion about the ideological trends. As shown in Figure 1.5, the two indicators are very close to one another in the five elections for which both these indicators can be computed. It is not even necessary to rescale them to convey the impression that they measure the same phenomenon.

Figure 1.5. Left/right balance in issue positions (o) and in respondents' self-placement (*) 1979-1994

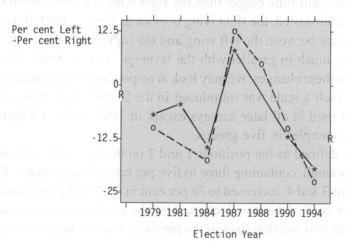

The left-right scale is available for the 1981 election, and so it reveals that the rightward change in attitudes between 1979 and 1984 took place after the 1981 election.

One explanation of these very considerable changes might be that they are reactions both to external events and to the policies of Danish governments. The rightward change from 1979 to 1984 is in a rather obvious way related to the mounting dissatisfaction with the Social Democratic government and the subsequent enthusiasm over the first years of the bourgeois coalition government. The dramatic leftward change between 1984 and 1987 would then be due to the public resentment of the (real or imagined) cuts in the welfare services instigated by the bourgeois government. The rightward change since 1987 then expresses the gradual adaptation of the public to liberal ideas of non-intervention on the part of the state.

The external factors might be visible in the form of a parallel development in other countries which may serve as reference countries for Danish politicians, newspapers, and the public. With regard to the major countries, the accession of Margaret Thatcher in Great Britain in 1979, Ronald Reagan in the United States in 1980, and Helmut Kohl in West Germany in 1982 suggests an international change in the direction of neo-liberal policies around 1980. Following these shifts toward conservative regimes we might expect some resistance to cutting accustomed public services and income transfers in the welfare countries. The prototype for this development is Great Britain, where the nineteen-eighties witnessed a soaring of public protest against the cuts in the welfare system resulting from Thatcherite policies, although the Conservative government continued in power.

Denmark's northern neighbours also exhibit marked shifts in political attitudes and government composition during the eighties. In Norway a clear shift to the right in economic attitudes took place between 1977 and 1981. The 1981 election brought the Right party to power for the next two years, and in 1983 the government was converted into a bourgeois four party coalition much like the Danish one of September 1982. During the bourgeois rule the attitudinal trend was reversed to a shift in the leftward direction between 1981 and 1985 (Aardal and Valen 1989, p. 92). This shift comes before the Danish shift to the left after the January 1984 election, but otherwise it is as close a parallel to the Danish development as can be imagined.

In Sweden a marked right swing in economic attitudes took place between the 1979 and 1982 elections, during a period of bourgeois government. This attitudinal shift is simultaneous with the Danish and Norwegian shifts, but the difference is that it occurs under bourgeois government. The rightward drift in Sweden continued between 1982 and 1985 (Holmberg and Gilljam 1987, p. 257), just as it did in Denmark until 1984. However, as the Social Democrats came to power in Sweden in 1985, we can hardly construct it as enthusiasm over a neo-liberal policy. By and large, Swedish economic attitudes as well as left-right identifications continued to move toward the right throughout the eighties until the conservative Carl Bildt government ran into the economic crisis which still characterises Swedish society by the mid-nineties.

1.4. Ideological and Partisan Change

The shifts toward the left and right in economic attitudes which we have observed in Figure 1.5 may contribute to explain the fate of the Danish parties. In a simple model of ideological voting in which left-right opinions are the underlying cause of party preferences, a shift to the left in public opinion on important issues is expected to strengthen the leftist party or parties. Conversely, a shift to the right should strengthen the party or parties of the right.

The hypothesis that aggregate partisan change between socialist and bourgeois parties is explained by parallel aggregate change in ideological attitudes presupposes that a fairly close and stable relationship exists at the micro level between ideological viewpoints and the socialist or bourgeois vote. Unless we can validate such an ideological issue voting model, we cannot expect the dynamic macro-level relationship to emerge. Previous research of the issue voting model (Borre 1984, pp. 162-165) has shown that the socialist vote increasingly became associated with ideological viewpoints between 1973 and 1984. By selecting three viewpoints from a larger set, it was found that they accounted for less than 20 per cent of the variance in the socialist vote at the 1973 election; by 1984 three such viewpoints explained more than 50 per cent of the corresponding variance. Thus over ten years the new party system, from a chaotic beginning, had become thoroughly ideologised.

Is this still the case in 1994? The answer is No. By repeating the procedure of selecting from the set of ideological viewpoints the three most efficient predictors, we obtain a variance reduction in the socialist (or bourgeois) vote of 32 per cent in 1990 and 26 per cent in 1994. That is, ten years of ideological rearmament were followed by ten years of almost as great ideological disarmament.

However, the loosening of the socialist vote from its ideological straightjacket does not necessarily mean that the issue voting model is no longer a valid one. First, it may turn out to work better within specific classes and generations than on the electorate as a whole; structural differences in the vote are pointed out and investigated in detail in chapters 5 and 6. Second, as we shall investigate in chapters 2 and 3, it is possible that traditional left-right voting is increasingly being replaced by voting along other issue dimensions. Thirdly, as studied in chapter 4, it is possible that partisan conflicts over ideological goals is being supplemented by conflicts over governments' and leaders' performance on these goals and the most efficient means of pursuing them. If that is the case, policy orientations and evaluations are still central to voter reactions, and the issue voting model should be refined to incorporate such factors. In any case the decline in ideological issue voting does not mean a return to the situation of the early 1970s.

Here we want to profit from looking at the simple left-right model so as to pinpoint the most important deviations from it. By comparing Figure 1.4 with Figure 1.5 we observe that the turn to the right in the period 1979 to 1984 coincided with a decline of the total socialist vote from 50.2 to 46.6 per cent of the vote cast. The subsequent shift to the left in the period 1984-1987 corresponded to a rise in the socialist vote to 49.7 per cent. During the last seven years the long pull toward the right from 1987 to 1994 has resulted in a decline in the socialist vote from 49.7 to 45.0 per cent of the vote, except that the line of decline was broken by the high point of 50.1 per cent socialist vote in 1990. Therefore a relationship in rough accordance with the simple model is found in five out of seven elections. The deviations are the 1979 and 1990 elections, both of which gave the Social Democrats a victory far exceeding that which would be expected from the simple ideological voting model.

If the simple model is applied to the left wing parties alone, it fares somewhat better. Figure 1.6 shows the voting strength of the left wing at the same elections as a function of the left-right attitudes.

Figure 1.6. *Relation between left/right attitudes and vote for the left-wing parties at Danish general elections 1979-1994*

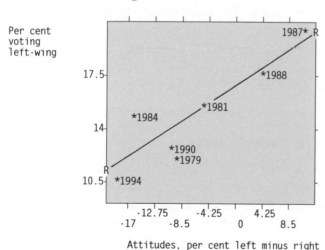

Attitudes, per cent left minus right

Note: Left/right attitudes are taken from Table 1.6, except the 1981 value which is taken from Table 1.7. Regression line: Y = 16.5 — .293 X with r = −.89**

The fit is clearly significant. The vote for the left wing rises by roughly .3 per cent for each shift of one scale point on the PDI measure of attitudes. That is, one per cent of the voters shifting their attitude from left to right means .6 per cent lost for the left-wing parties.

Thus the failure of the general socialist vote to conform to the drift of attitudes is caused by the Social Democratic vote. In 1979 and again in 1990 the Social Democratic party achieved electoral victories greatly surpassing the tendency of public attitudes. One can speculate about the reasons. In 1979 the bourgeois parties were split by the Liberal party taking part in a Social Democratic government, and Prime Minister Anker Jørgensen's strategy had thus proved successful. In 1988 the issue was security policy, which exposed the uncertain Social Democratic position on NATO membership. But in the 1990 election the new Social Democratic chairman Svend Auken was able to move into the centre, expressing his willingness to cooperate with bourgeois parties. It is possible that in this election the Social Democrats could profit from an international disarray of the left wing related to the fall of socialist states in east Europe (Borre 1991). As the Liberal leadership at the same time was moving toward the right, harnessing the ideological winds, the expected shift to the right evaporated in tactical manoeuvres.

This situation was unique, and the 1994 election fell back to the ideological trend which has favoured the right since 1987. The result is that the 1994 election stands out in all our diagrams and tables as the worst election for the socialist side in twenty years. This is so in spite of the advantage of having the government in a period of economic improvement. One of the problems for the following is to explain the rightward drift of the period 1987-94 in order to see whether it is rooted in enduring changes in value preferences and social structure. A place to begin such an analysis is to ask which parts of the electorate have been leading in that development.

1.5. The Vanguard and the Silent Majority

How are ideological shifts toward the left or right implemented? Ever since the beginning of large-scale voting research a distinction has been drawn between the ideologically involved voters and the rest (Campbell et al. 1960). The majority of voters are believed not to have any ideological understanding nor to be motivated by ideology in their political participation. In his classical article Converse (1962) showed that most American voters had little coherence or 'constraint' in their attitudes — and attitudinal coherence is a prerequisite for attaining a position on the left or right in the attitudinal left-right model we have referred to in the previous sections. Thus the lack of ideological coherence in their political attitudes ensures that the non-ideological voters as an aggregate do not deviate much from the centre on the left-right scale. On this point the Michigan studies, which pioneered the attitudinal approach in voting behaviour, were in agreement with the older studies made by the Columbia school of voting behaviour (Lazarsfeld, Berelson and Gaudet 1944; Berelson, Lazarsfeld, and McPhee 1954), which gave rise to the 'marginal voter' hypothesis; for according to that hypothesis the indifferent voters clustered in the middle of the political spectrum and were available to the party that succeeded in conquering the non-political centre.

Thus a minority of voters, who are ideologically conscious, occupy the positions on the left and right wings. This fact in itself does not rule out the possibility that the left and right wings balance each other numerically. But it means that the ideologically involved voters *potentially* may be skewed toward the left or right, and that a shift toward the left or right primarily will be caused by change among the ideologically involved voters. Thus the left-right model pictures a process of change in which the ideologically involved constitute a vanguard leading the change, while the silent majority constitute a fairly inert mass closer to the centre.

We shall apply this framework to the change in attitudes that we have witnessed among the Danish electorate for the period 1979-1987. As a simple measure of political involvement we classify the respondents into three groups according to their self-reported political interest. The 'vanguard' are defined as those who are very interested in politics. The 'silent majority are those who are somewhat or only a little interested in politics. We keep these two groups analytically apart from each other so as to certify whether the real difference lies between those with great interest and those with some interest, as the hypothesis implies.

Table 1.8 and Figure 1.7 show the left-right balance of opinion among the three groups in the 1979, 1984, 1987, 1990 and 1994 surveys.

The most plausible prediction would be that the vanguard deviated more from the zero line than the silent majority, and that the vanguard was thus responsible for the greater part of the attitudinal shifts which we observed in Figure 1.5. This prediction turns out not to be true. However, there is an interesting tendency for 1979 and 1984 in that the vanguard is on the left whereas the silent majority is on the right. This difference vanishes in 1987, not because of a change among the vanguard but because the silent majority made a strong turn to the left. An hypothesis which springs from this pattern would be that the anxiety over the cessation of the economic progress of the middle 1980s and the proposed cuts in the welfare system dominated the silent majority at that time.

Table 1.8. Ideological division of the interested/uninterested 1979-1994. Per cent

	1979	1984	1987	1990	1994
With Great Political Interest:					
Left Wing	43	43	43	29	22
Centre	25	23	29	38	33
Right Wing	32	34	28	33	45
Total	100	100	100	100	100
Difference, Left-Right	11	9	15	−4	−23
With Some Political Interest:					
Left Wing	26	24	39	27	19
Centre	33	31	34	36	37
Right Wing	41	45	27	37	44
Total	100	100	100	100	100
Difference, Left–Right	−15	−21	12	−10	−25
With Little or No Political Interest:					
Left Wing	23	13	34	21	21
Centre	37	44	43	48	40
Right Wing	40	43	23	31	39
Total	100	100	100	100	100
Difference, Left–Right	−17	−30	11	−10	−18

Note: The left wing is defined as those scoring 4-6, the centre as those scoring 7-9, and the right wing as those scoring 10-12 on an index composed of the responses to the four issues in Table 1.5 in which the left position was scored 1, the intermediate position or don't know responses 2, and the right position 3.

Figure 1.7.   Balance of left-right attitudes among respondents who are (A) very interested, (B) somewhat interested, and (C) only a little or not at all interested in politics, 1979-1994

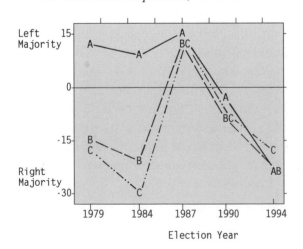

Voting and Political Attitudes in Denmark

From 1987 to 1994 the vanguard and the silent majority follow each other closely toward the right, from a left majority of 10-15 per cent in 1987 to a right majority of 20-25 per cent in 1994. For the silent majority this means a return to its 1984 position, while for the vanguard it is tempting to speak of a defection from socialism. In chapter 6, sections 6.5 and 6.6, we shall discuss this development further. For the present, we note that it fits with our earlier reference to the events in east Europe which began with the fall of the Berlin wall in November 1989 and continued with the dissolution of the Communist party in the Soviet Union in 1991. But certainly there are other elements in the 1990 and 1994 elections that impinge on the changes in left-right orientation, and we shall discuss them in subsequent chapters.

1.6. Conclusion

The Danish party system was deeply fragmented in 1973, and partisan change over the past two decades has been erratic at first glance. However, we have attempted to concentrate on two more general features of the electoral development. One is the recovery of the three old parties at the expense of the minor centre parties. The other is the shifts in the socialist vote from 1979 to 1994.

Concerning the former, our explanation is that the large parties have profited in the long run from their larger stock of party identification. Although they may have lost their character of class parties — a possibility we shall deal with in chapter 5 — they may have gained for other reasons, for example by a reputation for responsible government.

Concerning the latter, the rightward ideological pull over the last seven years from 1987 to 1994 is remarkable; but its impact on partisan change is partly concealed by the Social Democratic victory in 1990, and its impact on governmental power is concealed by the change from bourgeois to centre-left government in 1993. Apparently, the impact of ideological currents on Danish government formation is tempered by the fact that so far, all governments since 1945 have needed support from the small centre parties — even though these parties have been steadily reduced over the past two decades.

It is possible, however, that the traditional ideological left-right picture of Danish politics is in the process of being transformed, an idea that will be pursued in the next chapter.

2

OLD AND NEW POLITICS

2.1. The New Politics Thesis

The accustomed picture of European politics since the early part of the present century is one in which a socialist left struggles against a conservative right over the control of the economy and the distribution of its output. This struggle becomes the main issue of parliamentary politics at some point in the industrial development when the working class becomes sufficiently numerous and acquires the right to vote. This leads to an alignment of voters into a few parties both on the socialist and the bourgeois side. The party system tends to 'freeze', in Lipset and Rokkan's (1967) famous formulation, in a form defined by the early lines of conflicts, giving little scope for major new parties or cleavage lines.

During the 1970s, however, the party systems in mature west European polities exhibited signs of stress and instability, calling for reexamination of the 'freezing' hypothesis and offering new interpretations of the future developments. One of these interpretations was the 'new politics' thesis (Miller and Levitin 1976; Hildebrandt and Dalton 1978; Baker, Dalton and Hildebrandt 1981; Flanagan 1987). Briefly, it stated that economically advanced societies will experience a shift in political priorities and conflicts away from problems of economic growth and distribution and toward social, environmental, and ethical issues that reflect the negative side effects of advanced industrialism. In addition to (perhaps even replacing) the old politics dimension of political conflict, which represents the economic struggle, a new politics dimension will emerge to represent conflicts over the new non-economic issues. Just as the old left and old right emerged during the early phase of industrial society, a new left and new right emerge during the transition to the post-industrial society.

Furthermore, it was predicted that opinions were likely to drift toward the right on the old politics dimension because of the gradual depletion of economic demands originally put forward by socialist parties. On the new politics dimension, however, opinions are in the long run likely to drift toward the left as a consequence of the higher level of education. Thus the driving forces of the development were assumed to be the rising level of income and education.

The new politics thesis in its European version has received much inspiration from Inglehart's (1971, 1977, 1990) theory of postmaterialism, but differs from it on some points. Thus Inglehart originally relied on the Maslovian hypothesis of a hierarchy of human needs, and on the early socialisation of political values, to explain the generational progress of postmaterialism, and he does not anticipate a two-dimensional pattern of issue orientations to emerge — specifically, his theory has no need for a new right. However, Inglehart's postmaterialists correspond closely to the new left.

2.2. The Two Dimensions in 1990 and 1994

The Scandinavian countries belong to the group of advanced industrial countries in which a new politics dimension might be expected to emerge. But even though Denmark and Norway went through a period of political instability during the 1970s, and Sweden from the second half of the 1980s, no viable new politics dimension seemed to materialise until recently; for Denmark, such a new politics dimension was tentatively shown to exist at the 1990 election along with the traditional left-right dimension (Borre 1995b). It was suggested that the emergence of the new dimension in Denmark in the course of the 1980s was triggered by the parliamentary habits established during the bourgeois government of that period. The Radical Liberal party on many occasions failed to support the government in non-economic matters, siding instead with the Social Democrats and People's Socialists to form the so-called 'alternative majority'.

But although the impact of new politics on parliamentary politics (let alone government formations) had been slow to manifest itself, one could argue that new politics has been changing the political landscape for two decades. Grass roots activity has led to higher sensitivity of the population to elite decisions; and within the constituencies of the parties great structural change have taken place. These will be clearer in chapters 5 and 6. Since the validity of the new politics thesis seems to a great extent to depend on the stability of the new dimension, we first replicate the 1990 findings on the 1994 data.

Table 2.1 shows the result of a factor analysis of attitudes to eight political issues. Items 1-4 were selected to represent the old politics dimension and items 5-8 to represent the new politics dimension. The old politics items dealt with social reforms, reduction of income differences, state control of business, and the feasibility of wage increases. The new politics items dealt with issues of environment, financial aid to developing nations, the treatment of violent crimes, and the attitudes toward immigrants.

Table 2.1. Factor analysis of voter positions on eight issues in 1990 and 1994 (Varimax rotation)

	1990 Factor 1	1990 Factor 2	1994 Factor 1	1994 Factor 2
Old politics items:				
1. Social reforms	.19	.57	.12	.65
2. Economic equality	.00	.62	−.06	.63
3. State control of business	.16	.61	.22	.54
4. Wage increase	.04	.64	−.04	.54
New politics items:				
5. Aid to developing nations	.73	.02	.75	.03
6. Crimes of violence	.64	.16	.62	−.01
7. Environment v. growth	.56	.27	.50	.39
8. Immigration a threat	.82	.01	.78	.05
Average intercorrelations (r) between:				
Old politics items (N=6)	.18		.16	
New politics items (N=6)	.31		.29	
Old and new items (N=16)	.12		.10	

Note: The items were worded as follows: 1 — Which of these two statements comes closer to your own point of view, (a) Social reforms have gone too far; people should manage without social support and contributions from society, or (b) Those social reforms that have been carried through should be maintained to at least the same extent as now? Responses were scored a=5, b=1, neither or don't know=3 [v159 in 1990, v93 in 1994]. 2 — Which of these two statements comes closer to your own point of view, (a) The differences in incomes and living standards are still too large in our country, so people with small incomes should have a faster improvement of their living standards than those with higher incomes, or (b) The levelling of incomes has gone sufficiently far; the income differences that still exist should largely be maintained? Responses were scored a=1, b=5, neither or don't know=3 [v160 in 1990, v94 in 1994]. 3 — Which of these two statements comes closer to your own point of view, (a) Business people should to a larger be entitled to decide about their own business, or (b) The state should control and coordinate business life; at least, the state control should not be less than it is in Denmark today? Responses were scored a=5, b=1, neither or don't know=3 [v161 in 1990, v95 in 1994]. 4 — In the present economic situation we cannot afford wage increases. Responses were scored: agree completely=5, agree partly=4, neither agree nor disagree, or don't know=3, disagree partly=2, and disagree completely=1 [v217 in 1990, v182 in 1994]. 5 — Please indicate whether you think the state uses too much money, a suitable amount, or too little money on aid to underdeveloped countries. Responses were scored: too much=5, suitable or don't know=3, too little=1 [v185 in 1990, v132 in 1994]. 6 — Crimes of violence should be punished much more severely than they are today. Responses were scored: agree completely=5, agree partly=4, neither agree nor disagree, or don't know=3, disagree partly=2, and disagree completely=1 [v220 in 1990, v189 in 1994]. 7 — Economic growth should be secured by developing the industry even though this may be in conflict with environmental interests. Responses were scored: agree completely=5, agree partly=4, neither agree nor disagree, or don't know=3, disagree partly=2, and disagree completely=1 [v218 in 1990, v184 in 1994]. 8 — Immigration constitutes a serious threat to our national culture. Responses were scored: agree completely=5, agree partly=4, neither agree nor disagree, or don't know=3, disagree partly=2, and disagree completely=1 [v219 in 1990, v183 in 1994].

It is evident from the loadings on the two factors in 1990 and 1994 that items 5-8 load highly on factor 1 and items 1-4 on factor 2. Thus we interpret factor 1 as a new politics dimension and factor 2 as an old politics dimension. With one major exception, the items having high loadings on one factor have low loadings on the other. The exception is item 7, which trades off economic growth and environmental protection. This loads chiefly on the new politics dimension but also significantly on the old politics dimension. This result may suggest that environmental issues are not tightly integrated in either dimension. Goul Andersen (1990) has shown that Danish blue-collar workers are more 'green' than workers in Sweden and Norway.

The replication shows that the two dimensions are stable over the four year period. However, neither the old nor the new dimension are quite as coherent in 1994 as they were in 1990. The last section of the table presents the average intercorrelations of responses to the eight items. The average of the six correlation coefficients between the old politics items pairwise dropped from .18 to .16, and the average of the six coefficients for the new politics items dropped from .31 to .29. The result for the old politics items was expected, since it continues a trend from 1984 onward (Borre 1996) and fits with the hypothesis that the old politics dimension is slowly disintegrating. However, the new politics dimension would be theoretically assumed to crystallise further. It is possible, however, that this decline is a reflection of the changing content of the new politics dimension. By sticking to the same set of items we of course abstain from 'rejuvenating' the new politics dimension.

Figures 2.1 and 2.2 represent the loadings of the eight items on the two factors in 1990 and 1994, respectively.

The Y axis represents the loadings on the new politics factor, while the X axis represents the old politics factor. This is done in order to keep as close as possible to the familiar picture of the traditional left-right axis running across the page. Those expressing conservative opinions on the traditional issues of wage increase, income equality, state regulation, and social reforms therefore appear to the right in the figures. Those expressing conservative opinions on the new issues appear in the upper part of the figures.

Figure 2.1. Factor analysis of eight attitudinal items in 1990. Loadings on first (Y) and second (X) factor after rotation

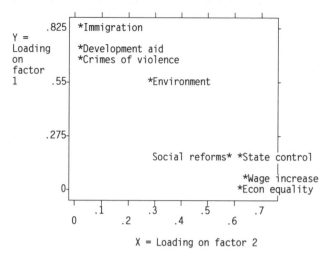

Note: For coordinates, see Table 2.1.

Figure 2.2. Factor analysis of eight attitudinal items in 1994. Loadings on first (Y) and second (X) factor after rotation

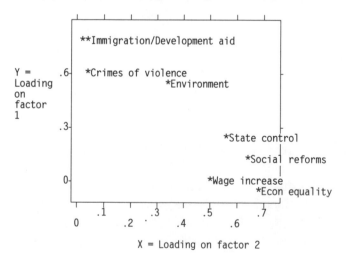

Note: For coordinates, see Table 2.1.

Voting and Political Attitudes in Denmark

The factor loadings in Table 2.1 are those of a varimax rotation, which means that the two factors extracted are uncorrelated.[1] All the same, the old and new politics items are on average correlated positively. This fact comes to the fore in the figures by the tendency of all issues to end up in the first quadrant with positive scores on both axes. Especially the environmental issue takes on a position somewhat in-between the old and the new dimension (particularly in 1994). Therefore the new politics dimension cannot without reservations be termed a 'green' dimension so far as Danish politics is concerned. The 'red' tend strongly to be 'green' too.

In comparing the two figures we observe that the issues fall less clearly into two clusters in 1994 than in 1990. We cannot know whether this tendency towards more confusion will continue into the future, but later in the chapter we shall study the partisan bases as well as the socioeconomic bases of the attitudinal dimensions in the hope of getting nearer to an answer.

2.3. Four Ideological Types

We shall represent the two-dimensional nature of Danish politics by means of a simple fourfold model in order to facilitate the following analysis. By splitting the old as well as the new politics into left and right and cross-tabulating these groups, we obtain four combinations: the old left/new left, the old left/new right, the old right/new left, and the old right/new right. Since these labels are cumbersome to work with, we shall adopt the following labels:

1. The Left Wing, combining old left with new left,
2. The Old Socialists, combining old left with new right,
3. The Green Bourgeois, combining new left with old right, and
4. The Right Wing, combining new right with old right.

The model is illustrated in Figure 2.3.

Figure 2.3.   *Model of four ideological voter types*

New Right	Old Socialists	Right Wing
New Left	Left Wing	Green Bourgeois
	Old Left	Old Right

---

1. Varimax rotation will be used for simplicity throughout this volume as the checks we have done with oblique rotation have produced substantially similar results.

The model resembles that of Middendorp (1978, p. 149), who sees Conservatism as based on the underlying values of equality versus freedom. According to him, Conservatism is in favour of freedom in the economic sense but equality in the non-economic sense that everybody is supposed to obey certain moral standards; this corresponds to the position of the Right Wing in the diagram. Diametrically opposed to them are those on the Left Wing who are in favour of economic equality but moral freedom. The Green Bourgeois share the value of economic freedom with the Right Wing and they share the value of moral freedom with the New Left. Their opposite numbers are the Old Socialists, who share the values of economic equality with a tendency to enforce moral standards on everybody.

We may first use our model to analyse the ideological change in the electorate from 1990 to 1994. The new politics thesis dissociates left and right attitudes into the old and the new set. Thereby it is imaginable that attitudes may shift in one direction on the old politics dimension while at the same shifting in the opposite direction on the new politics dimension. To investigate this, the responses on each item are scored from 1 to 5 and added up separately for the two groups of items. In this way an old politics index and a new politics index are computed, each giving a respondent a score between 4 and 20. Dividing the respondents into a left and a right group on each index, we then compute the size of the four groups at the two elections. The result is shown in Table 2.2.

The significant fact is that a right shift in attitudes is observed on the old politics issues but not on the new politics issues. The shift on the old politics issues fits with our hypothesis; but we might have expected a shift from the new right toward the new left as a consequence of the passing of four years in which new cohorts have entered the electorate. One explanation why this shift does not materialise is that it was counteracted by period effects in the form of worries about law-and-order. On the treatment of violent crime (item 6), there was a shift in favour of stronger punishment of no less than 11 percentage points. These concerns in turn might stem from cases of violence publicised by the media around the time of the survey.

However, period effects do not explain why right-wing parties have emerged as permanent members of many European party systems during the 1980s. As a common feature these parties are campaigning for law-and-order and restrictions on immigration. It appears that we are witnessing here side effects of a transformation of European national-states which are more general and enduring than the theory of postmaterialism is prepared to admit.

Table 2.2. Size of the ideological groups 1990 and 1994. Per cent

	1990	1994
Old politics Position:		
Left, scores 4-12	61	56
Right, scores 13-20	39	44
New politics division:		
Left, scores 4-12	39	40
Right, scores 13-20	61	60
Ideological types:		
Left Wing	27	26
Old Socialists	34	30
Green Bourgeois	12	14
Right Wing	27	30
Total/Average	100	100

Note: Of the ideological types or groups, the Left Wing is defined as those scoring 4-12 on both the old politics and the new politics index; the Old Socialists are those scoring 4-12 on the old politics index and 13-20 on the new politics index; the Green Bourgeois are those scoring 13-20 on the old politics index and 4-12 on the new politics index; and the Right Wing are those scoring 13-20 on both the old politics and the new politics index. Concerning these two indices, see Table 2.1.

The lower half of Table 2.2 indicates the size of our four ideological groups of voters by combining the two dimensions, the old and the new. The relative size of these groups depends on where we cut the axes but they are interesting for at least two reasons. In the first place they show the statistical association between the old and the new dimension. If we multiply the frequencies of the old left and right with those of the new left and right in the table, we find that the Left Wing and the Right Wing are each about four percentage points larger than would be expected from statistical independence; correspondingly, the Old Socialist and Green Bourgeois groups are four percentage points smaller than expected.

Second, the relative sizes of the groups reveal the change taking place between 1990 and 1994. It is seen that the Left Wing group diminished only insignificantly from 27 to 26 per cent while the Old Socialist group diminished from 34 to 30 per cent. The Green Bourgeois group increased from 12 to 14 per cent, and the Right Wing, from 27 to 30 per cent. New politics theory predicts a growth of the Green Bourgeois group, which combines right attitudes on economic issues with left attitudes on non-economic issues. It also predicts a decline of the Old Socialist group, which combines precisely the opposite views. Both of these predictions come true over the four year period. The growth of the Right Wing was not predicted; or perhaps one should say that new politics theory assumes this type of growth to be caused by short-term forces and therefore to be transitory. However, one may question this expectation, which does not take into account that internationalised crime, conflict between ethnic groups, a weakening of national states, and other tendencies toward a breakdown of the public order may accompany the emerging post-industrial society.

2.4. Ideological Type and Left-Right Placement

In this and the following section, our ideological types will be placed in the context of two well-known dimensions, namely the ideological left-right dimension and the materialist/postmaterialist values dimension.

We have termed the positions on the new politics dimension the new left and the new right, those on the old politics position the old left and old right, without validating the use of these labels. The most direct validation would come from the respondent's self-image, as it can be assessed from his or her self-placement on a left-right scale. According to prevailing opinion, which is based on empirical analyses of the meaning or content of the labels of left and right (Fuchs and Klingemann 1990; Inglehart and Klingemann 1976), the left-right dimension serves as a means of orientation and communication that summarises a varied set of bases of political conflict. Thus it is not to be understood as a 'super-issue' with a given content (such as social equality or social reform). Rather it serves as a schema whose content may vary from one country to another and change over time. When new issues are laid over older issues the meaning is apt to change so as to incorporate positions on the new issue.

When such a proposition is combined with the new politics theory, it follows that we could hypothesise a long-run change in the content of the left-right dimension in the direction of absorbing the new politics issues, and possibly a concomitant decline in old politics content.

In Danish politics the dominating interpretation of left and right is undoubtedly the traditional class conflict between working class interests and middle class interests. The latter may be taken to include the farmers' interests even though originally the farmers' party was considered to the left of the party of the urban bourgeoisie and still calls itself *Venstre* (Left) in opposition to the old *Højre* (Right). Because of the dominance of old politics in the interpretation of left and right, it is plausible to expect a greater impact of old politics position than of new politics position on the self-placement of our respondents. This is also brought out as the correlation of self-placement with old politics position was r=.43 in 1990 and .46 in 1994, whereas the correlations between self-placement and new politics position was r=.39 in 1990 and .34 in 1994. It is possible that the slight turn of the left-right axes in the direction of old politics in 1994 reflects the fact that the 1994 election campaign was dominated by economic politics, a fact we shall discuss further in chapter 4.

Table 2.3. Positions of the ideological types on the left/right self-placement scale 1990 and 1994

	1990	1994
Left Wing	4.41	4.86
Old Socialists	5.65	5.75
Green Bourgeois	6.45	6.39
Right Wing	7.13	6.94
All	5.81	5.94

Note: The left/right self-placement scale runs from 1 (left) to 10 (right). Concerning definitions of the ideological types, see note to Table 2.2.

Table 2.3 shows the mean positions of the four types on the left-right self-placement scale from 1 to 10. It is observed that within each of the two old politics groups, the new politics position plays a significant role in people's location on the left-right scale: the difference between the Left Wing and the Old Socialists was 1.24 point in 1990 and .89 in 1994, and that between the Green Bourgeois and the Right Wing was .68 point in 1990 and .55 in 1994. However, the old politics dimension seems more important for the self-location of the respondent: the difference between the Left Wing and the Green Bourgeois was 2.04 points in 1990 and 1.53 in 1994, and between the Old Socialists and the Right Wing, 1.48 point in 1990 and 1.19 in 1994. Consequently, of the two intermediate types, the Old Socialists are somewhat to the left of the Green Bourgeois in their left-right self-image. As a result the four types place themselves in Table 2.3 like pearls on a string on the left-right scale. The new politics dimension has entailed an extension of the old politics dimension toward both the left and the right pole. This impression is similar to that of Knutsen (1995), who argues that the new left and new right incorporate economic as well as non-economic values.

Looking at Table 2.3 we also observe that all distances between the types on the left-right scale became smaller in 1994 than they were in 1990. The Left Wing shifted markedly toward the centre. The Old Socialists also moved somewhat toward the right or centre, whereas the Green Bourgeois and the Right Wing moved toward the left. Thus there was a general convergence or drift toward the centre. The first-mentioned movement is the largest so that the total picture, as shown in the bottom row, is a shift toward the right. The rightward movement of the mean results in part from the reduced radicalism of the Left Wing and in part by the reduced size of the Old Socialist group.

On the whole, the correlations between the new politics position, the old politics position, and the complete left-right position, tended to become weaker between 1990 and 1994. A lapse of four years is a fairly short time to study long term trends. All that we can see is that during the elapsed four years there is no indication that new politics is replacing old politics in defining the content of left and right, but some evidence that both dimensions are gradually being loosened from the left/right self-image of respondents, as well as from each other.

2.5. New Politics and the MPM Dimension

Some writers on new politics theory, notably Flanagan, make a point of differentiating new politics from the materialist/postmaterialist or MPM value dimension proposed by Inglehart (1971); others treat the two concepts as synonymous. Our discussion of this point is necessarily sketchy. In the first place we have defined the new and old politics as attitudinal dimensions, not value priorities. Our respondents were not asked which of the eight items they considered more important than which. When asked to choose between two statements, such as (a) Businessmen should be permitted to decide in their own business, or (b) The state should control and coordinate industry, they are of course asked to choose between two lines of policy that represent contrasting values. However, a postmaterialist might respond that he was not concerned with either of these policies. Thus he would be likely to give indifferent or unstable responses to such items while instead giving straight and stable responses to non-materialist items such as whether crime should be fought by means of stronger punishment or by means of preventive and rehabilitative action.

Secondly the Danish data set includes the MPM battery only in the original short form which asks the respondent to select two out of four goals for society, (1) to maintain law-and-order, (2) to give the individual person a greater chance of affecting political decisions, (3) to fight rising prices, and (4) to protect freedom of speech. The first and third are assumed to be material values, the second and fourth postmaterial ones. Now, in the 1994 survey one can argue that there is no MPM dimension at all since only 15.6 per cent chose the two material goals and exactly the same number the two postmaterial goals. The remaining 68.8 per cent chose one material and one postmaterial goal and thereby placed themselves in the intermediate or mixed category. Chance alone would suggest that one out of six choose the materialist combination of goals and one out of six the postmaterialist combination while the remaining two-thirds would choose one material and one postmaterial goal.

Nonetheless the choice of goals should be related to our attitudinal dimensions, especially the new politics dimension. Those on the new left, whether Left Wing or Green Bourgeois, should tend to be the same as those who want to promote the individual person's influence in politics and to protect the freedom of speech, and so disproportionately sign up for postmaterialism. Conversely, those on the new right could be expected to value the law-and-order goal and stable prices.

In regard to the old politics dimension there is no such evident prediction to venture. None of the four Inglehart items appears to be associated with socialist values such as equality or solidarity, nor do they express liberal virtues of free markets or private initiative. Consequently we might expect the four items to be chosen rather indiscriminately on the old left and the old right.

Table 2.4. Division of ideological types into materialists and postmaterialists. Per cent

	Left Wing	Old Socialists	Green Bourg.	Right Wing
Postmaterialists	32	7	23	6
Mixed	62	70	69	74
Materialists	6	23	9	20
Total	100	100	100	100
N (100 per cent)	(499)	(571)	(270)	(580)
Difference PM-M	26	−16	14	−13

Note: For definition of the ideological types, see note of Table 2.2.

According to Table 2.4 this also seems to happen. Of our four voter types the Left Wing contains the highest number of postmaterialists, 32 per cent, followed by the Green Bourgeois with 23 per cent. The two remaining types have only six to seven per cent postmaterialists. Looking at the other end, the Old Socialists and the Right Wing have around twenty per cent materialists whereas the other two types have between six and nine per cent. It is clear that empirically the MPM dimension is close to the new politics dimension while it has much less to do with the old politics dimension. If we compute the number of postmaterialists minus the number of materialists (which Inglehart often does), the Left Wing leads the field with 26 per cent followed by the Green Bourgeois with 14 per cent, the Right Wing with −13 per cent and the Old Socialists with −16 per cent. In particular it is evident that the MPM index does not discriminate between the Old Socialists and the Right Wing, both of which are classified as materialists. Because of their similar position on the new politics dimension or, in other words, their sharing of non-materialist values, one understands how the Progress party can attract former

Social Democratic workers (cf. chapter 5). Still, we need to distinguish Old Socialists from the Right Wing, since these two types of voters may have very different attitudes towards such institutions as the trade unions and the welfare state.

However, the similarity between the new politics dimension and the MPM value dimension is reassuring since in the following we are going to discuss a number of hypotheses that are derived fairly indiscriminately from either conceptual framework.

2.6. The Generational Hypothesis

Most conceptualisations of values stress that values are long-term forces influencing behaviour. The theories disagree as to whether values are learnt early or late in people's childhood and youth, and it is only fair to say that the internalisation of different values stretches over a number of years with a tendency to crystallise during maturity. This means that individual or group differences in values that are observed a few years after the entrance of the voter into the electorate should be observable also many years later in the individual's life.

However, we do not postulate that the voter's new and old politics position — and hence his or her ideological type — is stable over the individual's life. In the first place we have already noted that issue positions, from which we derive that membership, are not values though probably attitudes lying close to values. Second, as we have seen in Table 2.2, some of these issue positions can change over a period of four years at a rate which suggests that besides reflecting values they are also subject to event-driven or policy-driven period effects.

New politics theory deviates from the original formulation of postmaterialism (Inglehart 1971, 1977) by claiming that contemporary change in industrial society influences those attitudinal dimensions that are relevant for policy preferences. Thus our new and old politics indices should reflect present concerns and opportunities as well as past socialisation. Such is undoubtedly the case also with Inglehart's value battery in the simple two-out-of-four version which is included in the Danish questionnaire. The international scare of inflation during the 1970s meant that more people chose the anti-inflation goal, with the result that 'postmaterialism' appeared to decline rather systematically between 1970 and 1980 (cf. Inglehart 1990, p. 85). Similarly, a fear of crime and violence during the 1980s and 1990s may mean a rising tendency to choose the law-and-order goal, again with the result that 'postmaterialism' declines (in Denmark, from 26 per cent postmaterialists in 1981 to 15 per cent in 1990, cf. Gundelach and Riis 1992, p. 189).

An hypothesis rivalling that of early socialisation is that value-laden policy attitudes reflect the general utility of these policies. This means, among other things, that policies which are patently successful may cause changes in attitudes and shape the entire political culture of nations. For example it has been claimed that the German economic miracle during the 1950s and 1960s eradicated nearly all traces of the Nazi past with its authoritarian values (Rogowsky 1974, p. 9). But it also means that the attainment of economic security gradually turns the public's attention toward other goals and reduces the marginal utility of further improvements in welfare programs. It has been established by means of several indicators that the more economically advanced west European countries are at the same time the least interested in socialist policies (Inglehart 1990, chap. 8; Borre and Viegas 1995). Thus the principle of marginal utility, used in economics, might be of use also in research on political behaviour, even though the risk is that it can be abused too. It should be noted that the marginal utility may also *rise*, as when an increase in the rate of crime gives a higher saliency, and hence a higher priority, to law-and-order policies.

In this more relaxed form the effect of values need not be a delayed response to childhood upbringing, especially when this upbringing seems irrelevant to the problems of contemporary society. The idea is maintained, however, that relatively stable generational differences can be observed and become part of the forecasting of future political behaviour. A new generation impressed by new politics views and problems will be less inhibited about giving them weight in political behaviour than will an older generation accustomed to thinking in old politics terms.

In regard to the party choice we shall study the generational differences in chapter 6; for now, we study the corresponding differences in the new and old politics perspective. Table 2.5 shows the result of a breakdown of both the 1990 and 1994 samples into fifteen-years cohorts.

In both 1994 and 1990 the Left Wing group is consistently stronger in the postwar generations than in the older ones, precisely as the theories of postmaterialism and new politics predict. However, the mobilisation of the so-called 1968-generation shows up here: Left Wing is strongest in the cohorts born 1945-1959 and is slightly weaker in the youngest generation born 1960 and after. Between 1990 and 1994 the Left Wing declined by three percentage points in the older cohorts, while keeping up its strength in the postwar generations.

Table 2.5. Ideological type by birth cohort, 1990 and 1994

	Born Bef.1930	Born 1930/44	Born 1945/59	Born 1960/76
1994 Data:				
Left Wing	11	21	34	31
Old Socialists	32	33	28	27
Green Bourgeois	9	9	14	21
Right Wing	48	38	24	21
Total	100	101	100	100
N (100 per cent)	(407)	(393)	(586)	(635)
Economic Left	43	54	62	58
Non-economic Left	20	30	48	52
1990 Data:				
Left Wing	14	24	34	31
Old Socialists	41	33	35	26
Green Bourgeois	9	13	13	15
Right Wing	36	30	18	28
Total	100	100	100	100
N (100 per cent)	(163)	(239)	(320)	(163)
Economic Left	55	57	69	57
Non-economic Left	23	37	47	46

Note: For definition of the ideological types, see note of Table 2.2.

The Old Socialists in 1990 were strongest in the oldest generation and weakest in the young generation; but this tendency has almost disappeared by 1994, leaving only a five per cent difference between prewar and postwar generations. The result is that by 1994 the Left Wing is clearly stronger than the Old Socialists in the postwar generations.

The Green Bourgeois is the smallest of the four groups, but like the Left Wing it increases in strength as we go from the older to the younger generations, a phenomenon that supports the postmaterialism and new politics theses. Unlike the Left Wing, the Green Bourgeois gained in strength among the youngest between 1990 and 1994.

Finally, the Right Wing declines in strength from the old to the young generations. By 1990 there was a tendency toward a revival of this type among the youngest voters; but by 1994, when all of the 1960-76 cohorts had entered the electorate, that tendency had disappeared again.

We observe here that the generational differences are somewhat larger in respect to the new left than in respect to the old left, and that the new left shows an upward course in the new generation whereas support for the old left is strongest in the 1945-59 generation.

The difference between the two postwar generations is that the youngest have turned toward the intermediate types of the Green Bourgeois and the Old Socialists relative to the first postwar generation.

Except for the variation caused by the left-wing mobilisation of the young during the 1970s, it appears from these data that the generation hypothesis is confirmed in its broad outline. The postwar generations have around twice as many supporters of the New Left as the older generations, the difference becoming even more pronounced in 1994 than it was in 1990. This clear generation gap on the new politics dimension will in all likelihood put the New Right on the defensive in the future. On the old politics dimension, however, the corresponding generation gap is much smaller, and so it is not difficult to imagine that shifts toward the right can take place here, as indeed happened between 1990 and 1994.

Let us look at the hypothesis in the postmaterialist version. Table 2.6 records the number of materialists, mixed, and postmaterialists in the same four generations.

Table 2.6. Materialists and postmaterialists by birth cohort, 1994. Per cent

	Born Bef.1930	Born 1930/44	Born 1945/59	Born 1960/76
Postmaterialists	4	13	21	21
Mixed	72	68	67	68
Materialists	24	19	12	11
Total	100	100	100	100
No. of Respondents (100 per cent)	(347)	(391)	(544)	(550)
Difference PM-M	−20	−6	9	10

It is obvious that Inglehart's generational hypothesis is supported in these data. The oldest generation, born before 1930, has six times as many materialists as postmaterialists, 24 per cent as against four per cent. By contrast the generations born after the second world war have twice as many postmaterialists as materialists, namely roughly twenty per cent postmaterialists compared with ten per cent materialists. The difference in number between the postmaterialists and the materialists, shown in the last row, rises from −20 per cent per cent in the oldest generation to −6 per cent in the middle generation and further to +9 per cent in the postwar generation, then levels off to +10 per cent in the youngest generation. So, in spite of the remarks about a materialist reaction among the young, postmaterialism seems not to have subsided in the young generation. For the moment it has merely taken a less leftist direction, favouring the Green Bourgeois more than the Left Wing.

2.7. New Politics and the Danish Party System

According to the new politics thesis the impact of new politics on the partisan choice should increase in the long run, as voters move away from indifferent centrist positions and toward the poles of the new left and new right. But of course, at this point the difference between party systems comes into play and creates a number of possible ways to express this development. Existing parties may respond with greater or lesser reluctance to new politics issues, more or less durable splits may occur in them, and new parties based on the new issues may or may not emerge, depending, among other things, on the ease of entry to the party system. The safest prediction seems to be that a period of instability will occur while the party system and the voters adapt to the new situation.

The Danish party system became fragmented during the 1960s and especially the 1970s as new parties emerged on the left wing, the right wing and in the centre, cutting slices of the three old class parties. However, as was pointed out in chapter 1, the development since the middle 1970s has entailed a recovery of the three old parties taken as a whole; their combined voting strength has grown from 47 per cent in 1973 to 67 per cent in 1984 and 73 per cent in the 1994 election (Table 1.1). This is not the development one would associate with the new politics thesis and a decline of class politics.

Therefore, the tendency towards new politics parties spreading toward the poles of the party system to represent its centrifugal forces may well be counterbalanced by the voters gravitating toward the old parties near the centre of the new politics spectrum, or by a tendency of the old parties to differentiate themselves on the new politics as well as the old politics dimension. We will first illustrate the centrifugal nature of the party system by means of Figure 2.4, which shows the mean positions of voters of different parties on the old and new politics dimension.

On the old politics dimension, which forms the horizontal axis, the voters of the Socialist People's party and those of the Left Wing list make up the left wing while the voters of the Conservative and Liberal parties make up the right wing. On the new politics dimension, forming the vertical axis, voters of the Socialist People's party, the Left Wing list, the Christian People's and Radical Liberal parties, make up the left wing in the lower area of the diagram, whereas the Progress party voters make up the right wing. It is characteristic that the Social Democratic voters differ quite a lot from the Liberal and Conservative voters on the old politics dimension but very little on the new politics dimension, except that the Social

Democratic voters are on the average more 'green' than the bourgeois voters. Thus these parties have little weight in accounting for the variance on the new politics position, whereas the extreme positions of the Progress party in the upper part, and four other parties in the lower part of the diagram are counterbalanced by their gradually diminishing voting support.

Figure 2.4.   Positions of the party groups on the old politics (X) and new politics dimension (Y) in 1994

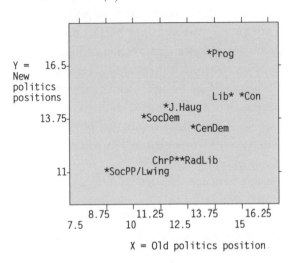

On the whole, there is a high tendency for voters of each party to cluster around the mean for that party. This tendency can be measured by one-way analysis of variance, or the correlation between individual position and mean position of the party. Table 2.7 shows these correlations for both the new and the old politics position.

Table 2.7.   Correlation between party mean and individual position on the old and new politics dimension. Etas

	1990	1994
Old politics position	.61	.52
New politics position	.46	.43

The correlation is strongest on the old politics position, eta=.61 in 1990 and .52 in 1994, but the new politics position is not much behind, eta=.46 in 1990 and .43 in 1994. Squaring these figures we find that partisan differences on the old politics position accounts for 37 per cent of the individual variance in 1990 and

27 per cent in 1994, whereas differences on the new politics position accounts for 21 per cent of the individual variance in 1990 and 18 per cent in 1994. On both dimensions the clustering of attitudes around the party means was more pronounced in 1990 than in 1994.

In the discussion of whether new politics is about to replace old politics as the leading dimension of political attitudes, or conversely whether new politics should be viewed as a merely a transitory and incoherent cluster of attitudes, we are led to take a middle position. In the course of a few elections new politics attitudes have asserted themselves as an important contribution to political thinking in the Danish electorate. Some, perhaps all, of the minor parties have taken stands on new politics issues as a basic strategy for survival while leaving it to the big parties to dominate the old politics issues. But there is no reality behind the idea that old politics is being replaced by new politics. Several issues that are regarded as new politics issues in other countries are actually closer to the old politics than to the new politics dimension in Danish politics. Environmental protection, for example, has become a leading issue in Social Democratic policy and in the Danish labour movement generally (Goul Andersen 1990).

We may study the relationship between the party system and the two dimensions in detail by breaking down the vote into our four ideological types (Table 2.8).

Table 2.8. Party distribution of the four ideological types 1994. Per cent

	Left Wing	Old Socialists	Green Bourg.	Right Wing
Unitary List	9	3	2	1
Socialist People's party	22	5	3	2
Social Democrats	41	50	18	20
J. Haugaard	1	1	0	1
Radical Liberals	6	2	9	2
Centre Democrats	3	3	5	2
Christian People's party	3	2	4	1
Conservatives	6	8	21	24
Liberals	9	19	37	39
Progressives	1	7	1	9
Total	101	100	100	101
N (100 per cent)	(471)	(513)	(253)	(533)

Note: For definition of the ideological types, see note of Table 2.2.

The two leftmost parties in the first two rows vary very considerably from the Left Wing at one end to the Right Wing: the vote for the Socialist People's party varies from 22 to two per cent, and the Unitary List, from nine to one per cent of the vote. The Social Democratic party has its strongest support among the Old Socialists (50 per cent) but gets a considerable share also on the Left Wing (41 per cent).

Turning to the small centre parties, all three of them reach their maximum support among the Green Bourgeois voters, where they collect almost twenty per cent of the vote between them, or the same as the support for the Social Democratic party. It is a little surprising that the Radical Liberals manage to get as much as six per cent of the Left Wing vote.

On the Right Wing the three bourgeois parties reach their maximum strength, with 39 per cent for the Liberals, 24 for the Conservatives, and 9 for the Progressives. Interestingly, the two large parties, the Liberals and the Conservatives, have their second stronghold among the Green Bourgeois whereas the Progress party relies on some measure of support from the Old Socialists. Again this underlines that it is the new right thinking rather than classical right thinking that underpins the Progress party, just as it is new left thinking which is the hallmark of the otherwise centrist Radical Liberal voters (cf. Goul Andersen and Bjørklund 1990).

The table reveals a deep schism that has developed between the two types of leftism. The Left Wing votes for the Socialist People's party or the Unitary List (31 per cent) rather than the three bourgeois parties (16 per cent); conversely, the Old Socialists prefer the bourgeois parties (34 per cent) to the two leftist parties (8 per cent). The Social Democratic party attempts to keep a balance between these two types and succeeds in the sense that its strength is almost the same in them (41 vs. 50 per cent). This strategy has sometimes paid off, as in 1990. At other times the Social Democratic party has suffered from the internal contradiction between these two types, losing voters to both sides. In the following we shall study the social cleavages underlying this political conflict.

2.8. New Politics and New Classes

The emergence of new politics issues is generally hypothesised to be related to structural changes in economically advanced societies. But there are many such changes, and the thesis is not too clear as to which are the relevant changes, and why. According to Inglehart the relative satisfaction of material needs in the new generations is at the core; these generations now turn to a pursuit of non-material needs for improving their quality of life. This might explain the emergence of the new left, but hardly that of the new right with its resistance to extending the welfare to immigrant groups or underdeveloped countries. Alternatively (cf. Goul Andersen 1990) one might speculate that the two poles of the new politics are opposite responses to the negative side effects of industrial society: when industrial growth along the accustomed lines no longer seems possible because of damage to the environment, or seems to carry too high social costs to family life or the local community, different strategies for countering the crisis may be developed. Here, the new left offers one utopia with a new set of values, whereas the new right offers another utopia, namely a return to values of the past. A third type of explanation, which takes post-industrial theory back to its point of departure (Bell 1973) focuses on the new types of professional organisation which are spreading both in the planning and administrative sectors of industry, in private service, and in public administration and service. These organisations are less hierarchical than earlier organisational forms, their emphasis being on cooperation, creativity and autonomy rather than obedience and diligence. The new left is here seen as a set of rising values congenial to this organisation, whereas the new right represents the values of the older industrial organisation which are gradually disappearing (Jenssen 1993). The reason why the older values are not simply represented by the old left and right is that old-fashioned sectors are now being marginalised more than previously by the advances of the new left.

While there may be some truth in each of these explanations, they also all have drawbacks. For example, the idea that the new left is a critique of the politics of modern society does not explain why political distrust is mainly found within the new right rather than the new left, a fact we shall discuss in chapter 11. On the other hand, the idea that the new right represents the backward and marginalised sectors does not square perfectly with the fact that the personnel of some new industrial enterprises, where trade unions have little importance, have a strong liking for the new right. Thus the commune of Billund, which is dominated by the Lego toy firm, is a stronghold of the Progress party.

At this stage our interest centres on locating our four ideological types in the social structure. We first look at the ideological preferences of occupational main classes (Table 2.9).

We find each of the four ideological types to have its stronghold in a different class. The Left Wing has its stronghold in the higher salariat, though it is also strongly represented in the lower salariat. The Old Socialists have their stronghold among the unskilled workers, while they are especially under-represented in the higher salariat. The stronghold of the Green Bourgeois is the higher salariat, while this ideology finds few adherents among the unskilled workers. Finally, the Right Wing clearly has its stronghold among the self-employed, a group including farmers, urban petty bourgeois, self-employed professionals, and an occasional capitalist.

Table 2.9. Ideological type of occupational groups. Per cent

	Unskilled workers	Skilled workers	Lower salariat	Higher salariat	Self-employed
Left Wing	24	25	35	40	21
Old Socialists	51	37	28	8	17
Green Bourgeois	6	12	14	25	17
Right Wing	19	26	23	27	44
Total	100	100	100	100	100
N (100 per cent)	(263)	(180)	(506)	(174)	(122)
Per cent Old Left	75	62	63	48	38
Per cent New Left	30	37	49	65	38

Note: For definition of the ideological groups or types, see note of Table 2.2. In the two last rows, Old Left=Left Wing+Old Socialists, and New Left=Left Wing+Green Bourgeois.

Consequently, in the row showing the per cent old left, one recognises the familiar picture of the workers (especially the unskilled) standing to the left and the self-employed, to the right. The salaried take a middle position with the lower salariat siding with the skilled workers and the higher salariat closer to the self-employed.

On the new politics dimension the situation is very different in that the higher salariat stand to the left whereas the unskilled workers are on the right, followed by the skilled workers and the self-employed. Consequently only one group is consistently on the right on both dimensions, namely the self-employed. Compared with the old politics dimension, workers (especially the unskilled) switch to the right on the new politics dimension, whereas higher salaried switch to the left on the same dimension.

While the class division of the industrial society thus stands in a straightforward relation to the old politics position, it partly fails to account for the new politics position. However, another stratifying factor is ready to take its place, namely level of education (Table 2.10).

It is evident that educational level is strongly correlated with left position on the new politics dimension, while it has little to do with the old politics position. Looking at the 1994 figures in the lower half of the table, the size of the new left increases from 20 to 68 per cent in the sample as we pass from those with seven years of schooling to those with twelve years or more. That increase falls almost evenly on the Left Wing and the Green Bourgeois, which means that very slight differences in old politics position are found between levels of education.

Table 2.10.   Ideological type by level of school education. Per cent, 1994

	Primary school 7 years	Primary school 8-9 years	Secondary 10 years	Higher, 12+ years
1990:				
Left Wing	10	21	32	44
Old Socialists	45	46	30	15
Green Bourgeois	6	11	14	20
Right Wing	39	22	24	21
Total	100	100	100	100
Per cent Old Left	55	67	62	59
Per cent New Left	16	32	46	64
1994:				
Left Wing	12	23	29	42
Old Socialists	37	39	30	12
Green Bourgeois	8	10	14	26
Right Wing	43	29	26	20
Total	100	100	100	100
Total Old Left	49	62	59	54
Total New Left	20	33	43	68

Note: For definition of the ideological types, see note of Table 2.2. In the two last rows, Old Left=Left Wing+Old Socialists, and New Left=Left Wing+Green Bourgeois.

We may here refer back to the generational differences which we observed in Table 2.5. Can the difference between generations in regard to new politics position be explained by the differential educational levels of these successive generations — or is it the other way round, so that educational differences are explained by these differences? The reasonable way to test these possibilities *vis-à-vis* one another is by means of regression analysis. When we enter the new politics index as the dependent variable, school education as one independent variable, and cohort as the other, the regression lines for the two years have the parameters shown in Table 2.11.

Table 2.11. *Effects of education and generation on new politics position. Unstandardised b's*

	1990		1994	
Education (4 levels)	−1.28	(.11)	−1.02	(.08)
Generation (4 cohorts)	−.12	(.12)	−.39	(.08)
Constant	16.76		17.06	

Note: See Table 2.10 for the definition of education, Table 2.5 for the definition of the cohorts, and Table 2.2 for the definition of new politics position. Entries are scale positions on the new politics index running from 4 to 20. Standard deviations in parentheses.

The coefficients show that the level of education is by far the stronger of the two independent variables in driving the new politics position of the respondent toward the new left pole. Controlling for cohorts, the difference between educational levels is still more than one scale point. Controlling for level of education the difference between successive cohorts is far below one-half scale position. As we have indicated the standard error of the estimates in parentheses, we may note that in 1990 the effect of respondent's cohort is not even significant when we control for level of school education. That is, even older persons, whose values are supposed to have been indoctrinated many years ago, tend to acquire the stands of the new left if they got a long school education, and the stands of the new right if they left school early. The limitations of our data prevent us from going further toward an exploration of the underlying differences in outlook and organisational values. However, such research has been carried out in Norway. Jenssen (1993) has established a basic distinction between two types of *relational* value which are promoted in educational institutions as well as in modern work organisations. A strongly competitive market environment promotes authoritarian and individualistic values such as are found on the new right. A more protected work environment favours what he calls egalitarian collectivism, that is, values represented on the new left. This conceptualisation fits with the scant data which the election surveys and other Danish surveys can yield. For example, Svensson and Togeby (1992) have shown how the new social order of post-industrial society gives rise to political cleavage in the young population along the attitudes of political tolerance, obviously an attitude strongly related to our new left attitude. In the election survey we have also found occupational subgroups with extremely high scores on new left attitudes (Borre 1995b). In particular the professional personnel in the welfare, health, and educational sectors were about the highest scorers in the new left direction in the 1990 sample.

2.9. Conclusion

In this chapter we have sought to clarify and test some hypotheses that are derived from new politics theory. Drawing on data from 1990 and 1994 we have found that indeed a new politics dimension can be discerned in the attitudinal data, giving the issue preferences and party preferences of the electorate a two-dimensional character. The labels of new left and new right seem justified by the evidence that both in 1990 and 1994 a new left and new right have supplemented the old left and right. Furthermore, the vote for the traditional large class parties in the Danish system are mainly differentiated on the old politics dimension whereas the vote for the minor parties are differentiated on the new politics dimension.

The new left/right issue dimension is related to such value dimensions as the libertarian/authoritarian and the postmaterialist/materialist dimensions, and voter positions on it are related above all to the voter's level of education, high education predisposing the voter toward the new left. Between 1990 and 1994 attitudes on the average turned toward the right on the old politics but not on the new politics dimension, and thus the distinction between the two dimensions helps clarify the nature of the shift to the right at the 1994 election.

3

ISSUE POSITION AND VOTING

3.1. Issue Voting

The party choice is the classical democratic means at the citizens' disposal for translating values, interests, and concerns into government action. Values and value change in civil society might therefore be expected to find their expression at the level of policy positions of the parliamentary parties. This linkage process has increasingly become the focus of electoral research, as several indications of a general rise in 'issue voting' and 'policy voting' began to be noticed about twenty years ago (Pomper 1972; Boyd 1972; Nie with Andersen 1974). The evidence generally points toward increasing issue voting in the crude sense of the term, i.e., conceived as correlations between issue positions and the vote. In that sense the tendency was also observed in Denmark for the period 1971-1984 (Borre 1984). However, an important link in that relationship has been missing, namely the voters' perceptions of the positions of the parties. Issue voting proper requires a double process: (1) the voter must take a position on some issue or issues, and (2) he or she must recognise the positions of at least some of the parties on these issues. Both are necessary for the translation process to function. The electoral process is supposed by democratic theory somehow to translate a complex set of values, interests and concerns into an extremely simple code, the choice of one party or candidate among a limited set of alternatives — in some party systems only two. In order to maximise the information, the voter in his or her role of communicator must be able to differentiate clearly between the meanings of these alternatives, that is, to predict the policy implications of the vote.

3.2. Proximity and Directional Models

The present chapter introduces the concept of policy distance and discusses the implications of it for the Danish 1994 election. The dominant paradigm for the attainment of public control of government policy includes a *proximity hypothesis*, which states that the utility of a party declines with increasing distance between the party's and the voter's issue position. In choosing among parties, other things being equal, the voter chooses the party with the highest utility. Under some simplifying assumptions concerning the shape of the utility function, this means choosing that party which is closest to his or her own position. In a more stochastic form of the hypothesis we would expect the vote for a party to attain its maximum support at the party's issue position and to decline with increasing distance in both directions from that position. However, the way the vote falls off will be influenced by the position of neighbouring parties: having a strong competitor on one side but not on the other, we should expect a party to display a sharper decline in support on the side where the competitor is.

Furthermore, there may be several issue dimensions involved, not all of them equally salient to the voter or the party. The hypothesis is expected to hold especially on those issues that are salient for the voter and stressed by the party. Thus the greatest likelihood of voting for a party should be found among voters who are near to the party on an issue which is important to both the voter and the party.

Space limitations will prevent us from testing all of these variants of the proximity hypothesis. However, a rival to the proximity hypothesis itself should be noted. This is the *directional* hypothesis (Rabinowitz and Mcdonald 1989), which states that the utility of a party increases with the extremeness of the party's position in the same direction as the voters' position. An exception is made for parties that are so extreme as to be irresponsible. But within a certain zone of responsibility, other things being equal a voter will choose the party which has the most extreme position in the same direction as the voter.

To illustrate the difference, the following line shows the position of a voter V and two parties P1 and P2, together with the central or neutral point 0 on an issue scale.

$$P1 \qquad 0 \quad V \qquad\qquad\qquad P2$$

According to proximity theory the voter should choose P1 rather than P2, even though it is on the other side of the neutral point, because P1 is nearer to the voter. According to directional theory the voter should choose P2 because that party represents the voter's view in a clearer form than P1.

While the perspective of proximity theory is one in which the major parties tend to converge on the centre position in order to conquer the in-between voters (cf. Downs 1957, pp. 115-117), the perspective of directional theory is one in which the large parties tend to move away from one another so as to present idealised and coherent pictures of the voter's positions. Obviously, the prospects for the centrist catch-all party are very different in the two perspectives. Since we have seen in the Danish case how the centrist parties have lost support since 1973 (cf. chapter 1), it will be plausible to investigate directional theory along with proximity theory in the following cases.

Voting and Political Attitudes in Denmark

How are the positions of the parties established? In computing policy distances we generally use as the position of the party the mean assessment of the whole sample. All respondents are, then, our judges of where the party stands. It is true that the voter's assessment conceals systematic variation such that those who like a party, and especially its own voters, draw the party nearer to their own position than the mean distance, whereas those who dislike the party very much push the party away from their own position so as to increase the distance. This tendency also follows from psychological theories of cognitive inconsistency or dissonance (cf. Heider 1958; Festinger 1957). Still, we may hope that as an aggregate result, these judgments provide a fair estimate of the party's position. In any case it would be hard to think of a more neutral evaluation than the one given by the electorate as a whole.

The tendency of the party's own voters to draw the party closer to their own position is one explanation why there are still voters for the party even at long distances. According to the proximity theory this can be explained by the lack of salience of the issue on which the policy distance is measured. But a rival explanation is that the long distances are not perceived as being long for the person who votes for the party. Misperception is one way out of the psychological inconsistency.

Using perceived distance instead of true distance will tend to increase our correlations between policy distance and support, for those reporting a very short distance will nearly all be the party's own supporters while those reporting a very long distance will be the party's most eager opponents. In the extreme case where all the voters of a party assimilate the party's position with their own, and nobody else does this, the vote will be 100 per cent at zero distance and decline immediately to 0 per cent at any other distance. Hence, using perceived distances rather than true distances will probably give a large and unfair advantage to the proximity theory relative to directional theory, and we shall not use them in the following.

The positional model of voting behaviour, whether of the proximity or directional variety, stands somewhat in opposition to the performance model to be discussed in chapter 4, as it assumes that the voters' goals may be opposed to those of other voters, whereas the performance model tends to impute certain goals as more or less shared by all voters, though with different emphasis or priority. Goals such as economic growth, full employment, a clean environment, or a well-functioning health sector, lead to what is commonly termed 'valence' issues. Since no one is likely to have the opposite goals, the controversies arise over the priority of the goals, the efficiency with which they are pursued by the government, the means by which they are pursued, etc. Some of these aspects of policy are discussed in later chapters, especially chapters 4 and 8-10. But in the present chapter we are dealing with 'position' issues, which entail an additional controversy over which goal should be pursued in government policy. These issues, of course, include most of those which have, through time, led to ideological clashes and to the emergence of new parties and social movements.

Already in the early debate about issue voting, the presence of valence issues led to severe criticism of the proximity hypothesis (Stokes 1963). Valence issues and position issues are, however, not sharply separated. In position voting the voter chooses one out of two or more positions on a scale, and proceeds to make a decision among parties which have taken different policy positions on the same scale. These positions may represent more or less state intervention in some policy area such as a welfare sector, more or less regulation of firms or the private lives of citizens, more or less power to a certain institution, etcetera; but they can also represent a trade-off between two 'valence issues' or political goals such as stable prices versus full employment, or environmental protection versus economic growth, asking the respondents to indicate which should have the highest priority. The notion of policy positions thereby has a wide range of application. Hence one can estimate a policy distance between the voter's position and each party's position on each pertinent issue or ideological dimension.

Nonetheless the requirement that voters in general have positions on issues and recognise the positions of the parties seems to imply a level of rationality which is seldom confirmed by voting studies. The directional theory is less demanding of the voter in this respect because it only asks for graded responses to opposite issue positions which may be little more than symbols (Rabinowitz and Macdonald 1989).

3.3. Selecting the Issues

It follows that in order to use the positional models in an analysis, one must have information on the positions of both voters and parties on the same issues. What issue scales should be used for a fairly adequate analysis of the Danish 1994 election? In the first place we saw in chapter 2 that the left-right scale is associated with a broad set of issues orientations on both old and new politics issues, though the economic issue referred primarily to the old politics dimension. Consequently, according to the proximity model we should expect a particularly strong negative relationship between party preference and policy distance on the general left-right dimension. In the Danish questionnaire, positions on that dimension were based on the question used by the Eurobarometer, 'In politics one often talks about left and right. Where do you place the parties on this scale [indicating a scale with points from one to ten]? And where do you place yourself?'

Left-right positions permit an overall test of our hypothesis. However, exactly because of its overall or summary nature, we also need to validate the positional models on various issues that are thought to enter people's minds when they make evaluations according to the left-right schema. Preferably these issues should include both old and new politics issues as they may be weakly related to the left-right scale, especially the new issues. In the following, therefore, besides the left-right positions on the ten point scale we shall rely on a set of items where the respondent is asked to indicate the position of each party, and of that of himself or herself, on an issue by means of a five-point scale such as the following:

'The parties disagree as to how many refugees we can take. Some think we take far too many refugees. Others say that we easily could take more refugees. Here is a scale from 1 to 5 [Show and explain card]. About where would you place [List of parties]? And where would you place yourself?'

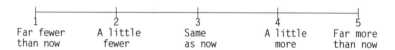

1	2	3	4	5
Far fewer than now	A little fewer	Same as now	A little more	Far more than now

Let us now illustrate how the two models work by reference to such a five-point scale. Proximity theory states that the voter's support for a party is a negative function of the numerical distance between the party's position and the voter's position. Accordingly, in theory this distance can assume any value between 0 and 4. Directional theory according to Rabinowitz and Macdonald (1989) states that the support is a positive function of both the party's and the voter's distance from a neutral point. This is because voters toward the ends of the scale have stronger feelings about the issue and because *parties* toward the end of the scale arouse stronger feelings than those in the centre. Thus for the purpose of testing the directional model we recode the positions so that it runs from −2 to +2 with 'same as now' taking the neutral value of 0. The utility is then computed as P*V, where P is the party's position and V, the voter's position. Obviously this product takes the maximum value of +4 when both P and V are at the same end, and the minimum value of −4 when they are at opposite ends on the scale. The utility will be 0 when either P or V, or both, are at the neutral middle position, 'same as now'. An interesting corollary of directional theory is that parties in the middle of the spectrum will have little support because they arouse no emotion at all.

Six issues were selected for a closer study of issue voting according to the proximity and directional models discussed above. Figure 3.1 shows the six issues and the distribution of the sample on each issue.

Figure 3.1.   Sample Distribution on Six Issues, 1994

1. Free market versus state intervention to control market forces

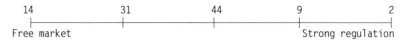

2. Tight economic policy, even in face of rising unemployment – versus increasing consumption
    and employment, even in the face of rising public debt.

3. Cutting public expenditures and revenues versus facing rising public income and expenses
    in the future

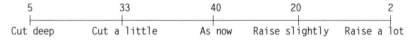

4. Take fewer or more refugees than now

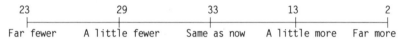

5. Putting more or less weight on environmental protection ('green dimension')

6. Maintaining law-and-order with more severe punishment versus preventing crime and treating
    criminals in a human way.

The choice of issues was inspired by the hypothesis of a change in priorities from economic to non-economic issues. Chapter 2 demonstrated that the parties, as groups of voters, differentiate themselves on the new politics as well as the old politics dimension. These findings suggest that the positions of voters on these issues would be influenced by their old and new politics position. Through this connection, furthermore, the themes of post-industrial change discussed in that chapter might be pursued further in the present one. New politics theory leads to an expectation that policy distances on new politics issues will gain importance relative to policy distances on old politics issues. However, the lack of comparability with earlier elections in our data makes it difficult to test the validity of these expectations.

The issues were conceived as three issues from the old politics (no. 1-3) and three from the new politics agenda (no. 4-6). In chapter 2 we defined four ideological types of voters by combining old and new politics attitudes. Table 3.1 reports the average positions of the four ideological types on each of the six issues. On each issue the leftmost position was coded –2 and the rightmost +2.

Table 3.1. Position of four ideological voter types on six issues

	Mean Position of			
	Left Wing	Old Socialists	Green Bourgeois	Right Wing
1. Free market	.01	.36	.61	.88
2. Tight economic policy	–.18	–.02	.47	.55
3. Cut public sector	–.30	.15	.38	.55
4. Fewer refugees	–.25	1.04	.11	1.05
5. Green policy	–1.09	–.66	–.56	–.25
6. Maintain law-and-order	–.27	.61	.14	.70

Note: See Figure 3.1 on the issue scales. The coding of the items was from –2 to +2, except for item 6 where the coding was reversed to run from +2 to –2.

We observe that for the three economic or old politics issues, 1-3, the order among the four voter types is similar to their positions on the left-right scale (cf. Table 3.3): the Left Wing has the lowest score followed by the Old Socialists, the Green Bourgeois, and lastly the Right Wing. That is, there is no tendency for the Left Wing and Old Socialists to stand close together with low scores, and the Green Socialists and Right Wing to be close together with high scores.

On the issues of refugees (no. 4) and law-and-order (no. 6) we find the new politics thinking confirmed in that the order of the two middle camps is reversed. Left Wing and Green Bourgeois voters tend to cluster at one end, and Old Socialist and Right Wing voters, at the other end of the scale. However, the environmental issue (no. 5) presents a mixture of the two tendencies. The Left Wing is clearly the most 'green' and the Right Wing the least 'green'. But the Old Socialists are close to the Green Bourgeois, and actually slightly more 'green' than the so-called Green Bourgeois! The tendency of the 'green' issue to be poorly integrated in the new politics agenda was observed in chapter 2 although to a smaller extent than here. That tendency fits with earlier research on the 'green discourse' (Goul Andersen 1990).

3.4. Positions on the Left-Right Scale

Our first analysis of the proximity and directional theories, however, will be carried out on the left-right scale rather than on individual issues. Table 3.2 shows in the first column the positions of the parties from left to right, as assessed by all the voters in the sample. The second column shows the positions of the party groups according to the data on the voters' self-placement.

Table 3.2. Left-right positions of the parties and their voters, 1994

	Party position	Mean of party's voters
Unitary List	1.80	3.74
Socialist People's party	2.91	4.09
Social Democratic	4.73	5.32
Radical Liberal	5.35	5.92
Centre Democratic	5.78	6.46
Christian People's party	5.85	6.35
Conservative	7.56	7.47
Liberal	7.91	7.71
Progressive	8.86	7.99
J. Haugaard		5.17
All	5.94	6.29

Note: Positions on the left-right scale ranged from 1 (left) to 10 (right).

In presenting the table, blank lines have been inserted where the distance between neighbouring parties approaches two points. This leads to a grouping in which the two opposition parties on the left stand apart from the four governing parties from the last period, which in turn stand apart from the three opposition parties on the right.

A characteristic feature is that the parties' positions in the first column are much more spread out over the scale than are the positions of the parties' voters in the second column. The parties range from 1.80 for the leftmost party to 8.86 for the rightmost, a range of over 7 points on the ten point scale. By contrast, the voters range from 3.74 for the leftmost party to 7.99 for the rightmost, a range of only 4.25 points. All the parties in the left opposition and the centre governing coalition are located to the left of their voters, whereas the three right opposition parties are located to the right of their voters.

The inclination of voters to cluster nearer to the centre position than the position of their preferred party suggests that many voters do not mind choosing a party which represents a clearer stand than their own. But it cannot be used as evidence against proximity theory, for a party may well have its maximum level of support in one or the other of the thinly populated tails of the left-right scale. It is, however, difficult to explain why the party does not move closer toward the more densely populated centre. A possible explanation for this fact will be offered in section

Voting and Political Attitudes in Denmark

5.7. For the present, however, the party positions in the first column of figures are to be used for computing the policy distances and hence, the proximity and directional scores for each respondent's relation to each party. The policy distances for a given party to be used as the independent variable in the proximity model are simply the absolute distance between the respondent's position (from 1 to 10) and the party's position. To illustrate, the distance from the Left-wing list is .80 for those at position 1, .20 for those at position 2, 1.20 for those at position 3, increasing to 8.20 for those at position 10, the rightmost position. The directional model requires that the positions of both parties and respondents be recomputed as distances from 5.5, the neutral midpoint of the left-right scale. The Left-wing list accordingly is scored −3.7, and this score is to be multiplied by the respondent's score, which ranges from −4.5 at position 1 to +4.5 at position 10.

The values thus obtained are predictors of the utility of that party for that respondent. In order to measure the dependent variable we turn to a set of questions measuring the respondent's general attitude toward the individual parties; the responses were graded from 1 (strongly dislike) to 11 (strongly like). In addition we analyse the effect of the predictor variables on the vote for the party.

Table 3.3 shows Pearson correlation coefficients at the level of the individual voter for the relation between on one hand the proximity score and the directional score, and on the other hand party support in the form of sympathy scores and voting.

Table 3.3. Correlation between party support, proximity and directional score on the left-right dimension

	Party sympathy and		Vote and	
	Proximity score	Directional score	Proximity score	Directional score
Unitary List	−.44	.45		
Socialist People's party	−.56	.54	−.33	.33
Social Democratic	−.46	.45	−.47	.37
Radical Liberal	−.30	.29	−.17	.04*
Centre Democrats	−.08	−.09		
Christian People's party	−.04*	.03*		
Conservative	−.51	.54	−.27	.30
Liberal	−.59	.61	−.42	.42
Progressive	−.45	.45		

Note: *=Not significant at five per cent level.

The two first columns deal with sympathy scores. It is evident that both the proximity hypothesis and the directional hypothesis receive overwhelming confirmation in these data. If we disregard the three minor centre parties, the correlations are all from .44 and upward to .61. For the Radical Liberals they are around .30. Only with respect to the Centre Democrats and the Christian People's parties, the correlations drop to insignificance or have the wrong sign.

It is also observed that the differences between the coefficients for the two models are indeed very small, no more than .03 except in the curious case of the Centre Democrats where the directional score is negatively related to sympathy for the party.

The two next columns of Table 3.3 shows correlations between the vote for a party and the two scores for five of the parties. For the Unitary list, the Progressive party, and the two small centre parties these correlations are omitted because of problems of sampling variance when the party is very small. We observe that also with regard to the vote, the correlations have the proper sign and are significant except in one case, involving the Radical Liberal party. Comparing the two models we find that the proximity model has the better fit in the case of the Social Democrats and the Radical Liberals, whereas the directional model has a slightly better fit in the case of the Conservative party. However, the vote correlations are generally smaller than the sympathy correlations, partly because party sympathy is graded into eleven positions whereas the vote is a binary variable.

Two other sets of correlations are not shown in the table but deserve to be noted anyway. In the first place, one reason why the two models tend to produce the same fit is that they are mutually related, especially for the extreme parties. Policy distance score and directional score are correlated with $r=.42$ for the Radical Liberals, $r=-.68$ for the Social Democrats, $r=-.89$ for the Liberals, $r=-.83$ for the Conservatives, $r=-.97$ for the Socialist People's party, $r=-.98$ for the Progressives, and $r=-.996$ for the Unitary List.

Second, our two measures of party support do not seem to measure the same thing. Actually vote and sympathy are correlated with $r=.61$ for the Social Democrats and $r=.59$ for the Liberals, but then correlation declines with declining party size to $r=.45$ for the Conservatives, $r=.40$ for the Socialist People's party, and $r=.26$ for the Radical Liberals. Apparently people may sympathise with smaller parties without voting for them; and the sympathy score in these cases tends to fit the models rather than does the voting choice.

3.5. Left-Right Placement and the Social Democratic Party

The Social Democratic party is extremely visible in its position as the chief governing party. In addition it is beleaguered by opposition parties both on its right and left. A good model of issue voting should therefore be able to account for the voters' choice of the Social Democratic party *vis-à-vis* other parties. However, both the proximity and the directional model perform rather poorly on the Social Democratic party, and hence we shall look more closely at this important case.

Proximity theory leads us to expect the support for the party to describe a curve with a maximum near the position of the party, that is, near 4.73. For each left-right position the first column of Table 3.4 records the Social Democratic support by left-right position in terms of the average sympathy shown toward the party (recomputed to range from −100 to +100); and the second column indicates Social Democratic support in terms of per cent of votes.

Table 3.4. Sympathy with and voting for SD party by the voter's position on the left-right scale

Left/Right position	Mean sympathy −100/+100	Votes per cent	Distance score	Directional score
1	5	22	3.73	3.5
2	42	14	2.73	2.8
3	44	42	1.73	2.0
4	40	61	.73	1.2
5	41	69	.27	.4
6	20	34	1.27	−.4
7	−5	7	2.27	−1.2
8	−18	6	3.27	−2.0
9	−13	4	4.27	−2.8
10	−25	8	5.27	−3.5

The table shows that both indicators of support have a maximum somewhere between the extreme positions on the left-right scale. The sympathy score reaches the 40 centigrade level at position 2 and remains there until position 5, after which it declines. The vote for the party reaches a maximum of 69 per cent at position 5, then drops off steeply to 7 per cent at position 7.

How well does this pattern of sympathy and voting fit proximity theory? Since from Table 3.2 we know the party's position to be 4.73, we may compute the distances to the positions toward left and right. Those voters who place themselves at position 5 are the nearest with a distance of .27 points; those at position 10 are the furthest removed with a distance of 5.27 points. These distances are entered in the third column of Table 3.3. The resulting relationship with sympathy score and voting for the Social Democratic party are seen in Figures 3.2 and 3.3, respectively.

Figure 3.2. Relation between distance from the Social Democratic party's position on the left/right dimension (X) and sympathy with SD party (Y)

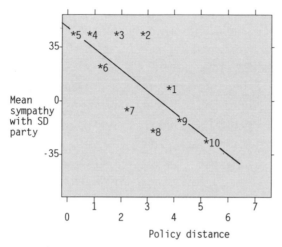

Note: The figures on the plot indicate position numbers. Regression line Y = 48.0 — 13.66 X with r=-.80 for N=10.

Figure 3.3. Relation between distance from the Social Democratic party's position on the left/right dimension (X) and per cent voting for SD party (Y)

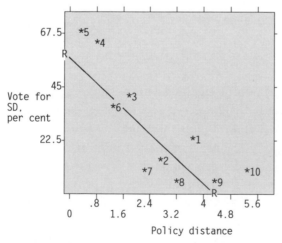

Note: The figures on the plot indicate position numbers. Regression line Y =58.4 — 12.41 X with r=-.84 for N=10.

Voting and Political Attitudes in Denmark

By and large the proximity hypothesis is confirmed in that the support tends to fall with increasing distance. However, it is also evident that left-right distance is not the whole truth in explaining the decline. In particular those located to the left of the Social Democratic party appear to like the party, and vote for it, much more than those to the right at approximately the same distance.

Now, one consequence of the proximity theory is that a party moving in a certain direction, left or right, will gain voters in that direction while losing voters in the opposite direction, other things being equal. The optimum place for a party should therefore be the position at which these two flows are equal in size. In the case of the Social Democratic party one is tempted to suggest that the party would fare better if it took up an even more centrist position than the present one. The reason is that the support appears more sensitive to distances toward the centre-right than to distances toward the left. In addition there are more voters to conquer in the centre than on the left. Thus it might gain in the aggregate by reducing distances to the centre at the expense of longer distances toward the left. As we shall see later though, there are arguments to the contrary.

How does the directional theory fit the pattern of Social Democratic sympathy and support? According to that theory we compute the directional factor at position 1 to be the product of the voter deviation from the centre, −4.5, and the party's deviation from the centre, −.77. The result is about 3.5. For the subsequent positions the directional factor decreases in a monotonous way to finish at −3.5 at position 10, the rightmost voter position. These directional scores are entered in Table 3.3 as the last column. The relations between that score and sympathy with, resp. voting support for, the Social Democratic party are seen in Figures 3.4 and 3.5.

In the case of the sympathy for the party, the directional theory appears to fit the data better than the proximity theory, were it not that the pattern is broken by the low sympathy shown at the rightmost position in Figure 3.4 (which is actually on the extreme left). In the case of voting for the party, however, the directional theory gives a hopeless misfit in Figure 3.5, since the maximum is reached in the middle position.

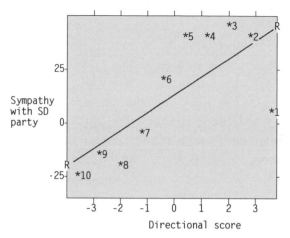

Note: The figures on the plot indicate position numbers. Regression line Y = 13.1 + 8.49 X with r=.75 for N=10.

Figure 3.5. Relation between directional score of Social Democratic party (X) and per cent voting for SD party (Y)

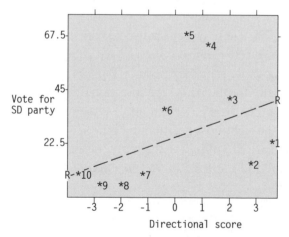

Note: The figures on the plot indicate position numbers. Regression line Y = 26.7 + 4.34 X with r=.44.

Until now we have studied left-right position. The left-right scale is expected to serve as a kind of short-hand representation of those issues that are important in the electorate. Therefore the problems that we encounter in fitting the Social Democratic party into these models can also be expected to originate in similar problems for the individual issues, indeed a detailed examination confirms this to be the case. Table 3.5 indicates the Social Democratic strength in per cent of the vote on each position of the six issues. These positions have been ordered from left to right.

Table 3.5. *Issue position and Social Democratic strength. Per cent voting Social Democratic at each issue position*

	Position				
	Left		Centre		Right
1. State regulation	26	41	47	18	13
2. Economic policy	44	51	44	12	10
3. Public budgets	31	42	45	18	11
4. Refugees	28	31	38	33	31
5. Environment	39	37	33	9	16
6. Law-and-order	28	35	44	23	36

Note: Per cent bases may be estimated from Figure 3.1.

It is observed, first, that on four of the six issues the party reaches its maximum at the middle position; on economic policy the strength culminates at the moderate left position, and only on the environmental issue is the maximum strength at the leftmost, 'most green' position. Thus the centre-left position of the Social Democratic party on the left-right scale seems well grounded in policy positions.

Secondly, the strength declines monotonously from the maximum in both directions except on the two last issues, where there is a slight anomaly. The monotonous course is of course encouraging for the policy distance model — that is, provided the party's own position is near the maximum point on each issue.

Thirdly, on the economic issues the minimum strength is reached at the far right position with 10-13 per cent Social Democrats. But on the three non-economic issues the situation is different. On the environmental and law-and-order issues the minimum is found at the moderate right position, and on the refugee issue the minimum is among those on the far left. By contrast, on the far right of the law-and-order and the refugee issue the party scores over thirty per cent of the vote!

We can immediately judge from these figures that the directional model represents no advance in relation to the proximity model, at least so far as the Social Democratic party is concerned. The directional model predicts a monotonous rise in utility of a party from one end of the continuum to the other — in the case of the Social Democratic party, from right to left. But only in one case, the case of the environmental issue, does the party obtain its maximum support on the extreme left; and even here the decline toward the right is broken, since the minimum is reached at position 4, not position 5. By further analysis it might be shown that the situation is better in the case of other parties, especially those with rather extreme positions. However, the proximity model and the directional model lead to the same prediction in the case of extreme parties; these parties give no grounds for assessing the merits of the two models. The real challenge for the directional model would therefore be to predict the pattern of support for parties on the moderate left and right, and for parties close to the centre. The Social Democratic party is by far the best test-case of a party with a moderate position, and as we have seen, the directional model does not work here.

3.6. Issue Proximity and Voting

The proximity model seems congruent with the two-dimensional issue space model that was sketched in chapter 2. Empirically, the directional model does not represent a significant advance over the proximity model in the case of Denmark, unlike some other countries where it has been tested (cf. Rabinowitz, Macdonald and Listhaug 1991; Merrill 1995; Maddens 1996). We shall therefore stick to the proximity model for the rest of the chapter.

The first step in testing the proximity hypothesis on our six issues is to compute the mean perceived position of the parties. The positions of all nine parties on the six issues are presented in Table 3.6.

Table 3.6. Mean positions of parties on six issues on a 1-5 scale

	Issue					
	State regul- ation	Econ- omic policy	Public bud- gets	Refu- gees	En- viron- ment	Law- and- order
Unitary List	4.45	4.35	4.37	4.02	4.47	1.81
Socialist People's party	4.21	4.16	4.15	3.96	4.38	1.91
Social Democratic	3.47	3.81	3.65	3.51	3.68	2.52
Radical Liberal	2.97	3.08	3.03	3.34	3.56	2.77
Christian People's party	2.88	2.97	3.05	3.45	3.42	2.81
Centre Democratic	2.80	3.01	2.98	3.28	3.27	3.07
Conservative	2.05	2.08	2.10	2.32	2.76	3.78
Liberal	1.87	1.86	1.85	2.15	2.58	3.90
Progressive	1.60	1.72	1.29	1.10	2.05	4.47
Weighted mean	2.62	2.76	2.68	2.91	3.25	3.12

Note: See Figure 3.1 for these issue scales.

Looking at the Social Democratic position on the economic issues, it is observed that this position is between 3 and 4 on all three issues. This is promising for the proximity model, for the party's voting strength is culminated between these two positions in Table 3.7. Looking at the non-economic issues, the last three columns, we find the party's position to be between 3 and 4 on the first two issues and between 2 and 3 on the law-and-order issue; again we find consistency between the party and its voters. It is true that on the issues of law-and-order and the number of refugees to be admitted to Denmark, there is a right wing including many Social Democratic voters. However, if the right wing is very small, this will just be a mole in the evidence supporting the directional theory.

The Unitary List and the Socialist People's party are consistently placed left of centre on each of the six issues, the Unitary List being placed slightly to the left of the Socialist People's party. The three small centre parties are placed slightly left-of-centre, but to the right of the Social Democratics party, on all issues. The Conservatives, Liberals, and Progressives are placed further to the right in that precise order on all issues. Indeed, the order among the parties hardly differs at all from one issue to the next, obviously reflecting a general left-right image of the Danish party system.

We may therefore fear that the individual issues do not count separately in explaining the partisan choice. However, we shall employ multiple regression analysis in order to explore this question. For each of six parties the vote was regressed on the policy distance on the six issues separately. Although we are here dealing with binary variables as dependent variables, the linear regression model rather than logit or probit models was chosen in order to facilitate the interpretation of the regression coefficients. Table 3.7 reports the result for the three old and large parties in columns 1-3 and for the three second-order parties in columns 4-6. These latter parties, it should be remembered, were claimed in chapter 2 to be the main representatives of new politics in the Danish party system.

The coefficients except in the last row are estimated vote changes associated with a change in policy distance of one position. For example, the Social Democratic vote declines by 13.2 per cent when the distance on the economic policy issue is increased by one position. Below these six rows, the 'Constant' row estimates the party's vote in per cent at zero distance: for example, 70.2 per cent are estimated to vote Social Democratic among those who agree completely with the party's stand on economic policy (since that stand lies inbetween two positions on the scale, complete agreement is not possible, however). In the bottom row the multiple correlation coefficient R is reported.

Table 3.7. Regression effects of policy distances on the vote

	Social Dem.	Conser- vative	Lib- eral	Soc. People	Radical Liberal	Progr. party
1. Gov. regulation	−.104	−.087	....	....	....	....
2. Economic policy	−.132	−.068	−.113	−.059	....	....
3. Public budgets	−.112	....	−.114	−.042	....	....
4. Refugees	....	....	....	....	....	−.051
5. Environment	....	−.046	....	....	....	....
6. Law-and-order	....	....	−.055	−.034	−.045	....
Constant	.702	.346	.547	.267	.096	.121
R	.41	.28	.38	.33	.14	.23

Note: Entries are unstandardised regression coefficients. Only coefficients that are significant on the five per cent level are shown.

We find that several issues influence the vote for these parties, and in every case the influence takes the form of a negative effect of policy distance. In the case of the three large parties, which we hypothesised to represent the old politics or economic issues, most of the significant effects comes from issues 1-3. Out of nine significant effects, seven belong to the cluster of economic issues. In the case of the three second-order parties, which we hypothesised to represent the new politics, only two of the five significant effects come from the economic issues. Though we would have preferred a clearer indication that support for a party varies with distance on just that dimension which the party is supposed to represent, the result points in the direction predicted by the new politics hypothesis.

3.7. The Role of Party Identification

We have established some evidence in favour of the proximity hypothesis, but we have also seen in the case of the left-right placement that voters tend to be 'on the inside', that is, in a less extreme position, than their parties. This principle turns out to apply to the majority of the individual issues as well. The typical relationship is that, on both the left and the right side of Danish politics, the parties are more extreme than their average voter. Thus the relationship we saw in Table 3.2 for the left-right placement is valid for each individual issue scale. Only one issue, the environmental issue, differs from this pattern in that even the left-wing parties are not as 'green' as their voters. But even in the case of the environmental issue, the range of positions from left to right is much greater for the parties than for their voters.

The tendency for parties to take more extreme stands than their voters fits with observations from Norway and Sweden (Rabinowitz, Macdonald and Listhaug 1991).

Putting the matter somewhat strongly, it appears as if the majority of voters were massed like a herd of antelopes on a savannah, surrounded on every side by lion-packs who take their share of the prey. This curious situation, however, is not a problem for the proximity theory because that theory does not imply that the party is in the middle of its voters. The voters may well be on the 'inner side' of the parties and yet vote for the nearest party. Indeed the voter may vote by proximity *no matter where the parties are located.* In the same way, the fact that people shop at the nearest shopping centre does not mean that the shopping centres are located where people live. This is an entirely different question. We still need to account for the parties' behaviour. What causes them to spread over the issue scale more than their voters?

We suggest that the party line is determined by the core voters and represents their views rather than the views of the party's average voter. Hence, we conceive of the relation between party position and voter position as one in which the parties attempt to draw voters to their positions rather than represent these voters in an unbiased way. Most of these voters will be the fairly uncommitted ones from the political centre; we saw already in Figure 3.1 that on the economic issues roughly 70 per cent of the voters are concentrated in the centre position or the one immediately to the right of it. On the new non-economic issues the situation is more complicated, but even here the centre position is the most popular.

This view assigns to the parties a more active role than the Downsian, according to which the parties conform to a given distribution of public opinion. Such a theory does not address the question how opinions are made. Directional theory is more helpful here since it implies that voters are mobilised by the parties. However, in this strategic game some of the voters must give more impetus to the party than the average. These would presumably be the active partisans who have an interest in seeing their policy goals fulfilled, and not a particular interest in maximising the party's share of the votes. Such voters are in our sample above all represented by the party identifiers. Our hypothesis is that the party identifiers tend to be close to the party line whereas the non-identifiers tend to be less extreme in their views than the party line. For reasons of space we shall test it only on the left-right self-placement. The result appears in Table 3.8.

From the first row we observe that the strong party identifiers have the largest share of voters (42 per cent) near to the party. They also divide evenly between the locations that are more extreme than the party and those that are more moderate than the party line (29 per cent each). The weak identifiers, the non-identifiers with a normal party choice, and most of all, the non identifiers without any commitment, deviate successively more from this pattern in the direction of being more moderate than the party line. Among the non-committed voters one half (50 per cent) are more moderate and only one in six (16 per cent) more extreme than their party. In short, the hypothesis is confirmed to a very significant extent.

Table 3.8. *Voter position relative to party position on a 1-10 left-right scale, by strength of party identification*

	More extreme	Near to party	More moderate	Total	N=100 per cent
Identifiers:					
Strong	29	42	29	100	(467)
Not strong	24	36	40	100	(419)
Non-identifiers:					
Party leaning	20	34	46	100	(573)
No leaning	16	34	50	100	(191)
All voters	23	37	40	100	(1650)

Note: 'Near to party' is defined as being at that scale position which is nearest to the party's position as indicated in Table 3.2, first column. 'More extreme' is defined as being between that position and that end of the scale (1 or 10) which is closest to the party's position. 'More moderate' is defined as the remaining positions.

Thus party identifiers tend to cluster around the party's position, whereas non-identifiers who vote for the party cluster at the 'inside' of that party's position. What we saw in Table 3.2 was a linear relation between party position (X) and voter position (Y) which has a slope somewhat less than one. For strong party identifiers the slope should be a steeper and approximate one. For non-identifying voters the slope should be much less than one. This expectation comes true in Table 3.9.

Table 3.9. *Regression analysis of the relation between a party's position (X) and the voter's position (Y) on the left-right dimension by level of party identification*

Strong Identifiers	$Y = .38 + .963 X$	(r=.77)
Weak Identifiers	$Y = 1.22 + .790 X$	(r=.72)
Party Leaners	$Y = 1.57 + .721 X$	(r=.76)
Non-Identifiers	$Y = 2.54 + .559 X$	(r=.64)

The table shows the results of regression analyses with Y=voter position and X=party position conducted separately on strong identifiers, weak identifiers, party 'leaners' and non-identifying voters of the same party. We observe here that the slope of the relation rises systematically from b=.559 among non-identifiers to b=.721 among party leaners, to b=.790 among weak identifiers and finally to b=.963 among strong identifiers. At the same time the constant parameter drops from 2.54 to .38, indicating that with rising strength of party identification the linear relation approaches the Y=X line; this line of course represents an unbiased translation of party position into voter position, or the reverse.

3.8. Conclusion

The party choice is presumed to be an important first link in the process of translating the *input* of societal values and interests, problems and concerns, into an *output* of policies. Issue voting is a very direct way to conduct this process in which the translation takes place issue by issue rather than by means of the parties' results in government or their affiliation with particular social groups. We have demonstrated in this chapter that a fair deal of issue voting takes place in the Danish electorate, and that proximity voting is an important mechanism for matching party positions and voter positions on issues or policies. However, the mechanism is not simply one in which the parties act as instructed delegates. They tend to take positions that are more articulate than those of their medium voters, and to resist tendencies to be drawn toward the position of the indifferent centrist voter. We have shown this tendency to be related to the attitude of party identification: party identifiers are significantly more true to their party on general left-right orientation than are non-identifiers voting for the same party. Thus, in the Danish electorate it seems that party identification functions as an attitude which reinforces issue voting and contributes to a sharper issue profile of the parties.

4

PERFORMANCE AND LEADERSHIP

4.1. Introduction

Budge and Farlie (1983, p. 37) note that 'Government record and prospects have been salient at all Danish elections'. So, like other Danish election campaigns, the 1994 campaign was a trial of the government and a debate about possible alternatives to it. But this time the electorate was in a particularly fortunate position. Half-way through the election period, the government had changed hand from Conservatives and Liberals to a Social Democratic government with participation of the small centre parties. This created an almost ideal occasion for comparing the policies, performance, and leadership qualities of the bourgeois and social democratic alternatives. Early in the campaign the Liberal leader Uffe Ellemann-Jensen proposed a 'blue' government consisting of Liberals, Conservatives, and Progressives, as an alternative to the present 'red' government consisting of Social Democrats and candidates of the three centre parties. Though the idea was not pursued consistently throughout the campaign by the three parties, it played a role among the voters, and if the three parties had managed to get a majority of seats it would no doubt have been revived, being the logical alternative once the centre parties had committed themselves to a continuation of the present government.

The election campaign was dominated by economic problems. The new government defended its economic reforms and pointed to the growth and optimism in the economy. It was attacked by the bourgeois opposition from a neo-liberal position critical of the expanding public budgets. Of the bourgeois parties, particularly the Liberal party had shown an amazing growth in the opinion polls. The Conservative party was handicapped by the credibility problems aroused in the Tamilian affair, which led to Mr Schlüter's resignation and the change of government in January 1993. Their new leader Hans Engell chose a fairly low profile not too far from the political centre. This pitted the incumbent Prime Minister Poul Nyrup Rasmussen and former Foreign Minister Uffe Ellemann-Jensen against one another as the chief contestants.

In this chapter we turn to the voters' perceptions of the issues of the day and their evaluations of the government in an attempt to throw light on the short-term forces operating in the 1994 election. Our analysis will make use of three main types of questionnaire item. One type has questions about which political goals and problems were important to the voter — that is, items on the political agenda.

Another type has questions rating the capacity or efficiency of the government, compared to an alternative bourgeois government, in tackling these goals and problems. The third type of question concerns the respondents' ratings of the party leaders on a sympathy scale.

Our general hypothesis is that the government will profit from being seen as superior to the alternative government in dealing with important goals and problems. It will tend to lose from an unfavourable rating, relative to the bourgeois alternative, on important matters. It will neither gain nor lose from ratings on unimportant matters or matters where the voters perceive no difference between these governments. Hence, we seek to relate the vote for these alternatives to the expected performance of the government, compared to a rival government, on a set of political goals. Ratings of party leaders, especially P. Nyrup Rasmussen and U. Ellemann-Jensen are hypothesised to influence the choice between the present government and the alternative bourgeois government partly because they are considered a component of the expected performance of the governments.

The importance of various goals and problems are expected to condition the effects of the performance ratings, and therefore we begin by examining which goals and problems were foremost in the voters' minds during the election campaign.

4.2. The Agenda of the 1994 Election

Although economic issues dominated the campaigns of especially the big parties, and the electors therefore must have thought they were choosing between two distinct schools of economic policy, it does not follow that these problems were the most important ones in the eyes of the electors. It seems logical that in order to influence the voting choice, a problem or a political goal must both be important to the voter and be stressed by the parties during the election campaign. Beginning with the voters' agenda, Table 4.1 shows that unemployment was mentioned by almost half the voters as being one of the three most important problems which the politicians should deal with. The unemployment problem was even more dominant than in the 1990 election, where about one third of the electors placed it among the most important problems.

Other important items on the voters' agenda were conditions for the elderly, immigration, the environment, and the general economic condition. Problems of the elderly and of immigration made a significant leap forward on the agenda compared with the previous election whereas taxes and the general economic condition dropped from their prominent positions as no. 2 and 3 on the agenda. Economic problems that had dominated in former periods, such as foreign debt or the risk of inflation (Goul Andersen 1994, pp. 46-53), completely dropped out of the voters' agenda. Thus we should not expect taxes, inflation or balance of payment to affect the vote division in the 1994 election, even though the preceding bourgeois government might boast of having overcome these problems successfully. Our hypothesis implies that people vote on the *present* goals and problem, and not out of gratitude.

Table 4.1. Important issues spontaneously mentioned by respondents. Per cent of sample

	1994	1990
Unemployment	47	31
Conditions of the elderly	22	12
Immigration	16	4
Environment	15	12
Economy	15	19
Social problems and policy	10	11
Balance of payment, foreign debt	6	12

Source: Thomsen 1995.

In studying the 'effects' of the political agenda, one should realise that agenda items such as those in Table 4.1 typically deal with goals that are universally accepted. They are 'valence' issues rather than 'position' issues (Stokes 1963). The voters therefore do not differ with regard to the stands or positions they prefer; instead they may differ with regard to the priority of a particular goal, the political means or costs of attaining the goal, and the efficiency of particular parties or governments in working for the goal. In following the campaign the voter may find that to some parties, full employment appears more important than stable prices, whereas to others it is the reverse, and to still others both of these goals appear less important than fighting pollution or limiting immigration. But given the voter's agreement with these goals, the voter may still wonder whether a particular party or government is going to work efficiently in the direction of them.

In an attempt to bring the political agenda of the public to bear more directly on the vote, we asked our respondents how important various issue areas were to them when deciding how to vote. Table 4.2 sets out these data.

A surprising fact emerges from these data. When put in order of importance, classical economic issues such as taxes and the public debt fell far below social issues such as health care and problems of the elderly. Also environmental issues, law and order, immigration, and culture and education take precedence over economic problems, among which only unemployment (partly a social problem) ranks high. Therefore it is possible that the election campaign dealt with problems that meant little to the general public.

Voting and Political Attitudes in Denmark

Table 4.2. Importance of various issues for the vote decision, 1994. Per cent of sample

Issue	Great importance	Less importance	No importance	Total
1. Health care	73	17	10	100
2. Unemployment	72	17	11	100
3. Elderly, pensions	67	22	11	100
4. Environment	63	25	12	100
5. Law and order, justice	57	29	14	100
6. Immigrants, refugees	48	35	17	100
7. Culture and education	44	37	19	100
8. Public deficit and debt	43	33	24	100
9. EU relations	42	37	21	100
10. Taxes	38	45	17	100

Note: N's (corresponding to 100 per cent) between 1778 and 1724.

If the popular agenda differs from the agenda which the media and parties have set for the election campaign, what are the forces shaping the popular agenda? Research in political agendas (Baker, Dalton and Hildebrandt 1981; Roller 1995) has suggested that the political priorities of the public are subject to long run societal change. These ideas were discussed in chapter 2. On the basis of them one would expect the agenda in Table 4.2 to split into an old and a new agenda. The old agenda, focussed on economic problems, would include the issues of tax, public debt, health care, unemployment, old age pensions, and law and order, whereas the new agenda, dealing with quality-of-life problems, would include the environment, immigration, relations with EU, culture and education.

Table 4.3 brings the results of a factor analysis of responses to the ten items in Table 4.2.

The unrotated solution indicates a strong first factor or principal component on which all items load positively. This factor therefore expresses the tendency of some respondents to claim that all issues, or issues in general, were important for their vote whereas other respondents do not attach importance to issues (at least not to these ten items). Such a factor tends to disappear when the solution is rotated, but since we have a straightforward interpretation of it, we should stick to the unrotated solution. The second unrotated factor splits the items into those with positive loadings, those with negative loadings, and those with loadings around zero. Positive loadings are assigned to public debt and EU relations and, to some extent, taxes. We may interpret them as representing an economic agenda focused on Denmark's competitive position. Negative loadings are assigned to the problems of the elderly and health care problems and, again to some extent, law and order.

This seems to express a welfare agenda with particular focus on the problems of the older part of the population.

Table 4.3. Factor analysis of importance of issues for the vote. Loadings on unrotated factors

	Factor 1	Factor 2
Care of elderly, pensions	.72	−.50
Health care	.77	−.38
Law and order, justice	.70	−.19
Immigrants, refugees	.59	.01
Environment	.67	.02
Unemployment	.68	.06
Culture and education	.66	.07
Taxes	.59	.25
Public deficit and debt	.51	.50
EU relations	.50	.54

Note: Issues were scored 3=very important, 2=less important, 1=unimportant.

There are no more factors of any importance in these data. Thus we do not find a separation of the items into an old and a new agenda. When the loadings are plotted in a diagram with the factors forming the X and Y axes, all items tend to cluster around an almost vertical line, as shown in Figure 4.1. The agenda items describe a fan from the economic concerns in the upper part to the social concerns in the lower part of the figure. Therefore, we prefer to say that the issues on the agenda tend to fall into a one-dimensional continuum from social to economic issues, once the first unrotated factor is eliminated.

It is characteristic that of the 'new issues', the environment, culture & education, and immigration take intermediate positions similar to unemployment, whereas EU relations side completely with the economic issues. In chapter 7 we shall see that the picture changes when we turn to attitudinal data. But as far as the agenda items are concerned, the Danish 1994 election did not feature a 'new' versus 'old' politics distinction.

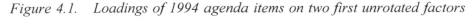

Figure 4.1. Loadings of 1994 agenda items on two first unrotated factors

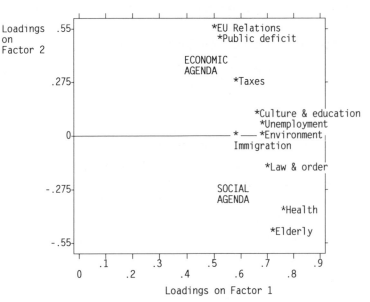

Note: The variables are responses to the items, 'I will now mention some topics that were discussed during the election campaign. How important were these topics for you when you decided which party to vote for — very important, less important, or not important at all?' Responses were coded 3=very important, 2=less important, and 1=not at all important or don't know.

Rather, our interpretation is that two major agenda dimensions existed in the Danish 1994 electorate. One dimension described the distinction between those who attach great importance to issues (issue voters) and those who attach little importance. The other dimension described a distinction between those stressing social welfare issues and those stressing national economic issues. Moreover, if we compare the factor solution with the list of priorities in Table 4.2, it is fairly evident that on this second dimension, the social agenda dominated over the economic agenda. In the 1994 election there was a pressure 'from below' to give first priority to such social issues as health care and problems of the aged, plus to some extent also crime problems and problems related with immigration. Among the economic problems, the only one reaching the same level of public attention was unemployment, which of course has an important social angle too.

Yet the politicians' agenda seemed to be dominated by debates about taxes, interest rates, wages and profits. Hence, the question of what issues were *important* when the voters made up their minds about the governments cannot be answered with confidence; our best guess is that in weighing the governments the voters

Performance and Leadership

struck a balance between their own agenda and that of the politicians; such a guess has some support from a prior study on agenda-setting (Siune and Borre 1975).

4.3. Performance Ratings of Alternative Governments

We may now proceed to the main actors on the political scene. Given the importance attached to a given goal on the political agenda, voters are expected to be affected in their vote decisions by their perceptions of which parties, governments, or leaders would perform better in pursuing that goal. These perceptions will be called performance ratings. These ratings are not retrospective, since we ask the respondent to judge who would be best in solving various specific problems. However, the respondent may of course react 'empirically' by basing his or her rating on past records. This is especially plausible in a situation where two different governments had ruled within a short period. In the present survey particularly the social democratic and bourgeois alternatives should be evaluated since voters had had a chance to see for themselves that these governmental alternatives would differ in their approach to problems and goals. These governments will naturally be dominated by the big parties, and therefore the ratings of the two governments also provides a rough rating of the Social Democratic policy *vis-à-vis* a Conservative-Liberal policy. Ratings of minor parties on particular goals not only would be extremely difficult for the respondent but also largely irrelevant for our purpose, since a small party would have to compromise with others in one of these governments. Indeed, voting for a small party with idealistic goals but no chance of carrying them out is not what we would consider as 'performance' voting. We therefore asked people to compare 'the present government led by social democrats' with 'a bourgeois government' in various policy fields.

It is clear, however, that measuring the impact of agenda items in this way is confounded by a generally high amount of selective perception such that the voter tends to claim that his or her own party is superior to other parties, whatever the goal to be pursued. Such a tendency is particularly tempting because the labels of the governments have to be included in the wording of the question and because responding to the item does not presuppose any knowledge about the different policies of the parties; a voter may claim to prefer a bourgeois policy to a social democratic one, or the reverse, without knowing what these policies are. Thus, a fairly high correlation between the preference for a party on a number of policy fields and voting for that party may express loyalty or party identification.

Similarly, the opposite situation where the voter expresses indifference to the choice among the two governments does not mean that the voter cannot tell the difference between them. Distrustful voters tend to think that all governments —

at least, all those that are the options in an election — will be equally inefficient. The politically disinterested are often heard to claim that it really makes no difference whichever government is appointed. This impression may be reinforced by a campaign in which all parties follow a catch-all strategy of mentioning every goal which they know to be of relevance for the voters.

Because of the selective perception argument many researchers abstain from analysing the impact of performance evaluations on the vote; Holmberg (1981, p. 157), for example, finds that voter evaluations of the parties' competence in government or opposition 'often coincided with how much they appreciated the parties. The *most likely* reason for this result is that party sympathies colour the evaluations of competence in government and opposition'.

We must therefore anticipate a great deal of rationalisation in the performance data. However, both party strategists and political reporters often talk about the *image* which a party or government tries to impress on the electorate, or to erase from the public's memory. The image seems to allude to the public's perceptions of the general policy or ideology which the party stands for, its reputed success or failure in solving certain problems when in government, or the kinds of people who vote for the party. Thus the party may promote its image as a 'green' party, a party in favour of cutting public expenses, a party for the young, and so forth. Such an image is implicitly assumed to operate across the electorate, not just on the party's own followers. It should therefore not to be subject to rationalisation.

In a crude sense the empirical validity of the objections against the 'performance' items may be judged merely from the aggregated distribution of responses to these items. Before starting our analysis at the level of the individual respondent, we may therefore look at the results of comparing two governments, the present one and a bourgeois alternative, on their presumed performance on various political goals (Table 4.4).

These marginal distributions are encouraging for our purposes. Suppose all voters of the government parties claim that the present government is best, while the voters of the bourgeois opposition claim that a bourgeois government would be better, and the voters of the left opposition claim that there is no difference between the two governments. Such a situation would then lead to an aggregated distribution of ratings on every goal which is equal to the vote distribution. Obviously this is not the case. The marginals differ very much from one goal to the next, and from the aggregate vote division. So, at least some of the respondents must have 'admitted' that the other government is better on at least some points.

Table 4.4. Perceived performance of governments on political goals. Percentages

	Present Gov'ment best	Bourgeois Gov'ment best	No diff-erence	Don't know	Total
Solving the country's economic problems generally	22	50	20	8	100
Fighting unemployment	50	19	24	7	100
Securing the country a modern industry	16	52	21	11	100
Fighting inflation	11	54	19	14	100
Fighting the deficit on the public budgets	10	62	17	11	100
Securing the social balance in the economic policy	47	23	17	12	100
Caring for Denmark's interests in the EU	20	40	29	11	100
Securing the environment	53	12	27	8	100
Securing law and order	14	29	48	9	100
Securing citizen influence in society	29	18	43	10	100
Securing individual freedom	22	28	39	11	100
Securing a proper balance between the tax burden and social security	40	25	23	12	100
Giving yourself the most money at your disposal	34	30	23	13	100

Also, the fear that few voters will recognise a difference between the governments seems unfounded. The 'no difference' and 'don't know' categories are of modest size and never approach a majority between them. Whether as a result of selective perception or sound judgement, people do make up their minds about which government would be the best in a given policy field.

Furthermore, one notices that the responses tend systematically to be biased in favour of the present government on one set of items and the bourgeois government on another set. The largest difference in favour of the present government is found in regard to the goals of securing the environment (41 per cent), fighting unemployment (31 per cent), and securing the social balance (24 per cent). The largest difference in the opposite direction is found on the goals of fighting the budget deficit (52 per cent), fighting inflation (43 per cent), securing a modern industry (36 per cent), and solving the country's economic problems generally (28 per cent). On the goals of law and order, citizen influence, and securing individual

Voting and Political Attitudes in Denmark

freedom the largest number thought there was no difference between the two governments.

Such differences are evidence that there are limits to the rationalisation effect; and Brody and Page (1972, pp. 452-455) also observe that strangely, the aggregate distribution is rarely used as an argument against rationalisation. In our case the aggregate distribution points towards the conclusion that the two governments were seen as representing two different fields of competence: the present government was seen as superior in solving environmental and social problems while the alternative bourgeois government was seen as superior in promoting economic growth and private initiative. When seen in the light of Tables 4.2 and 4.3, such images of the governments open the possibility of a simplistic model of the turnover of governments which does not depend at all on opinion change (cf. the 'Salience Model' discussed by Budge and Farlie 1983). We may speculate that when economic problems are in the forefront, the public budgets are getting out of hand, and inflation is lurking, a bourgeois government will be elected; but when unemployment is getting too high or the welfare society is threatened, a social-democratic government will be preferred by the majority. Different problems call for different leaders.

In a model of this kind, the priority of political goals and problems — that is, the changing political agenda — is the main dynamic element. However, it would not be fair to the efforts of politicians to leave out changes in their competence as dynamic elements in the model. That is, we do not want to exclude the possibility that a social-democratic government might show an astounding success in improving the Danish trade balance and hold down inflation, nor the possibility that a bourgeois government might generate full employment and wipe out poverty. The public image of the two opposing governments may change over time — as indeed it has done. With respect to competence in solving the country's economic problems in general, the positive image of the bourgeois government dates only from the early part of 1991 — the date when the deficit on the balance of payment was turned into a surplus (Goul Andersen 1994). Thereafter, two years of Conservative/Liberal government served to imprint this idea of the bourgeois government's economic competence on the voters.

On two other economic issues, namely inflation control and caring about a modern industry, the positive image of bourgeois government appears to be of a more enduring quality. Its pro-industrial image has even been steadily improved over the years since early 1989. By contrast, the voters have lost faith in bourgeois initiatives to fight unemployment, and one has to go back at least to 1988 to find something like a tie between the two types of government on this count.

In the following we analyse the performance data from 1994 as they relate to the voting choice. Here, the overriding problem is to control for the causality which is due to selective perception. In most cases we must suspect that a difference between partisan camps in their ratings of the government and bourgeois opposition expresses a degree of loyalty or opposition to the government which overrides the actual performance of the two governments. Before turning to an analytic model of short-term effects that will take account of these loyalties we shall, however, look at another set of short-term factors that must be included in such a model, namely the voters' orientations towards the party leaders.

4.4. Ratings of Party Leaders

The performance of a government, or a would-be government, can be expected to depend on leadership factors such as the party leaders' competence and motivation, their capacity for coordinating policies and for generating trust in the public, and so forth. Research on elections in Britain and Australia from the eighties (Bean and Mughan 1989; Stewart and Clarke 1992) has indicated the significant effects of notions of party leaders on the voting choice, and suggested that leadership has two main dimensions, competence and responsiveness, in the eyes of the public. Ratings of the leaders of major parties are therefore hypothesised to be intertwined with those data on problems, issue priorities and policy evaluations which we have surveyed in Tables 4.1-4.3. In particular this should be so in the case of the Social Democratic Prime Minister Poul Nyrup Rasmussen and the leader of the largest opposition party, the Liberal Uffe Ellemann-Jensen. But since they would have to include other parties in their government or at least depend on them for outside support, the quality of leaders of other significant parties probably also enter in the public's ratings of the performance of the government alternatives. For example, an Ellemann-Jensen government would depend on support from the Progress party, and thereby a low rating of the Progress party leader Mrs Pia Kjærsgaard might well harm the expected performance of such a government. On the opposite side of the spectrum, a low rating of the Socialist People's party leader Mr Holger K. Nielsen might harm the expected future performance of the Nyrup government if that government came to be dependent on left-wing support.

Ratings of the party leaders were made by respondents on an eleven-point scale. Table 4.5 divides the ratings into those positive, neutral, and negative. In addition a mean rating between +100 and –100 is computed.

We note here that even though Prime Minister Nyrup Rasmussen was the leader of the largest party, his rating was inferior to the leaders of the bourgeois opposition Mr Ellemann-Jensen and particularly Mr Hans Engell. Moreover the Prime Minister elicited the greatest number of neutral ratings, while Mr Ellemann elicited by far the fewest, only ten per cent.

Table 4.5. Ratings of party leaders. Per cent distribution and average scores

	Per cent positive	Per cent neutral	Per cent negative	Per cent pos–neg	Ave. score
Hans Engell (Con.)	55	22	23	32	+17
Uffe Ellemann-Jensen (Lib.)	55	10	35	20	+12
Poul Nyrup Rasmussen (Soc.D)	41	26	33	8	+2
Mimi Jakobsen (Cen.D)	42	22	36	6	−1
Marianne Jelved (Rad.)	36	22	42	−6	−7
Holger K. Nielsen (Soc.P)	32	22	46	−14	−13
Pia Kjærsgaard (Prog.)	27	17	56	−29	−25

Note: Based on the item, "Here are some questions about how much you like the parties, party leaders, and the policy which the parties have pursued. Even though you may view a party, its leader and policy as a whole, we ask you to try and answer each question. Beginning with the leaders, here is a card with a scale running from 0 to 10. The more you like the person, the higher mark you give. If you neither like nor dislike a person, you should give 5." Negative scores were 0-4, neutral score 5, and positive scores 6-10. For the average score, the coding was 0=−100, 1=−80, 2=−60, 3=−40, 4=−20, 5=0, 6=+20, 7=+40, 8=+60, 9=+80, and 10=+100. Observe, however, that in the datafile, all codes were increased by one because zeroes were counted as missing values. Don't Know responses were excluded, N's were around 1050.

In the following we shall discuss to what extent these ratings represent short-term forces influencing the election outcome. It is plausible to speculate that the moderate popularity of the Prime Minister compared with the great popularity of the two bourgeois party leaders was a factor in the decrease of the government's vote from 48 to 44 per cent and the increase of the combined Liberal-Conservative vote from 31 to 38 per cent in 1994 compared with the previous election (cf. Table 1.1). However, it would indeed be facile to interpret the election in this way without a more thorough analysis. We have already offered a more general explanation in chapter 1, namely, that the 1994 election exhibited a strong rightist turn in political attitudes; such ideological factors may be imagined to operate in various subtle ways, one of them being their tendency to colour the public's evaluations of the chief political actors on the political scene. We therefore need to differentiate between various aspects of these evaluations and to pinpoint those which seen to have the greatest relevance for the 1994 election.

4.5. Partisan Differences in Ratings

Our general hypothesis as stated in the introduction to this chapter is that the perceived performance of the government relative to alternative governments on the handling of important political issues has an impact on the outcome of the election. Based on the data and discussion in sections 4.3 and 4.4 we shall argue that performance includes both a policy aspect and a leadership aspect. The campaign focuses on certain political goals or problems and on certain actors who are supposed to do something about them. The voters are induced to compare the credibility and competence of different leaders in working towards these goals. However, the long term predispositions of the voters mean that their comparisons are biased, and this bias has to be eliminated in the analysis.

The problem of separating long-term from short-term effects is basic to voting research. To assess the magnitude of the problem in relation to the election we are studying, let us look at a few tables which report the vote division in relation to the ratings we have discussed in the foregoing sections. In respect of the vote division we shall distinguish three groups or camps of voters: those voting for parties in the present government, for parties in the alternative bourgeois or 'blue' government, and for the left-wing opposition parties. To illustrate the relation of the vote to ratings on policy performance, we select one of the items in Table 4.4, namely "Securing a proper balance between the tax burden and social security". It seems likely that socialist and bourgeois voters mean different things by 'proper balance'. Therefore, the opinion is divided as to which government is best, as Table 4.4 shows. But precisely because of this flexibility of the item, it might be interesting to demonstrate that it has an independent effect on the vote. Table 4.6 shows how the vote division varies with the perceptions of government performance on that item.

According to the first row of figures for the 1994 vote, 68 per cent of those who thought the present government best in attaining such a balance voted for one of the parties in that government. The second and third rows show that 12 per cent voted for the bourgeois opposition and 20 per cent for the left-wing opposition parties in the same group. The set of figures in the middle portion of the table deals with those who thought there was little difference between the two governments. One might have expected the left wing to recruit more voters in this category, but this is not the case. The bourgeois parties dominate with more than half the votes, while the Social Democratic party together with the centre parties receive 38 per cent. The lower set of figures shows the party preferences of those who believed a bourgeois government to be better than the present. Almost nine out of ten in this group vote bourgeois, almost all of the rest Social Democratic or centrist, and almost no one (2 per cent) left-wing.

Voting and Political Attitudes in Denmark

Table 4.6. 1994 and recalled 1990 vote in per cent, by rating of government performance on tax burden/social security balance

	1994	1990	Change
Present government best:			
Voted SD or centre	68	64	4
Voted bourgeois	12	14	−2
Voted left-wing	20	22	−2
Total	100	100	0
No. of respondents	(737)	(696)	
Almost no difference:			
Voted SD or centre	38	41	−3
Voted bourgeois	51	48	3
Voted left-wing	11	11	0
Total	100	100	0
No. of respondents	(469)	(447)	
Bourgeois alternative best:			
Voted SD or centre	10	14	−4
Voted bourgeois	88	84	4
Voted left-wing	2	2	0
Total	100	100	0
No. of respondents	(564)	(532)	

Note: Based on the item: "Who do you think is best in solving the problems I shall now read to you, either the present government led by Social Democrats, or a bourgeois government? Who would best attain the right balance between the tax burden and social welfare?"

The differences between the three groups are enormous, but of course it would be naive to regard them as 'effects' of the performance ratings. Rather we suspect the causality to operate the other way round, so that voters predisposed towards the present government tend to perceive that government to be superior to a bourgeois government, whereas bourgeois voters perceive a bourgeois government as better; the left-wing opposition voters in this case side with the government voters in their ratings of the alternative governments. Thus the difference is to a large extent caused by what we termed selective perceptions.

This suspicion grows to certainty when we find in the second column of figures that the major part of the differences existed already in the 1990 election, if we can believe the vote recalls of our respondents. Looking at the strength of the Social Democrats and centre parties, we find the difference between the upper and the lower group in 1994 to be 68–10=58 percentage points; however, 50 percentage points difference existed already in the 1990 election, over two years before the government was formed. There remains 8 per cent which may be ascribed to the rating of the governments. This 8 per cent takes the form of an increase of 4 per cent in the group who think the present government is better and a *decrease* of 4 per cent in the opposite group. Still, even though by this calculation fifty out of fifty-eight percentage points in the vote is due to long-run factors, we are encouraged to find that eight percentage points may be due to the short term factors whose existence we are arguing. Looking at the change in the two opposition camps, we find that of the eight percentage points, about six were offset in the bourgeois vote and two in the left-wing camp.

Turning now to the ratings of party leaders by the voters, much the same can be said as with respect to the performance of governments. We are not surprised to find that Prime Minister Nyrup Rasmussen is more popular among Social Democratic voters than among Liberal voters, while the reverse is the case with opposition leader Ellemann-Jensen. These correlations are to be regarded as effects of partisanship upon leadership ratings rather than the other way round. By setting out the data in Tables 4.7 and 4.8 in parallel with the way it is done in Table 4.6 we may, however, attempt to control for the effect of partisanship. The 1990 vote cannot have been caused by evaluations of the performance of these two leaders during the 1990-1994 period; and their performance prior to 1990 should be a minor factor since Mr Nyrup Rasmussen first became the leader of the Social Democratic party in 1992, whereas Mr Ellemann-Jensen only became the leader of the opposition after the resignation of Prime Minister Schlüter and the change of government in 1993.

In Table 4.7 we distinguish three groups of voters: those positive, indifferent, and negative towards the Social Democratic prime minster.

The upper set of figures indicate that among those rating the Prime Minister positively, the vote for the government rose by four percentage points, of which three were taken from the bourgeois parties and one from the left wing. According to the middle section, among those neutral towards the PM the government gained three percentage points and the bourgeois opposition one percentage point, lost by the left wing. Finally, among those with a negative rating of the PM, the government lost four percentage points, all of which went to the bourgeois opposition.

Table 4.7. 1994 and recalled 1990 vote in per cent, by rating of Prime Minister Poul Nyrup Rasmussen

	1994	1990	Change
With positive rating of PNR:			
Voted SD or centre	69	65	4
Voted bourgeois	18	19	−1
Voted left-wing	13	16	−3
Total	100	100	0
No. of respondents	(389)	(376)	
With neutral rating of PNR:			
Voted SD or centre	31	28	3
Voted bourgeois	55	54	1
Voted left-wing	14	18	−4
Total	100	100	0
No. of respondents	(230)	(218)	
With negative rating of PNR:			
Voted SD or centre	17	21	−4
Voted bourgeois	73	69	4
Voted left-wing	10	10	0
Total	100	100	0
No. of respondents	(304)	(282)	

Note: Rating of Prime Minister Nyrup Rasmussen on an eleven point scale, here collapsed to three: ngative=0-4, neutral=5, and positive=6-10.

The effects of the ratings of Ellemann-Jensen (Table 4.8) are somewhat weaker: a gain for the bourgeois parties of two percentage points in the group who were positive or neutral towards him, and a loss of one percentage point in the group who were negative towards him. Interestingly, in the latter group it was the government that triumphed, not the left wing. The numbers in parentheses indicate that Mr Ellemann-Jensen elicited far more positive ratings than did the Prime Minister, but also slightly more negative evaluations, leaving few in the neutral category. These differences are quite in agreement with the popular picture of the two contestants; the media missed no opportunity to contrast the colourful personality of the opposition leader with the somewhat colourless Prime Minister, often caricatured with wool in his mouth.

Table 4.8. 1994 and recalled 1990 vote in per cent, by rating of opposition leader Uffe Ellemann-Jensen

	1994	1990	Change
With positive rating of UEJ:			
Voted SD or centre	23	24	−1
Voted bourgeois	72	70	2
Voted left-wing	5	6	−1
Total	100	100	0
No. of respondents	(512)	(477)	
With neutral rating of UEJ:			
Voted SD or centre	60	58	2
Voted bourgeois	26	24	2
Voted left-wing	14	18	−4
Total	100	100	0
No. of respondents	(85)	(83)	
With negative rating of UEJ:			
Voted SD or centre	68	64	4
Voted bourgeois	9	10	−1
Voted left-wing	23	26	−3
Total	100	100	0
No. of respondents	(326)	(316)	

Note: Rating of Uffe Ellemann-Jensen on an eleven point scale, here collapsed to three: negative=0-4, neutral=5, and positive=6-10.

Our conclusion so far is that probably there are short-term effects both of some agenda items and of the ratings of major party leaders. We have reached this conclusion by breaking down the 1994 vote into groups of respondents with different ratings and subtracting those group differences that existed already in 1990; so, only changes in the aggregated vote from 1990 to 1994 are regarded as indicating an effect of the performance ratings. This is by far the simplest method, but it is not unproblematic. In the first place the 1990 vote may not be a valid indicator of long-term partisan loyalty, being itself influenced by the circumstances of the 1990 election. As we saw in chapter 1, the Social Democratic party had an unusually good election in 1990.

Secondly, we have access to the 1990 vote only as recalled four years later, and such recalls suffer from validity problems of their own. They are usually distorted in the direction of present partisan preferences and therefore are likely to underrate the amount of vote switching. Admittedly this tendency reduces the first problem, namely that the recalled 1990 vote would be dependent on transitory campaign forces. But it does not follow that the 1990 vote comes nearer to being a valid indicator of enduring loyalties.

Thirdly, the method does not permit us to compare the effects of different ratings overlapping one another. For example, do the positive rating effect of Mr Nyrup Rasmussen and the negative effect of Mr Ellemann-Jensen on the Social Democratic vote duplicate one another? In order to generate estimates of such effects the sample would have to be broken down into many subgroups, and the effects on the vote change could only be estimated with large sampling errors. As our hypothesis requires such comparisons, we have to turn to a different method of analysis.

4.6. Party Identification and Ratings of Governments

In the following we deal with the vote for the present government as the dependent variable. Ratings of performance and leaders are inserted among the independent variables in order to study their effects on the choice of government. To control for the partisan predisposition of the respondent, which will surely colour these ratings, we shall rely on party identification. This is in accord with an influential research tradition which uses party identifications to estimate an expected or 'normal' vote (Converse 1966; Boyd 1972; Brody and Page 1972). Even though earlier research has suggested that party identification in the Danish electorate is itself rather unstable (Borre and Katz 1973), at least it is not likely to be influenced by the short-term forces of the foregoing election.

Consequently respondent's identification with a party in government (in most cases the Social Democratic party) or a party in opposition was scored in five categories. Table 4.9 shows the support for the government in each of these five categories.

Table 4.9. Per cent voting for government, by party identification

Identifies with a government party	97	(418)
Feels closer to a government party	89	(298)
Does not feel closer to any party	42	(338)
Feels closer to a non-government party	10	(391)
Identifies with a non-government party	2	(543)

Note: Figures in parentheses indicate no. of respondents (=100 per cent).

According to the first column of figures, the vote for government varied from 97 per cent among those identifying with a government party to only 2 per cent among those identifying with an opposition party which may be either a bourgeois or a left wing party. Of those in the middle, 42 per cent voted for a government party.

Evidently the two groups of identifiers vote *en bloc* for or against the government, leaving almost no space for the impact of short-term forces of the kinds we are studying in this chapter. Such impact can come only from the three middle categories, and especially the uncommitted middle category can be expected to be swayed by short-term forces. In the next two tables we show these expectations to hold true. First, Table 4.10 shows how the government vote varies within categories of party identifiers with ratings of the government and bourgeois government on the issue of attaining a balance between taxes and social security.

Table 4.10. *Per cent voting for government, by party identification party identification and rating on tax burden/social security balance*

	Present Government best	No diff- erence	Bourgeois Government best
Identifies with a government party	99 (279)	95 (95)	87 (23)
Feels closer to a government party	92 (160)	88 (86)	68 (19)
Does not feel closer to any party	59 (83)	39 (103)	19 (48)
Feels closer to a non-government party	22 (109)	5 (131)	3 (104)
Identifies with a non-government party	7 (104)	1 (147)	0 (275)

Note: Number of respondents (=100 per cent) in parentheses.

The variation in the vote for government due to respondent's rating is considerable, amounting to 40 percentage points among the independents, 19-24 among those leaning towards a party, and 7-12 percentage points among the identifiers. However, the figures in parentheses, indicating the percentage base, show that some of these differences are measured with a rather large sampling error. Especially the small cells in the upper right corner demonstrate that very few identifiers of the government parties are prepared to admit that a bourgeois government would be better than the present government in balancing taxes with welfare.

Table 4.11.   *Per cent voting for government, by party identification and rating of prime minister*

	Rating of Prime Minister		
	Positive	Neutral	Negative
Identifies with a government party	99 (154)	94 (33)	100 (10)
Feels closer to a government party	92 (89)	86 (22)	80 (35)
Does not feel closer to any party	59 (37)	46 (37)	19 (48)
Feels closer to a non-government party	21 (41)	5 (58)	6 (80)
Identifies with a non-government party	3 (67)	1 (80)	1 (277)

Note: Number of respondents (=100 per cent) in parentheses. Rating of prime minister on an eleven point scale, here collapsed to three: negative=0-4, neutral=5, and positive=6-10.

Table 4.11 shows the effects of the rating of Prime Minister Nyrup Rasmussen on the vote for the parties in his government. Like the preceding table, this one shows unmistakeable effects of the rating, but in a different way. The effect is by far the strongest (40 percentage points) in the middle category of noncommitted voters. It is far weaker (12-15 percentage points) in the categories of voters who feel closer to one party than to others. It vanishes completely among the party identifiers in the outer categories.

These results are largely consistent with those in Tables 4.7-4.9. In both cases some effect of short term forces are apparent. Ratings of government performance on an issue as well as ratings of at least one political leader, the Prime Minister, unmistakeably make a difference in the voting choice. The difference is not a spurious effect of the voter's partisanship. A certain proportion of the electors, probably between five and fifteen per cent, seemingly vote in accordance with their ratings of the contesting governments and leaders of government. Table 4.11 suggests that these people are to be found among voters who do not identify with any party. While the rating of government or Prime Minister made a difference of forty per cent in the government's vote within that share of the electorate who are uncommitted to any party, this rating made little difference to the vote of that half of the electorate which identifies with the parties. Whatever the finer nuances in the causality, it seems almost impossible for a party identifier to vote for another government, no matter how well he may like the leader of that other government.

To obtain an estimate of the net effects of performance and leadership ratings on the government vote controlling for party identification, we apply the percentages in Table 4.9 as standards in Tables 4.10 and 4.11 for computing an expected government vote for each column of these tables. These expected vote figures may then be compared with the actual government vote, which we know from Tables 4.6 and 4.7 respectively. The result is presented in Table 4.12.

Table 4.12.   Actual and expected vote for government (per cent) by performance rating and rating of prime minister

	Actual	Expected	Difference
Performance:			
Present government best	68	63	+5
Almost no difference	38	41	−3
Bourgeois government best	10	16	−6
Rating of Prime Minister:			
Positive	69	64	+5
Neutral	31	32	−1
Negative	17	17	0

Note: Expected percentages are calculated by multiplying the percentages in Table 4.9 by the raw numbers of respondents in Table 4.10 and 4.11, e.g. .97x279 + .89x160 + .42x83 + .10x109 + .02x104, and dividing by the no. of respondents, e.g. 279+160+83+109+104, yielding 63 per cent in the first table row.

By means of this standard calculation we find that indeed the government did better than expected among respondents who rated it superior to a bourgeois governemt in balancing the tax burden with social security. This short-term effect is not large, however, amounting to a vote of 68 per cent as against an expected vote of 63 per cent. Those rating a bourgeois government superior gave only 10 per cent to the present government, where 16 per cent would be expected from the pattern of party identification. Those who saw no difference between these governments gave only 38 per cent of their votes to the present government, where 41 per cent was expected; thus the perception that the governments were equal counted to the advantage of the bourgeois opposition.

The positive effect of rating the prime minister positively is visible in the lower part of the table: here, 69 per cent of the positive gave their vote to the government, vs. an expected 64 per cent. A negative or neutral evaluation of the prime minister, however, had little adverse effect.

Voting and Political Attitudes in Denmark

4.7. Regression Analysis of the Government Vote

According to our hypothesis, the effects of performance ratings should be influenced by the agenda in the sense that the importance of a goal or problem determines how much it will affect the vote. Therefore we need to compare the performance effects on various problems or goals. Furthermore, we need to take into account the leadership effects in order to ensure that they do not duplicate each other. Such an analysis would become extremely cumbersome unless we resort to regression analysis.

The regression models in Table 4.13 estimate the vote differences due to the ratings we have discussed. Party identifications and rating variables are coded from +1 to -1, positive values indicating preference for the Social Democratic government. The estimates are presented in the form of unstandardised regression coefficients; this means that they estimate how many percentage points the vote is affected by a positive or negative rating compared with a neutral one. It is true that the foregoing analysis has shown these effects to be themselves dependent on the strength of respondent's party identification: they are larger for those without party identification than for those with party identification. To incorporate such interaction between the independent variables would make our regression model somewhat more complicated. Instead we have chosen to rely on the simple additive and linear regression model, computing the effects of rating as the average effects of the ratings across groups of party identifiers. Along with the regression estimates, significance levels are indicated even though this can only be a rough guide to the importance of an issue, given that the dichotomous choice of voting for or against the government is not well suited to linear regression technique.

For Model I, ratings of the government on the twelve items in Table 4.4 (all except the last) were entered in the regression equation. Only three turned out to have significant coefficients: ratings on the tax/welfare balance, economic problems, and the fight against unemployment. That the tax/welfare balance became the most important of the twelve items, we will argue, is consistent with our findings in Table 4.2 that the social agenda predominated. No other item among the twelve options expresses better the goal of the social agenda. That economic problems came second is not quite consistent with our finding that the social agenda dominated over the economic agenda; it probably reflects the fact that to a great extent the election campaign dealt with general economic problems. The position of unemployment as the third item should be expected, of course, from its prominent role in the campaign debate and the public agenda.

Table 4.13.   *Regression analysis of the vote for government parties. Unstandardised b coefficients*

	Model I	Model II	Model III
Identification with gov. party	.463**	.464**	.446**
Government's performance on:			
- Economic problems in general	.041**		.016
- Fighting unemployment	.025*		.032*
- Balancing taxes w. welfare	.053**		.042**
Sympathy rating of:			
- PM Poul Nyrup Rasmussen		.116**	.083**
- Uffe Ellemann-Jensen		−.044*	−.013
- Hans Engell		−.028	−.007
Constant	.471	.480	.462
Multiple correlation	.826	.828	.833
No. of cases	1765	919	919

Note: Identification with government party was coded 1=identifies with Social Democratic or one of the centre parties, .5=feels closer to one of these parties, 0=does not feel closer to any party, −.5=feels closer to a non-government party, and −1=identifies with a non-government party. Ratings of government performance were coded 1=better than bourgeois government, 0=no difference or don't know, and −1=worse than bourgeois government. Sympathy ratings were graded in eleven categories from 1.0=highest position, .8=second highest position .... −1.0=lowest position.
** = Significant at 1 per cent level, * = At 5 per cent level.

Model II deals with the party leaders. As we expected, sympathy towards the prime minister turned out to have a significant effect on the vote for government. Weaker, negative effects were estimated for sympathy towards the opposition leaders Ellemann-Jensen and Engell.

In Model III these rating variables are brought together in the regression equation. Such a procedure is likely to decrease the effects because they duplicate one another. In the event there are two rating variables which seem more important than others, namely, sympathy for the prime minister and rating of the government on the goal of attaining a proper balance between taxes and welfare. A third variable of some importance seems to be the rating of the government's efforts in fighting unemployment. All other rating and sympathy variables in Tables 4.2 and 4.4 were inefficient after control for the long term variable, party identification.

We will argue that this result lends support to our hypothesis in three ways. First and most generally the result indicates that ratings of the government's performance and as well as sympathy for its leader did have separate effects on the vote for the government in 1994. Second, the issues on which the voters concentrated in judging the present government relative to its bourgeois predecessor were not the purely economic ones but those with social implications. Solving the economic problems of the country lost importance when sympathies for the prime minister and the prominent bourgeois politicians were brought into the analysis. This suggests that these politicians became identified with the economic success or failure of the government, whereas they did not become identified with the 'social' success or failure to the same degree.

How much did the modest popularity of the Prime Minister harm the government's election result? According to Model III, had the Prime Minister been able to raise his popularity from the actual level of around zero to the high level of +.5, corresponding to an average score of +50 in Table 4.5, the government would have profited by about 4 percentage points, that is, from the actual 44 per cent to 48 per cent. This means that it would not have suffered any loss in the election. Thus, with the present analysis we cannot neglect the influence of personality factors. These do not decide elections, contrary to what is often claimed by the media; but they cannot be discarded either.

4.8. Regression Analysis of the Bourgeois Vote

A similar model will now be applied to the vote for the three bourgeois parties combined — Liberals, Conservatives, and Progressives — as a function of the rating of an hypothetical bourgeois government. This will not yield coefficients that are merely the mirror image of those in Table 4.13 because of the presence of the left-wing opposition as a third block of parties. We are indeed able to specify fairly precisely what should come out of the regression analysis.

With regard to the effects of the leadership ratings, because of the split opposition we expect to find a weaker effect of the rating of Prime Minister Nyrup Rasmussen on the bourgeois vote: those who do not fancy his leadership need not vote bourgeois but may instead defect the opposite way to vote for the left-wing opposition. For the same reason we expect to find a *stronger* effect of the bourgeois leaders Ellemann-Jensen and Engell: those who do not like them may not have defected to the Social Democrats or centre parties, thereby appearing in the models in Table 4.13, but may instead have defected all the way to the left-wing parties.

In respect of the performance ratings of the Social Democratic-centre government relative to a bourgeois government, it is plausible to expect a strengthening of the coefficients. This is because the left-wing voters are likely to rate the present government higher than the preceding bourgeois government. Therefore, rating the present government above the bourgeois government may not result in a vote for the present government but instead a vote for the left wing. These people disappear out of the models in Table 4.13, but they would be included in a model of the bourgeois vote. To put it briefly, in estimating coefficients for the bourgeois opposition parties we are looking at a more clearcut left-right or socialist-bourgeois vote division which bundles the government with the left-wing parties against the bourgeois parties.

Table 4.14 reports the coefficients of the regression equations taking the bourgeois vote as their dependent variable. As control for partisan predisposition we use party identification as in Table 4.13, but now identification with the three parties counts positively, identification with a socialist party or centre party, negatively.

Table 4.14. Regression analysis of the vote for the bourgeois opposition parties.
Unstandardised b coefficients

	Model I	Model II	Model III
Identification with bourgeois parties	.419**	.451**	.387**
Bourgeois government's performance on:			
- General economic problems	.067**		.042**
- Fighting unemployment	.039**		.040**
- Keeping tax/welfare balance	.089**		.075**
Sympathy rating of			
- PM Nyrup Rasmussen (Soc.Dem.)		−.071**	−.027
- Ellemann-Jensen (Lib.)		.096**	.061**
- Engell (Cons.)		.066**	.047*
Constant	.477	.453	.467
Multiple correlation	.86	.87	.88
No. of cases	1765	919	919

Note: Coding of the independent variables between +1 and −1, see note of previous table. **
= Significant at 1 per cent level, * = At 5 per cent level.

We observe a somewhat clearer set of short term effects of performance ratings than in the previous table. In Model I the same three ratings as in Table 4.13 emerge with significant effects, and in the same order of magnitude, but they all make a greater difference than in Table 4.13. 'Balancing taxes with welfare' now attains a comparatively high coefficient, shifting the bourgeois vote almost nine per cent one way or the other. In Model II the changes are as we predicted. The difference caused by the rating of the Prime Minister is cut to seven per cent, evidently because its impact is split between the left-wing and the bourgeois opposition. Conversely, the rating of Liberal leader Ellemann-Jensen now emerges with the greatest impact on the vote, and that of Conservative leader Engell grows to almost the same level as the rating of Nyrup Rasmussen. In Model III the effect of the sympathy for Prime Minister Nyrup Rasmussen on the bourgeois vote dwindles to below two per cent. It seems that the effect of liking the PM is to a great extent a duplication of the effect of rating the results of his policy favourably.

4.9. Personal Economy

Finally, we shall briefly analyse a variable which was included among the political goals in Table 4.4 but stands apart from the 'societal' goals. This is the goal of 'giving yourself the most money at your disposal'. The economic school of voting research implies that there is a fixed agenda at every election: everybody wants the economy to grow, unemployment to disappear, and inflation to be kept at bay; and in particular, everybody wants to maximise his or her personal real income (Nannestad & Paldam 1995, 1997). We have argued that the importance of economic problems differs from one election to the next and from one voter to the next. In short, we have stressed the agenda as an intervening variable between objective conditions — in society or in the individual — and the voting choice.

Perhaps the clearest test of the status of economic self-interest as a motivating force in voting is provided by the last item in Table 4.4. To what extent does the respondent choose sides according to which government will benefit himself or herself economically? Until now we have left out this item from our analysis because it is the only one referring explicitly to the voter as an individual. Allowing it in the regression model produces the result in Table 4.15.

Table 4.15. *Regression analysis of the vote for the government, using egoistic evaluation. Unstandardised b coefficients*

	Model I	Model II
Identification with government parties	.494**	.458**
Government better at:		
- Improving your personal economy	.067**	.036**
- Solving general economic problems		.033**
- Fighting unemployment		.020*
- Keeping tax/welfare balance		.044**
Constant	.475**	.469**

Note: Independent variables coded between +1 and −1, see note of Table 4.12. ** = Significant
        at 1 per cent level, * = At 5 per cent level.

As Model I shows, when the item is permitted to stand alone (save for the control for partisan predisposition), it makes a considerable difference: voters who thought that the social democratic government was superior to a bourgeois one produced a vote for government that was 6-7 percentage points higher than those who thought there was no difference, whereas voters who thought a bourgeois government would be better for them voted 6-7 per cent less for the government.

However, when the societal goals are entered in the equation (Model II), the difference shrinks to between 3 and 4 per cent of the vote cast. Attaining a balance between taxes and welfare remains the most important goal, causing a difference of 4-5 per cent. The 'sociotropic' economic goal of solving the country's general economic problems is then on the same level as the 'egotropic' goal with a differentiating effect of 3-4 per cent. Finally, the effect of handling the unemployment declines to 2 per cent.

Thus there certainly is evidence of egoistic voting, but the government's capacity for increasing the citizens' income does not seem to have any particularly prominent standing among the performance variables. Our conclusion concerning the effect of the 'pocketbook item', after we have controlled for partisan predisposition is more modest than that of Nannestad and Paldam (1997) and rather supports the earlier scepticism expressed by Hibbs (1993). It is not a 'hidden agenda' from which the voter derives his interest in cutting taxes or increasing the welfare budget. According to these data one might as well argue in favour of the reverse causality: a voter who judges the government by its capacity for attaining a proper balance between taxes and welfare tends to assume that such a policy will also provide himself with a suitable income.

4.10. Conclusion

Our approach in this chapter has relied on the perceived qualities of governments and leaders as sources of the voting choice. Thereby it has supplemented the model of issue voting which we pursued in chapters 2 and 3. There we showed that to a great extent people vote for parties which express the same political goals as themselves. It was necessary to supplement that view with the reservation that in order to pursue a political goal in practice, a party first must enter into a government coalition and then manifest its capacity for working successfully towards that goal. Thus it becomes important to measure the perceived performance of alternative governments in various policy areas, as well as the confidence in the leadership of these governments. These evaluations also contain a clue to a theory of electoral change that differs from the ordinary issue voting theory, for as the political agenda changes, the performance of a government in a given policy area may not be as relevant in a particular election as it was in the prior one. Concretely we suspect that economic performance counted little in the 1994 election, and so the economic growth did not bring the government the political success it had hoped. Unfortunately we do not have similar data for 1990 which could substantiate this finding. We did, however, demonstrate effects of performance and leadership ratings which could not be explained by rationalisation of party loyalties. The public's images of parties and leaders constitute separate factors affecting the election outcome.

CHANGING CLASS CLEAVAGES

5.1. Introduction

Until the 1960s, the political stability and the strength of the old parties derived mainly from the underlying association between social class and party choice, and long-term political change largely corresponded with class structural change. In spite of peaceful social relations and an early 'domesticated' Social Democratic party (Lipset & Rokkan 1967), Denmark was among the world's most class-polarised countries, partly because of a massive mobilisation of the working class, partly because of the absence of other cleavages. The same holds for Sweden whereas Norway, with its lower level of unionisation and somewhat more complicated cleavage structure (Rokkan 1970) lagged a little behind.[1]

If Denmark used to be prototypical of class-based politics, however, it has also been known as prototypical of the *decline* of class voting (e.g. Worre 1980; Lipset 1981). The decline of class voting thesis is not entirely undisputed (Glans 1989, 1993; Sainsbury 1987; Bartolini & Mair 1991; Goul Andersen 1992a) but in this chapter we concentrate on its specification and interpretation.

As to the *specification* of the decline of class voting, we shall point out that social divisions in party choice in Denmark remain strong but have changed. We believe that conventional concepts of class and class voting are inappropriate to describe the association between occupational position and political behaviour today (Goul Andersen 1984d) but others might prefer to see our findings as *explanations* of the decline of class voting in the conventional sense. Rather than entering into endless discussions over this question, we find it more fruitful to spell out exactly what has happened. This specification attacks those *interpretations* of the decline in class voting which are based on the premise that there is a radical weakening of the association between social position (broadly speaking) and political behaviour. Next, we intend to show that even some of the most widely shared interpretations

---

1. Denmark and Sweden have the highest unionisation rates in the OECD (some 85 per cent), mainly because of the 'Ghent system' of unemployment insurance (based on voluntary membership of unemployment insurance funds largely controlled by the trade unions). However, Norway has the highest unionisation rates among the European countries with obligatory, state-controlled unemployment insurance systems (Visser 1991; Goul Andersen 1996a).

of changing voting patterns of particular classes are far less plausible than they might appear at first glance.

To *specify* the decline of class voting, we have to consider, firstly, the proper measurement of class voting; secondly, the changing social divisions in political behaviour; and thirdly, the changes in the class structure (the changing composition of the middle class and the integration of women at the labour market). As to the measurement problems, we shall not discuss alternative measures of class voting or social attraction here (Alford 1963; Janda 1980; Glans 1989) but as two simple supplementary measures, we shall speak of class voting of particular groups (defined as the difference between the proportion of left voters in the group and in the electorate), and of the working-class bias of particular parties (difference between the proportion of workers among the supporters of the party and in the entire electorate).

The problem of changing social divisions is a more serious one: are the traditional working class/middle class divisions still politically relevant (if they ever were)? Such discussions of class concepts, and of underlying theoretical conceptions of social class, have never had any prominent place in electoral research. However, if class voting is defined as a relationship between social position and party choice, the starting point must be a theoretically and empirically adequate classification of social positions. Otherwise the 'decline of class voting' might simply reflect obsolence of traditional class concepts.

It has been suggested that conventional class divisions are increasingly replaced by divisions between groups which are integrated on the labour market and groups which are marginalised or excluded (Gorz 1981; Dahrendorf 1988); this question is addressed in chapter 8. As we do not find these divisions decisive, we focus in the following on new divisions between occupational positions. At this point, we shall follow the basic assumption rooted in structural class theory that what matters is not how much people *have* but what they *do*.[2] Thus class relations are multidimensional, not a question of unidimensional ranking. This means, firstly, that the frequently used concept of a 'middle class' (or various 'lower middle class'/'higher middle class' subdivisions) should be abandoned in favour of a *basic distinction between the 'old middle class' of self-employed and the 'new middle class' of non-manual employees*, both of which may be internally stratified.[3]

---

2. See also Wright (1978), and Wright and Shin (1988). The class conception below is developed at length in Goul Andersen (1991a).
3. Below, we use the terms 'non-manual employees' and 'salariat' interchangeably. This includes not only ordinary white collar workers but also professionals, except self-employed.

Secondly, a contemporary conception of social class has to take account of the modern welfare state and distinguish between *public and private employees*.

The last-mentioned sector distinction does not replace the conventional class divisions; rather, the two types of divisions interact. As far as manual workers are concerned, such public vs. private sector affiliations are likely to be relatively weak but among non-manual employees (not least among higher-level or professional groups) political behaviour and outlooks are likely to be influenced by sector position. At the same time, however, ordinary, vertical class relations (in particular managerial power) also differentiate between public employees.

This is not to suggest any simple, deterministic theory of self-interests predicting that public employees will inevitably be attracted to the parties to the left. This may be relevant in particular conjunctures where the public sector is 'contested terrain', and this may even have long-term implications, but the political position of public employees is contingent upon a number of other contextual factors as well. To spell out such contextual factors at the macro level is beyond the scope of this chapter where we concentrate on a single country. What matters here is to recognise that the public sector is 'different', and that it is impossible to speak of 'the new middle class' as a homogeneous entity; if we fail to distinguish between public and private employees, we simply lead to misleading descriptions as intra-class variations become larger than inter-class variations.

Finally, even class voting in the conventional sense needs elaboration. Thus, we have to specify the effects of class structural change, in particular the growth of the 'new middle class' and the decline of the 'old middle class'. And we also have to examine the effects of the integration of women in to the labour market for the changes in, and for the measurement of class voting.

Having specified the association between class (occupational position) and voting behaviour, we examine the *interpretations* of the 'decline of class voting', especially the turn to the right among manual workers. Electoral research contains surprisingly few speculations about what *mediates* the relationship between occupational position and party choice (Oskarson 1994). Usually, some vague notions of class interests or reference group are implied. However, only the working class has a tradition of class identification and explicit consciousness of *class* interests. The arche-typical 'class consciousness' among other classes does not include a conscious class identification; the very existence of classes may even be denied.[4] Nevertheless,

---

4. See Poulantzas (1978); Goul Andersen (1979). Therefore it is misleading to say that the class struggle is a struggle *about* class before it is a struggle *between* classes (Przeworski 1977). The same holds for postmodernist, subjectivist conceptions of social class as a discursively constituted phenomenon. In fact, it repeats a classic failure of election studies

Voting and Political Attitudes in Denmark

it is among such middle-class groups that we find the strongest pattern of class-determined voting. We believe that this is rooted in general outlooks, rather than conscious attachment to some reference group. Such outlooks may, of course, correspond with class interests, but they cannot be reduced to narrow, myopic self-interests.

Various attempts to explain declining class voting not only suggest different explanatory variables; they also diverge in their interpretation of the phenomenon to be explained. According to the '*embourgeoisement theory*', decline of class voting is mainly a matter of declining socialist sentiments within the working class. This change, in turn, is attributed to increasing wealth and equality and/or to the achievement of a middle-class life style. In short: as class divisions are modified, workers become less attached to the socialist parties.

The '*value change*' theory acknowledges that increasing wealth and equality may have softened old conflicts but claim that this change has at the same time generated new, value-based conflicts as the middle classes have achieved new, 'postmaterialist' aspirations. According to this theory, decline of class voting is mainly a matter of middle class radicalisation and (to a lesser degree) a counter-movement among 'materialist' social groups, including the working class.

Unlike the other theories, *issue voting* theory is not based on the assumption that values or attitudes within classes have changed. Declining class voting may be a simple effect of a *changing relationship between attitudes and behaviour*: voters have become more rational and vote increasingly in accordance with their issue preferences rather than in accordance with their class positions.

Finally, whereas the explanations above are based on the assumption that changes in class voting must be rooted in changing voter characteristics, a *policy explanation* would suggest that class political behaviour is also dependent on policies that political parties adopt. In particular, short-term fluctuations may be explained by changes in policy or policy outcome (Hibbs 1987), or by changes in the political agenda (Hibbs 1987); but as suggested by Esping-Andersen (1980), even long-term patterns may reflect either conscious attempts by bourgeois parties to create new divisions among workers (e.g. between house-owners and tenants) or conscious attempts by socialist parties to attract middle class voters, e.g. by lowering marginal taxes.

---

by equating class with class consciousness (Hoff 1989; Goul Andersen 1991a). As the 'images of society' (Goldthorpe, Lockwood et al. 1968-9) among the old and new middle classes is not a class image, we should expect strength of class identification with the working class to be highly correlated with socialist party choice whereas we should find little or no association between strength of middle class identification and bourgeois party choice.

But first we must specify the changing voting patterns in detail. This is done in the three following sections which also explore the effects of class structural change and the changing labour market position of women. Section 5.5 examines theories of working-class 'embourgeoisement' as well as the effects of housing policies. Section 5.6 examines whether class-specific changes in *issue positions* may account for the changes in voting behaviour, and section 5.7 explores the declining class identification. Section 5.8 describes the changing social composition of the supporters of the Danish parties, and finally, section 5.9 seeks to provide a class-theoretical explanation of the decline in class voting in 1994.

5.2. Class Structure and Party Choice, 1964-1994

a. An Overview: The 1990s

Table 5.1 describes the association between social class and support for individual parties in the 1990s (most tables in the following are based on a dichotomisation of party choice). Beginning with the working class, we may observe that there are no significant differences between the voting patterns of unskilled and skilled workers. This contrasts with the situation in the 1960s when skilled workers still had a slight flavour of 'labour aristocracy', as compared with the unskilled; in particular, skilled workers were more inclined to vote for the Conservatives (Glans 1977). But since the 1970s, the proportion voting socialist has differed by only some 0-3 percentage points (Hoff & Goul Andersen 1986; Glans 1989). Thus, contrary to many speculations, the working class seems to have become more politically homogeneous (see also Goul Andersen 1988).[5] We also observe that workers still gravitate towards the Social Democrats, although the party rarely obtains more than 50 per cent of the workers' votes.

However, the elections in the 1990s also illustrate the fact that the working class has become politically unstable. Traditional theories of class and electoral behaviour assumed that people with 'ambivalent' class positions such as the 'new middle class' are more politically rootless and tend to be floating voters (Wright 1978, 1985; Poulantzas 1978; see also Goul Andersen 1991a). From 1990 to 1994, it was the other way around: working-class support for the Social Democrats dropped

---

5. By the same token, we observe few, if any effects of technological change (Goul Andersen 1988). Only sector differences seem to have increased: in 1994, the proportions of workers voting socialist were 62 per cent within the public sector, 56 per cent within manufacture and construction but only 44 per cent within private services. Among unemployed, the proportion was 66 per cent.

significantly whereas the party's losses among the 'middle classes' in 1994 were marginal. This swing to the right is discussed in section 5.9 below.[6]

Table 5.1. Occupational class and party choice, 1990 and 1994. Percentages

		Left-wing parties		SD	Centre parties			Right parties			Other lists[1]	(N)
		UnitL	SocPP		RL	CD	Chr	Lib	Con	Prog		
Unskilled Worker	1990	1	9	57	1	3	2	8	4	9	6	306
	1994	4	8	45	2	2	2	18	6	10	3	398
Skilled Worker	1990	2	8	55	1	6	2	5	7	10	4	207
	1994	5	7	44	2	4	1	21	8	6	2	317
Lower Non-manual Employee	1990	2	13	36	4	7	2	13	17	5	1	765
	1994	4	11	34	4	3	2	23	15	3	1	857
Higher Non-manual Employee	1990	4	9	21	5	9	1	22	28	1	–	199
	1994	5	12	16	9	4	2	29	22	1	0	272
Farmer	1990	–	–	4	2	–	–	66	19	7	2	55
	1994	1	2	4	2	–	–	65	12	14	–	55
Other self-employed	1990	1	6	12	4	5	1	25	34	11	1	111
	1994	4	2	8	5	6	1	35	28	11	–	153
Worker, total	1990	1	9	57	1	4	2	7	5	9	5	515
	1994	4	8	45	2	3	2	19	7	8	2	714
Non-manual employee, total	1990	2	12	33	5	7	2	15	19	4	1	965
	1994	4	12	29	6	3	2	24	17	3	1	1129
Self-employed, total[2]	1990	1	3	8	3	3	1	42	29	9	1	211
	1994	3	2	7	5	4	1	44	23	11	0	248
Election Result	1990	1.7	8.3	37.4	3.5	5.1	2.3	15.8	16.0	6.4	3.5	
	1994	3.1	7.3	34.6	4.6	2.8	1.9	23.3	15.0	6.4	1.0	

1) 1990: 'Common Course' party (left wing populist), 'The Greens', 'Justice party' (Georgist, single-tax party), and candidates outside the parties.
   1994: Candidates outside the parties (among whom the comedian Jacob Haugaard was elected).
2) Including 'assisting spouse'.

Lower-level non-manuals are more politically divided. The Social Democrats are slightly over-represented but the group is quite evenly divided between socialist and bourgeois votes. Higher-level non-manuals (including managers), on the other hand, are strongly attracted to the right-wing parties, that is, the Liberals and the Conservatives but certainly not the populist Progress party. Both lower-level and

6. The dramatic change in the 1994 election is confirmed by three large surveys of some 3500, 3000 and 7000 respondents, carried out by AIM Nielsen in March/April 1995, January/February 1996, and May/August 1996, respectively. These surveys indicate that the class-specific losses among workers have been reinforced since the 1994 election (the weekly *Mandag Morgen*, no. 7 and 30/1996).

higher-level non-manuals are disproportionately attracted to centre parties (in particular the Radical Liberals and the Centre Democrats).

The 'old middle class' reveals far the strongest class-determined party choice. Among farmers, only some 4-7 per cent prefer socialist parties, and among other self-employed, the figure is below 20 per cent. Farmers are the only social group with a stable support above 50 per cent for a single party, i.e. for the Liberals which was supported by two-thirds of the farmers in 1990 and 1994. Together, the parties to the right (Liberals, Conservatives, and the Progress party) receive more than 90 per cent of the farmers' votes.

Self-employed outside agriculture do not hold stable preferences for any individual party but tend to oscillate between the Conservatives (which used to be the major party), the Liberals and the Progress party which has always had a stronghold here (in the 1970s, it frequently obtained one-third of the votes, see Goul Andersen & Bjørklund 1990). The stable element is the strong combined support for these three parties: in 1990 and 1994, they received around three-quarters of the votes among the self-employed.

The class profiles of individual parties are described further below (section 5.8).

b. Long-Term Trends in Class Voting, in a Scandinavian Perspective
As it emerges from Table 5.2, Denmark used to be a highly class-polarised country in terms of party choice. Until the mid-1960s, about 80 per cent of the workers voted for socialist parties; among farmers, the proportion was some 5 per cent or less, and among self-employed, a highest point was encountered in 1964 when 26 per cent voted socialist (for survey data from the 1950s, see Glans 1989). The 'new middle class' of non-manual employees was more divided as some 40 per cent preferred the socialist parties; but numerically, this group was still relatively small in the 1960s. Consequently, the Alford index of class voting, calculated as the difference in 'left voting' between the working class and the middle class (Alford 1963), was high: 50 percentage points or more in 1964 and 1966.

Voting and Political Attitudes in Denmark

Table 5.2. Social class[1] and party choice, 1964-1994. Proportions voting socialist. Percentages

	1964	1966	1968	1971	1973	1975	1977	1979	1981	1984	1987	1988	1990	1994
Working class	78	81	71	74	56	62	64	66	64	64	67	62	71	57
New middle class	40	42	36	39	30	37	46	52	46	45	52	47	48	45
Farmers	5	5	3	2	1	3	1	6	3	1	3	.	6	7
Other self-employed	26	23	16	12	12	14	14	20	15	12	23	.	20	14
Whole population[2]	49	50	44	49	37	40	47	50	48	46	50	48	50	44
Middle class, total	28	29	24	31	21	27	37	40	38	38	44	39	42	39
Alford Index[3]	50	52	47	43	35	35	27	26	26	26	23	23	29	18

1) Own present occupation. Pensioners and housewives not included. Based on Gallup's occupational code.

2) The Greens and the 'Common Course'-party are recorded as socialist parties. 'Outside the parties' are not recorded as socialists.

3) Assisting wives working in their husband's firm are included in the 'middle class' but not in the figures for farmers and self-employed as we have no precise information on husband's occupation.

Sources: Based on monthly Gallup polls after the elections, typically carried out as special sections of the Danish Election Project (1977, 1979, 1984-1994). The 1973 figures are based on a special survey conducted by Ingemar Glans in April/May 1974. Ingemar Glans also kindly provided the data from the 1960s. 1984 figures are based on a combination of the 1984 election survey and a 'class survey' from August/September 1985 conducted by Jørgen Goul Andersen and Jens Hoff. Sample size: about 2000 in 1979, 3000 in 1973, 1977, 1988 and 1990, 4000 in 1984, 1987 and 1994, otherwise above 10000. All data is weighted by party choice (see also Goul Andersen 1989).

From Figure 5.1 it emerges that class voting in Denmark was even stronger than in Norway and Sweden in the 1960s, mainly because of an extremely low level of socialist voting among Danish farmers. It seems that workers were also slightly more socialist in Denmark but this may derive from different dividing lines between workers and non-manual employees. Another country difference in coding practices which affects recent figures, is the Norwegian and Swedish practice of classifying pensioners according to their former occupation. As pensioners tend to follow their voting habits in the past, this introduces an element of inertia in to the Norwegian and Swedish data.[7]

At any rate, Denmark experienced a marked decline in class voting in 1973 and again in 1977; from 1968 to 1977, the Alford index of class voting declined from 47 to 27 (or from 50 to 28 if housewives are included). In the 'earthquake' election of 1973 when the socialist parties obtained only 36.4 per cent of the votes, workers defected from the Socialist parties a little more than other groups; and in 1977 when the socialist parties regained their traditional strength, workers did not return as frequently as other voters. From 1977 to 1990, the Alford index varied between 23 and 29 without any clear trend. After a peak value of 29 in 1990, the index reached a new lowest point of 18 in the 1994 election when only 57 per cent of the workers voted socialist.

To a large degree, the other Scandinavian countries have followed a similar pattern. However, excepting the 1991 election, class voting of the working class as well as class voting in general has remained higher in Sweden than in the two other countries. Both in Sweden and Norway, however, the decline of class voting have taken a more gradual course than in Denmark. The inclusion of pensioners in Norway and Sweden does contribute to modifying the changes but the main part of the difference is genuine.

---

7.   Danish election studies classify the respondents according to their own present occupation, i.e. pensioners are classified as pensioners and are not included in calculations of class voting. Married women are classified according to their own occupation if they are employed and previously home-working housewives were classified according to husbands' class. However, as housewives have disappeared, the occupation of 'head of household' was dropped as a standard variable from the mid-1980s. Accordingly, we have dropped housewives from the tables in this chapter. As housewives were older and not exposed to the cross-pressures of cross-class families, class voting among housewives was higher than among the employed. Besides, as there used to be more housewives in the old middle class than in other classes, this class obtained a higher weight in the aggregation of middle class voting. Consequently, the figures on class voting presented here are 1 to 3 percentage points lower from 1964 to 1979, as compared to previous calculations where housewives are included (see e.g. Goul Andersen 1992a).

Figure 5.1.a. Alford's Index of class voting. Denmark, Norway, and Sweden

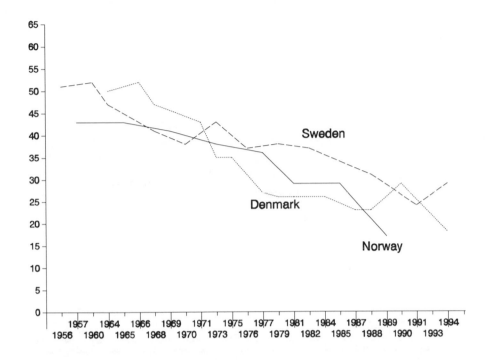

Sources: Norway: 1957-1985: Listhaug 1989, p. 41) 1989: Valen, Aardal, Vogt 1990, p. 70)
FMS counted as non-socialist.
Sweden: 1956-1991: Oskarson (1994, pp. 42-45).
1994: (Gilljam & Holmberg 1995, pp. 100-01). Greens counted as non-socialist.

Figure 5.1.b. Class voting of the working class: Percentages voting socialist. Denmark, Norway and Sweden

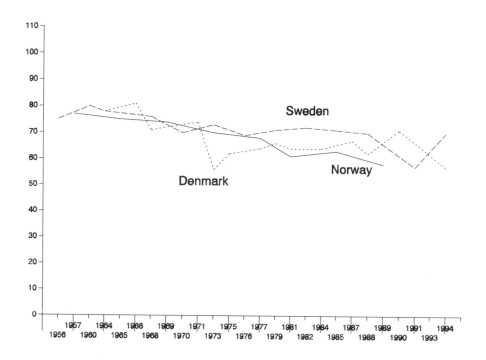

Sources: Norway: 1957-1985: Listhaug 1989, p. 41) 1989: Valen, Aardal, Vogt 1990, p. 70)
FMS counted as non-socialist.
Sweden: 1956-1991: Oskarson (1994, pp. 42-45).
1994: (Gilljam & Holmberg 1995, pp. 100-01). Greens counted as non-socialist.

In all three countries, class structural change is part of the explanation (Goul Andersen 1984d; Listhaug 1989; Oskarson 1994): the class composition of the middle class has changed as farmers and other self-employed are replaced by much more politically divided groups of non-manual employees. As it emerges from Table 5.3, changing class composition explains roughly 10 percentage points of the decline in class voting in the 1980s, that is, nearly one-half of the decline from 1964 to 1990, and one-third of the decline from 1964 to 1994.

Voting and Political Attitudes in Denmark

Table 5.3. *Alford Index of class voting. Denmark 1964-1994. Unstandardised and standardised.[1] Percentage points*

Alford Index	1964	1966	1968	1971	1973	1975	1979	1981	1984	1987	1990	1994
Unstandardised	50	52	47	43	35	35	26	26	26	23	29	18
Standardised	50	52	47	49	37	38	33	35	37	33	39	28
Total change since 1964	.	+2	–3	–7	–15	–15	–24	–24	–24	–27	–21	–32
Explained by class structural change	.	0	0	–6	–2	–3	–7	–9	–11	–10	–10	–10
Rest: 'Real' change	.	+2	–3	–1	–13	–12	–17	–15	–13	–17	–11	–22

1)   Standardised figures assume same class composition of the 'middle class' as in 1964.

This does not mean that the decline in class voting is spurious in any substantial sense. The changing class structure is a real fact, and being evenly divided between left and right, the growing 'new middle class' does not contribute to class voting at all. The question is, however, if there are class divisions *within* the new middle class.

As to such divisions, it is trivial to point out that the 'new middle class' is *vertically* stratified. As revealed by the dichotomisation of the new middle class in Table 5.1, voting patterns vary accordingly, and such divisions are standard variables in electoral research. They may add to the explained variance[8] but they hardly increase our understanding of the social changes. The important division is the *horizontal* division between the public and the private sector which questions the very concept of 'the new middle class', at least from the criterion that a classification should produce larger inter-class differences than intra-class differences.

5.3. Sector Classes: Private and Public Employees

The changes in class voting above are strongly influenced by an emerging new political division between public and private employees, along with a significant growth in the number of public employees. In the Danish welfare state, about one-third of the (employed) labour force are public employees, mainly in non-manual occupations.

---

8.   Attempts to improve measurement of the vertical divisions add very little, on the other hand. Thus, changing the 'class boundaries' adds nothing except what is gained from improved reliability when occupation is coded from open-ended questions (Goul Andersen 1989). Replacing standard occupational classifications (as in Table 2.1) with a social status index or with elaborate marxist class concepts adds nothing at all; rather, the explained variance declines (Hoff & Goul Andersen 1986). At best, such divisions may serve as a supplement to occupational classifications, not as an alternative.

Table 5.4. Party choice among public and private employees, 1971-94. Per cent voting socialist

	1971	1973	1975	1979	1981	1984	1987	1990	1994
Total, manual+non-manual									
Privately employed, total	62	45	48	56	49	47	51	48	39
Public employees, total	47	37	50	61	57	53	62	62	57
Difference public — private	−15	−8	+2	+5	+8	+6	+11	+14	+18
Manual workers									
Privately employed	74	57	62	64	62	61	64	68	52
Public employees	74	52	66	72	65	61	69	75	62
Difference public — private	0	−5	+4	+8	+3	0	+5	+7	+10
Non-manual employees									
Privately employed	41	28	31	45	36	35	39	33	27
Public employees	37	33	45	57	54	52	60	59	56
Difference public — private	−4	+5	+14	+12	+18	+17	+21	+26	+29
Class difference manual-non-manual									
private sector	33	29	31	19	26	26	25	35	25
public sector	37	19	21	15	11	9	9	16	6
total	35	26	25	14	18	19	15	23	12
(N)									
manual, private	272	598	2065	278	2404	395	450	302	433
manual, public	48	72	381	93	1073	144	120	102	101
non-manual, private	154	445	1630	212	2318	459	460	415	431
non-manual, public	144	371	1274	267	2991	613	579	483	452

The changes in party choice are presented in Table 5.4. In 1971, a large majority of 62 per cent of the privately employed wage earners voted for socialist parties, as compared to only 47 per cent among public employees. However, this difference evaporated in the 1970s; from 1975, public employees have voted further to the left, and since then, the sector difference has increased almost monotonously. By 1994, only 39 per cent of the privately employed voted socialist — a decline of 23 percentage points since 1971. Among public employees, 57 per cent preferred a socialist party, that is, an increase of 10 percentage points. Besides, the left-wing parties have got a stronghold among public employees: in 1971, left-wing parties gained 18 per cent among privately employed and 15 per cent among public employees. By 1994, they received only 7 per cent among the privately employed, as compared to 20 per cent among public employees.

Like the political divisions between the 'new' and the 'old' middle class, these divisions confirm the basic assumption of structural class theory that what matters is not how much people have but what they do. From structural class theory, one would, furthermore, assume that such divisions are more likely to occur among specialised groups who also identify more with their jobs than among workers who may more easily move in or out of the public sector. The table confirms this assumption as the sector difference is mainly concentrated among non-manual employees. In 1971 and even in the welfare backlash election of 1973, there was no significant difference. But by 1994, only 27 per cent of the privately employed non-manuals voted for socialist parties whereas 56 per cent of the public employees preferred a socialist party, i.e. a difference of 29 percentage points. This means that the sector difference among non-manual employees has become one of the most important social divisions among Danish voters in the 1980s and 1990s.

It would be tempting to interpret this division as an effect of simple self-interests in the welfare state. However, as discussed in section 5.6 and in chapter 8, our data do not lend much support to such an interpretation. From Table 5.4, we may, furthermore, observe that the emerging division is a movement in two steps: a significant movement to the left among public employees in the 1970s, and an equally significant movement to the right among the privately employed non-manuals in the 1980s and 1990s. This indicates that we are faced with two separate waves of mobilisation rather than a single process of polarisation over the public sector. This is also confirmed by the voting patterns of workers.

Among workers, there has been a stable sector difference since the mid-1970s. But it is small, and it turns out that the movement to the right among workers from 1990 to 1994 was equally strong in the private and the public sector (even among unemployed workers, the proportion voting socialist declined from 75 to 66 per cent). Thus, the major part of the movement to the right in the 1994 election seems to derive from a class-specific movement to the right among workers, regardless of sector; we return to this point later on.

Returning to the question of class differences between manual and non-manual employees, we finally observe that there is a considerable interaction with sector. In the public sector, class differences have almost evaporated but class voting remains high in the private sector: the 1990 election reveals the highest working class/new middle class difference for the entire period, and even in 1994, class differences remained considerable.

At the same time, contrary to what might be expected from theories of value change, we face a very significant movement to the right among higher-level non-manuals in the private sector. In 1994, socialist voting in this group had declined to only 17 per cent, and among men in such positions, the figure was as low as

11 per cent, i.e. exactly the same as among self-employed. By contrast, some 30 per cent of higher-level non-manuals in the private sector (regardless of gender) voted socialist by 1971.

A similar pattern of increasing sector differences is encountered in Norway and Sweden (Listhaug 1989, p. 45; Aardal & Valen 1989; Oskarson 1994, p. 88; Gilljam & Holmberg 1995, p. 104) but the timing is different, and the Danish figures are far the most significant. In Norway, the sector difference among non-manuals has fluctuated between 12 and 19 percentage points since 1969, without any clear trend. In Sweden, the sector variable was not introduced until 1976, and it was not until the 1994 election that the sector difference exceeded 10 percentage points. Again, it is tempting to suggest that the country difference is sparked off by the different timing and strengths of welfare retrenchment policies in the Scandinavian countries but as we shall see below, attitudinal data are not consistent with such a simple explanation.

5.4. Changes in Class Voting: What is to be Explained?

As demonstrated above, the highest level of class voting in Denmark was encountered in the mid-1960s. Since then, four related social processes have taken place: (1) class structural change: expansion of the 'new middle class' and a significant change in the composition of the 'middle class'; (2) expansion of the public sector; (3) expansion of female labour market participation; and (4) increasing unemployment and exclusion from the labour market (the last two processes are further analysed in chapter 6 and 8, respectively).

At this point, we may ask: how much would class voting have declined if these processes had not taken place? This contrafactual question may be answered if we look at the *voting patterns among the former core group of privately employed men* and standardise for the changes in the composition of the 'middle class'. The figures in Table 5.5 reveal that until 1990, there was very little change in class voting among privately employed men. Even the class difference between workers and non-manual employees was constant (37 to 39 percentage points). The Alford index declined from 53 in 1964 to 45 in 1990 but if we standardise for a change in the composition of the middle class, most of this decline disappears.[9] Whether the 1994 data signals a short-term deviance or a more definitive break with previous developments remains to be seen.

---

9. These computations rest upon the plausible (probably even conservative) assumption that there was no sector difference in voting in 1964.

Table 5.5. Class voting among privately employed men, 1964(1971)-1994. Per cent voting socialist

	1964[1]	1966[1]	1971	1990	1994
Workers	(80)	(83)	76	69	52
Non-manual employees	(43)	(46)	40	30	22
Farmers	6	5	2	7	8
Self-employed	25	21	14	17	15
Workers minus non-manual employees	(37)	(37)	37	39	30
Alford index: workers minus middle class	(53)	(56)	51	45	33
Alford index/standardised by 1964 weights[2]	(53)	(56)	55	50	36
Alford index/standardised by 1994 weights[2]	(46)	(48)	51	45	33

1) Under the assumption of no sector differences in 1964 and 1966.
2) Standardisation for changing composition of the middle class (as Table 5.3), using 1964 and 1994 weights, respectively.

In short, until 1990, it was possible to argue that the apparent decline in class voting was an effect of the changing composition of the 'middle class', the expansion of the public sector, and the entrance of women into the labour market; what remains to be explained is the class-specific move to the right among manual workers in the 1994 election. Alternatively, if we define class voting of particular groups as deviation from the election result, it emerges that some groups have maintained a high level of class voting, even in 1994:

(1) Among self-employed, class voting is permanently high.
(2) Among non-manual employees in the private sector, class voting is steadily increasing. The proportion of socialists among men has halved since the 1960s.
(3) Non-manual employees in the public sector deviate only slightly from the overall average but the sign of this deviation has changed.
(4) Thus it is only among workers that we discover a genuine *decline* of class voting. This calls for class-specific explanations, and so does the class-specific decline in socialist voting among workers in the 1994 election.

In short, the conventional interpretation of decline of class voting as a *general* weakening of the association between occupational position and political behaviour is wrong. The argument is flawed as it is based on an illegitimate aggregation of middle class groups among whom some vote even further to the left than privately employed workers. Thus the relevant research question is not what explains the declining importance of class but rather what explains the changing behaviour of particular groups:

(1) What explains the move to the right/the declining class voting of workers?
(2) What explains the leftward move of public employees in the 1970s?
(3) What explains the rightward move among private employees in the 1980s and 1990s?

We are not able to provide definitive answers to these questions. But we may give some clues, and in particular, we shall demonstrate that some widely shared assumptions are not confirmed in the Danish case.

5.5. Class Inequality, Class Voting and the 'Embourgeoisement' Theory

In sociology, a main concern of class theories is to explain social inequality, and even in studies of political behaviour it is frequently assumed, at least indirectly, that inequality is the decisive component of social class. Thus the classical explanation of the decline in working class radicalism is increasing wealth and the achievement of middle-class life styles, although it was not always implied that this would lead workers to vote for bourgeois parties. Thus Lipset (1964) concluded that revolutionary class struggle was replaced by a 'democratic class struggle' in the fully-fledged industrial society. However, a few years later another classical study concluded that workers' relationship to trade unions and Socialist parties was becoming increasingly instrumental (Goldthorpe & Lockwood 1968-9) and that this might also lead workers to vote for bourgeois parties. The 'embourgeoisement' theory was also echoed by Inglehart (1977) in the argument that increasing wealth had softened the demands of the traditional working class but generated new demands within the (new) middle class. But does increasing wealth and changing life-styles affect political behaviour? And does it explain class differences? Structural class theory would suggest that what matters is not the *amount* of income earned, absolutely or relatively, but the *way* it is earned.

To examine these questions, we have chosen two indicators: income and home ownership. Strictly speaking, it is problematical to infer macro-level effects of increasing wealth from micro-level differences in income as the latter may simply reflect enduring divisions between various occupations with different wage levels and trade union traditions. However, home ownership is not subject to the same criticism as it has increased considerably in the period we have analysed.

a. Income and Partisanship
The effects of income and social class upon the proportion voting socialist are examined in Table 5.6. In order to avoid disturbing effects of household size and gender differences in wages or working hours, we have chosen *personal* income among economically active *men* as our main indicator. Data from 1971 and 1979

are included to indicate changes over time. To begin with the 'embourgeoisement' theory, we find no sign of decreasing support for socialist parties among workers with higher incomes; rather, there seems to be a *positive* relationship. Now, this is mainly a spurious association, explained by regional differences, but at least, the data allow us to conclude that at the individual level, higher income is not a source of bourgeois orientations among workers.

This finding also speaks against the assumption that income is a decisive component of social class. We, furthermore, find that the proportion voting socialist among self-employed is negligible, regardless of income.[10] Only among non-manual employees do we find a significant correlation between income and party choice; in particular, there are few socialists in the 'very high' income group. However, as income is largely a reflection of vertical class divisions within the new middle class (qualifications and hierarchical position), we are faced with a problem of multicollinearity: if our subdivision along vertical class lines is sufficiently detailed, there is almost no independent variation.

Table 5.6. Class, personal income and party choice among men, 1971, 1979 and 1994. Per cent voting socialist

(a)	1971			1979			1994		
Income	Worker	Non-man.	Self-empl.	Worker	Non-man.	Self-empl.	Worker	Non-man.	Self-empl.
Low	72	58	4	66	72	16	50	51	9
Medium	77	39	(6)	70	44	(21)	59	48	24
High	81	49	(25)	71	38	–	60	31	(18)
Very high	.	(13)	(0)	.	29	4	(71)	17	6
Total	76	43	8	68	46	13	56	456	14
(N)	96	39	41	111	42	54	154	78	44
	91	44	14	90	69	18	203	176	40
	37	60	15	23	58	12	57	134	27
	1	23	14	6	36	21	10	68	33
	226	167	84	231	205	105	425	456	144

Income intervals (thousand DkK)	1971	1979	1994
Low	< 30	< 90	< 200
Medium	30-39	90-119	200-299
High	40-59.	120-149	300-399
Very high	60 +	150 +	400 +

10. Because of shortage of cases, we have collapsed farmers and other self-employed in the table. This tends to suppress income effects, however, as farmers are more to the right and typically have lower incomes than other self-employed. However, even among self-employed outside agriculture, larger surveys consistently reveal that the proportion voting socialist is small, even in the lowest income group.

Changing Class Cleavages

It may be added that an equivalent analysis among women reveals no income effects at all (regardless of control for working hours). An equivalent analysis based on family income among married or cohabiting couples yields approximately identical results but with the modification that we encounter a weak but bell-shaped relationship between family income and socialist voting among workers whereas the relationship between income and socialist voting becomes weaker than above among non-manual employees.

In short, income does not as such seem to be a relevant determinant of political behaviour in Denmark,[11] and at the individual level, there is nothing to confirm the embourgeoisement theory among workers. Still, we have to make a reservation concerning the last point: the question is whether we can infer from our findings that a *general* increase in standards of living over time will not affect working-class voting behaviour.

b. Home Ownership and Party Choice

This reservation is much less relevant when it comes to home ownership which has changed considerably since the 1960s. Further, we may also easily falsify any assumption that home ownership is an intervening variable between social class and party choice, as there were no class differences in home ownership between manual and non-manual employees until 1979. Since then, a small difference has emerged along with mass unemployment which has been much more widespread among workers than in the middle classes. In 1994, the proportion of home owners was 66 per cent among workers, 73 per cent among non-manual employees, and 90 per cent among self-employed.

Nevertheless, increasing home ownership among workers would be a plausible explanation of working class 'embourgeoisement' as the theory would predict that political effects of home ownership are class-dependent. For workers, home ownership may entail a break with a 'proletarian' life-style whereas middle class tenants are unlikely to adopt a proletarian life-style. Furthermore, the increase in home ownership among workers took place within a short span of years: by 1968, only some 40 per cent of all workers were home owners; by the mid-1970s, the proportion was about 60 per cent. This increase in home ownership coincides perfectly in time with the move to the right among workers from the mid-1960s to the mid-1970s.

---

11. This is a quite consistent finding in nearly all types of analyses. Even in the 1990 election which was called because of disagreement over marginal taxes for medium and higher incomes, the income effects were exactly the same as in 1979 and 1994, and it even turned out that there was no significant association between income and attitudes towards taxation policies, except among the very highest incomes (Goul Andersen 1992b).

It has also been demonstrated that in a purely statistical sense, the increasing proportion of home owners is able to 'explain' most of the move to the right in the working class from the 1960s to the 1970s: had the proportion of home owners remained constant, there would only have been an insignificant move to the right, given the voting patterns of working class tenants and home owners (Hoff & Goul Andersen 1986, pp. 64-67).

However, an alternative *policy explanation* may be derived from Esping-Andersen's (1980) considerations of policy tactics in the political class struggle: building on Swedish experience, Esping-Andersen argued that home ownership does not *as such* entail bourgeois orientations; rather it was the privileges of Danish home owners (full tax deductions for interests, alongside with high inflation and untaxed capital gains) — and the political struggle between left and right over these privileges — that explained why home owners moved to the right in the 1970s.

As these privileges of home owners largely disappeared from the mid-1980s to 1994,[12] it has now become possible to test this alternative explanation, and the data in Table 5.7 leave little doubt about the conclusion: the political effects of home ownership among workers had almost disappeared by 1994. Besides, the data reveals that for the first time, the socialist parties experienced severe losses among working class tenants in 1994. A control for age modifies the picture slightly but the conclusion remains that what seemed for a long time to be a satisfactory 'explanation' of embourgeoisement, was a misinterpretation that conflated life style effects with rational voting in relation to policy effects.

Table 5.7. Home ownership and party choice among workers, 1968-1994. Per cent voting socialist

	1968	1971	1979	1984	1990	1994	N(1994)
Home owners	62	62	56	58	65	54	492
Tenants	78	84	81	79	81	63	222
Difference	16	22	25	21	16	9	
Proportion of home owners in sample	40	50	62	65	65	66	

Note: 1968 data are based on type of dwelling rather than ownership. However, at that time, this was an almost perfect approximation as owner-apartments were not allowed. Furthermore, even by 1984, the two variables were nearly coincidental (Hoff & Goul Andersen 1986, p. 66).

12. Since 1993/94, there have been considerable capital gains among house-owners but attitudes are not very likely to have changed before the 1994 election; besides, tax deductions have been lowered considerably since 1987.

This also makes macro-level inferences from individual-level income effects a bit less hazardous. We may conclude that income and home ownership are not mediating variables between social class and party choice, and it also seems safe to conclude that increasing wealth and changing life-styles has not had much effect upon working-class political behaviour: it is not these variables that explain the declining political cohesiveness.

c. Weakening of Working-Class Community

If there is any relationship between changing life-styles and changing voter patterns, it is, at best, a more indirect one. It may be suggested that the changing voting pattern among workers reflects a disintegration of the working-class subculture which is only indirectly related to changing life-styles.

From this perspective, the classical pattern of working class behaviour should be a pattern of strong group interactions and strong effects of the collective upon the individual whereas an erosion of working class subculture would mean privatisation, i.e. less politically relevant interaction with colleagues and smaller or no effects of the collective upon the individual. Arguing along the same lines, we should expect an 'awakening' among non-manual employees and opposite effects of interaction among privately employed and public employees. In Table 5.8, this is shown by means of a question indicating political discussions with colleagues during the election campaign.

To quite a large degree, the data confirm our expectations. In particular from 1971 to 1984, there were clear signs of a declining political interaction among workers and a decreasing impact of the collectivity upon the individual. From 1971 to 1984, the proportion of workers participating in discussions declined from 64 to 42 per cent whereas it remained constant in the two other groups. Besides, political discussions with colleagues had a radicalising effect among workers in 1971 but this effect nearly evaporated in the following years. Among non-manuals, political discussions had opposite effects on private and public employees, as predicted: a radicalising impact on public employees and a conservative impact on the privately employed.

Table 5.8. Per cent voting socialist, by social class and discussions with colleagues during campaign

	Manual Workers			Non-manuals, private sector			Non-manuals, public sector		
	Discussed with colleagues		Effect	Discussed with colleagues		Effect	Discussed with colleagues		Effect
	yes	no[1]		yes	no[1]		yes	no	
1971	81	63	+18	43	43	0	35	46	−11
1975	64	52	+12	33	39	−6	49	(28)	(+21)
1979	73	67	+6	43	47	−4	60	56	+4
1984	66	65	+1	29	39	−10	56	38	+18
1994	59	51	+8	26	39	−13	56	54	+2
(N)			per cent yes[2]			per cent yes			per cent yes
1971	208	116	64	87	61	59	88	46	66
1975	109	84	56	88	36	71	53	18	75
1979	181	177	51	111	109	50	159	112	59
1984	72	101	42	76	49	61	109	58	65
1994	223	118	65	162	63	72	234	80	75

Source: Data 1971-1984 quoted from Goul Andersen (1984c, p. 26).
1)   Including unemployed 1971-84 (but unemployment was relatively small until 1979).
2)   Have discussed politics with colleagues.

During the 1994 campaign, however, there was far more discussion with colleagues than in previous elections, and this holds also for the working class where a weak positive relationship between political discussions and socialist party choice reemerged. Still, the relationship seems to be weaker than in the early 1970s, and since 1975, workers have discussed less politics with colleagues than the two other groups. The signs of the effects among the two other groups also come out as predicted. But it must be acknowledged that the pattern is somewhat less clear in 1994 than is was ten years earlier. Thus, even though our predictions are confirmed, the results do not allow us to conclude that we have found the *major* explanation of working class embourgeoisement, nor of the political changes in the two other groups.

However, *sociological* theories of social change seem to hold no other relevant explanation of working class embourgeoisement; as we see it, the decisive variables are to be found elsewhere. In line with our general efforts in this book to see voting as reactions to policies advocated by different parties and more or less successfully implemented by different governments, we now turn to various *political sociological* interpretations of changing voting patterns among social classes.

5.6. Ideological Changes

A first question is to what degree the changes in class voting — increasing sector polarisation and lower class voting among workers — are related to class-specific changes in attitudes. Because of space limitations, we concentrate on three major ideological indicators which have been strongly related to the economic changes and to the political debates within the past twenty years:

- support for the welfare state
- support for state regulation of business
- support for economic equality.

The *'embourgeoisement'* theory implicitly assumes that workers move ideologically to the right — and more so than other social groups — along with the achievement of a 'middle class' or a 'middle mass' status. Interpreted this way, the 'embourgeoisement' may encompass all workers, not only the better-off strata. In particular, we might expect that workers develop a more achievement-oriented mentality and accordingly less favourable attitudes to economic equality. From the point of view of *issue voting* theory, on the other hand, it may be the association between attitudes and party choice that has changed among workers, rather than the attitudes themselves.

As far as the increasing *sector polarisation* is concerned, it would seem obvious to suggest that this was rooted in conflicting welfare state interests, and, to a lesser degree, in different attitudes to state regulation. Therefore we should expect to find an increasing ideological polarisation between private and public employees exactly at these issues along with the increasing sector polarisation in party choice. One might even imagine that welfare conflict contributes to declining class polarisation. Workers in Denmark pay high and visible income taxes, not the least to cover expenses for public services that are consumed just as much as upper-middle class groups.[13] This might generate negative welfare state feelings among workers, perhaps even among workers in the public sector.

---

13. The Danish tax system is unique in the European Union in that social contributions are negligible whereas ordinary income taxes are very high. Further, public service expenditures are much higher than in most other countries outside Scandinavia (Goul Andersen & Munk Christiansen 1991; Goul Andersen 1996a). Nevertheless, the public sector seems to be unusually redistributive in Denmark (Ministry of Finance 1995b).

Alternatively, sector polarisation may be more associated with value change. Postmaterialism, mainly among public employees, could be a possible explanation. However, as the strongest force behind the increasing sector polarisation is a move to the right among the privately employed, it is more interesting to examine whether increasingly *individualist, achievement-oriented values* in Danish society (Gundelach & Riis 1992) are becoming especially intense or widespread among the privately employed. Indeed, this could be supported by institutional changes at the labour market — decentralised bargaining and performance-related wage systems. Such institutional changes have proceeded quite far in the private sector whereas traditional wage systems and centralised bargaining still predominate within the public sector. Thus conflicts over equality rather than controversy over the welfare state may be at the core of sector polarisation.

Below, we begin by examining if class polarisation in attitudes between workers and others has declined. At this point, it is possible to carry the analysis back to 1969, i.e. to the period when the swing to the right among workers began. The results presented in Table 5.9 are quite astonishing. It turns out that *from 1969 to 1994, nothing has happened at all in terms of class polarisation.* There are no signs of declining welfare state support among workers — if anything, it is the middle classes who have become a bit less enthusiastic about the welfare state. On the other two issues, there is a move to the right but this change is entirely parallel in all class categories. In short, there are no signs of a class-specific ideological move to the right among manual workers. Thus we may safely conclude that the long-term swing to the right among manual workers is not rooted in (class-specific) ideological change along the conventional aspects of the left-right dimension.

Table 5.9. Class positions on ideological left-right issues, 1969-1994. PDI (Percentage Difference Indexes), in percentage points

	Social reforms				Economic equality				State control of business			
	1969	1979	1994	Change 1969-94	1969	1979	1994	Change 1969-94	1969	1979	1994	Change 1969-94
Workers	53	33	53	0	60	38	28	−32	16	8	−4	−22
Non-manual employees	58	32	44	−14	30	16	4	−26	5	−3	−16	−21
Self-employed	12	−16	3	−9	28	−3	−8	−36	−47	−52	−61	−14
(N)	171	443	443									
	112	553	680									
	120	227	147									

Wordings: See Table 1.5, items 1-3.

At the same time, however, we may note that the class differences in ideology have always been *small*, as compared to the differences in voting patterns. Only the issue of economic equality produce a significant class polarisation in attitudes. In other words, workers seem to have voted further to the left in 1969 than was justified by their ideological orientations. Thus we are able to bury any sort of conventional 'embourgeoisement' interpretation of the decline in class voting: declining socialist voting among workers is not related to income or middle class-status, and it is not related to class-specific ideological movements to the right.

Table 5.10. *Class/sector positions on ideological left-right issues, 1969-1994.*
PDI (Percentage Difference Indexes), in percentage points

Class/ sector	Social reforms				Economic equality				State control of business			
	1974	1979	1994	Change 1974-94	1974	1979	1994	Change 1974-94	1974	1979	1994	Change 1974-94
Workers, private	−3	35	48	+51	46	40	23	−23	−1	6	−7	−6
Workers, public	−12	28	47	+59	51	33	29	−22	9	14	−1	−10
Non-manuals, private	−22	14	26	+48	24	5	−23	−47	−22	−24	−24	−2
Non-manuals, public	6	28	47	+41	45	25	18	−27	4	14	−13	−17
	786	328	252									
	90	114	92									
	460	250	251									
	341	302	352									

Wordings: See Table 1.5, items 1-3.

Turning to the sector cleavages, our data only allow us to go back to 1974 but the analysis nevertheless covers most of the period where the sector polarisation took place. The results which are presented in Table 5.10, are quite surprising. Firstly, support for the welfare state has increased, and it has increased almost proportionately in all groups from 1974 (1979) to 1994. Secondly, even though privately employed non-manuals remain the most sceptical, there is a considerable preponderance of favourable welfare state attitudes even in this group by 1994. Thus it seems that the political polarisation between private and public employees is *not* rooted in increasing controversy over the welfare state.

The same holds for state regulation. Since 1979, there has been a general decline in belief in state regulation of the economy but this decline is most pronounced among *public* employees. Among privately employed non-manuals, on the other

Voting and Political Attitudes in Denmark

hand, attitudes to state regulation of business do not seem to have changed at all since 1979, in spite of a dramatic swing to the right. Thus, rather than increasing sector polarisation over state regulation of business, we find a convergence.

The sector changes in attitudes towards economic equality, on the other hand, are consistent with the sector change in voting patterns. Here, we find a marked sector polarisation in attitudes as well as a quite definitive break with social democratic values among privately employed non-manuals. As attitudes towards equality are strongly related to party choice, it seems likely that this may be *one* of the major explanations of the sector polarisation in party choice.[14]

Of course, this small sample of attitudes does not allow us to draw too far-reaching conclusions but the finding that changing attitudes to equality is related to increasing sector polarisation whereas welfare state attitudes are not, is nevertheless a significant one. When it comes to *class polarisation*, on the other hand, we found no evidence of any class-specific move to the right among workers but at the same time, class differences in attitudes have always been too small to account for the propensity of workers to vote for left parties; the only major class difference is the difference in attitudes to economic equality.[15] These findings would be consistent with an issue voting explanation of declining class voting.

5.7. From Class Identification to Issue Voting?

Sometimes the question of class voting vs. issue voting is examined by comparing the (direct) effects of class and political attitudes on party choice. As pointed out by Knutsen (1988), however, this sort of operationalisation is misleading as these variables occupy very different positions in the causal chain. Rather, a proper comparison could take place at the social psychological level, i.e. by comparing

---

14. Changing beliefs about economic competence may also play a role. The most significant swing to the right among the privately employed took place around 1980 when Denmark experienced a severe economic crisis. This crisis was traumatic for Danish voters: even by 1990, most voters still blamed the Social Democratic governments before 1982 for the country's economic problems (Goul Andersen 1992), and even privately employed non-manuals who voted for the Social Democrats were uncertain about the economic competence of the Social Democrats in the mid-1980s (Goul Andersen 1988, pp. 36-37).
15. Although the items above cover the core aspects of the left-right dimension, we cannot rule out the possibility that the selection of items gives a somewhat biased impression of class differences in attitudes. Thus our items may not discriminate too well between socialist and social liberal positions. At this point, questions that relate to trade union consciousness, collectivism or strike activity were proved in the 1970s to relate very strongly to social class, on the one hand, and to party choice on the other (Goul Andersen 1979). But the 1970s was a period of industrial unrest, and it is likely that such attitudes are less salient today.

the effect of issue positions with the effect of class identification. In this section, we put up some simple models based on a working class — middle class dichotomy, thus ignoring the complexities of modern class structures.

Typically, the ideal predictions of an issue voting explanation would be the following:

(1) Class identification is generally declining, in particular class identification of workers.
(2) Class identification is losing ground to issue positions as determinant of party choice.
(3) Consequently, the mediating link between social class, class consciousness and party choice is weakening.

These predictions are examined below.

a. The Decline in Class Identification

The first prediction is that class identification declines. Class identification has been given little attention in Danish electoral research (from 1979 to 1994, it was not even included in the election surveys but we are able to use data from an equivalent 'class survey' from 1985). The question has been posed in two different formats, each of which were repeated in one-half of the 1994 survey. This gives us a possibility to 'translate' between the two question formats (although the translation may not be perfect because of sample errors). Table 5.11 compares the results of the two techniques and describe the changes over time. The major difference is that the 1979 (b) version explicitly mentioned that 'most people would say they belonged to either the working class or the middle class' whereas the 1971 (a) version simply asked if the respondent felt that he or she 'belong(s) to a particular social class'. In both versions, non-identifiers were subsequently asked if they could indicate some class affiliation if they had to choose.

Both time series confirm that there has been a long-term decline in class identification. According to the (a) format, the proportion of class identifiers among the electorate at large has declined from 52 per cent in 1971 to 47 per cent in 1994. Working class identification has declined from 23 per cent to 16 per cent, with the 1985 figures fitting in between. Not surprisingly, the (b) format produces higher figures but the overall trend is the same.

Table 5.11.   *Class identification, 1971-1994. Among the population at large, and among manual workers. Percentages*

	Entire population					Manual Workers				
	(a) format			(b) format		(a) format			(b) format	
	1971	1985	1994	1979	1994	1971	1985	1994	1979	1994
1. Strong working class identification	13	} 20	8	19	11	22	} 35	16	32	19
2. Working class identification	10		8	14	11	15		14	26	18
3. Belong to working class	17	16	13	11	11	26	28	22	18	23
4. Belong to middle class	31	33	40	19	27	20	20	28	10	19
5. Middle class identification	18	} 31	21	23	27	12	} 17	14	8	15
6. Strong middle class identification	11		10	14	13	5		6	6	6
Total 'valid' answers	100	100	100	100	100	100	100	100	100	100
(N)	1095	1655	950	1586	846	328	322	218	379	177
7. Other answer/dk (percentage of total sample)	16	20	10	17	13	12	20	6	14	16
Class id. total (1+2+5+6)	52	51	47	70	62	54	52	50	72	58
Strong class id. (1+6)	24	.	18	33	24	27	.	22	38	25
Working class id. (1+2+3)	23	20	16	33	22	37	35	30	58	37

Wording: (a) "One often talks of social classes in Denmark. Do you feel you belong to a social class? [if yes:] Which class? — Do you feel strongly or less strongly attached to [class]? [if no:] If you had to place yourself in a social class anyway, which would it be?"

(b) "One often talks of social classes in Denmark. Most people would say that they belong either to the *working class* or to the *middle class*. Do you feel you belong to a social class? [if yes]: Which class? — Do you feel very strongly, strongly or less strongly attached to [class]? [if no]: If you were to chose, would you say you belonged mostly to the working class or to the middle class?"

Now, these figures could be a spurious effect of the declining proportion of manual workers in the class structure. But this is not the case. As predicted, it is working class identification among workers that has changed mostly: from 37 per cent in 1971 to 30 per cent in 1994, according to the (a) format and from 58 in 1979 to 37 per cent in 1994, according to the (b) format.[16]

---

16. Among nonworkers, working class identification is a relatively rare phenomenon. Even if we include those who feel close to the working class, only some 16-17 per cent of non-manual employees felt any attachment to the working class in 1994; in 1971 and 1979,

At the same time, however, these figures reveal that the decline in class identification is not an entirely linear one: from 1971 to 1979, the proportion of working-class identifiers increased from 37 to 58 per cent among manual workers, and the proportion of strong identifiers increased from 22 to 32 per cent. The difference in question wording only explains a minor part of this change: according to the 1994 survey, the (b) format only exaggerates the proportion of working-class identifiers with some 7 per cent and the proportion of strong working-class identifiers with about 3 per cent, as compared with the (a) format. It is not difficult to explain the increasing class identification in Denmark in the 1970s. This was a period of an unprecedented resurgence of class conflict manifested in frequent and massive political strikes against the government, and a large number of wildcat strikes at the workplace level. But this means that mobilisation makes a difference, and the 1979 figures should warn against too deterministic interpretations. Further, it must be acknowledged that the long-term change from 1971 to 1994 is a bit lower than expected. Thus it is premature to dismiss class identification entirely — at least if it is still relevant for party choice.

b. *Class Identification and Party Choice*
As witnessed by Table 5.12, the association between class identification and party choice has remained quite strong. Even in 1994, support for socialist parties was some 80-90 per cent among strong working class identifiers as compared to 25-35 per cent among strong middle class identifiers, depending on the question format. Still, the effect is decreasing: from 1971 to 1994 (a), the eta coefficient has declined from .51 to .32, with the 1985 result falling in between. However, the (b) version produce a little more ambiguous results as the association has only been marginally weakened, from eta=.45 in 1979 to eta=.41 in 1994.[17]

It was suggested earlier that middle class identification is not really a matter of class consciousness but rather an expression of absence of working class identification. This is confirmed by the fact that the degree of middle class identification is almost irrelevant for party choice.[18] Therefore we collapse the categories 4-6 in the following.

---

the figures were 19 and 25 per cent, respectively. Not surprisingly, the figures for self-employed are even lower.

17. Part of this ambiguity may derive from sampling variations as class effects in general exhibit some variations between the two interview rounds in 1994.

18. This is also confirmed by the fact that there is no significant difference in class identification between privately and publicly employed non-manuals even though the last-mentioned group is twice as likely to vote socialist as the first-mentioned.

To maintain a sufficient number of cases, we have merged the two subsets of the 1994 sample in the following, unless otherwise indicated. The next section of Table 5.12 describes the association of class identification and party choice among workers. The results are quite surprising: from 1971 to 1985, the association was weakened, as predicted. But in 1994, the association between class identification and party choice among workers is about as strong as in 1971. There was a significantly lower support for socialist parties at all levels of class identification in 1994, and fewer class identifiers, but the strength of the association was surprisingly stable. We may thus conclude that our hypotheses about declining class identification and declining political relevance of class identification are confirmed but not quite to the extent we had expected.

Table 5.12. *Class identification and party choice. 1971, 1979, 1985[1] and 1994.*
(1) All respondents; (2) Manual workers. Percentages voting socialist

	Proportions voting socialist					(N)				
(1) All respondents	1971 (a)	1979 (b)	1985 (a)	1994 (a)	1994 (b)	1971	1979	1985	1994 (a)	1994 (b)
1. Strong working class id.	93	85	} 81	81	88	130	274	} 267	65	78
2. Weak working class id.	83	72		70	73	89	177		67	84
3. Lean towards working class	74	62	64	65	59	157	152	211	109	78
4. Lean tow. middle class	32	31	30	35	32	310	262	442	341	201
5. Weak middle class id.	34	38	} 40	40	37	188	309	} 413	181	210
6. Strong middle class id.	25	25		36	26	102	199		83	101
eta	.51	.45	.39	.32	.41					
(2) Manual Workers										
1. Strong working class id.	94	81	} 76		88	68	110	} 89		60
2. Weak working class id.	81	74			69	39	80			56
3. Lean tow. working class	78	71	66		54	70	56	68		72
4.6. Middle class attachm.	59	47	52		45	107	75	91		147
eta	.32	.28	.22		.32					

1) Party choice 1984.

c. Social Class, Class Identification and Voting

The next step is to examine what has happened with the causal chain between class, class identification and voting. Our expectations are that this causal chain has weakened and that this is the main explanation of decline of class voting. The results are presented in Figure 5.4 where we have dichotomised class (working class/middle classes) and class identification (working class identifiers or leaners vs. middle class identifiers or leaners). Our data confirm the first expectation but not the second: according to both the (a) and (b) versions of class identification, the causal chain between class, class identification and party choice is weakened. But the change is surprisingly moderate and only explains a minor share of the declining effect of social class. Rather, it is the direct causal effect of social class on party choice (which summarise all other possible paths) that is dramatically reduced, from beta=.28 in 1971 to beta=.01. in 1994, according to the (a) version. The (b) version also show a much lower direct effect than in 1971 but no decline from 1979 to 1994.[19]

In other words: class identification seems to be the only stable element in class voting, in accordance with the reference group perspective on class identification. Other effects of social class seem to have evaporated since 1971.

---

19. It is a well-known problem in path analyses that the direct effects are overestimated unless the intervening variables are perfectly reliable. However, as we have only one intervening variable here, and as the direct effect in 1994 (a) is as low as beta=.01, this cannot be a very serious problem here.

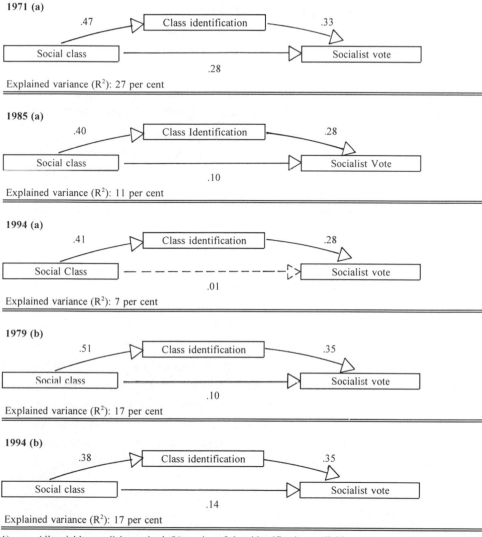

Figure 5.4. Path analysis of the effects of social class and class identification on the proportion voting socialist[1], 1971, 1979 and 1994. Standardised regression coefficients (betas)

1971 (a)

.47   Class identification   .33

Social class   Socialist vote

.28

Explained variance (R²): 27 per cent

1985 (a)

.40   Class Identification   .28

Social class   Socialist Vote

.10

Explained variance (R²): 11 per cent

1994 (a)

.41   Class identification   .28

Social Class   Socialist vote

.01

Explained variance (R²): 7 per cent

1979 (b)

.51   Class identification   .35

Social class   Socialist vote

.10

Explained variance (R²): 17 per cent

1994 (b)

.38   Class identification   .35

Social class   Socialist vote

.14

Explained variance (R²): 17 per cent

1)   All variables are dichotomised. (b) version of class identification explicitly mentions working class/middle class.

d. Social Class, Class Identification and Issue Voting

The findings above need not contradict an issue voting explanation, however, if the association between social class and issue position is weak. And our data in section 5.6 indicated that this was the case. The predictions from an issue voting interpretation are the following:

-   effects of issue positions are increasing
-   effects of class identification are declining
-   what remains of class effects is increasingly mediated by issue positions; as class differences in issue positions are relatively small, this means that class voting is declining.

In the following, we have merged the two subsets of the 1994 sample. We have used three different indices of left-right position in order to obtain comparability:

-   Index 1 (1971 and 1979), based on four Likert-format items on equality, tax progression, state control with investments, and NATO membership. The index is a simple additive index, with 'agree' coded 1, 'disagree' coded −1, and 'don't know'/'neither agree or disagree' coded 0. Subsequently, the index was recoded to five categories in order to ensure an approximately linear relationship with proportion voting socialist.[20] Respondents with three or more neutral answers are coded missing.
-   Index 2 (1979, 1985, and 1994), based on the four A/B items presented in Table 1.5. Same construction as index 1 above (this index was used only for controls).
-   Self-placement on left-right scale from 1 or 0 to 10 (1979, 1985 and 1994), recoded to 4 or 5 categories.[21] As mentioned earlier, this scale tends to summarise issue position on old and new politics simultaneously.

As it emerges from Table 5.13, our data do not unambiguously confirm the first assumption that issue voting has increased, neither for the electorate at large, nor for manual workers. On index 1, we observe a small decline for the electorate at large from 1971 to 1979,[22] and on index 2, we observe a quite significant decline for manual workers from 1979/1985 to 1994. But on the left-right self-placement index, we observe an increasing association with party choice, also among manual

---

20. −4 and −3 recoded to −2, −2 and −1 recoded to −1, and so forth.
21. 1-10 scale: 1-4, 5, 6, 7-10; 0-10 scale (1985): 0-3,4,5,6,7-10.
22. In fact, these results are a bit surprising as the correlation between individual items, as well as between individual items and party choice increased dramatically from 1971 to 1979 (Nielsen 1976; Goul Andersen 1984b). However, when the four items are combined into an index, the opposite result emerges.

workers.[23] It may be the case that the other measures have become obsolete or inadequate to tap all relevant aspects of left-right polarisation today.

Table 5.13.   *The association between position on economic left-right scale and socialist party choice, 1971, 1984, 1979 and 1994. Eta*

	Index 1		Index 2			Left-Right self-placement		
	1971	1979	1979	1985	1994	1979	1985	1994
All respondents	.51	.45	.52	.51	.48	.65	.70	.70
Manual workers	.35	.35	.39	.40	.30	.60	.54	.64

Wordings:
Index 1): 1) High incomes ought to be taxed more strongly than they are today.
        2) We should get out of NATO as soon as possible.
        3) The state has too little control with private investments.
        4) In politics, one should strike for obtaining equal economic conditions for everybody, regardless of education and occupation.
Index 2): See Table 1.5.
Additive indexes from trichotomised items. Persons with three 'don't know' answers or more are excluded.

Further, whereas the two first measures indicate that workers have never become genuine issue voters as far as traditional left-right attitudes are concerned, the left-right self-placement scale shows that they are nevertheless aware of their overall position to the right or to the left. There are several possible interpretations: there may be less consistency in attitudes or between attitudes and voting among workers; workers may emphasise other aspects of left-right attitudes; there may be class-specific reliability problems of measurement; or workers may vote more according to their position on the new politics-dimension than do the rest of the population. As to the last-mentioned interpretation, however, the evidence is negative: we found quite a strong association between new politics position and voting among the middle class(es) but not among workers. But as revealed in section 5.9 below, the associations among workers are much more significant when it comes to the effects in terms of *change* in party choice from 1990 to 1994.

Turning to the causal models in Figures 5.5 and 5.6, we observe a definite break between the 1971 survey and all the others. In 1971, there were strong class effects on socialist voting on all possible paths: via class identification, via issues, and via both. Finally, there also remained a moderately strong direct effect. In all

---

23 Although the causal order between self-placement and party choice is more ambiguous than the association between issue positions and party choice, it seems reasonable to suggest that the main source of difference is the fact that self-placement is a more general measure which may tap both old and new politics cleavages (see also chapter 2 above).

other surveys, direct class effects are small, and class effects on issue positions are negligible. What remains of social class effects is mediated by class identification, partly as a direct effect of class identification, partly as an effect mediated by the effect of class identification on left-right positions.[24]

In relation to an issue voting interpretation, our results are ambiguous: it is questionable whether issue voting has increased while, also, the (direct) association between social class and issue position has almost evaporated. But on the other hand, the effect of class identification appears to quite a large degree to be mediated by issue position.

Figure 5.5. Path analysis of the effects of class, class identification and issue position (Attitude index) on the proportion voting socialist, 1971 and 1979. Beta-coefficients

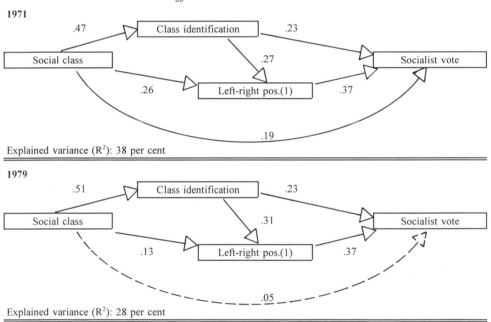

1971

.47 → Class identification → .23
Social class → .26 → Left-right pos.(1) → .37 → Socialist vote
.27
.19

Explained variance (R²): 38 per cent

1979

.51 → Class identification → .23
Social class → .13 → Left-right pos.(1) → .37 → Socialist vote
.31
.05

Explained variance (R²): 28 per cent

24. The only differences between the results based on index 2 and left-right self-placement is a stronger effect of issue position according to the self-placement question, along with a somewhat lower direct effect of class identification.

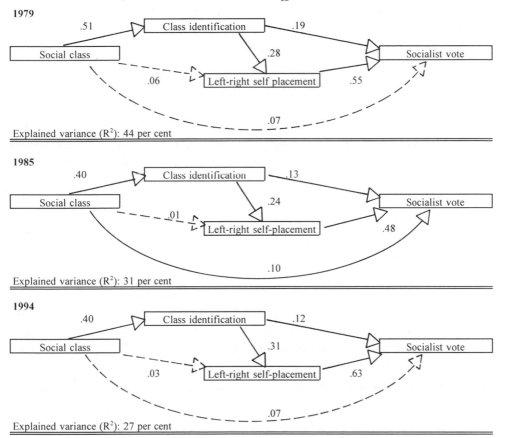

Figure 5.6.   Path analysis of the effects of class, class identification and issue position (Left-Right self-placement) on the proportion voting socialist, 1971, 1979 and 1994. Beta-coefficients

1979

.51   Class identification   .19

Social class

.06   .28   Left-right self placement   .55

Socialist vote

.07

Explained variance (R²): 44 per cent

1985

.40   Class identification   .13

Social class

.01   .24   Left-right self-placement   .48

Socialist vote

.10

Explained variance (R²): 31 per cent

1994

.40   Class identification   .12

Social class

.03   .31   Left-right self-placement   .63

Socialist vote

.07

Explained variance (R²): 27 per cent

e. Conclusions

To sum up, our findings are ambiguous. On the one hand, class identification has remained a bit stronger than expected, and this holds also for the path between social class, class identification and party choice. On the other hand, the effect of class identification appears to a large degree to be mediated by left-right position — a sort of 'rational', class-conscious voting. Next, the direct (residual) effect of social class on party choice, mainly reflecting simple habits, has disappeared. Thus it is legitimate to conclude that the main trend is a weakening of working class identifications, combined with a quite strong tendency only to vote in accordance with class positions if it is also compatible with issue positions.

As a note of caution it must be mentioned, though, that we have not examined all relevant issues. In particular, trade union consciousness may have been an important element in raising the level of working class identification in the 1970s, and in explaining the residual (direct) effects of class upon party choice. As such issues have without doubt become less salient in the 1990s, and as attitudes have become far less radical, there are good reasons for the weakening of this residual (direct) relationship between class and voting.

Besides, new politics issues have become more salient in recent years. As demonstrated below, there are also significant class differences in welfare priorities which do not unambiguously pull workers in leftist directions. Insufficient time series prevents us from pursuing such problems very far here but it turned out that in 1994, we could not observe a significant effect of new politics issues upon party choice among workers, only among the middle classes. Nevertheless, such issues may make a difference, not the least among workers. Whereas Lipset (1960) could safely assume that 'working class authoritarianism' had little political impact in practice because workers voted out of economic self-interests or from class identification, such assumptions can no longer be taken for granted when the cohesion of the working class declines. Indeed, from what has been described in the Marxist literature as 'spontaneous class consciousness' it should be expected that workers may feel attracted by quite other political forces than the socialist ones if they react on the basis of spontaneous class consciousness. As a first approximation to such perspectives, we may look upon the changing social basis of the party system.

5.8. Changes in the Party System: Class and Sector Composition of Parties

Class polarisation is one type of measure of the association between social class and partisanship. Another measure is the social composition of individual parties and the relationship between social structure and the party system. In Table 5.14, the parties are ranked according to their relative left-right position on old politics issues, according to conventional judgements among political observers. In 1964, the proportion of workers among the supporters of the parties almost monotonously followed the ranking of the parties on a left-right dimension: two out of three supporters for the left wing parties and the Social Democrats were recruited from the working class; among the supporters of the Radical Liberals and Liberals the figure was one out of five, and among Conservative supporters, it was only one out of six.

In 1994, the ranking and the distinction between labour parties and bourgeois parties is blurred: the highest proportion of workers is found in the populist Progress party, closely followed by the Social Democrats. Next, we find the left-wing 'Unitary

List' (which recruits a relatively large number of former communists), followed by the Christian People's party. The next group of parties include the Socialist People's party, the Liberal party and the Centre Democrats where some 27-28 per cent of the supporters are workers, i.e. slightly below average. Finally, we find the Radical Liberals and the Conservatives at the bottom, with roughly the same proportion of working-class supporters as in 1964.

Table 5.14.   *Social composition of individual parties. 1964 (1971) and 1994. Proportions, in percentages*

	Manual workers[1]		Public employees[2]		(N)
	1964	1994	1971	1994	1994
Unitary List (1964: Comm.)	89	39	36	48	109
Soc.People's party	65	28	23	65	280
Social Democrats	67	48	24	41	1155
Radical Liberals	20	19	33	41	141
Christian People's party	.	34	.	41	70
Centre Democrats	.	28	.	27	91
Liberals	20	27	17	25	834
Conservatives	16	17	32	23	449
Progress party (1964: Independent party)	21	50	.	9	170
Electorate	43	34	26	33	3326

1)   Proportion of voters in the labour force (including unemployed, etc.).
2)   Proportion of gainfully employed voters (excluding unemployed).

It is especially the new parties (Progress party, Centre Democrats, Christian People's party) that blur the distinctions, and it must be admitted that they are all very small parties (at present). But even the Liberal party also obtained an unusually high proportion of working-class supporters in 1994. At the same time, the major socialist party on the left wing, i.e. the Socialist People's party, has clearly lost its working-class profile.

Table 5.15 shows that this is the result of a gradual but systematic change: the over-representation of workers among the supporters of the left-wing parties disappeared in the 1970s along with a crisis in the major party where a new, young and postmaterialist leadership took over. At the other end of the spectrum, the Progress party began as a tax revolt party with an unusually broad social base but afterall with a certain under-representation of workers. From the 1980s, however, immigration has been at the top of the party's agenda, and the over-representation of workers has been steadily increasing (for equivalent Norwegian data, see Goul Andersen and Bjørklund 1990, 1997; see also Betz 1994).

Table 5.15. *Over- or under- representation of manual workers in various party groups. Percentage points deviation from mean[1)]*

	1966	1973	1977	1979	1981	1984	1987	1988	1990	1994
Left Wing party	+26	+17	+6	+3	+4	0	+2	+4	+1	−3
Social Democrats	+27	+26	+20	+15	+18	+20	+19	+16	+16	+13
Bourgeois party	−26	−15	−20	−17	−15	−12	−12	−15	−16	−11
Progress party	.	−4	−1	+2	+6	+9	+4	+14	+15	+16

1) Difference in percentage points between the proportion of workers among the party group's supporters and the overall mean. Voters in the labour force only (1966-1988 including housewives classified according to husband's class position).

Turning to the proportion of public employees in Table 5.14, we find quite the opposite development, from a scattered and chaotic pattern towards an ordering. In 1971, Conservatives, Radical Liberals and Left Socialists were the parties with the highest proportion of public employees whereas the proportion among the supporters of the Socialist People's party and the Social Democrats was slightly below average. By 1994, two-thirds of the supporters of the Socialist People's party are public employees, and the proportion of public employees declines almost monotonously from left to right.

At first sight, the figures seem to support an interpretation that interest conflicts over the public sector constitute a new major cleavage in Danish politics. As indicated by the analysis of attitudes above (section 5.6), the situation is far more complicated. But clearly, the social basis of the Danish party system has changed dramatically, and the emergence of new working-class parties at the 'extreme' right is a qualitative change which is probably more important than the quantitative changes observed above. This also means that a simple analysis of the effects of 'old politics' and 'new politics' upon workers' party choice between socialist and non-socialist parties is an insufficient measure of the changes in working class political behaviour. This point may be further substantiated by an analysis of the short-term changes in party choice in the 1994 election which completes this chapter.

5.9. Issues and Social Class: Interpreting Short-Term Changes

As pointed out in the beginning of this chapter, the defeat of the socialist parties in the 1994 election was mainly the result of a class-specific move to the right among manual workers, regardless of sector and employment status. Table 5.16 summarises the evidence and adds a survey of voting intentions from May/August

1996 to substantiate the interpretation: among manual workers, there is a dramatic swing to the right of some 22 percentage points from 1990 to 1996; among the lower salariat, there is a change of only 6 percentage points; among the higher salariat, there is no change at all; and among self-employed, the socialist parties may even appear to have improved their position.

Table 5.16. *Party choice 1990-1994 and party preference 1996 by social class. Percentages voting socialist (N's=100 per cent in parentheses)*

	Election 1990		Election 1994		Voting intention 1996		Change 1990-96
Manual Worker	70	(515)	57	(714)	48	(1250)	−22
Lower Salariat	52	(765)	49	(857)	46	(1145)	−6
Higher Salariat	33	(199)	33	(272)	34	(479)	+1
Self-Employed	13	(211)	12	(248)	17	(341)	+4

Note: 1996 figures are based on telephone interviews with 7061 randomly sampled voters, conducted by AIM Nielsen in May and August, 1996 (weighted by social criteria and by party choice 1994). As 'salariat' is defined a bit more narrowly *vis-à-vis* manual workers in the AIM Nielsen survey, this may explain one or two percentage points of the decrease in support for socialist parties among manual workers, 1994-1996.

Now, the question of course is what made workers so attracted to the non-socialist parties.[25] From chapter 2 above, we would expect that workers' rightist position on new politics issues could be a major explanation. Furthermore, the government alliance between the Social Democrats and the centre parties which tends to pull the Social Democrats to the right on old politics issues, pulls in the very opposite direction when it comes to new politics: on these issues (except the environment), the centre parties typically occupy more leftist positions than the Social Democrats.

Workers' attraction to rightist positions on new politics issues is not a new phenomenon, rather it is rather a modern equivalent of 'working class authoritarianism'. Even Karl Marx wrote about the 'spontaneous class consciousness' of workers and about the clashes between English and Irish workers in the 19th century. It was pointed out in several studies in the 1950s and probably also reflected in the negative correlations between liberal attitudes towards welfare and towards the cold war reported in Nie and Andersen (1974). But whereas Lipset could safely

---

25. The change in social composition 1990-1994 (1996) is parallel for Liberals, the Conservatives, and the Progress party, i.e. it is difficult to ascribe the change to the popularity of particular party leaders. It is also noteworthy that the social composition of the Centre parties who are all exposed on new politics issues does not reveal a change in favour of more workers. in the 1990s.

conclude in 1960 that it had little practical importance in the fully-fledged industrial society as workers typically voted for non-authoritarian socialist (liberal) parties because of class interests or class identification (Lipset 1960), this can no longer be taken for granted. If people come to vote more in accordance with issue positions than previously, however, and if new politics issues become increasingly salient, working-class voting behaviour may take quite other directions. For the Socialist parties it is a permanent latent threat which may be activated not only by increasing saliency and change in the voter's agenda (but perhaps also by dissatisfaction with leadership as a catalysing factor).[26]

To test these propositions, we may begin by comparing the voting patterns 1990 and 1994 within the four ideological types defined in chapter 2: 'Left Wing', 'Old Socialists', 'Green Bourgeois', and 'Right Wing'. From the considerations above, we should expect particularly strong losses for the socialist parties among 'Old Socialists', that is, among voters with a leftist position on old politics issues and a rightist position on new politics issues. Among 'Green Bourgeois' voters, we should expect the opposite pattern, i.e. stable or even increasing support. Finally, we should expect the two remaining categories to fall in-between.

As it emerges from the three first columns of Table 5.17, these predictions are largely confirmed. Among 'Old Socialists', the proportion voting socialist declined from 69 to 57 per cent, that is, by 12 percentage points. Among 'Green Bourgeois' voters, on the other hand, support for socialist parties increased by six percentage points. Thus, our main prediction is clearly confirmed. The prediction that the remaining two types would fall in-between is also confirmed; however, if anything, we would have expected more substantial losses among Right Wing voters than among Left Wing voters but at this point our data indicate the opposite.

Now, these patterns might be simple reflections of the social changes in voting patterns: workers are predominantly 'Old Socialists', and workers were most inclined to move to the right in 1994. The question is if similar patterns may be observed among working class voters. However, as the three last columns in Table 5.17 show, we do not face a spurious correlation. On the contrary, the changes among workers come out exactly as predicted: among 'Old Socialist' workers, support for socialist parties declined with no less than 20 percentage points. As there were virtually no 'Green Bourgeois' workers in the 1990 sample, we are unable to measure if

---

26. We shall not explore these questions here; we only want to warn against too deterministic interpretations suggesting that socialist parties will necessarily lose working class support. Apart from changing policies, they have e.g. the opportunities of changing policy images (i.e. by symbolic reactions); they may change the political agenda; and they may overcome troubles by improving their leadership or general images.

there has been any changes here. However, among 'Left Wing' workers, support for socialist parties declined only marginally, whereas there was a decline of nine percentage points among 'Right Wing' workers. In short, the figures among workers come out exactly as predicted.

Table 5.17.   *Proportion voting socialist among four ideological types, 1990 and 1994. (a) Electorate at large; (b) Manual workers. Percentages*

	Entire electorate			Manual workers		
	1990	1994	change	1990	1994	change
Left Wing	77	70	−7	75	71	−4
Old Socialist	69	57	−12	82	62	−20
Green Bourgeois	17	23	+6	.	40	.
Right Wing	21	22	+1	49	40	−9
(N)	192	461		41	96	
	252	519		79	168	
	98	251		2	30	
	228	540		37	81	

For definitions, see Table 2.2.

It must be acknowledged, however, that the number of observations in the 1990 sample is small and that most of the changes fall slightly below statistical significance. However, we may also exploit the opportunities of the 1994 sample more intensively. Firstly, we may compare the position of workers and the perceived position ('policy image') of the Social Democratic party; and secondly, we may examine the association between policy position on new politics issues and voting behaviour among those workers who, according to their own (recall) information, voted for the Social Democratic party in 1990. To improve our data basis, we include not only those who defected from the Social Democrats but also those who considered doing so.

We begin by examining the average issue positions of the working class and the new middle class, and workers' perception of the policy positions of the Social Democrats and the Liberals, respectively (i.e. the *policy images* of these parties among workers). From Table 5.18 it turns out that on the issues of law-and-order and refugee policies, workers are, on average, much to the right of the new middle class, and extremely deviant from what they believe to be the positions of the Social Democrats; rather, they come very close to what they believe to be the position of the Liberals on these issues. On the issue of environmental policy, on the other hand, workers are just as 'green' as the new middle class, the Social Democrats is considered a 'green' party, and the Liberals have a problem with their policy image. Finally, on conventional left-right issues concerning the public sector, economic policies and state regulation, workers tend to be more in accordance with the Social Democrats than the Liberals even though the Social Democratic party is considered too far to the left. At these points, class differences between workers and salariat are negligible.

Table 5.18.   Average issue positions of workers and the new middle class, workers' perception of the issue positions of the Social Democrats and the Liberals, and distance of these two parties from the workers. Measured on a scale from −100 (extreme right) to +100 (extreme left)

	Issue position of new middle class	Manual workers				
		Issue position of manual workers	Workers' perception of the position of the Social Democrats	Workers' perception of the position of the Liberals	Distance of Soc.Dem. party from workers	Distance of Liberal party from workers
Issue position items[1]						
1. Refugee policies	−17	−35	+24	−37	+59	−2
2. Law-and-order	−2	−28	+21	−41	+49	−13
3. Environmental policy	+39	+37	+36	−16	−1	−53
4. State regulation of markets	−17	−19	+13	−44	+32	−25
5. Soft vs. tight economic policy	−7	+2	+40	−56	+38	−58
6. Size public sector	−3	−2	+26	−49	+28	−47
Public expenditure items[2]						
Refugees	−22	−45	.	.	.	.
Foreign Aid	−22	−43	.	.	.	.

1)   See chapter 3 section 3 for the wording of those items. For the present purposes responses were recoded to range from −100 l (extreme right) to +100 (extreme left).
2)   See chapter 7 section 4 on those items. Here coded from −100 (gov. spends too much) to +100 (gov. spends too little).

Now the question is if this deviance between own positions and perceived party positions has any effect on the propensity of workers to switch from the Social Democrats to one of the right-wing parties. We therefore combined stable Social Democratic workers with party switchers across a very large number of issues.

Apart from the associations reported below, there were absolutely no significant differences, neither on conventional left-right issues, nor on economic policy issues, welfare state issues or public expenditure questions. In other words, the party switchers among workers were not further to the right in any conventional sense. By the same token, we found no association with sociotropic or egotropic evaluations of economic policies, including a tax reform which gave tax relief to middle- and upper-incomes but which was nevertheless opposed by the bourgeois parties to the right.

Table 5.19. *Association between policy positions and behaviour in 1994 election among workers who voted for the Social Democrats in 1990. Percentages*

Manual workers who voted for the Social Democrats in 1990 election	Loyal to government party or left-wing party in 1994	Considered voting for Liberals, Cons. or Progr.party in 1994	Switched to Liberals, Cons. or Progr.party in 1994	N (=100 per cent)
Position on law-and-order issues				
Same as or left of Social Dem. party	97	3	–	39
To the right of Soc.Dem. party	72	10	18	40
On foreign aid and/or refugees government should:[1]				
Spend more or the same as now	96	–	4	55
Save on one of these items	84	14	2	43
Save on both	82	7	11	73
Political distrust index:[2]				
0 Trustful	100	–	–	24
1	90	6	4	49
2	86	8	6	51
3 Distrustful	76	11	13	46

1) Excluding 'don't know' answers.
2) Excluding 'don't know' answers. The index measures the number of 'distrust' answers on three questions:
   "In general, one can be confident that our political leaders make the right decisions for the country" (disagree);
   "The politicians are too lavish with the taxpayers' money" (agree);
   "How much confidence to you, generally speaking, have in Danish politicians?" (little/very little).

However, on new politics issues, we did find significant deviances. Among workers who perceived themselves to be to the right of the Social Democrats on the law-and-order issue, 28 per cent switched to the right-wing opposition or considered doing so; among other workers, the proportion was barely three per cent (Table 5.19). A similar, but statistically insignificant, deviation was found on the refugee issue (both these questions were posed only to one sample subset of about 1000 respondents). By the same token, we found a significant association between the propensity to switch and the wish to save on public expenses for refugees and foreign aid. Less surprisingly, we also found an association between political distrust and propensity to switch party.

Thus we have strong indications of dissatisfaction with government policies among the Social Democrats' working-class constituencies on these new politics issues, and we have strong indications that it leads to changes in party preferences. Even though new politics position in general did not seem to be causally related to party choice among workers in 1994 (when we control for old politics position), there are significant changes from 1990 to 1994, and these are the only variables in our survey which are able to account for the class-specific move to the right among manual workers in the 1994 election.

Now, a note of caution should be mentioned. In the first place, we do not necessarily imply any *deterministic* political decomposition of the working class. Next, even if we are able to identify the attitudinal distinctiveness of workers who defected from the Social Democrats, it does not follow unconditionally that this is also the *cause* of their defection. It is imaginable that an underlying dissatisfaction with government competence, with leadership etc. may act as a precondition or as a catalyst which make voters defect from government parties; when people defect, it may simply be the most 'ideologically deviant' that are the first to switch party. The new tendency, then, is the fact that workers are by now among the most 'ideologically deviant' groups. But this encounters a more general problem of drawing macro-level implications from individual-level data in survey research which we are unable to pursue further here. Nevertheless, our findings in Tables 5.17 to 5.19 do strongly confirm the predictions of new politics theory that workers move toward the right when new politics are activated (cf. chapter 2, especially Table 2.9 above).

5.10. Conclusions

This chapter began by noting that Denmark is among the prototypical countries in terms of decline of class voting, at least if this is defined as the difference in voting between the so-called middle class and the working class. However, it turns out that the description is based on obsolete and inadequate class concepts that fail to take account of the changes in the social structure. Thus on closer inspection it turned out that the changing composition of the so-called 'middle class' account for much of the change, and that there are new, very significant social differences in party choice that are entirely neglected by the conventional class concepts. Even if it remains that social background variables have a somewhat smaller impact upon party choice, it nevertheless seems that changing class voting is a more adequate description than declining class voting.

We explored some possible explanations of these changes and demonstrated that the forces behind the public/private sector cleavage among non-manual employees are much more complicated than commonly believed. This involves also consideration of the mobilisation processes in the 1970s, to which we turn in the following chapter. What is to be explained, apart from the radicalisation of public employees, is class-specific changes within the working class and among privately employed non-manuals.

It turned out that the last-mentioned change could not be explained by changing political preferences on left-right issues in general; rather, changing values concerning equality seemed to be a core variable. However, lack of trust in Social Democratic economic policy competence also stands out as a possible explanation, and finally, we have not been able to measure whether some sense of identification with the private sector or with business life may also be involved; at any rate, the movement to the right is very significant even among low-income non-manuals in the private sector.

The swing to the right among manual workers cannot be explained by a general 'embourgeoisement'. Thus explanations in terms of increasing wealth and changing life-styles could be falsified. Declining class identification, and declining effects of class identities in favour of issue positions is a more reasonable explanation but at the same time, the data warn against a too easy dismissal of this classical variable: class identification remains a strong predictor of party choice among workers, even though the number of class identifiers declines. But it must be noted that much of the effect of class identification is mediated by issue positions.

However, the last sections indicated that it may more be the 'proletarian' side of the working class than the achievement of a middle class status that pull workers to the right. At least in the 1994 election, there were clear indications that workers who were, in accordance with their working-class position, dissatisfied with too leftist positions of the Social Democrats on new politics (or authoritarian) issues were the most inclined to switch to the right. At the macro level, and more basically, such sentiments among manual workers are also reflected in the fact that new working class parties of a very unconventional nature have emerged: in Denmark, the right-wing populist Progress party has become the most clear-cut working class party, if measured by the social composition of its supporters.

6

GENERATIONAL AND GENDER VARIATIONS

6.1. Introduction

Age may be seen both as a life cycle variable and as a generation variable. During the life cycle, people gain more experiences with politics as they assume more roles in society, they form political identities and participate in politics until they may eventually withdraw at the last stage. There is also a folklore, first expressed by Disraëli (1804-81), but rarely examined systematically, that people tend to become more conservative or at least more moderate as they grow older. In developed welfare states, people also have changing interests *vis-à-vis* the welfare state at different stages of life (as consumers of public services, as receivers of transfer incomes, or as taxpayers). Life-cycle effects on political behaviour is a classic issue which is treated below in section 6.2 and 6.3.

However, more interest is usually attached to the generational aspect: to which degree is it possible to speak of different political generations with enduring, generation-specific values, attitudes and behaviour? From this perspective, one would stress political socialisation during adolescence as a core variable: young people enter the political world with a sort of *tabula rasa* political mind, perhaps modified by political identities or attitudes transmitted from their parents. Gradually, the table is filled with their own experiences. Therefore early socialisation during adolescence is critical as it tends to have long-term effects. Unlike Inglehart's (1977, 1990) theory of postmaterialism which stresses the satisfaction of material needs during adolescence, one could point at the *political* influences. This may be political influence from processes of political mobilisation — processes which, in turn, are frequently related to more basic societal changes, problems or conflicts (Goul Andersen 1990a).

Changing conditions of political socialisation may catalyse the development of generational differences. In the first place, nearly all aspects of modernisation (increasing social and spatial mobility, cross-pressures of information, and increasing levels of education) are likely to reduce the transmission of political identities from parents to children. Secondly, the educational revolution means that people frequently have their first (and, presumably, most basic) political experiences before entering the labour market. This should increase the influence of processes of political mobilisation upon the young who act with less constraint than earlier and interact mainly with each other.

160

Still, adult socialisation may also play an important role and perhaps even eliminate such generational differences which appear at an early stage of the life-cycle. This chapter seeks to single out some of the main generational and life-cycle effects in Danish politics. We have a sort of 'zero point' as there were virtually no differences in voting patterns between age groups in 1964 when all age groups were evenly distributed between socialists and non-socialists.

Since then, the picture has changed. Danish politics has been marked by quite significant differences between age groups — differences which have, furthermore, had a clear gender profile. Therefore electoral research in Denmark has put considerable effort into the analysis of such changes. This holds in particular for the leftist mobilisation among the young in the 1970s (Goul Andersen 1984a; Svensson & Togeby 1986; Borre 1989) but attention has also been directed to the subsequent ideological move to the right among the young, especially among young males, in the 1980s and 1990s (Borre 1989; Svensson & Togeby 1991; Gundelach & Riis 1992). Just as the youth and student rebellion was more than a short breeze in Denmark, value changes associated with the bourgeois governments and the triumph of the yuppies in the mid-1980s seem to have left a more permanent imprint on the younger generations.

In this chapter, we shall focus mainly on the long-term perspectives. What has happened to the generations who were mobilised to the left in the 1970s? Have they maintained their leftist ideals, or have they become more and more domesticated alongside with adult socialisation in new occupational roles? In short: What is the interplay between life-cycle and generational processes? Are particular parties (such as the Social Democrats) victims of generational replacement or are they able to catch up during the life cycle? Do people become more 'conservative' as they grow older; do they become more 'moderate'; or do they rather become alienated in a rapidly changing society? These themes are treated in sections 6.4, 6.5 and 6.6.

As far as generational changes are concerned, Svensson & Togeby (1986, 1991) have argued convincingly that the contours of societal changes become more clear when we focus on the younger generations. However, we might perhaps achieve an even more condensed picture of the changes by looking at the better-educated young who may be assumed in several respects to be trend-setting among the young. Thus we shall devote section 6.5 to the study of better-educated young in a long-term perspective.

Another theme is the nature of mobilisation processes. What does mobilisation mean at the individual level? How does it manifest itself? And how can it be measured? Is the rightward mobilisation in the 1990s akin to the leftward mobilisation in the 1970s, and if not, what are the differences? These questions are addressed in section 6.6.

Finally, the chapter addresses briefly the question of the gender gap in Danish politics and its relation to generational change. Gender-related differences in party choice in Scandinavia have generally been analysed under the headlines of mobilisation and radicalisation: women became conscious of common interests and were mobilised and radicalised in the 1970s and far into the 1980s (Goul Andersen 1984b; Togeby 1994; Christensen 1994) — on the basis of shared gender interests, and to a large degree on the basis also of shared values and common class interests. But are these headlines still adequate in the 1990s, or have women rather become more 'conservative' i.e., reluctant to change, while young men mobilise to the right? Section 6.7 deal with gender variations and their interaction with generational differences. Section 6.8 summarises new and old social divisions in party choice: to which degree have social factors analysed in this and the previous chapter remained a key to the understanding of electoral behaviour?

6.2. Life Cycle Effects on Party Identification and Political Stability

Even though age may be particularly relevant to a generational perspective, there are also interesting questions relating to age as a life cycle phenomenon. Besides, the life cycle itself has changed meaning within the last thirty or forty years. As mentioned above, modernisation and educational revolution brought with them changing conditions of socialisation which leave room for more autonomous and self-reinforcing ideological movements among the young. Besides, as students or pupils, more and more young people begin their adult life with a strong dependency on the welfare state, both as consumers of welfare services and as dependents on allowances from the state.[1]

Because of early retirement arrangements and higher public pensions, elderly people have also become more dependent on the welfare state than previously. Another change is the increasingly rapid technological, economic and social changes which may devalue the value of life experience. If there is a folklore that people tend to become more 'conservative' or at least more 'moderate' as they grow older, one might alternatively imagine that older people become more alienated or more oriented towards the welfare state. Such welfare state attachments might also be expected among the young where one may, furthermore, expect to find increasingly uncertain political identities as a consequence of changing conditions of socialisation. The question of an emerging U-curve association between age and welfare state

---

1. Educational allowances are unusually generous in Denmark, as students aged 20 years or more receive an allowance (independently of parents' income) which covers basic living expenses though not an 'acceptable' standard of living.

support is treated in chapter 8 whereas we shall examine below the association between age, political identities and political alienation.

To begin with the young, it is among the most well-documented political facts that young people have more uncertain political identities and less commitments to particular parties than the middle-aged and elderly. But considering the changing conditions of socialisation and the changes in the party system from the early 1970s to the mid-1990s, it is relevant to ask if this has changed.

As revealed by the bottom line of Table 6.1, there has been a decline in political affiliations from 1971 to 1994 (see for Scandinavian comparisons Goul Andersen & Hoff 1997). Thus, the proportion of voters who postponed their final voting decision until the campaign has increased from 15 to 27 per cent; the proportion who considered voting for another party has increased from 22 to 43 per cent; and the proportion of party switchers has nearly doubled, from 13 to 24 per cent. Although the last-mentioned figure reflects the rich substitution possibilities of the Danish multiparty system it remains the case that even the proportion of voters who cross the border between socialist and non-socialist parties has doubled; however, at this point the figures are very small, from 4 per cent by 1971 to 8 per cent in 1994.[2] Thus, in all these indicators, we find signs of declining party attachments in the population at large. Rather than being the consequence of gradual change, most of this change took the form of an irreversible decline in the 1973 election where the old five-party system broke down (Bille, Nielsen & Sauerberg 1992). Although the old parties have recovered considerably, the loyalties of voters have never been fully reestablished (see also chapter 1).

Only the figures on party identification have remained relatively stable: the proportion of party identification declined from 54 per cent by 1971 to 49 per cent in 1994 (an all-time low figure). The proportions of strong identifiers has declined from 29 to 26 per cent.

Turning from the gross figures to the question of age variations, however, there does not seem to be much of a change. Party loyalties and political identities seem to have become weaker at all levels, across generations and life cycle positions. The conventional picture that young people have weaker bonds to the political parties is confirmed but there are few, if any signs of an increasing difference between age groups. The only figure which may indicate such changes is the proportion

---

2. These figures are unweighted and probably underestimated as they are based on recall of voting in last election which took place nearly four years before the interview. However, as it is the relative rather than the absolute figures which interest us here, it is safest to avoid weighting which may easily produce biased estimates exactly of such age effects.

of party switchers, which has doubled in all groups under 50 years whereas the changes among the remaining age groups are more moderate.

The decreasing party loyalties may reflect the fact that parties face increasing difficulties in representing the increasingly complex and cross-cutting cleavages of contemporary society. This is confirmed by the fact that 43 per cent of the voters answered that they voted with mixed feelings for their party, or even felt that they had to choose the least of evils. However, the age differences on this question are very moderate, and our data do not confirm the suspicion that elderly people might become politically alienated in a rapidly changing society. The elderly were quite happy about their party choice, and there were no significant age differences in political distrust in 1994.

Table 6.1. Age and political commitments, 1994. Percentages

Age	Party identification		Decided during campaign[1]		Considered voting for another party[1]		Switched party (un-weighted)[2]		Switched between socialist and non-soc.party[2]		Voted with mixed feelings/for the least of evils[1]	(N)
	1971	1994	1971	1994	1971	1994	1971	1994	1971	1994	1994	1994
18-19	.	33	.	32	.	61	.	.	.	.	24	52
20-29	37	39	27	41	34	45	17	34	7	13	44	389
30-39	47	39	19	35	29	44	16	31	5	8	50	396
40-49	54	47	13	30	23	35	12	24	4	7	45	384
50-59	58	60	6	18	16	27	9	16	4	6	45	267
60-69	70	60	8	19	12	30	11	18	3	4	40	260
70+	75	65	5	16	6	19	11	14	2	6	30	273
All voters	54	49	15	27	22	43	13	24	4	8	43	2021

1) Only respondents who participated in the election.
2) Only respondents who participated in both elections and indicate which party they voted for.

Finally, there is the well-known tendency for young people to be particularly sensitive to the changes in popularity of the parties, young people tend to support the 'winning' parties. As we shall see below, this pattern was partly broken in the 1970s when the young generation mobilised leftwards. But it is more visible in the 1990s. In the 1994 election, the four winning parties gained an overall increase in support of 11 per cent. According to a comparison between the 1990 and 1994 election survey, the increase in support for these parties among the 18-24 years old was 16 per cent. The relative proportions in the 1990 election seem to be of a similar size which also roughly reflects the ratio of party switchers among the young and the population at large — about 2:3 according to Table 6.1.

Voting and Political Attitudes in Denmark

To sum up, life-cycle differences in Denmark confirm the conventional picture, and at this point, there seems to be nothing new under the sun within the last 25 years, except for a general increase in instability and a decline of party loyalties across all age groups and generations.

6.3. Age and Partisanship: An Overview

It emerges from Table 6.2 that there was a quite strong association between age and party choice in the 1994 election. In spite of the welfare state dependency of young and old voters which might pull such groups to the left, support for the socialist parties follows the very opposite pattern, i.e. an inverse U-curve. Among young voters aged less than 25 years, only one-third voted for socialist parties, and among voters aged 70 years or more, the figure is only slightly higher to 37 per cent. Among the 35-44 years old, on the other hand, 55 per cent preferred a socialist party. Popularly speaking, young people and their grandparents prefer bourgeois parties, whereas the age groups in-between are more inclined to vote socialist.

Support for individual parties and party groups deviate somewhat from the overall pattern:

- *Left-wing parties* have a stronghold among the 30-44 years old and, to a lesser degree, among the young. Support for these parties is very low among voters aged more than 50 years and nearly absent among the old.
- *The Social Democrats* have little support among young voters whereas support is nearly the same in all age groups above 35 years.
- *Centre parties* as a whole enjoy approximately the same level of support in all age groups, although slightly higher among the younger voters.
- Support for *the Liberals and the Conservatives* follow a U-shaped curve, that is, it is very high among voters aged less than 30 years or more than 70 years whereas it is very low among 35-44 years old voters.
- *The Progress party* has a stronghold among older voters; otherwise, support for the party is rather evenly distributed.

For the first time since 1929, a candidate who ran for election outside the parties, was elected in the 1994 election. Along with a few other candidates outside the parties, the comedian Jacob Haugaard was supported mainly by young voters.[3]

---

3. As parties within the same party group are frequently in mutual competition, and as young voters are more volatile, it could be expected that parties within the same 'family' would exhibit a very different age profile. With a few exceptions, however, the same patterns are found among individual parties within the above-mentioned age groups. Among left-wing parties, the List of Unity is less skewed towards the 35-44 years old than the Socialist People's

Not surprisingly, nonvoters are also relatively young but it is noteworthy that voters who left a blank ballot (this group has been increasing considerably in recent elections) are also much younger than the electorate at large.

Table 6.2. Age and party choice 1994. Party groups. Percentages

Age	Left-wing	Soc.Dem.	Soc. parties, total	Centre parties	Lib. and Cons.	Progr.	Other cand. parties	Total	(N)
18-24	13	21	34	12	46	6	2	100	315
25-29	10	31	41	10	42	5	2	100	341
30-34	16	27	43	11	38	5	3	100	316
35-39	17	38	55	10	29	5	1	100	328
40-44	19	36	55	10	29	5	1	100	315
45-49	13	35	48	8	38	6	0	100	323
50-59	6	43	49	8	38	5	0	100	475
60-69	5	40	45	8	38	9	–	100	438
70+	2	35	37	9	44	10	–	100	478

Average age of supporters:
> Left-wing: List of Unity, 40 years (N=109); Socialist People's party, 40 years (N=280); Social Democrats, 49 years (N=1155).
> Centre parties: Radical Liberals, 46 years (N=141); Centre Democrats, 43 years (N=91); Christian People's party, 48 years (N=70).
> Right-wing: Conservatives, 50 years (N=449); Liberals, 46 years (N=834); Progress party, 52 years (N=170).
> Outside the parties, 34 years (N=27); Blanks, 39 years (N=33); Nonvoters, 42 years (N=290).

The difference between age groups in the 1994 election is a relatively recent phenomenon, however. As it emerges from Table 6.3, there was only one election from 1971 to 1988 with a non-socialist majority among the 18-24 years old: the 'earthquake' election of 1973 where the socialist parties obtained only 36.7 per cent of the votes. In spite of higher volatility among young voters who tend to follow the general trend in elections, young voters became the most leftist for a long period, regardless of election outcome. This move to the left among the young had begun by 1966, and in all elections until 1979, the 18-24 years old was the most socialist age group. From 1979, the most leftist group was the 25-29 years old, in 1988 and 1990, it was the 30-39 years old, and in the 1994 election, the

---

party but the average age is almost the same. Among centre parties, Radical Liberals enjoy slightly higher support among young voters whereas the Christian People's party has a stronghold among the old but again, the average age deviates only with 2 years. Finally, Liberal voters are somewhat younger than the Conservatives, due to a strong over-representation among the youngest age groups. The age profile of support for both parties, however, follows a U-shaped curve.

Voting and Political Attitudes in Denmark

age group between 40 and 49 years had the largest proportion of socialists. This certainly indicates a generation effect to which we shall return below. The first clear signals of a move to the right among young voters were recorded in 1987 when the entire electorate moved leftwards whereas young voters moved to the right. In 1994 when there was a strong general movement to the right, the changes among the young became really visible, and at the same time even the age groups between 25 and 39 years moved very significantly to the right whereas the age groups above 40 years barely changed.

At the other end of the life cycle, there was an opposite movement in the 1970s. All age groups moved to the right in the 1968 election, but the older age groups never fully returned to support the Social Democrats and the left-wing parties, and from 1971 (with the 1973 election as a partial exception), a permanent generation gap between younger and older voters became visible. From 1973 onwards, there has only occasionally have more than 40 per cent of voters aged more than 65 supported the socialist parties.

Table 6.3. Support for socialist parties, by age, 1964-1994. Percentages

Age	1964	1966	1968	1971	1973	1975	1979	1981	1984	1987	1988	1990	1994
18-24	49	61	47	62	40	54	60	60	54	52	50	47	34
25-29		51	44	60	36	46	66	61	62	63	53	55	40
30-39	49	49	41	49	35	38	52	50	50	61	58	60	49
40-49	50	49	43	43	37	40	42	43	39	46	50	50	51
50-64	49	50	42	49	37	40	47	45	46	46	42	45	47
65+		48	44	43	37	39	46	42	38	39	37	44	39
Total	48.9	49.9	43.3	49.4	36.7	41.2	50.1	48.2	46.6	49.9	47.5	50.0	45.0

Note: Socialists include Greens, Common Course (left-wing populist), Humanist party, and a variety of small Marxist splinters at the extreme left.

This derives to a large degree from a mobilisation of the left-wing parties, and from a changing support base of these parties. Table 6.4 shows the equivalent figures for support for left-wing parties from 1964 to 1994. From the mid-1960s to 1979, left-wing support was increasingly concentrated among the young. From 1966 to 1979, left-wing support was halved among voters aged more than 40 years but it nearly doubled among the young. The relatively stable left-wing support in the elections thus concealed a massive mobilisation and concentration of voters among the young. In 1979, about one-third of all voters aged less than 30 years voted for a left-wing party; a similar proportion supported the Social Democrats and the non-socialists parties, respectively. This explains the explosion of left-wing support in the 1980s, and for some time, it seemed that simple generation replacement would allow the left-wing to match the Social Democrats in electoral support within a couple of decades (Svensson & Togeby 1986). However, after support peaked in 1987 when more than one-third of all voters aged less than 40 years voted for a left-wing party, a rapid decline took place. Among young voters (18-29 years), support for left-wing parties declined with two-thirds from 1987 to 1994, and in 1994, left-wing support among the young reached its lowest level since 1964. Among the 30-39 years old, support declined by one-half but remained at a higher level than within the same age group in the 1960s and 1970s. On the other hand, the 40-49 years old were quite resistant to change. Clearly, the changing support for the left-wing parties calls for a generational explanation.

Table 6.4. Support for left-wing parties, by age, 1964-1994. Percentages

Age	1964	1966	1968	1971	1973	1975	1979	1981	1984	1987	1988	1990	1994
18-24	} 10	19	15	24	23	33	31	35	30	31	32	18	13
25-29		16	14	17	19	23	32	34	34	37	28	18	10
30-39	9	13	11	14	11	12	13	19	23	34	30	20	17
40-49	9	12	10	11	9	9	6	9	8	19	16	13	16
50-64	} 5	10	7	9	9	6	4	7	7	10	6	6	6
65+		6	3	2	6	3	4	4	2	5	4	4	3
Total	7	12	9	12	11	11	12	15	15	21	18	13	10

6.4. Generational Change in a Long-term Perspective

As mentioned earlier, we have a 'zero point' for the analysis of generational effects as there were virtually no generational differences in 1964. The proportion of socialists was the same in all age groups whereas there was a minor difference in left-wing support between voters aged more or less than 50 years; among non-socialist parties, the Conservatives were a bit stronger among the young whereas Liberals and Radical Liberals were strongest among the old, — probably reflecting urbanisation and class-structural changes. There did not seem to be any generational effect of the crisis in the 1930s, or of the Second World War (except for the difference in left-wing support).

In our cohort analysis we begin by looking at support for left-wing parties as it seems to be the dynamic factor from 1966 onwards. The relevant figures are presented in Table 6.5. As most surveys operate with fixed age intervals, it has been necessary to limit the number of elections covered by the analysis. But it is quite obvious that generation effects are very strong. The hard-core left-wing generations are the cohorts born between 1951 and 1960. In 1987, the support for left-wing parties among this generation peaked at a level close to 40 per cent, and

Voting and Political Attitudes in Denmark

in all previous elections except the first that they participated in, it has been above 30 per cent. This generation has also proved relatively resistant to change in the 1990s as left-wing support has remained close to 20 per cent.

Table 6.5. Support for left-wing parties, 1966-1994, by birth cohort. Percentages

Year of birth	1966[1]	1971	1973	1975[1]	1979	1984	1987	1990	1994
1976-1980	.	.	.	.	.	.	.	.	(13)
1971-1975	.	.	.	.	.	.	.	(21)	13
1966-1970	.	.	.	.	.	.	29*	17*	11
1961-1965	.	.	.	.	.	29	33	18	13
1956-1960	.	.	.	.	27*	36	38	21	18
1951-1955	.	.	24*	33	36*	31	38	19	18
1946-1950	.	24*	19	23	19*	21	24	17	17
1941-1945	19	17*	14	[12]²	14*	12	21	8	8
1936-1940	16	13*	12	[12]²	8*	10	14	10*	6
1926-1935	13	16	10	9	4	7	10	6	4
1916-1925	12	8	9	[6]³	4	6	6	6	3
1901-1915	10	7	8	[3]⁴	4	2	4	4*	2*
-1900	6	1*	1*	[3]⁴	(2)	0⁺	.	.	.
Election	11.7	12.1	11.1	11.2	11.8	15.0	20.6	12.6	10.4

Notes:
1) Fixed age groups, approximated to birth cohorts. Deviances are, on average, about half a year in 1975 and about 1½ year in 1966.
2) Figures refer to birth cohorts 1936-1945 as a whole (30-39 years old).
3) Birth cohorts 1911-1925.
4) All cohorts born 1910 or earlier.
Signatures: * N < 200
+ N < 100
() N < 50

In everyday language, the label '1968 generation' has most frequently been applied to the cohorts born in the 1940s, and it was certainly from this generation that the mobilising pioneers of the student and youth rebellion were recruited in the 1960s. However, in Denmark, this mobilisation was prolonged until about 1980, and it was mainly the birth cohorts from the 1950s that were mobilised. The cohorts born during the second world war were hardly affected. Among the pioneering birth cohorts born from 1946 to 1950, we find an astonishing stability: from 1971 to 1994, support for left wing parties has varied only between 17 and 24 per cent. This is consistent with the assumption that as trend-setting 'pioneers', the left-wing activists in this generation were more committed to their cause than the generation from the 1950s where there were many more 'followers'.

In spite of varying distributions between 'pioneers' and 'followers', the cohorts born between 1946 and 1960 may be described as a single political generation, 'the first postwar generation'. To an even larger degree, the notion of 'followers' may be applied to the second postwar generation (born 1961 or later). In the 1980s, it seemed that this generation would simply follow in the footsteps of the first postwar generation. But in the 1990s when the ideological winds changed, these birth cohorts rapidly abandoned their links with the left-wing parties, and from 1987 to 1994, their support for the left-wing parties declined by two-thirds. Thus the decline of left-wing support among the young is not only a matter of generational replacement; it also reflects weak convictions that were easily changed among the birth cohorts of the 1960s.

However, there also seems to be a universal effect of ageing. Among all birth cohorts, we observe a decline in left-wing support as people grow older. This holds even for the 1987 election where all surviving prewar cohorts gave less support to the left-wing parties than in 1966 even though the left-wing parties' share in the elections had nearly doubled. We return to this problem below. First, we shall analyse support for the socialist parties as a whole, in a generational perspective.

The relevant data are presented in Table 6.6. The generations with over-representation of left-wing voters are roughly the same as the generations with disproportional support for socialist parties. In order to eliminate the effects of fluctuations in election results, the entries in the table are percentage point deviations from the election result in respective age groups. Thus all figures are immediately comparable.

Among the two oldest generations (born 1915 or earlier), we observe a marked decline in socialist support over the life cycle. This may reflect changing voting behaviour among individual voters but perhaps the figures may also be affected by social differences in mortality (which are quite large). Besides, we cannot exclude the fact that social differences in health mean that a larger proportion from the lower classes live in institutions where they are not sampled for the survey.

Table 6.6. Support for socialist parties, 1966-1994, by birth cohort. Deviation from overall mean. Percentage points

Year of birth	1966[1]	1971	1973	1975[1]	1979	1984	1987	1990	1994
1976-1980	.	.	.	.	.	.	.	.	(−20)
1971-1975	.	.	.	.	.	.	.	(+7)	−9
1966-1970	.	.	.	.	.	.	+3*	−5*	−4
1961-1965	.	.	.	.	.	+5	+5	+5	−4
1956-1960	.	.	.	.	+7*	+15	+14	+11	+9
1951-1955	.	.	+4*	+13	+20*	+10	+14	+9	+9
1946-1950	.	+13*	0	+5	+4*	0	+2	+3	+5
1941-1945	+11	+6*	−5	[−3]²	−2*	−1	−4	−3	+5
1936-1940	+1	−3*	+1	[−3]²	−5*	−11	−6	−5*	+2
1926-1935	−1	0	+1	−1	−6	−5	−4	−4	−2
1916-1925	−1	−5*	+2	[−1]³	−3	+2	−6	−3	−4
1901-1915	0	−1	0	[−2]⁴	−1	−10	−15	−11*	−11*
-1900	−2	−7*	−12*	[−2]⁴	(−12)	−28⁺	.	.	.
Election	50	49	37	41	50	47	50	50	45

Notes:
1) Fixed age groups, approximated to birth cohorts. Deviances are, on average, about half a year in 1975 and about 1½ year in 1966.
2) Figures refer to birth cohorts 1936-1945 as a whole (30-39 years old).
3) Birth cohorts 1911-1925.
4) All cohorts born 1910 or earlier.
Signatures: * N < 200
  + N < 100
  () N < 50

Among the other age groups, the result is more uncertain but at least it seems certain that the very leftist generations from the 1950s have moved rightwards, even relatively speaking, in the 1990s. Until 1994, a similar trend was found among the generations born between 1926 and 1945 but at this point, the 1994 data disturb the picture, in particular for the 1936-1945 cohort. It is possible that this is a special period effect since the tax reform of 1992, promoted by the government, seems to have been particularly favourable for this group. On the other hand, we have few indications of an subjective awareness of these generational advantages.

We may analyse the problem from yet another angle, however, by comparing the voting pattern of young voters (aged less than 30 years) in each election from 1964 to 1990 with the party choice of the same cohorts in 1994. The figures are presented in Table 6.7, as deviance in percentage points from aggregate election results, for left-wing parties, Social Democrats, and non-socialist parties, respectively. In 1964 when voting age was 21 years, the youngest age group includes the 21-29 years old, i.e. the birth cohorts from 1935 to 1943. Correspondingly, the 21-29 years old voters in 1966 include the birth cohorts from 1937 to 1945, and so on. If voting did not change over the life cycle, the deviations for each cohort should remain constant. By comparing the deviations for the young in each election with the deviations for the relevant birth cohorts in 1994, we thus obtain a measure of change over the life cycle. For example, support for left-wing parties was 3 percentage points above the population mean among those voters aged less than 30 years in 1964. In 1994, these birth cohorts (1935-1943) were less inclined to vote for leftist parties than the average population (–4 percentage point). Accordingly, left-wing parties have suffered an (adjusted) loss of (3+4) 7 percentage points in this cohort.

Table 6.7. *Party choice among voters aged less than 30 years (deviation from election result) at the elections 1964-1994, party choice among the corresponding birth cohorts in 1994, resulting ageing effect. Percentage points*

Election year	a. Party choice among voters aged less than 30 years: deviation from election result			b. Party choice for same birth cohorts in 1994: deviation from election result			c. Ageing effect (b minus a)		
	Left-wing	Social Dem.	Bourg. party	Left-wing	Social Dem.	Bourg. party	Left-wing	Social Dem.	Bourg. party
1964	+3	–3	0	–4	+8	–4	–7	+11	–4
1966	+5	–1	–4	–3	+7	–4	–8	+8	0
1968	+6	–3	–3	–2	+5	–3	–8	+8	0
1971	+10	+2	–12	+4	+2	–6	–6	0	+6
1973	+13	–5	–8	+5	+1	–6	–8	+6	+2
1975	+15	–7	–8	+6	0	–6	–9	+7	+2
1977	+14	–4	–10	+8	+1	–9	–6	+5	+1
1979	+19	–6	–13	+9	0	–9	–10	+6	+4
1981	+19	–7	–12	+7	–2	–5	–12	+5	+7
1984	+17	–6	–11	+6	–3	–3	–11	+3	+8
1987	+13	–6	–7	+4	–6	+2	–9	0	+9
1988	+12	–9	–3	+4	–6	+2	–8	+3	+5
1990	+5	–4	–1	+2	–8	+6	–3	+4	+7
1994	+1	–9	+8	+1	–9	+8	.	.	.

The results are pretty clear. Among all birth cohorts, there is quite a strong defection from the left-wing parties as they grow older. Among all birth cohorts from 1935 onwards, people have been more inclined than the average voter to vote for left-wing parties in their first elections (from +3 for the 21-29 years old in 1964, to +19 for the 18-29 years old in 1979 and 1981). But among the birth cohorts born 1938-1946 or earlier, people have ended up being less inclined to vote for left-wing parties than the average voter. In other words: left-wing voting was a simple life cycle phenomenon. This holds also for the following birth cohorts but here we observe a generational effect, too. The left-wing parties have suffered severe losses but in 1994, they have remained over-represented, in particular among the voters who were young (less than 30 years) in the 1970s. Among voters who were young in the 1980s, however, the losses have been extraordinarily severe. For instance, among the cohorts born between 1954 and 1965, the left-wing parties were over-represented by 17 percentage points in the 1984 election (January) but in 1994, there was an over-representation of only 6 percentage points, i.e. an adjusted loss of 11 percentage points (as election results were worse for the left-wing parties in 1994 than in 1984, the real, uncorrected, loss is even larger, of course).

Turning to the Social Democrats, we observe that apart from 1971, this party has been under-represented among the young in all elections over a 30-year period. However, this is not necessarily a sign of weakness: among all cohorts, the Social Democrats have gained increasing support over the life cycle, and the party has ended up being over-represented among all cohorts born 1950-1961 or earlier. So far, this has not happened among the younger generations, and considering the relatively low support for the left-wing parties, it is likely the Social Democrats will remain under-represented here. As it has been quite abnormal for young people to prefer bourgeois parties, we have no experience as to what happens to such voters when they become older. The present mobilisation on the right is clearly a threat to the Social Democrats. *But the mobilisation of the 'new left' in the 1960s and 1970s, contrary to what is often believed, has been highly beneficial to the Social Democratic party.*

Finally, the non-socialist parties have remained under-represented among those voters who were young in the 1960s, 1970s and early 1980s; still, apart from the birth cohorts that were young in the 1960s, the bourgeois parties have been successful in catching up, i.e. the under-representation has become smaller as people grow older. Whereas the Social Democrats have been most advantaged by ageing/maturation among those who were young in the 1960s and 1970s, the bourgeois parties have so far been the main winners among those cohorts that were young in the 1980s.

To sum up, we can clearly identify two political generations: the first postwar generation (born 1946-1960) and the second postwar generation (born 1961-), the first voting disproportionately to the left, the second voting disproportionately to the right. The formation of the first postwar generation as a distinct political generation seems to have been associated with a counter-reaction among the older generations, thus contributing to an increasing polarisation between generations. It is difficult to speculate what will happen to the second postwar generation during the course of its life. But the distinctiveness of the first postwar generation has weakened: it has become more Social Democratic, and it has become more bourgeois. To some degree this probably reflects the fact that the Social Democrats and the bourgeois parties have changed, in particular by adapting to postmaterialist value change. But as we shall see below, it also reflects a change in political attitudes with ageing.

To provide an explanation of the formation of these two political generations is outside the scope of this chapter. Rather than explaining why this took place, we concentrate below — as a first step — on the description of *how* it happened. We shall argue that it follows a simple cultural diffusion model, involving the notion of better-educated young as a trend-setting group.

6.5. Intellectuals and the Better-Educated

Unlike theories of stratification or Weberian conceptions of social class, Marxist and other macro-level perspectives on social class have always included the notion of intellectuals as a particular group in the class structure.[4] Narrowly speaking, the concept of intellectuals or intelligentsia designates the group of people who are occupied with ideological, political and cultural tasks, including education — 'teachers, writers, celebrities' to quote a book title of Regis Debray (1980) — a group which should not be conflated with 'technic-scientific intelligence'.

However, it is a group with very fluid class boundaries, and it is not really important to utilise the exact concept here, nor is it necessary to discuss the determinants of the group's behaviour. The important distinguishing characteristic is that intellectuals do not act on the basis of their own, narrow class interests — at least not to the same degree as other groups. Rather, the political behaviour of intellectuals is strongly influenced by political and ideological movements in society.

This is deriven partly from a professional preoccupation with ideology, partly from the particular conditions of socialisation as students, i.e. outside usual class relations. According to Marxist class theories, intellectuals will 'normally' be attached to bourgeois class interests — because of class origins, because of future class positions, or because of their role in the reproduction of the dominant ideology in society. However, in periods of political/ideological mobilisation, and under

---

4. In Denmark, the Radical Liberals have been based, historically, on an odd alliance between smallholders and urban intellectuals.

various conditions which are difficult to specify, they may become radicalised — either to the right or to the left (Brym 1980).[5]

Now, the attachment to ideology is characteristic only of intellectuals in the narrow sense. But in relation to the analysis of political generations, the most important aspect is perhaps the particular conditions of socialisation, and these conditions to a large degree extend to the better-educated at large. Attending high schools, universities or other educations during their politically formative years, the better-educated are particularly likely to be influenced by the waves of ideological mobilisation. Besides, as the group of better-educated has exploded in size, the emergence of distinct political generations is very much facilitated. In addition, the better-educated are likely to be trend-setters within their generations.

Below, we simply look at the group having completed a high school exam ('gymnasium' which is usually completed at about the age of 19), i.e. a group that is broader than intellectuals in the conventional sense. Perhaps one may say that we have utilised the *notion* of intellectuals, rather than the *concept* of intellectuals. At any rate, Table 6.8 reveals that the notion of intellectuals is more necessary than ever for political sociology. Again, we have a good starting point in 1964 when four-fifths of all better-educated voted for bourgeois parties, regardless of age. Less than 10 per cent voted for left-wing parties. From 1966, the young generation began moving leftwards but still in 1968, in the year of the student rebellion, two-thirds of the 20-29 years old voted for non-socialist parties. However, the mobilisation continued: by 1975, a socialist majority was reached among the 20-29 years old, and for the first time, a strong move to the left was also observable among the 30-39 years old.

This mobilisation among the young peaked between 1977 to 1981 when two-thirds voted for socialist parties, and in 1979 and 1981, there was even an absolute majority voting for left-wing parties. A closer inspection of support for individual left-wing parties reveals that the culmination point of mobilisation was 1979. In 1979, 35 per cent among the 18-29 years old voted for revolutionary left-wing parties (left socialists, communists, maoists, or trotskiists), 17 per cent for the more reformist Socialist People's party. In 1981, only 18 per cent voted for the revolutionary left, 34 per cent for the Socialist People's party.

---

5.   This radicalism may take almost any direction. It would be tempting to argue that intellectuals were bound to be supporters of civil and democratic rights — free speech, tolerance, etc. However, history provides many instances of deviance from this tendency: for instance, the association of German students was among the very first to support nazism, and at the zenith of the anti-authoritarian Danish student rebellion of the 1970s, political intolerance (or at least an extreme version of 'political correctness') was quite widespread.

Table 6.8. Party choice among better-educated, by age, 1964-94. Percentages

Year	Age	Left-wing	Social Dem.	Socialist, total	Non-socialists	(N)
1964	20-29	8	10	18	82	204
	30-39	10	11	21	79	142
	40+	6	12	18	82	348
1966	20-29	18	6	24	76	243
	30-39	14	8	22	78	133
	40+	5	4	9	91	303
1968	20-29	24	11	35	65	301
	30-39	10	9	19	81	192
	40+	5	6	11	89	375
1971	20-29	(42)	(5)	(47)	(53)	18
	30-39	(23)	(10)	(33)	(67)	17
	40+	(7)	(5)	(12)	(88)	18
1973	20-29	35	8	43	57	144
	30-39	6	7	13	87	64
	40+	6	7	13	87	100
1975	20-29	42	14	56	44	379
	30-39	19	14	33	67	269
	40+	8	6	14	86	385
1977	20-29	42	27	69	31	66
	30-39	19	34	53	47	42
	40+	2	16	18	82	52
1979	18-29	51	19	70	30	95
	30-39	27	26	53	47	48
	40+	7	22	29	71	52
1981	18-29	52	14	66	34	1052
	30-39	35	17	52	48	692
	40+	10	12	22	78	766
1984	18-29	46	11	57	43	216
	30-39	41	18	59	41	142
	40+	9	10	19	81	110
1987	18-29	41	9	50	50	206
	30-39	56	12	68	32	142
	40-49	28	9	37	63	66
	50+	6	15	21	79	65
1988	18-29	33	12	45	55	203
	30-39	47	15	62	38	97
	40+	16	8	24	76	127
1990	18-29	18	25	43	57	180
	30-39	31	27	58	42	133
	40-49	25	18	43	57	91
	50+	10	13	23	77	84
1994	18-29	12	18	30	70	262
	30-39	25	18	43	56	197
	40-49	31	25	56	42	138
	50+	10	15	25	75	96
1994	35-39	30	23	53	46	82
	40-44	33	27	60	38	78
	45-49	28	23	51	47	60
	50-54	18	22	40	60	31

In the electorate at large, the left-wing parties did not peak until 1987 when nearly 21 per cent voted for a party to the left of the Social Democrats. Among the young generation of better-educated, however, there was a movement to the right already by 1984; in 1987, bourgeois parties had captured one-half of the votes, and from 1988, a majority has voted for non-socialist parties. In 1994, there was a non-socialist majority of 70 per cent among the 18-29 years old, and only 12 per cent voted for a left-wing party.

At the same time it may be observed how the leftist generation move through the age groups. From 1977, there was also a socialist majority among the 30-39 years old, culminating in 1987 when 68 per cent of the 30-39 years old voted for a socialist party and 56 per cent for a left-wing party. From 1987, a leftward movement also becomes observable among the 40-49 years old, and by 1994, there is a socialist majority for the first time among the 40-49 years old whereas the non-socialist parties hold the majority among the 30-39 years old in 1994 — for the first time since 1975. Even in 1994, however, there is little change among better-educated aged more than 50 years as 75 per cent prefer a non-socialist party.

Finally, a more detailed classification into five-years age groups in 1994 indicates that there remains a socialist majority among the 35-39 years old and that a few left-wingers are now entering the age group 50-54 years. Thus, we are faced with an unusually strong generational effect though it does seem that the effect is weakening somewhat. To get a more precise description, we turn to an analysis of the behaviour of various birth cohorts over time.

Table 6.9. *Party choice among better-educated, by year of birth. Proportion voting socialist, as deviation from election result. Percentages*

Year of birth	1966	1973	1975	1979	1984	1987	1990	1994
1971-	.	.	.	.	.	.	(–14)	–16
1961-70	.	.	.	.	–3	–5	–17	–13
1946-60	.	+5	+15	+21	+15	+14	+4	+9
1936-45	–26	–13	–8	(–17)	–18	–16	–8	0
-1935	–37	–23	–27	–18	–28	–25	–31	–32
Election	49.9	36.9	41.1	50.1	46.6	49.9	50.0	45.0
(N)	.						13	118
	.				90	154	180	242
	.	112	379	105	248	209	184	246
	243	75	268	27	54	55	62	56
	436	105	385	38	73	61	62	52

From the data presented in Table 6.9 we can clearly identify two political generations among the better-educated. The first is the generation born before 1935 which has consistently voted much further to the right than the population at large, in accordance with the privileged socioeconomic position of the better-educated. This generation appears entirely unaffected by the political changes in the last decades. Next, we find the postwar generation 1946-1960 which has not only voted much further to the left than other generations of better-educated but also to the left of the population at large (this has not occurred in any other generation at any time). The data do indicate, however, that the socialist orientations are weakening in the 1990s, and a closer inspection reveals that defections from socialist parties in this generation are strongly related to income — people in leading positions rarely maintain socialist ideals.

Finally, everything seems to indicate that the youngest generation of better-educated will follow a political course to the right and become a third distinct generation. The data also indicate, however, that there may be significant intra-generational change. Thus the age cohort born in the 1960s has moved significantly to the right in the 1990s. And the generation born between 1936 and 1945 which began its political trajectory far to the right seems to have moved to the left. Probably there is a sort of 'contagion effect' between the generations, i.e. a strong mobilisation within a particular generation tends to affect the neighbouring generations. This could explain both the move to the left among the 1936-1945 generation and the move to the right among the generation born in the 1960s.

6.6. Political Mobilisation in the 1970s and 1990s

Above, we have spoken of mobilisation effects, in particular about the mobilisation of the young generation in the 1970s — a mobilisation that had its core and its point of departure among the better-educated youth. Broadly speaking, the same pattern is found, with opposite signs, among the young in the 1990s.

But what does mobilisation actually mean? Is the mobilisation in the 1990s simply a repetition of the mobilisation in the 1970s with opposite signs? And how far does it go: is it a simple matter of following the voting habits of a reference group, perhaps even a matter of fashion, or are there significant changes in ideological convictions at play?

'Mobilisation' is a difficult concept to handle in individual-level analyses and easily becomes a more or less tautological residual explanation as it is measured by the same variables as it seeks to explain. Indeed, this reflects the self-reinforcing nature of political mobilisation (Togeby 1994). However, one may seek to define mobilisation operationally also by other variables. Thus we suggest as an operational definition that the strength of a mobilisation process may be measured by its ability to generate political interest among the groups that are affected, as well as by its ability to capture the politically interested persons with the group that is mobilised. Finally, the strength of mobiliation may be measured by the strength of attitudinal change or attitudinal deviation that it entails.

If we follow this definition, the mobilisation process in the 1970s must be characterised as extremely strong whereas one can hardly speak of any political mobilisation in the 1990s. Thus from Table 6.10 we observe a significant decline in political interest among the young from 1979 to 1994.[6] In 1979, 20 per cent were much interested in politics. In 1994, the figure was only 12 per cent. This decline was particularly significant among the better-educated where the proportion indicating that they were 'much' interested in politics dropped from 44 per cent to only 18 per cent, i.e. below population average.

Table 6.10.   *Political interest by age in 1979 and 1994 among all voters, and among better-educated. Percentages*

Age	Political interest, 1979			Political interest, 1994			(N)	
	Much	Some	Little/ none	Much	Some	Little/ none	1979	1994
All voters								
18-29	20	40	40	12	48	40	394	441
30-39	21	45	34	15	47	38	417	396
40 +	20	41	39	25	40	35	1103	1184
Better-educated								
18-29	44	44	12	18	57	25	107	184
30-39	37	46	17	21	56	23	60	124
40 +	26	56	18	45	40	15	62	126

Among the group of better-educated aged more than 40 years, on the other hand, the proportion of 'much' politically interested has increased from 26 to 45 per cent, mainly due to generational replacement.

Clearly, it was the situation in 1979 that was unusual; among the better-educated, there was a quite strong *negative* association between age and political interest. This interpretation is also confirmed by the fact that there is no increase in political

---

6.   A similar trend is reported in Svensson and Togeby (1991) on the basis of two very large but not country-wide surveys of young people in 1979 (Svensson and Togeby 1986) and 1988.

apathy except among the better-educated — in sharp contrast to popular images of polarisation and increasing apathy among the less educated.

The next question is to what degree political interest is related to party choice, i.e. to left-wing party preference in 1979, and to preference for non-socialist parties in 1994. We touched on this subject in section 1.5 but may now take a closer look at it. As revealed by Table 6.11, there was a very strong association between political interest and left-wing voting. In fact, political interest was one of the most important determinants of left-wing voting in 1979. Among the 18-29 years old who were much interested in politics, a majority of 53 per cent voted for left-wing parties (as compared to 12 per cent in the electorate at large). And among the better-educated youth with much interest in politics, two out of three voted for left-wing parties; only one out of six voted for a non-socialist party. In other words, among the better-educated youth, political interest was almost tantamount to strong socialist sentiments.

In 1994, the group of highly interested among the better-educated is even too small to allow a calculation of percentages. And for the age group at large, there is only a weak association between political interest and party choice in 1994. By and large, this holds also for individual parties within the bourgeois bloc. Thus whereas the strength of the left-wing among the young in the 1970s was clearly related to a process of political mobilisation, there is little genuine political mobilisation in the 1990s although there is a positive association between political interest and non-socialist party choice, unlike in the 1970s.

Table 6.11.   Party choice among 18-29 years old, by political interest, 1979 and 1994. Percentages

Year	Political interest	Left-wing	Social Dem.	Socialist, total	Non-socialist	n (=100 per cent)
1979						
All	much	53	18	71	29	78
voters	some	29	32	61	39	131
	little/none	19	41	60	40	110
Better-						
educated	much	66	17	83	17	45
	some	39	24	62	38	40
1994						
All voters	much	13	22	35	65	47
	some	13	22	35	65	191
	little/none	8	33	41	59	131

Finally, there is the question of political attitudes. Were young left-wing voters really that radical in 1979, and are young Liberal/Conservative as far to the right as indicated by their party choice? As far as the young left-wing voters in the aftermath of the youth and student rebellion is concerned, it has been claimed that they were 'really' more of a 'green' (i.e. postmaterialist) opposition than a 'red' (socialist) one; only because of the absence of alternatives, they tended to identify with the existing opposition to the regime such as the communist parties in France and Italy (Inglehart & Rabier 1986).

Table 6.12.   Left-right attitudes among left-wing and conservative/liberal voters in 1979 and 1994, by age. PDI (per cent difference index) in favour of leftist responses

	Left-wing voters		Liberal/Conservative		All voters	
	1979	1994	1979	1994	1979	1994
18-29	64	30	−33	−43	19	−13
30-39	61	39	−38	−40	0	−5
40-49	51	33	−44	−48	−16	−13
50+	45	38	−47	−48	−13	−22
(N)	97	46	48	172	303	437
	45	62	91	120	347	391
	17	62	95	122	282	383
	30	34	218	275	655	784

Note: Left-right attitudes measured on a four-item scale of four forced choice-questions on economic equality, state regulation of business, socialisation of business, and maintenance of welfare arrangements (see Table 1.5 for wordings).

This argument has much to it; however, Denmark was different. The two largest left-wing parties (the Socialist People's party and the Left Socialists) were both socialist and postmaterialist and were ready to absorb and represent the protest, as well as to give it political direction (Logue 1982). And the young postmaterialist protesters certainly succeeded in convincing themselves that they were also socialist. Thus, in spite of the fact that left-wing voting was a mass phenomenon among the young but a small minority phenomenon among the older, the young were nevertheless the most radical, as measured by a left-right scale (see Table 6.12). On a question of total nationalisation of business, the differences were (even more) marked. Among the 18-29 years old left-wingers, there was a PDI of +32 in favour of nationalisation; among left-wing voters aged more than 40 years, the PDI was −11. By 1994, however, the situation is back to normal: the young left-wing voters even appear slightly less radical than the older but the difference is not significant.

On the right-wing, there is not an equivalent radicalisation among the young in 1994 but young people in general have clearly moved ideologically to the right, and in spite of a dramatic increase in support for the Liberals and the Conservatives among the young to more than three times the level in 1979, even the supporters of these two parties are more to the right than in 1979. But unlike the young left-wing supporters in 1979, the young liberals and conservatives are not more radical than the older voters within their parties.[7]

But it has been demonstrated that both in the 1970s and 1990s, the changes in party politics between the generations is more than a question of fashion. The generational differences reflect quite deep-seated ideological changes. This holds in particular for the socialist mobilisation of the first postwar generation which was very successful whereas the liberal/conservative swing to the right among the second postwar generation is less of a mobilisation at all, and less radical, but nevertheless involves significant changes in political values that follow the changes in party choice.

6.7. Gender Variations and Gender Mobilisation

A mobilisation perspective also applies to the emerging or increasing gender differences in Danish politics (Togeby 1994). From a structural perspective, one may point to gender differences in class interests, in values, and in gender interests (equal rights/women's liberation) as factors which tend to pull women to the political left, provided that basically women react most according to their own interests (Goul Andersen 1984b). The basic dynamic factor, viewed from this perspective, is women's increasing labour market participation and increasing labour market integration as (almost) full-time, life-long wage labourers, as well as the adaptation of the (Scandinavian) welfare states to meet the changing needs of women. However, to fully understand the changes in the 1970s, 1980s, and 1990s, it is also necessary to understand the dynamics of mobilisation itself.

First a recapitulation of the findings of previous research. They are well-established facts that women are almost fully integrated into the labour market, that housewives have nearly disappeared, that part-time labour is rapidly declining, and that women are more unionised than men (Goul Andersen 1996d). By the same token, women are slightly more interested in union politics than men, and the political behaviour of married women is at least as much determined by their own class

---

7.   Besides, on a number of welfare state issues and postmaterialist issues, young Liberals and Conservatives deviate strongly from their older fellow-partisans, i.e. they are more of the 'green bourgeois' type of voters, c.f. chapter 8.

interests as by their husband's class interests. Married women are influenced by the class interests of their spouse but the same holds true for married men. This also explains why the occupation of 'head of household' has been dropped as a standard variable by Danish survey collectors.

Table 6.13 reveals the proportion voting socialist among men and women, 1964-1994. Unlike as in many other countries, there has not been any systematic tendency for women to be more 'conservative' than men in Denmark for the last 30 years. Until 1975, there was no systematic gender difference at all. The gender differences that are recorded until 1975 may be explained either by sampling errors, or by a slightly higher volatility among men. But from 1977 onwards, a trend emerges, and from 1981, the proportion voting socialist has consistently been 3-4 percentage points higher among women than among men. In the 1990s the gender gap has grown to 6 percentage points.

Table 6.13.   Gender and party choice, 1964-1994. Per cent voting socialist

	1964	1966	1968	1971	1973	1975	1977	1979	1981	1984	1987	1988	1990	1994
Men	49	51	43	52	35	41	46	50	46	45	48	46	47	42
Women	49	49	44	47	39	41	48	50	50	48	51	49	53	48
Diff.	0	−2	+1	−5	+4	0	+2	0	+4	+3	+3	+3	+6	+6

Table 6.14.   Gender composition of individual parties. 1964 and 1994. Proportion of women, in percentages

	Proportion of women[2]		(N)
	1964	1994	1994
Left soc.[1] (1964: Comm.)	49	48	109
Soc. People's party	43	62	280
Social Democrats	51	52	1155
Radical Liberals	45	53	141
Christian People's party	.	66	70
Centre Democrats	.	60	91
Liberals	46	47	834
Conservatives	57	45	449
Progress party (1964: Independent p.)	45	35	170
Electorate	50	50	3326

1)   Alliance between former communists, left socialists and socialists without former party affiliation.

2)   Figures are standardised by setting the overall proportion of women in both samples to 50 per cent and adding/subtracting deviations from respective sample means.

This dichotomy between socialists and non-socialists does not fully describe the changing association between gender and party choice, however. Table 6.14 presents the gender composition of individual parties in 1964 and 1994. It appears that there are quite significant changes: the Socialist People's party used to be a male-dominated party, not the least representing workers with a radical trade union consciousness. In 1994, however, it is the most women-dominated party next to the Christian People's party as 62 per cent of the party's supporters are women. It also turns out that the other new centre party, the Centre Democrats, had an over-representation of women, along with the third centre party, the Radical Liberals. Thus the dividing line is between centre-left parties on the one hand and right-wing parties on the other.

Among the right-wing parties, the semi-populist Progress party has always been male-dominated, even though a women (Pia Kjærsgaard) has been the leading figure since the mid-1980s (furthermore, when the party broke into two separate parties by 1995, both parties were led by women). Next, the Conservative party which used to have a strong over-representation of women, has a significant male bias in the 1990s. This holds also for the mobilising Liberal party but somewhat surprisingly, the male over-representation in 1994 is not stronger than 30 years earlier.

This gender difference in party choice is strongly related to gender differences in class position. It in fact turns out that if we control for gender differences in occupation and sector, the gender difference of 8 percentage points in proportions voting socialist among the gainfully employed disappears: statistically speaking, the gender difference in voting may be completely explained by the fact that a much larger proportion of women are employed in the public sector, whereas a huge majority of self-employed and higher-level non-manuals are men. But this does not apply to political attitudes.

It is well-known that there are characteristic gender differences in political attitudes, in particular attitudes towards the welfare state, towards foreign policies (including NATO and the European Union), and, to a lesser degree, towards the environment (Goul Andersen 1984b; Togeby 1994; Christensen 1994; see also chapter 10). It is less well-known, however, that this gender difference also extends to the choice of economic policy strategies and that it is at this point we find by far the most significant gender effects (see chapter 9, Tables 9.10 and 9.11). Thus, with fundamental gender differences in class interests and fundamental gender differences in values that relate not only to 'soft' policy areas but even enters the core of disagreement over economic policies, it certainly comes as no surprise that there are gender differences in party choice. On the contrary, such differences should be expected to become even larger, and as we shall see below, it is indeed likely that they will.

What remains is the question of political mobilisation. From the notion of political mobilisation, we should expect a declining gender difference in political interest, in particular among the younger generations. Next, we should expect the gender gap in party choice to be largest among the politically interested with politically interested women voting far to the left. Finally, we should expect that the gender gap in party choice was largest among the younger generations.

Beginning with the mobilisation of political interest, we do observe a decline in the gender gap in political interest between 1979 and 1994 (Table 6.15). In 1971 and 1979, there was a 19 percentage point difference in the proportion of politically interested ('much' or 'some'). In 1994, the figure was only 12 percentage points. But the assumption that this reflects a political mobilisation among younger women is not confirmed. On the contrary, political interest has increased among all women *except* the younger age groups. This implies that the gender difference in political interest is contingent on age but in the opposite way than was expected: gender differences have nearly disappeared among people over 60 years but have remained very strong among the young (18-29 years).

Before commenting further on these data, we turn to the association between political interest and party choice (see Table 6.16).

Table 6.15.   *Political interest among men and women, by age. 1971, 1979 and 1994. Percentages*

	1971		1979		1994		Gender difference Women — men		
Political interest:	Men	Women	Men	Women	Men	Women	1971	1979	1994
Much	19	9	26	15	24	15	−10	−11	−9
Some	50	41	46	38	45	42	−9	−8	−3
Little/none	31	50	28	47	31	43	19	19	12
Total	100	100	100	100	100	100	.	.	.
Percentage with much or some interest:									
18-29 years	61	40	71	50	70	49	−21	−21	−21
30-39 years	72	53	77	57	70	55	−19	−23	−15
40-49 years	79	50	73	51	75	61	−29	−22	−14
50-59 years	72	54	71	52	69	59	−18	−19	−10
60-69 years	64	55	66	51	66	61	−9	−15	−5
70 + years	60	48	72	56	64	63	−12	−16	−1
Total	69	50	72	53	69	57	−19	−19	−12

Here the results roughly come out as predicted. In 1979, there was a particularly strong radicalisation among the most politically interested women under 40 years of whom almost three quarters voted socialist. This pattern is maintained in 1994 but it seems to have weakened quite a lot.

Table 6.16.   Political interest and party choice among men and women, by age. 1971, 1979 and 1994. Percentages voting socialist

	Proportions that vote socialist						Gender difference Women — men		
	1971		1979		1994				
A. By political interest, entire sample	Men	Women	Men	Women	Men	Women	1971	1979	1994
Much interest	56	47	55	53	42	51	−9	−2	9
Some interest	49	47	48	48	40	46	−2	0	6
Little/none	60	47	48	51	46	49	−13	3	3
Total	52	47	50	50	42	48	−5	0	6
B. Among much interested, by age									
18-39	64*	()	59	72	38	63*	()	13	25
40-59	54*	(49)	51	47*	45	50	(−5)	−4	5
60 +	46*	(50)	54	30*	42	43*	(4)	−24	1
Total	56	47	55	53	42	51	−9	−2	9

Figures with an asterisk indicate N < 50. Figures in parentheses indicate N < 30. Figures not calculated when N < 20.

It must be acknowledged, however, that the apparent radicalisation among politically interested women in 1994 hinges upon women over 30 years. Among women under 30 there are too few politically interested respondents to allow any conclusions.

Thus we have a somewhat blurred picture of the mobilisation of women. On the one hand, women have become politically mobilised. The gender gap in politics is especially large among the most politically interested, and this effect is strongest among the younger women. On the other hand, among women under 30, we find few signs of increasing political interest. This indicates that the mobilisation has come to an end. To examine this suggestion, we turn to an analysis of age and generational variations in gender differences in party choice.

Table 6.17.   Party choice, by age and gender, 1994. Per cent

		Left-wing	Social Dem.	Socialist total	Centre parties	Lib/Cons/ Progr.p.	Outside parties	(N)
18-24	Men	12	19	31	10	58	1	172
	Women	15	24	39	14	45	2	143
25-29	Men	10	24	34	7	57	2	167
	Women	10	37	47	13	39	1	174
30-34	Men	12	26	38	8	50	4	151
	Women	20	28	48	15	36	1	165
35-44	Men	13	38	51	9	39	1	305
	Women	23	36	59	11	29	1	338
45-49	Men	9	40	49	8	43	–	171
	Women	17	29	46	8	45	1	153
50-59	Men	6	40	46	5	48	1	346
	Women	5	44	49	9	41	1	344
60+	Men	5	34	39	9	53	–	366
	Women	1	39	40	10	50	–	336
Total	Men	9	33	42	8	49	1	1677
	Women	12	36	48	11	40	1	1653

The association between gender, age and party choice is revealed in Table 6.17. It turns out that in all groups up to 45 years, women vote to the left of men whereas the gender difference is negligible among the older age groups. Among those under forty-five, women are, furthermore, inclined to prefer centre parties rather than the parties to the right — Conservatives, Liberals and the Progress party. Among the 25-29 years old, where the gender gap is widest, there is difference of 13 percentage points in the proportion voting socialist, and a difference of 18 percentage points in the proportion voting for the right-wing parties.

Table 6.18, furthermore, reveals that we are faced here with generational differences and that the gender gap among the electorate at large is widening because of generational replacement. Among the generations born before 1920, there are no consistent gender difference in voting patterns at all. Among the generations born between 1921 and 1950, there seems to have emerged a modest preference for socialist parties among women and an increasingly negative preference for right-wing parties. Among the birth cohorts from the 1950s, we find a very significant and consistent pattern, i.e. a gender gap in proportions voting socialist of some 5-9 percentage points, and a gap in the opposite direction in voting for right-wing parties of some 8-10 percentage points (with 1987 as an exception).

It is, however, among the birth cohorts from the 1960s that we find the most significant gender gap, as well as a significant widening of the gap in the 1990s. Among the birth cohorts from the 1970s, on the other hand, the gender gap is a bit little less marked in our data. With the possible exception of the last finding, the data are compatible with the notion of mobilisation. However, it is important to notice that the increasing gender gap among the birth cohorts of the 1960s does not occur because of a radicalisation of women; it stems from a strong rightward move among men. Next, if we return to Table 6.17, we observe that for the first time since the mid-1970s, there was a bourgeois majority among young women in 1994, not only for the 18-24 years old but even among the 25-29 years old.

Table 6.18.   Gender differences in party choice 1971-1994, by birth cohorts. Per cent women minus per cent men voting for particular parties

Year of birth	1971	1979	1984	1987	1990	1994
A. Socialist parties						
1971-	.	.	.	.	(+4)	−7
1961-1970	.	.	+9	+7	+11	+14
1951-1960	.	+5	+9	+6	+9	+6
1941-1950	−2	+5	+2	+7	+3	+3
1921-1940	−7	+1	+1	+1	+3	+4
- 1920	−2	−5	−3	+1	+1	−4
B. Liberal, Conservative, or Progress party						
1971-	.	.	.	.	(−30)	−12
1961-1970	.	.	−4	−8	−12	−19
1951-1960	.	−8	−9	−2	−10	−8
1941-1950	+2	−5	−3	−4	−2	−6
1921-1940	+1	0	0	+1	−1	−5
-1920	+5	−2	+1	−1	0	−1

Figures in parentheses are calculated on the basis of less than 2 x 100 respondents.

Thus it seems that young women follow the move to the right among men, only more reluctantly. Furthermore, they are not very interested in politics. Thus it seems misleading to speak of a mobilisation of women in the 1990s; there was a mobilisation in the 1970s and 1980s which has left its imprint on a generation of women, and contrary to some expectations, the achievement of a (more) equal status at the labour market has not made gender differences in politics disappear — quite the contrary. But since the mid-1980s there has been a political mobilisation among men which did not affect women much in the first place. Gradually, however, this ideological change has also spread to women, and although women may be more 'resistant', they seem, basically, to follow the same trend.

6.8. Social Cleavages in Danish Politics — a Summary

We began the previous chapter with by a discussion of the decline in class voting which decline is sometimes taken to mean that social differences in party choice have become unimportant altogether. Our data show that this is much of an exaggeration:

* To begin with social class, simple aggregation errors of two middle classes produce a biased impression of the decline in class voting.
* Class voting among self-employed has not decreased, and among higher-level employees in the private sector, it has increased.
* The changes in class voting 1990-1994 may to quite a large degree be explained from a class theoretical perspective.
* New divisions between occupational groups have emerged, in particular a division between private and public employees (mainly among non-manuals).
* Intellectuals constitute a particular social category in the class structure which is ignored in conventional analyses of voting behaviour.
* New divisions between generations have emerged which were entirely absent in the 1960s.
* New gender divisions appeared from the mid-1970s; such divisions were also absent in the 1960s.

No matter how we measure the association between social background factors and party choice, even if we take account of the numerous interaction effects, it still remains that the association between party choice and social background factors has declined, mainly because of a change in the class structure (i.e., replacement of the old middle class with a more heterogeneous new middle class). But the decline is far less outspoken than is commonly assumed, and the social changes in voting patterns link voting behaviour to broader analyses of social change and social movements. At least in the Danish case it emerges that elucidating such changes in social patterns is much more interesting than simply noting that such patterns have weakened in general.

7

BELIEFS ABOUT THE SCOPE OF GOVERNMENT

The main objective of chapters 1-6 was to account for the party choice in the Danish 1994 election and the foregoing elections. We have shown that to a great extent the vote can be seen as determined by the voter's issue orientations and as a reaction to the policy alternatives presented by different parties and governments. Whereas chapters 2-4 discussed the internal relationships of such a policy voting model, chapters 5 and 6 went on to relate it to the perspective of social development. Policy voting was seen as a set of intervening variables between the social position and the partisan choice of the voter.

In chapters 7-10 the party choice will no longer be the central dependent variable. Instead we turn to a study in which individual and aggregated policy preferences stand in the centre of the analysis. For that purpose we need to consult a broader theoretical framework than the ones offered in traditional election research. The recently published Beliefs in Government series of five volumes[1] illustrates the breadth of comparative research in political attitudes. Among these attitudes we select for the following chapters those dealing with the scope of government — that is, beliefs about what the government should do or not do, what it can do, and what it is already doing.

Beliefs about the scope of government were at the heart of the traditional ideologies of conservatism, liberalism, and socialism. But it is open to doubt whether these ideas are still viable today. On the one hand it is often said that politics has become practical problem-solving, every serious political movement or party recognising the need for some measure of centralised decision-making and coordination. In so doing, the decision-makers take account of the costs and benefits accruing to themselves as well as their clients. Consequently we have a rational school of research attempting to replace ideology with self-interest or utility in explaining attitudes toward government efforts in various policy fields. But on the other hand it is also often held that politics in modern society has a strong symbolic content, the mass media running campaigns for or against government action based on single cases that suit the style of the human interest story. These views have led some post-modernist scholars to deny almost any element of rationality in the political thinking of mass electorates. The approach we shall pursue is neither

---

1. Oxford University Press, 1995.

of the two. The values school maintains that voters need to ground their opinions and political behaviour in meaningful belief systems. It leads to a set of theses and analytical models which, if validated, argue an intermediate position between the other two approaches.

7.1. Key Concepts

Analytically one can separate normative beliefs from cognitive beliefs about the scope of government. Normative beliefs about what the government should do and should not do are reflections in the public that may lead to *demands* in Easton's sense: "Articulated statements, directed toward the authorities, proposing that some kind of authoritative allocation ought to be undertaken" (Easton 1965, p. 120). Such demands, in theory, are supposed to affect the *policy output* — either directly, as when a government mainly launches programs that are known to be in accordance with the majority of the voters, or indirectly, as when the voters' issue positions influence their partisan choice so that a new governing coalition can take over. Cognitive beliefs about what the government is doing, what it will do in the future, what it possibly can do, etcetera, are evaluations of the policy output.

Demand input originates in, and policy output is directed towards, the *environment* of the political system, that is, the society over which it resides, and other political systems. The perceived relationship of demand input to policy output gives rise to a third key concept in Easton's framework: where demands for government action are frustrated, this may result in the loss of *political support*. What Easton terms specific support "reflects the satisfaction a member feels when he perceives his demands as having been met" (Easton 1965, p. 125). The key concepts in Easton's conceptual framework for the political system may be imagined to be related as follows:

(1)   Aggregated demands are positively related to actual government policies;
(2)   Consistency between individual demands and government policies is positively related to support for the political system.

The first relation implies that mass attitudes toward the scope of government are related to the scope of government itself. On the other hand policy demands by the mass electorate will normally influence actual policies; at least to some extent people get what they want. One has to admit though that the findings from the so-called linkage studies (e.g., Luttbeg 1981) are not optimistic with regard to the strength of this relationship; autonomous political and bureaucratic elites, corporate bargaining, economic necessities, implementation problems, and pressures from the international environment often interfere with the process of translating input demands into output policies. One approach has been to correlate majority opinion with policy across a great number of issues. However, this seems to lead to a zero or even negative correlation. In under half the cases were government policies in accord with the balance of public opinion at the mass level; this result was valid for the United States as well as France, West Germany, and Britain (Brooks 1985, 1987, 1990).

In so far as there is a positive relation, it may also be hypothesised to work the other way round. Actual government policy may become integrated in the political culture of a society so that after a while demands adapt to what people actually get. Policies may lead to a build-up of institutions, public as well as private, which influence the habits of people. Especially one might suggest that policies which are successful gradually will swing public opinion in favour of them. For example, the public health sector in Switzerland or the United States is small compared with that of Britain or Germany, but since it seems to work, Swiss or American public opinion is much less in favour of raising the public expenditures for health than is British or German public opinion. More generally, western capitalist countries have succeeded in increasing the living standards so that the inclination for radical change in these countries is much lower than in either former communist countries or developing countries of the third world.

The second relation implies that where the translation from input demands to output policy functions smoothly, the result will be a general trust in the political system. But again, the relation may also work the other way round: where people have a strong trust in the political system, they will abstain from demanding more than the system can give. In a political system which enjoys a high level of support, public opinion is more likely to be realistic and well-informed than in a system which the public distrusts.

These two basic relations are derived from Easton's very abstract conceptual system. If we look at them from the perspective of values theory, we reach different hypotheses (in the case of Denmark, generally more optimistic ones) than if we apply rational theory. From the perspective of values theory, beliefs about the scope of government vary in a characteristic way with the economic level of the society. Comparative studies of the scope of government in west European countries (Borre and Scarbrough 1995) suggest that in general, wealthy countries have managed to attain a balance of demand input and policy output so as to keep the political support at a high level, whereas poorer countries have had difficulties in satisfying the expectations of their electorates and therefore suffer from lower support. Denmark, along with the other Scandinavian countries, and also Germany and the Netherlands, unambiguously belong in the former category.

From the perspective of rational, or public choice, theory, one problem with public control of policy — relation 1 above — is that mass demands are contradictory, so that, even if the decision-makers did their best in translating demands into policy, they would fail in one or other respect. Notably, demands are claimed to be asymmetrical, demands for government spending in different fields adding up to a much larger government budget than the majority of the public would tolerate (Kristensen 1980, 1982, 1984). Taking these diverse demands for spending at face value might explain both the long-term rise of the public budgets as well as the dissatisfaction with the high tax level. In other words, the asymmetry thesis claims that the separate demands for expenditures are translated fairly correctly, the demands for low taxes incorrectly. The reason for this, it is argued, is that most taxpayers have a larger stake in a particular demand than their stake in the total aggregated demand.

Thus the propellers driving the public sector forward are in part a rising demand on every particular item and in part a permanent tendency toward inconsistent demands. It will be seen that this explanation makes the assumption that certain mass opinions are fulfilled — namely, those on particularised items — whereas others are not — namely, those on the aggregate budget or the tax rate. This is explained by the logic of decision-making. Public choice theory is generally scornful about the effects of appeals to solidarity. However, in the name of logic the possibility should be mentioned that the public expenditures have increased because the majority of the voters wanted them to increase and did not mind paying the taxes. If this could be shown, we would need no bureaucratic distortion nor asymmetry in public opinion to explain the rise. The rising budget would be what the median voter wanted.

Following rational theory further, public reactions may well depend on the budget size itself as well as on the general state and direction of the economy. Wilensky (1975) hypothesised that a high or steeply rising tax level causes a tax protest, and liberal economists such as Laffer have argued that taxes above a certain level are detrimental to the work ethic and to the division of labour necessary in a modern economy. As to the effect of the state of the economy, in times of economic prosperity the mass public may be expected to be more tolerant toward rising public expenses than during economic recession because their own living standard may not decline in spite of the higher taxes. The argument is that when the economy grows, the state must also grow — indeed it may grow disproportionably, as formulated in Wagner's Law at the turn of the century. Thus it is especially in times of economic crisis that the pessimistic predictions of public choice theory confront the more optimistic predictions of values theory. The optimism of values theory rests on the ideas that demands can be satisfied, that they can be directed toward non-material and presumably less costly budget items, and that they are not necessarily egoistic as values refer to what 'ought' to be done — i.e., there is a moral side to demands.

Some years ago these contrasting views became especially relevant because of the effects of the first and second oil crises on the economy of most western nations. The result was a debate from 1975 onward about demand overload, legitimacy crisis, and political bankruptcy (King 1975; Crozier, Huntington and Watanuki 1975; Rose and Peters 1978). The overload theory argued that people had become increasingly dependent on governments to solve their problems, and would therefore turn to governments to relieve their economic distress — precisely at a time when the governments ran into a fiscal crisis. Similarly, the concept of rising expectations suggested that the attempt to saturate one demand merely leads to a new demand. The theory of legitimacy crisis held that this tendency was reinforced by the democratic process whereby different parties compete for votes, and would therefore lead to discontent with the democratic process itself.

New politics theory advances a different scenario for government growth than the theories of rising expectations, overload, crises-of-democracy — a less gloomy scenario, one feels inclined to say. New politics theory anticipates that the large welfare state demands characterising the past generation will gradually subside, along with traditional Social Democratic ideology which has promoted that demand. In later versions of postmaterialist theory Inglehart advances this idea in the form of a theory of declining marginal utility of economic policies (Inglehart 1990, chap. 8). However, the reduced need for economic policy does not mean a return to economic liberalism, for economic liberalism stresses economic factors just as much as did economic interventionism. According to Inglehart, the declining marginal utility of economic factors signals a declining interest in economic factors generally, the emphasis shifting toward non-economic issues. The solution for the future is not economic liberalism as the antithesis of socialism, but rather a shift in the tasks of government toward enhancing people's quality of life.

For the rest of the chapter we shall discuss the nature and determinants of attitudes to the scope of government, whereas the relation involving political support (relation 2) will be discussed in chapter 11. Sorting out the various theories about crisis and overload, we begin with a premise that seems to underpin all of them, namely the notion of rising expectations. It states that demands are not satisfied by policies which relieve social or economic problems. These demands may either be unrelated with past policies or outright positively related such that attempts to satisfy one demand entail the articulation of new demands. The fulfilment of one demand teaches people, as it were, that it pays to pressure the government. Once having embarked on a policy of expanding the state, the process never stops; the growth of the state is an irreversible process. At least, stopping the growth will lead to a crisis of democracy since it has to be done against the will of the majority. A causal chain of participation leading to polarisation, and polarisation leading to a loss of support, may have to be stopped by limiting participation (Huntington 1975).

Those proclaiming the growth of the state have often been vague in their conceptualisation. Sometimes it seems to mean an increasing tendency to regulate people's lives, sometimes a growth in government personnel, sometimes an increase in public budgets (including income transfers) or in taxes. It has been pointed out by Roller (1995) that the scope of government has at least two dimensions, *range* and *degree*. The scope may grow either in breadth by extending its activities to new fields, or it may grow in depth or intensity within existing fields of intervention with the lives of citizens. For example, a health programme may be stretched to cover new diseases or it may provide more intensive treatment of diseases already covered; collective transportation may be extended to new routes or more intensively cultivate existing routes, and so forth.

At a more general level, survey data can be found that touch on both these dimensions. A demand for a greater range of government is reflected in questions on whether it is the responsibility of government to take care of certain societal or individual needs. A demand for a higher degree of government intervention is reflected in questions of whether the government should do more or spend more in certain policy fields. In the following we turn first to the responsibility items and then, in more detail, to the spending items.

7.2. The Responsibility of Government

Mass opinions on the range of government can be gauged from responses to survey items asking whether, in the respondent's opinion, it should be the government's responsibility to pursue some societal goal, such as full employment, a clean environment, adequate housing, or economic growth. The response may be graded into four categories, 'definitely should be', 'probably should be', 'probably should not be', or 'definitely should not be'. In this form the items appeared in the ISSP Role of Government survey in 1985 and 1990. They were also included in the Danish 1994 election survey. Table 7.1 shows in the left-hand column the Danish responses and in the other columns comparable data from West Germany and Norway.

Table 7.1. Opinion balance on government responsibility in various policy fields.
Per cent definitely yes minus per cent definitely no

	Denmark 1994	W.Ger. 1985	W.Ger. 1990	Norway 1990
Provide jobs for everyone	30.2	32.7	25.2	48.4
Keep prices under control	17.6	20.3	13.5	56.4
Provide health care	94.2	53.4	56.0	83.3
Living standard for the old	91.7	55.4	53.6	85.5
Industrial growth	22.4	4.5	−.2	16.8
Support unemployed	53.5	20.8	14.5	41.1
Reduce income differences	15.0	20.4	14.0	29.9
Average of 7 items	46.4	29.6	25.2	51.6

Now it is possible that the West German system of financing welfare services conceals the hand of government in social policies. But the impression from the bottom figures is that people in Denmark and Norway, much more than those in West Germany, assign responsibility to the government for a great deal of policy goals. The liberal attitude of West Germans became even more pronounced between 1985 and 1990. If demand overload is a problem, it should be a much bigger problem in the two Scandinavian countries than in West Germany. Indeed, the hypothesis of rising expectations does not seem consistent with these data. In West Germany, where a comparison over time is possible, the hypothesis does not hold. In Scandinavia, the expectations are so dramatically higher than in West Germany that one wonders why the Scandinavian way does not lower the political support markedly compared with the West German way.

Instead, the table fits the view that expectations are determined in part by institutional arrangements and in part by transitory problems of the society. One observes that they differ very much from country to country and from one policy field to another. In the case of Denmark it is clear that with respect to care for the sick and elderly, the government is held responsible by the huge majority, whereas on such goals as income levelling and industrial growth the opinion is much more divided. This may be seen in connection with the fact that Denmark on the one hand has become a bit of a laggard in regard to health expenses, but on the other hand has an unusually high and even increasing level of equality in after-tax income (Goul Andersen 1997). With regard to keeping prices under control, we find that few make the government responsible for this in Denmark at present, but on the other hand, anti-inflation policies were in strong demand in Norway in 1990. Therefore we suggest that expectations in this field vary with the actual magnitude of the problem — that is, it may be related to recent experience of price rise rather than being a permanent feature of the national political culture.

Our conclusion concerning this point is that in some policy fields, expectations for government action probably rise and fall in relation to the size of the problem; in other fields expectations are extremely high and seem integrated into the political culture, and therefore are fairly constant over time.

7.3. Structure of Responsibility Attitudes

Let us look now at the responsibility items from the perspective of the new politics thesis described in chapter 2. That thesis suggests a typology of voters based on their political goals and preferences. The two types of interventionists on the old left and new left, respectively, should align themselves against the old right and new right. Further, the old left and the new left should differ as to the main purpose of intervention, the old left being primarily occupied with economic intervention and the new left, with intervention to preserve the quality of life.

For such a test, factor analysis seems appropriate, and Table 7.2 presents the unrotated and varimax-rotated solutions for ten items, whereas Figure 7.1 is a diagram of the unrotated solution.

Table 7.2. *Factor analysis of government responsibility in various policy fields, 1994. Loadings on unrotated and rotated factors*

	Unrotated			Rotated		
	Factor 1	Factor 2		Factor 1	Factor 2	Factor 3
Provide jobs	.63	−.39		.72		
Control prices	.53	−.54		.78		
Industrial growth	.36	−.35		.52		
Income levelling	.66	−.27		.61	.36	
Support students	.51	.27			.76	
Housing	.59	.26			.77	
Unemployed	.68	.12			.64	
Health care	.40	.48				.82
Older people	.48	.43				.78
Environment	.42	.17				.35
Variance explained	29 %	12 %		29 %	12 %	11 %

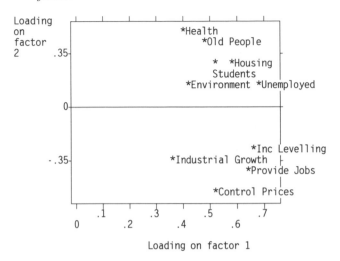

Figure 7.1. Principal components solution for attitudes to the responsibilities of government. X=Loadings on first factor, Y=Loadings on second factor

The unrotated factor solution shows a principal component with positive loadings of all ten items, a finding which confirms a general interventionist as opposed to a general liberal attitude. Crosscutting this dimension we find the second factor to be one that tends to differentiate between economic goals (full employment, stable prices, industrial growth) and social goals (health care, care of older people). The social goals load positively, and the economic goals negatively, on that factor.

There is a fairly strong resemblance between this structure and the one we found in chapter 4 regarding the election agenda (cf. Table 4.3 and Figure 4.1). In both cases all items load positively on the first factor but fan out from positive to negative loadings on the second factor. The two agenda items loading most negatively in Figure 4.1 are health care problems and problems of the older population. These correspond with the two fields of responsibility which load most positively in Figure 7.1. Conversely, national economic problems load positively in Figure 4.1 and corresponding fields of responsibility load negatively in Figure 7.1. Thus in both figures the second factor represents a dimension running from social to economic problems or policy fields, respectively. The fact that its direction is the opposite in Figure 7.1 is not relevant, as it depends on mere technicalities of factor analysis. We can conclude that also with regard to assigning responsibility to their government, voters divide, first, into those assigning a broad range of responsibilities and those assigning a narrow range; and second, the former divide into those assigning responsibility for social (welfare) policy and those assigning responsibility for economic policy.

Voting and Political Attitudes in Denmark

How does this result square with the theory of values? With some reservations we will argue that the first factor (principal component) represents two contrasting values, interventionism versus liberalism, whereas the second factor represents a further differentiation of interventionism into economic and social interventionism. Our reservation stems from using the label of liberalism to those who do not think the government has many responsibilities, as they may be mixed with respondents who were less motivated to answer our questions about the responsibility of government.

All the same, the result of the factor analysis clearly invites an interpretation in terms of value theory. It is too early to judge to what extent it may be fitted more specifically into Inglehart's (1977) postmaterialism theory. One could argue that the second factor, the economic vs. social agenda or responsibility, indicates a materialist versus postmaterialist dimension. This amounts to considering inflation control the most typically materialist concern while considering health care the most typically postmaterialist concern. With respect to inflation control we have no reservation because this is actually one of the two materialist items in Inglehart's MPM battery. The other is law and order, a policy goal which was not included among the responsibility items because it can be taken for granted that the state is responsible for the security of its citizens. With regard to health care we are more in doubt as to its status on the MPM dimension. Welfare goals express values of material security as well as quality of life values. We shall therefore postpone our conclusion about this point until we have studied another set of items representing beliefs about the scope of government.

7.4. Spending Attitudes

Turning from the range dimension toward the degree dimension of the scope of government, we will analyse a series of survey items which have figured both in international surveys (ISSP Role of Government 1985 and 1990) and in several Danish surveys. These items present the respondent with a list of policy areas. The ISSP survey uses eight policy areas and asks whether the respondent would like to see more or less government spending in each area, the response being chosen among five categories from 'spend much more' to 'spend much less'. The Danish surveys use a varying number of policy areas and ask whether the respondent thinks too much, too little, or that a suitable amount is being spent in each area.

Those countries participating in the ISSP survey both in 1985 and in 1990 exhibit rising demands over these five years. If we define the net demand as the per cent who want to spend more minus the per cent who want to spend less, averaged over all eight items, we find that the net demand rose from 22 to 29 per cent in

West Germany, from 34 to 38 per cent in Britain, from 21 to 28 per cent in the United States, and from 36 to 44 per cent in Italy, while in Australia it stayed at 25 per cent (ISSP Role of Government survey 1985 and 1990).

For Denmark, Table 7.3 shows the aggregate responses to various items for 1979, 1985, 1990 and 1994. The table contains those items that were asked more than once, and the first seven lines contain items that were asked all four times.

Table 7.3. Opinion balance on government spending in various policy fields. Per cent who want more minus per cent who want less spending

	1979	1985	1990	1994
Defence	−44	−36	−38	−35
Health	28	61	61	73
Education	22	44	45	42
Old age pensions	56	64	57	51
Environmental protection	37	57	49	42
Day care for children	26	24	29	32
Cultural purposes	−30	−12	−21	−34
Average of 7 items	13	29	26	24
Unemployment benefits	...	17	2	−1
Police	41		...	52
Poor relief	...	30	−11	−11
Aid to developing nations	...	−14	−26	−36
Refugees	...		−30	−35
Highways	−35		...	−47

Source: For 1979 and 1985, Goul Andersen (1991a); for 1990 and 1994, election surveys. In the two election surveys, respondents giving Don't Know responses to an item have been regarded as responding 'a suitable amount'.

From the row indicating the average of the first seven items it is clear that budget demands expanded in the first half of the nineteen-eighties. The rise of the average opinion balance from 13 per cent in 1979 to 29 per cent in 1990, indicating the net per cent of voters wanting more expenditure, cannot be written off as sampling error. Thus far the hypothesis of rising expectations is supported. The later figures of 24-26, though slightly lower than the 1985 figure, actually serve to consolidate the finding about rising expectations, for the confirm that the level of demand is higher in the eighties and nineties than it was in the seventies.

Looking at the individual items we find that the health sector accounts for about half of the average increase. But demands have also risen in the fields of defence, education, and perhaps children's day care.

On the strength of these data we conclude that expectations indeed rose in Denmark between 1979 and 1985. In other economically advanced countries there

Voting and Political Attitudes in Denmark

was a rise between 1985 and 1990. This is interesting because in several of these countries the political trend favoured liberalism at the expense of socialism — in Denmark the bourgeois government replaced the Social Democratic government in 1982. If we assume (rightly, as will be shown later) that bourgeois voters tend to have lower budget demands than socialist voters, then we are faced with the paradox that public opinion turned toward the left while party preferences turned toward the right. Denmark in this respect echoes the development in Great Britain, where public protest over the cuts in welfare soared, without, however, bringing down Mrs Thatcher's government.

From a superficial comparison of the net demand in Denmark with that of the countries represented by the ISSP survey it may seem that Denmark is not characterised by a high demand level. However, such a comparison is doubtful. Even though the eight items included in the ISSP are all included in the Danish 1994 survey, and seven of them are also included in the 1979 and 1990 surveys, in comparing those items that are common to these surveys it should be remembered that the wording is not the same and particularly that the Danish items only provide three response categories whereas the ISSP provides five. Thereby the Danish items probably induce more respondents to choose the middle response category of spending the same as now than does the ISSP wording. As the result, the net demand will probably be less positive when the Danish wording is used rather than the ISSP wording.

But the difference in wording does not prevent us from comparing the items with one another in regard to their popularity or internal relationship. It is clear from Table 7.3 that the aggregate demand differs strongly between policy areas. Both in 1990 and in 1994 the demands for government spending for health and old age pensions is at the top of the list, while spending for military purposes is at the bottom. This rating of priorities for government spending is certainly not unique to Denmark; an impressive correlation of r=.99 is found for example between the Danish 1990 data in Table 7.3 and the Norwegian data from the ISSP 1990 survey (N=7). Smaller but still significant correlations are found with the West German, Dutch, or British data. Hence the rating in Table 7.3 is rather typical of the European welfare states of the past and present decade in spite of the substantial differences in welfare arrangements and in priorities between various welfare state models (e.g. Esping-Andersen 1990, 1996; Kolberg and Esping-Andersen 1991).

As the evidence is that expectations about the state have indeed risen, we must ask how this evidence affects the new politics thesis. That thesis anticipates a shift in political priorities, mainly from economic to non-economic policy goals, to occur in economically advanced societies. One may hypothesise that such a shift will also be reflected in budget demands even though the non-economic goals must here be formulated in economic terms. To illustrate, the postmaterialist or adherent of the new left will advocate that the government allot more means for such purposes as cleaning the environment, solving the problems of immigrants and refugees, and promoting culture and the arts; the adherent of the new right will oppose such expenditure as a waste of taxpayers' money.

The debate about overload, ungovernability, etc., began in 1975 and so precedes the debate about new politics. One can claim that the two theses are inconsistent with one another. The notion of rising expectations seems to imply that values do not change. The arguments in favour of rising expectations rest on an assumption that present demands continue into the future whether or not they are satisfied. However, the logic of asymmetry, according to which item-by-item expenditures will always add up to a budget increase, must imply that certain values with high priority will come to dominate the budget at the cost of other values with lower priority; how else can the budget be financed? In a sense, value change theory is a way out of the dilemma which the thesis of asymmetry has raised.

However, when looking at the budgetary demands from a new politics perspective, we observe immediately the broad similarity between the policy demands in 1979 and 1994. The main rise, as we noted, occurred in the field of health policy, a traditional concern of welfare societies. It is rather unsatisfactory to describe this as a case of value change. In order to keep on surer ground, however, we have to study the 'spending' items more closely.

7.5. The Structure of Spending Attitudes

Closely related to new politics theory is the theorising about political agendas, the aim of which is to predict which issues will be given highest attention and priority in political decision-making. These were discussed in the beginning of chapter 4 as a preliminary step toward analysis of short term forces in the 1994 election. However, the priority of issues may also be viewed in a value change perspective. According to that perspective agendas are not determined exclusively by political elites (or the necessities of the economic system, as traditional Marxist thinking concludes) and neither by pseudo-events invented by the mass media (as the theory of mass society assumes). Instead agendas are reflections of political values, taking into account the capacity and willingness of the prevailing political regime for satisfying those values. Thus, Inglehart's theory of postmaterialism leads more or less directly to an expectation that agenda items can be classified into two types, materialist and postmaterialist, and that in the long run the latter will replace the former. However, research has repeatedly found (Roller 1995) that there are not two but three main agendas in advanced western societies, (1) material security,

(2) physical security, and (3) the satisfaction of higher-order needs for self-fulfilment. Thus the materialist agenda breaks down into two, physical and material security (Flanagan 1987).

The priority of issues, or political agenda, can be expected to be reflected in budget demands. Just as people have different concerns, which give rise to different priorities or policy goals, we can suppose that they attempt to implement these goals by allotting the means for pursuing them — for example, to support different budget demands. We therefore hypothesise these types to emerge from a factor analysis of budget demands.

There are, however, various ways of conducting the factor analysis. Table 7.4 shows the result of a rotated factor analysis in 1994 of eight items indicating budget demands. The items chosen for analysis are those appearing also in the ISSP surveys of 1985 and 1990.

Table 7.4. Factor analysis of budget demands in eight policy areas 1994. (Varimax rotation)

	Factor 1	Factor 2	Factor 3
1. Old age pensions	.71	−.10	−.03
2. Health	.67	.16	.11
3. Unemployment benefits	.51	.13	−.30
4. Culture and arts	−.16	.77	−.01
5. Education	.40	.57	.08
6. Environmental protection	.18	.56	−.36
7. Defence	.25	.06	.76
8. Law enforcement	.31	.13	.63
Variance explained	23 %	15 %	13 %

The analysis resulted in three factors with eigenvalues above 1. These factors are fairly easy to interpret. Factor 1 includes spending on health, old age pensions, and unemployment benefits. These are the three policy fields most closely identified with the material security dimension for which the welfare state has been constructed.

Factor 2 includes spending on education, environment, and culture and the arts. Evidently this corresponds to needs for self-actualisation or self-fulfilment.

Factor 3 includes spending on the police and the defence. This is of course associated with the need for physical security.

Figure 7.2 plots the eight spending items on the two first factors. On the first factor the three welfare items cluster in the lower right corner of the diagram. The three items that concern nature and culture occupy the upper part of the diagram. Defence spending stands out in the lower left corner, while law enforcement seems to be aligned with welfare spending in the diagram because the diagram does not represent the third factor.

Figure 7.2.   *Rotated solution for attitudes to government spending in various policy fields. Denmark, 1994. X=Loadings on first factor, Y=Loadings on second factor*

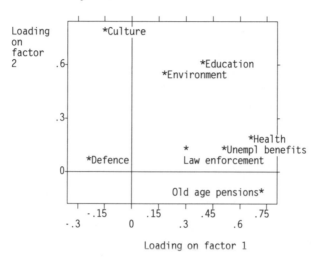

These eight items, as we said, were selected from our assortment of twenty because they matched the items in the ISSP survey. Factor analysis of that survey (Huseby 1995) indicates that typically the same three factors emerge in all countries. For convenience these factors have been termed *welfare-seeking*, *beauty-seeking*, and *order-seeking*, respectively (Borre 1995a). The only difference between countries worth mentioning is that in Britain and Italy, education policy belonged to the first dimension of welfare-seeking whereas in West Germany and Norway education belongs to the second dimension of beauty-seeking. Our guess is that as a policy field, education can be looked at either way, as some have suggested (e.g. Baker, Dalton, and Hildebrandt 1981, p. 142). It is not unreasonable to suggest that Italians and Britons look at education policy as satisfying material needs whereas West Germans, Norwegians and Danes look at it as satisfaction of higher needs.

7.6. Spending Attitudes and the MPM Dimension

Because postmaterialist theory argues that need-related values affect issue preferences, we need to clarify how these factors are related to Inglehart's value types. This can be done by constructing an index for each of the three factors that we found. For the next table, the responses to the spending items on old age pensions, health policy, and unemployment benefits were added into an index on welfare-seeking; the responses to the items on education policy, environmental protection and cultural policy were added into an index of beauty-seeking; and the responses to the items on law enforcement and defence policy were added into an index of order-seeking. Table 7.5 shows the correlations between these spending types and the value types devised by Inglehart.

Table 7.5.   Spending attitudes by value type. 1994. Per cent

	Materialist	Mixed	Postmaterialist	Corr. with PM
Welfare-seeking				
Positive score	79	78	76	
0 or negative	21	22	24	
Total	100	100	100	−.03
Beauty-seeking				
Positive score	35	49	72	
0 or negative	65	51	28	
Total	100	100	100	.25
Order-seeking				
Positive score	34	40	17	
0 or negative	66	60	83	
Total	100	100	100	−.16
Per cent of sample	15.6	68.9	15.6	

Note: Welfare-seeking is the no. of items out of nos. 1-3 in Table 7.4 on which the respondent would spend more, minus the no. on which he would spend less. Beauty-seeking is the corresponding measure for items 4-6, and order seeking the measure for items 7-8. Welfare- and beauty-seeking thus range from +3 to −3, order-seeking from +2 to −2. The three value types in the table heading are based on the conventional Inglehart items (Inglehart 1990, p. 74, items A-D).

It turns out that welfare-seeking is uncorrelated with postmaterialism (r=−.03), whereas beauty-seeking is fairly well positively correlated (r=.25) and order-seeking negatively correlated (r=−.16) with postmaterialism. The figures in the table also indicate that the proportion who may be called 'welfare-seekers' (as having a positive score on welfare-seeking) is 76-79 per cent among all three value types, while the proportion who are 'beauty-seekers' varies from 72 per cent among the postmaterialists to 35 among the materialists. Finally, the proportion who are 'order-seekers' is 34-40 per cent in the materialist and mixed categories but only 17 per cent among the postmaterialists.

It is quite as hypothesised that postmaterialists tend to demand spending on environmental protection, education, and culture, whereas materialists (and the mixed category) tend to demand spending on law enforcement and defence. The question of who are the welfare spenders is salomonically resolved: they occur with the same frequency in all three categories. Thus, two of the three factors of the rotated factor solution correspond roughly to Inglehart's value types while the third factor is neutral toward the value types. Unfortunately this factor deals with those policy fields which are particularly heavy in cost and on which nearly four-fifth of the voters demand more spending. Inglehart's value types are a good guide as long as we are talking about the relatively small items on the budget of the welfare state, but a poor guide when it comes to the big items which loom large on the public budgets.

7.7. Spending Attitudes and New Politics

Why is the postmaterialist theory inadequate in analysing welfare issues, at least in the Danish context? We suspect that the reason is, simply, that it argues a dimension which was designed to cut across the old left-right dimension; however, welfare issues are part of that older dimension. Therefore we expect these issues to be better handled within the new politics-old politics framework which we examined in chapter 2. That framework should also be adequate for treating the other agendas, beauty-seeking and order-seeking: we expect beauty-seeking to be associated with the new left, and order-seeking, with the new right. We shall therefore base our analysis on a distinction between the four ideological types defined in chapter 2:

1. *Left Wing*, combining the old left with new left positions,
2. *Old Socialists*, combining old left and new right positions,
3. *Green Bourgeois*, combining old right and new left positions, and
4. *Right Wing*, combining old right and new right positions.

Table 7.6 examines the difference in demands between these four ideological types.

The different items have been grouped according to which left-right dimension they fit into. The first set are mainly related to the old left-right dimension.

Job creation and *unemployment benefits* belong exclusively to the old left-right dimension: the group differences are 26-36 percentage points along the old dimension but only 1-5 points along the new dimension.

Also *Child care* expenses belong in the old dimension, with group differences of 24-28 points along that dimension vs. only 4-8 points along the new dimension; it is mainly an issue of the old left. Almost the same pattern occurs for *Job leaves*, which yield group differences of 28-29 points along the old dimension and only 9-10 along the new one. We may also classify *Public transportation* in the same category, as it shows 15-21 per cent differences along the old left-right dimension as against 10-16 per cent differences along the new dimension. Finally, *Large family support* and *Poor reliefs* are found in this category.

Table 7.6. *Spending attitudes of ideological types, 1994. Per cent favouring more spending minus per cent favouring less spending*

Spending on:	Ideological Type			
	Left Wing	Old Soc- ialists	Green Bourg.	Right Wing
1. Old politics items				
Job creation	16	15	−20	−15
Unemployment benefits	12	11	−18	−15
Child care	46	42	22	14
Job leaves	3	−12	−31	−41
Public transportation	26	10	5	−5
Child allowances	11	5	−5	−10
Poor reliefs	11	−7	−21	−29
Health care	80	81	51	67
Highways	−57	−49	−41	−39
2. Mixed items				
Education	58	44	42	27
Old age pensions	51	64	31	49
3. New politics items				
Anti-pollution	63	40	48	22
Culture	−11	−47	−23	−46
Refugees	6	−57	−9	−60
Defence	−48	−43	−29	−18
Police	37	58	47	61

The last two items in the set differ at some point from the others.

Health care expenditures belong to the old politics dimension as the group differences along that dimension are greater (14-29 percentage points) than along the new politics dimension (1-16 points). But they differ from the previous group of items in that the Right Wing is more inclined than the Green Bourgeois to demand increased spending.

Finally, *Highways* are the only budget item which belongs to the old left-right dimension and is, at the same time, a right-wing item.

Two important items exhibit a mixture of old and new politics differences.

Old age pensions belong equally in the old and the new dimensions, as group differences along the old dimension are 15-20 percentage points and along the new dimension, 13-18 points; the New Right here join forces with the Old Left, thus making pensions the favourite issue of the Old Socialists.

Education belongs equally in the two dimensions, as this item shows group differences of 16-17 percentage points along the old left-right dimension and 14-15 along the new one. But its direction on the new dimension is the reverse of the direction of old age pensions. It is primarily a demand pressed for by the Left Wing and resisted by the Right Wing.

The last set consist of five items belonging chiefly to the new left-right dimension. The first three are favoured especially by the new left, the last two by the new right.

Anti-pollution measures belong more to the new left-right dimension than to the old, as the group differences are 23-26 per cent in that direction vs. only 15-18 in the direction of the old left-right.

Cultural expenses, although not regarded with great sympathy by any of the groups, definitely belong to the new left-right dimension; the group differences are 23-36 per cent in that dimension but only 1-12 along the old dimension. The resistance is strong among both Old Socialists and the Right Wing.

Even more than cultural expenses, resistance against expenses for *Refugees* unites the new right against the new left. The group differences are no less than 51-63 percentage points along the new politics dimension and only 3-15 along the old dimension.

Of the two items favoured, relatively speaking, by the new right, expenditures for the *Police* are generally accepted. Their pattern shows that they chiefly belong to the new dimension, with group differences of 14-21 per cent against 3-10 per cent along the old dimension. *Defence* expenditures, by contrast, seem universally resisted, but display the same pattern as the police expenses, group differences of 19-25 percentage points along the new dimension vs. only 5-9 points along the old dimension.

As a general conclusion from Table 7.6, there appears to be a reasonable fit between the ideological types we derived from factor analysis of left-right ideological attitudes in chapter 2 and the latent axes underlying budget demands. However, one apparent difficulty in matching these two frameworks is to explain how the findings of *three* factors in Table 7.4 can be made to square with our concept of *two* politics dimensions leading to *four* ideological camps? For example one might expect factor 2 and factor 3 in Table 7.2 to coincide on the same factor, as they seem to be much like the new left and new right, respectively.

The connection may be hypothesised to be analogous to that which we proposed for the responsibility items. Since we are dealing with inclinations for raising or lowering the budget, we assume that the political left — whether of the old left or the new left variety — tends to be interventionist, while their opposite numbers on the old and new right tend to be liberal in the sense of advocating as little state activity as possible.

This view is confirmed if we study the total spending demands of the four ideological types (Table 7.7).

Table 7.7. Spending attitudes of ideological voter types, 1994. No. of items on which R wanted to spend more and spend less

	No. of Items			
	Spend more	Spend less	Diff-erence	No.
Left Wing	6.59	2.42	4.17	523
Old Socialists	6.43	3.71	2.72	601
Green Bourgeois	4.63	3.44	1.19	285
Right Wing	4.81	4.36	.45	612
All	5.73	3.53	2.20	2021

Note: A total of 20 items were asked; however, one (aid to developing countries) has been omitted because it also enters the definition of the ideological types.

The number of items on which the respondent wants the government to spend more is highest among the Left Wing (6.59) followed by the Old Socialists, while the Green Bourgeois mention the smallest number (4.63). The number of items on which the respondent wants the government to cut expenses is lowest on the Left Wing (2.42) and highest on the Right Wing (4.36), the Old Socialists being slightly more inclined to save than the Green Bourgeois. When the second number is subtracted from the first, however, the result is a consistent decline of the net no. of items singled out for expansion from 4.17 among the Left Wing to .45 among the Right Wing. That is, leftist position on both the old politics scale and the new politics scale are related with spending attitude, although the old politics position seems to be the more important of the two. This also becomes clear if we look at the correlations (not shown) between spending attitudes and the old and new politics positions from which the ideological camps were operationally defined. The Pearson correlation between the net no. of items suggested for expanding the budget and leftist position is substantial, especially its correlation with old politics position ($r=.42$), whereas its correlation with new politics position is somewhat lower ($r=.26$), exactly what Table 7.7 suggests.

Thus there may well be an overall interventionist-liberal dimension constituting the main dimension in responses to spending items. When this dimension is taken care of, the next question is: spending for what purpose? This is the point where we should expect the new left and the old left to part company. The old left should advocate spending for the traditional welfare purposes and particularly for the purpose of promoting economic equality. The old right naturally opposes spending for these purposes, whereas the new left and right do not have quite so strong feelings in this regard.

The new left, however, should advocate spending for different purposes, namely protection of the environment and cultural purposes. Here they are vehemently opposed by the new right. The old left and right are expected to remain fairly neutral on these policy items. For example, spending on culture may be attractive to some people on the old right both because they represent the classical taste in art and because supporting culture may mean creating national symbols, which is quite in the style of traditional conservatism.

According to this reasoning we should turn to the *unrotated* factor solution for a test. The first factor (principal component) should be a general interventionist/-liberal factor on which all kinds of expenditure load positively except items that are associated with the liberal minimal state: defence and law enforcement. The second factor, running at a right angle to the first, should be a new politics factor sorting out old left interventionism from new left interventionism.

Table 7.8 and Figure 7.3 present the unrotated solution for the same eight items that Table 7.4 analysed.

Figure 7.3. *Principal components solution for attitudes to government spending in various policy fields. Denmark, 1994. X=Loadings on first factor, Y=Loadings on second factor*

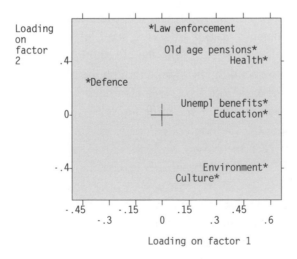

Voting and Political Attitudes in Denmark

Table 7.8. Factor analysis of budget demands in eight policy areas 1994 (unrotated)

	Factor 1	Factor 2
1. Old age pensions	.51	.48
2. Health	.56	.40
3. Unemployment benefits	.57	.09
4. Education	.58	.00
5. Environmental protection	.56	−.39
6. Culture and arts	.29	−.50
7. Law enforcement	−.07	.64
8. Defence	−.43	.24
Variance explained	23 %	16 %

Looking at Table 7.8 we observe that the first factor or principal component shows positive loadings for six policy items and negative for law enforcement and defence. Consequently it is clearly the old interventionist factor dividing left and right. The hallmark of economic liberalism, which found its political expression in Denmark from the middle of the 19th century, was precisely that it favoured state expenditure for no other purposes than internal and external security. This basic principle has carried over from the old politics to the new politics dimension with the result that the first factor separates the old and new right (with low scores) from the old and new left (with high scores).

The second factor gives high positive loadings to old age pension and health, loadings around zero for unemployment benefits and education, and high negative loadings for cultural purposes and environmental protection. This reflects the conflict between the old left and the new left as to which direction the budget ought to take. The old left emphasises the material security items of the welfare state whereas the new left pushes forward towards quality of life items. In the diagram the priorities of the old left are located in the upper right quadrangle, and the priorities of the new left, in the lower right quadrangle. In the upper right quadrangle we find the liberalist's agenda of limiting government spending to external and internal security.

Although the pattern could be better clustered in accordance with our expectations, it roughly fits the line of reasoning underlying the old politics-new politics scheme. Long-term shifts in the tasks of government have taken place, first from an original emphasis on physical security (represented in the upper left corner of Figure 7.3) toward an emphasis on welfare (the upper right corner), and lately toward an emphasis on environmental and cultural matters (the lower right corner). Thus the hypothesis of the three-way agenda is supported by the factor analysis.

The precise relationship between the three-way agenda, as based on the factor analysis, and the two issue dimensions and four ideological types which we defined in chapter 2, is given in Table 7.9.

Table 7.9. Spending attitudes of ideological types, 1994

	Welfare items	Beauty items	Order items	(N)
Opinion balance of ideological type:				
Left Wing	+53	+28	−5	(441)
Old socialists	+53	−4	+9	(509)
Green Bourgeois	+27	+14	+9	(247)
Right Wing	+33	−14	+22	(518)
Regression effect of:				
Old politics position (beta)	−.41**	−.11**	.19**	
New politics position (beta)	.05*	−.40**	.20**	
Multiple correlation (R)	.41	.44	.31	

Notes: Welfare items are old-age pensioners, health, unemployment benefits, and education. Beauty items are environmental protection, culture and arts. Order items are law enforcement and defence. — The opinion balance is the per cent who think government is spending too little minus the per cent who think it is spending too much, averaged for the items in the index. — For the definition of ideological types, old and new politics position, see chapter 2, Tables 2.1 and 2.2. — Positive beta effects indicate that the items are preferred by voters on the right, negative effects, that they are preferred on the left.

Although among all four ideological types there is a majority in favour of greater government expenditures for the welfare items, the Left Wing and the Old Socialist are clearly in the lead with opinion balances of +53 percentage points each. Thus the spending attitude on these items is influenced almost solely by the respondent's old politics position, which is also observed in the regression equation in the lower half of the table.

As regards expenditures for 'beauty items' (environmental protection, culture and the arts) there is a majority in favour of spending among the Left Wing and the Green Bourgeois, but a majority in favour of saving among the Old socialists and the Right Wing. The attitude is therefore mainly influenced by the respondent's new politics position, although the old politics position also is seen to have a significant effect.

Finally, as regards order items (law enforcement and defence) those on the Left Wing tend to be against, whereas those on the Right Wing tend to be in favour of greater expenditures. The two remaining categories take a middle position. Consequently the regression analysis shows that both the old and the new politics position influence the stand of the respondent. As we hypothesised, the old and the new right join forces in strengthening the institutions belonging to these policy areas.

7.8. Spending Attitudes of Government and Opposition Voters

The government, formed by the Social Democratic party in coalition with three smaller centre parties, was suspended between the main opposition on its right and the smaller left wing opposition. The views on the public budgets naturally differed between these three main blocks. It is of some interest to pinpoint the policy items on which this conflict was particularly acute, and those where alliances between any two of these three blocks were possible; in addition we might answer the hypothetical question, on which items would a take-over by a bourgeois government make the greatest difference.

Table 7.10 divides the respondents into the three camps of voters and indicates the attitude to spending on the eight items we have used for the purpose of defining the three types of spenders.

Table 7.10. *Spending attitudes among government and opposition voters, 1994. Net no. of items on which R wants to spend more*

	Left-wing opposition	Government voters	Bourgeois opposition
Spending on:			
Welfare policies	1.63	1.43	.91
Beauty policies	1.25	.62	.16
Order policies	−.45	.09	.43

Note: On the definition of welfare, beauty and order policies, see note of Table 7.4.

In all three areas, the mean position of government voters lies between the means of the left and right opposition. However, with respect to spending on welfare items they are fairly near to the left wing voters, whereas with respect to spending on police and defence, as well as on culture and environment, government voters take a more straight down the middle position between the two sides of the opposition.

In fact there is not a single item out of the twenty spending items in the Danish 1994 questionnaire on which the mean of government voters is not located between the two means of the opposition camps. The responses of the three camps of voters have almost the appearance of spinal reactions based on indoctrinated left-right ideology. Those on the left wing overbid the government voters in every policy field apart from the police and defence. Those to the right of government underbid the government voters in every policy field except police and defence.

This does not mean that the bourgeois opposition voters on balance want to cut expenses. It is evident from Table 7.10 that even bourgeois voters take a positive stand on the expansion of welfare expenditures (.91). However, they are more positive toward a 'politics of order' than toward a 'politics of beauty' (.43 against .16). The general picture, one might say, is one of unabashed overspending — the only instance of net saving is the left wing attitude toward the police and defence.

The uniformity of the positions of these three voter camps, no matter in which policy field we are dealing, once again points to the strong impact of left-right ideology on the spending attitudes.

7.9. Impact of Ideology and Social Background on Beliefs in Government

We began this chapter by arguing that rather than income or specific interest tied to social positions, ideology and values were the chief determinants of the role which the citizens assign to their government. In the course of our analysis we have differentiated between policy areas indicating different functions of government or types of demand so as to demonstrate that these demands are consistent with the ideological types which we earlier introduced and which are related to basic political values. The new left nurtures different ideas about society than did the old left, just as the new right manifests different ideas than did the old right.

Consequently the left-right axis has come to incorporate positions on the new, mainly non-material issues in addition to expressing positions on the older economic issues. These positions also reflect beliefs about the proper role of government, or the state. Put simply, the new left wants an even more active state than did the old left, whereas the new right wants an even less active state than did the old right (cf. Table 7.7).

Following our approach in this chapter we expect these ideological viewpoints to override the usual social background variables in accounting for the two types of beliefs in government discussed in this chapter. For a summary test of this hypothesis we have confronted left-right ideological position with four types of socioeconomic position in two regression models in Table 7.11.

The two regression models deal with the *degree* and *range* dimension of government respectively, but it should be noted from the outset that these two dimensions are fairly highly correlated in people's minds: the correlation between the two dependent variables is r=.45.

Table 7.11.   *Impact of ideological and social position on beliefs about the scope of government, 1994 (beta effects and T values)*

	Net spending		Gov. responsibility	
	Beta	T	Beta	T
Left-Right Position	−.35	−15.1	−.29	−12.3
Household Income	−.02	−.7	−.11	−4.8
School Education	.06	2.6	−.02	−.9
Working Class Id.	.07	3.1	.10	4.0
Female Sex	.11	4.9	.05	2.3
Multiple Correlation	.40		.37	
N	1674		1674	

Note: Left-right position coded from 1 (left) through 10 (right), household income coded 1-8, school education 1-4, and class identification from 5 (working class id.) through 1 (middle class id.). Net spending is the no. of budget items on which respondent wanted to spend more minus the no. on which he/she wanted to spend less, coded from +20 to −20. Government responsibility is an additive index of responses to ten items, each coded 5=definitely yes, 4=probably yes, 3=don't know, 2=probably no, and 1=definitely no.

The table shows that by far the strongest impact on both of these types of beliefs or demands comes from respondent's left-right self-placement, resulting in T values over 10 in both regression models. Of the social position variables gender is particularly important for the spending demands, women demanding more government spending than men (T value close to 5). In respect to assigning responsibilities to the government, people with working-class identification and people with low income are more likely to demand an active state (T values between 4 and 5). It is therefore the workers and the low-income groups who want to extend the government's responsibility whereas it is particularly the women who want a bigger budget. This is broadly consistent with public choice theory, but the importance of these social factors is to a great extent eclipsed by the ideological factor, which alone accounts for more than four-fifths of the multiple correlation.

7.10. Conclusion

Both spending and responsibility attitudes have turned out to have a strong ideological or value component, making them part of larger belief structures. The old conflict between socialism and liberalism over the economic tasks of the state is carried on in these structures and supplemented with a newer conflict over tasks in the fields of quality of life.

However, we have noticed that spending attitudes also have another component, cutting across the ideological or value component. This is the policy-driven tendency of spending demands in some fields to rise, in others to decline. During the 1980s spending demands rose seemingly in reaction to declared or actually executed cuts in the health sector and the educational sector (Table 7.3); during the early 1990s expenditures for cultural purposes and aid to developing countries fell in public disgrace, although they are favoured by the fast-growing share of the population with higher education. However, no direct paths of causality run from these changing demands to aggregate vote changes. The bourgeois four-party government was able to continue until 1988; when at last it fell, this was because it overplayed its hand on the foreign policy. And when the Social Democratic government came to power early in 1993, the direct reason again was not dissatisfaction with the previous government's budget or economic results but a case in which its administration of the refugee policy had been ruled illegal. Apparently we should not regard it as a major threat to a government that it cannot satisfy its customers' economic demands every time, as rational theory tends to assume. This chapter has treated voter's expectations of the government in a very general way. It has established certain properties of the overall level and structure of these expectations. But referring to the relations that were sketched in the beginning of the chapter (section 7.1), we must anticipate that demands are not causally related to policy output or political support in any simple and direct fashion. We need to study these demands more closely in conjunction with real and perceived policies and policy outcomes. This will be done for three critical policy areas in the next three chapters.

8

WELFARE STATE LEGITIMACY AND NEW SOCIAL DIVISIONS

8.1. Introduction

Whereas the previous chapter analysed the political divisions in attitudes to the scope of government, this chapter is concerned with the role of the welfare state in the cohesion of society. Whereas it is generally acknowledged that the welfare state has played a major role in integrating the working class and extending full citizenship to all groups in society (Marshall 1949), the intellectual debate since the 1970s has been more concerned with the internal and external threats to the maintenance of the welfare state and its integrating capabilities.

The optimistic arguments of the 1960s about the role of the welfare state in moderating class conflicts, even towards an 'end of ideology' (Bell 1960; Lipset 1964) were soon to be challenged. The first generation of criticism was mainly concerned with change or resurgence of class conflicts. Thus Wilensky (1975) predicted that the rise of the 'middle mass' of white collar workers and better-off manuals would gradually undermine welfare state support. However, while having some plausibility in the context of residual welfare states, this argument was far less relevant to European welfare states as 'the middle mass' is as much a part of the welfare state as the lower classes — be it through social insurance arrangements of the continental European type or through the universalism and extensive service provision of the Scandinavian welfare model (Esping-Andersen 1990).

Unlike the 'industrial society'/'end of ideology' theorists, Marxists did not believe that the class struggle had died. The integration of the working class by welfare arrangements was essentially seen as a sort of 'bribery' — a 'cash nexus' legitimacy which would erode as the welfare state became unable to satisfy rising expectations (Habermas 1973).

By these arguments, the Marxists anticipated the second generation of theories questioning the legitimacy of the welfare state. Thus, the 'demand overload' literature (King 1975; Birch 1984) expected that the inability to meet rising expectations under conditions of low economic growth, combined with fiscal illusions, would leave government in a state of economic and moral bankruptcy (Rose & Peters 1978). By now, we know that these arguments were exaggerated: the welfare state survived the economic crises of the 1980s, legitimacy was maintained, and if anything, governments were strengthened *vis-à-vis* organised interests in society. Although important dynamics were identified, the literature failed to take account of the mobilisation of crisis awareness, of learning processes, and of adjustment of expectations that could make retrenchment policies acceptable (Petersen et al. 1987; Goul Andersen 1994; Confalonieri & Newton 1995; Borre and Scarbrough 1995).

Although the discussion about 'demand overload' has survived in the 1990s, new critical arguments over and above overload and legitimacy problems are also brought to the forefront.[1]

One major complex of problems is concerned with the changes at the labour market, which, in turn, are related to deep-reaching technological changes as well to changes in the international division of labour. Thus, one of the most influential debates among sociologists has been about the visions of a 'two thirds society' (Dahrendorf 1988) where large groups of the low-productive segments of the labour force are marginalised, not only at the labour market but also in society at large. Among economists, concern is more with financing social transfers for the marginalised along with the increasing members of pensioners and other groups outside the labour market. But the two traditions often meet in the prediction of an increasing political polarisation between the 'insiders' and 'outsiders' at the labour market. Whereas the maintenance of political trust and system legitimacy among the 'outsiders' was the major concern in the 1970s and 1980s, recent discussions are more concerned with the maintenance of solidarity among the 'outsiders'. Next, not least in a Scandinavian contest, this discussion must also include the public employees (Dunleavy 1980; Pöntinen & Uusitalo 1986; Kristensen 1987) who increasingly distinguish themselves politically from the privately employed, in particular in Denmark (cf. chapter 5). Are we facing a decline in welfare legitimacy due to an increasing polarisation between 'insiders' and 'outsiders', or between privately employed 'insiders' on the one hand and public employers and publicly supported 'outsiders' on the other? This is one of the main questions of this chapter.

Finally, we shall briefly consider another argument which also originated in the Marxist critique of the 1970s (Offe 1984) and is concerned with the dangers of paternalism. This includes Habermas' (1981) classic arguments about the 'colonisation of the life world by the system world', or, more specifically, arguments that the welfare state tends to turn people into clients (Rold Andersen 1984; Ministry of Finance 1988). Again, social change may be an important conditioning factor:

---

1. We are of course unable to discuss all relevant welfare state problems here. In particular, we shall leave aside (1) the question of the effects of immigration; (2) the question of whether people undermine the welfare state through fraud and abuse; and (3) the economic problems *as such*, i.e. the question of financial pressures due to ageing populations, labour market exclusion, economic disincentives and inflexible labour markets (for an overview, see Goul Andersen 1997).

other things being equal, increasing social differentiation and individualisation make it more difficult for public service institutions to satisfy ever more different demands, while higher educational attainments increase the level of expectations.

As to the last argument, we hypothesise that the feeling of paternalism among welfare state clients as well as among the citizens at large may depend very much on institutional characteristics. 'Empowerment' factors such as the amount of influence opportunities (voice and exit) granted to clients and citizens may be decisive. This does not only imply differences over time or between countries but also significant differences between different parts of the public sector (Hoff 1993). Although the danger of paternalism is always present, we hypothesise that this is not considered a major problem among Danish voters.

As to the other arguments, we have two major objections. The first is the question of models which seem to converge on assumptions of self-interested, and myopic, actors akin came to those of rational choice theory. Although self-interests are undoubtedly relevant for welfare state attitudes, we assume that people are also guided by internalised values, sometimes by conflicting values. This focuses attention on shared values in society, as well as to values rooted in differences in (way of) life-experiences: generation, gender and social class are among the potentially important variables here (Goul Andersen 1992b).

Secondly, welfare states differ. Employing the ideal types of Esping-Andersen (1990) and others, we may suggest that residual/liberal welfare states tend to produce strong divisions between the poor and the better-off; corporative/conservative welfare states tend to produce strong divisions between insiders and outsiders; and the universalist/social democratic welfare states in Scandinavia tend to be the most integrative. This derives partly from the relatively generous social security for the poor and the outsiders in the Scandinavian model, partly from its emphasis on services which are consumed more or less equally by all groups in society. It goes without saying that unemployment is a cause of serious social problems but nevertheless, the Danish welfare state has been relatively successful in preventing labour market marginalisation from developing into social marginalisation, at least as judged from the economic conditions, the social and political participation, and the typical well-being of the unemployed (Goul Andersen & Hoff 1995; Goul Andersen 1996b).[2] Both the emphasis on service provisions and the measures against social

---

2. For instance, only three per cent of the households where the head of household is unemployed fall below the poverty line in Denmark; in the UK, the equivalent figure is nearly 50 per cent (Commission 1995; quoted in Goul Andersen 1996b).

marginalisation[3] lead us to expect a very limited polarisation in the Danish case. Finally, the unusually high labour market participation of women — most frequently on an (almost) full-time basis — along with social rights basically tied to the individual, limit the social consequences of unemployment as there is typically only one unemployed person within each family (though at the same time, more people experience unemployment within the family).

However, the very nature of the welfare state might also have the very opposite consequences. An unusually large segment of the economically active are public employees, and as demonstrated in chapter 5, the political divisions between private and public employees have widened almost constantly since the early 1970s. This could mean that, although Denmark may have turned into a one-third society in which the privately employed insiders constitute only one-third and public employees along with the outsiders constitute the remaining two-thirds of the population, it is still far from being a two-thirds society in which the reverse is the case. From a public choice perspective, one would certainly expect a one-third society to be a main source of division — such division might even make democracy impossible. Below, we also examine this scenario.

8.2. Welfare State Legitimacy — Basic Patterns

Earlier chapters have shown that welfare state attitudes constitute a separate and important cluster within mass attitudes to the scope of government in general (chapter 7), and that they relate to issues with high priority in the electoral choice (chapter 4). The present chapter therefore confronts the choice of welfare strategies or policies, that is, people's beliefs about the level, development, cost, effects, etc. of various programmes in the Danish welfare system and the concomitant support for these programmes from various sectors of society.

a. General Support
Like other studies, the 1994 election survey reveals a broad popular support for the welfare state (see also Nannestad & Paldam 1990; Goul Andersen 1992b). When asked if social reforms have gone too far, 63 per cent of the adult population in 1994 answered that the reforms should be maintained at least at the present level whereas only 28 per cent believed that reforms had gone too far (Table 8.1).[4]

---

3.   The list is longer: integration of the unemployed in the trade unions, emphasis on participatory values in the education system, and high priority to basic education should pull in the same direction.

4.   The changes over time are described in Table 1.5 and Table 7.3.

A standard argument against this 'conventional' interpretation is that it would be more accurate to ask explicitly about *preferences* as between welfare and taxes. However, in spite of several attempts by governing or opposition parties to put tax relief on the political agenda, it has not really been on the voters' agenda since 1975.[5] Furthermore, people have frequently declared themselves willing to pay higher taxes in order to improve particular public services (Goul Andersen 1995b, p. 33). However, yet another standard argument against the last-mentioned type of measures is they may involve an asymmetry as each spending item means very little to taxation; it is the aggregated effects that count for taxpayers (Kristensen 1987).

To solve this disagreement, two more questions were included in the survey. The first question was part of a battery where the respondents were asked which government alternative they regarded as the best to solve various problems. On the item 'ensure a proper balance between tax burden and social security', 40 per cent preferred the Social Democratic government whereas only 25 per cent preferred a bourgeois government, the rest being indifferent or in doubt. Responses/answers to the next question show that about one-half of the voters not only want to maintain but even want to expand the welfare state: when asked whether they would prefer lower taxes or improved public services if it became possible to lower taxes in the future, 47 per cent assigned priority to lower taxes but about the same proportion (44 per cent) preferred improved public services. This validates the interpretation of the first question, i.e. that most people really *do* want to maintain the welfare state. However, as the explicit reference to taxes in the two last-mentioned questions may differentiate more adequately, they have been combined into a simple additive index to be used in the analyses below.

---

5.   In 1990, the bourgeois minority government called for an election on a proposal for a (largely unfinanced) tax relief. 54 per cent of the voters answered that taxes was the most important issue in the *electoral campaign in the media* (Bille, Nielsen & Sauerberg 1992, p. 89) but although the voters were clearly aware of their personal advantages from the proposal (Goul Andersen 1994, p. 85), the proportion of voters regarding taxes as the most important issue declined from 20 to 9 per cent during the election campaign. In the 1990 election survey conducted immediately after the election, the proportion had dropped further to only 6 per cent. Unemployment, the economy, welfare and the environment were considered much more important.

Table 8.1. Basic welfare state attitudes, 1994. Percentages and PDI's in favour of welfare (percentage difference indexes)

	Agree	Dis-agree	Indifferent/Don't know	Total	PDI (in favour of welfare state)
1. Social reforms have gone too far*)	28	63	9	100	+35
2. Prefer bourgeois balance welfare and tax*)	25	40	35	100	+15
3. Prefer tax relief before improved public service*)	47	44	9	100	−3
Index: tax relief or more welfare (2+3)					+6
4. In the long run, we cannot afford to maintain the welfare state we have known	50	36	14	100	−14
5. The income transfers are getting beyond control	58	20	22	100	−38
Index: can Afford Welfare (4+5)					−27
6. The welfare state imposes paternalism guardianship upon its citizens	31	51	18	100	+20

*)   Wordings 1-3:
1.   "First a question about government spending on social programs.
      A says: we have gone too far with social reforms in this country. People should to a larger extent manage without social welfare and public contributions.
      B says: the social reforms already adopted in our country should be maintained, at least at the present level.
      — Do you agree mostly with A or with B?"
2.   "Who do you think are the best to solve the (following) problems... — The present government with its Social Democratic leadership, or a bourgeois government? ... To ensure a proper balance between tax burden and social security?"
3.   "If it becomes possible in the long run to lower taxation, what would you prefer: ... A: tax relief or B: improved public services?".
Combined index of 2 and 3: categories assigned values 1 (positive to welfare state); — 1 (negative to welfare state); 0 (neutral). Persons with don't know on both questions are treated as missing. The index is a simple additive index, divided by 2. This means that the figures are almost equivalent to PDI's.

b. Paternalism

Another classical argument, originally derived from Marxist theory, is concerned with paternalism guardianship as a source of legitimacy problems. Not the least in the Scandinavian model, with its extensive service provisions, citizens may be alienated by the frequent experiences with the bureaucratic rationality of the state (Rold Andersen 1984). However, as pointed out by Hoff (1993), the welfare state may be organised in many different ways: the availability of voice or exit mechanisms is an important determinant of the dependency of citizens, and may even change the bureaucratic rationality itself.[6] As measured by these criteria, the Danish welfare state must be judged as unusually responsive, and also most people are satisfied with their influence in most welfare institutions (Hoff 1993, 1995). By the same token, user satisfaction generally tends to be high; dissatisfaction is typically related to insufficient economic resources, not to problems of influence and responsiveness (Ministry of Finance 1993, 1995a).

In the election survey 1994, we have included only a single question about this aspect of legitimacy: an item stating that "The welfare state imposes guardianship upon its citizens". At this point, however, only a minority of 31 per cent answer affirmatively, and as we shall see below, affirmative answers are mainly found among the older generations. We may thus conclude that the Danish welfare state does not experience any serious legitimacy problems in this field.

c. Fiscal Problems

Rather than being concerned with taxes and guardianship, people are responsive to the argument that the welfare state is threatened by increasing burdens of income transfers. 58 per cent agreed that 'income transfers are getting beyond control', and 50 per cent agreed that "if we take a long view, it becomes impossible to maintain the welfare state as we know it today".[7] Of course, there may be an element of persuasion in these questions, and it is 'easy' to answer affirmatively. But it nevertheless appears to be a potentially important source of lower legitimacy. For further use, these two highly correlated questions are also combined into an additive index (constructed as above).

To sum up so far, most people appear satisfied with present welfare arrangements, satisfied with the balance between welfare and taxation, but troubled by the expected long-term economic implications.

d. Efficiency and Abuse

This description is incomplete, however, unless it is added that people also want 'value for money'. As pointed out by Svallfors (1989; see equivalent Danish data

---

6. Besides, as pointed out by Rothstein (1993), a guiding principle in the development of the Scandinavian welfare states since the 1930s was to provide the individual with resources in order to strengthen his or her autonomy rather than interfering with the clients' use of the transfers (see also Sandmo 1991).

7. These findings are analogous to our findings from a 1990 survey where people were asked about the causes of Denmark's economic problems. Here, the three most important items were 'The public sector is too large' (68 per cent), 'Too heavy burden of taxation' (56 per cent), and 'The policies of the Social Democratic governments before 1982' (54 per cent) (Goul Andersen 1991b).

in Hviid Nielsen 1994), general welfare state support is analytically and empirically distinct from the questions of efficiency and abuse. The questions concerning these dimensions are presented in Table 8.2.

Table 8.2. Attitudes towards welfare state efficiency, abuse, and redistribution. 1994. Percentages

	Agree	Dis-agree	Indifferent/ Don't know	Total	PDI (in favour of welfare state)
1. Higher productivity in private sector*)	72	4	24	100	–68
2. Many public activities could be performed better and cheaper if they were privatised	62	23	15	100	–39
3. It is still possible to save a lot of money by making the public sector more efficient without damaging the service delivered to citizens	62	26	12	100	–36
Index: efficiency					–49
4a. Too many people receive welfare services without really needing it	63	20	17	100	–43
4b. Far too many people abuse social systems	79	15	6	100	–64
5. Many unemployed don't really want a job	52	39	9	100	–13
Index: abuse					–33
6. High incomes should be taxed higher than today	46	37	17	100	+9
7. Child allowances should be abolished for people with good incomes	62	29	9	100	(+33)

*)   Wording: "In general, where do you think productivity is highest — in the public or in the private sector?"

Questions 4a and 4b were posed as alternative questions in the first and the second interview round (split-half) but are treated in indexes as a single question as variations in the two subsets of the sample are identical.

Not surprisingly, the public sector has a reputation for being less efficient than the private sector (question 1). More remarkably, a large majority also agree that a lot of services could be performed better and with lower costs if they were privatised (question 2). And despite much discussion about unbearable cuts in budgets, most people still believe that it would be possible to increase productivity without damaging the quality of the services delivered to citizens. Furthermore, a battery of privatisation questions in the survey (not presented) reveal that most people are quite positive towards experiments with privatisation of public services.

The scepticism about efficiency is confirmed by a concrete question concerning the health sector which has been subject to much public debate. Denmark is among the few countries that have been able to lower the proportion of GDP assigned to health expenditures, and public opinion has changed accordingly: since 1979 when only 35 per cent wanted to spend more on health care, demands have increased consistently, and by 1994, 74 per cent wanted to increase the health budgets (see also Table 7.3). But when asked about the main causes of crowded hospitals and long waiting lists, more people nevertheless believed that inefficiency was a problem (see Table 8.3): 75 per cent acknowledged the need for more resources but 82 per cent believed that lack of efficiency was part of the problem.

Table 8.3. Perceived causes of problems with overcrowded hospitals and waiting lists. Percentages

	Very important	Rather important	Less important	Don't know
Problems with work planning and poor exploitation of resources	49	33	14	4
Problems with insufficient budgets	39	36	23	3

Our questions on *abuse* (questions 4-5 in Table 8.2) may be too easy to answer affirmatively but indicate that people may be very critical towards abuse in spite of general support for the welfare state. As suspicion of abuse furthermore tends to spread into the working class and other low-status groups who normally support the welfare state, abuse is sometimes described as the Achilles heel of welfare state legitimacy (Svallfors 1989; see also for a distinction between substantial and procedural justice, Rothstein 1993). As pointed out above, it is not the only potential source of declining legitimacy, however. As far as the present level is concerned, time series show that perceptions of abuse were more widespread in the mid-1970s and have remained almost constant in recent years. Consequently, it does not seem that abuse is presently considered a very serious problem.

e. Specific Programmes

Voter attitudes to public expenditures were described in general in chapter 7. When we limit ourselves to the ten items concerning welfare expenditures, a factor analysis reveals three dimensions of welfare spending preferences,[8] revealed in Table 8.4.

---

8. Spending on unemployment benefits and on social assistance now constitute one common factor, and culture is dissociated from education because of a large number of questions of particular concern to families with children (questions of kindergartens, child allowances, and leave arrangements).

* *Care for the elderly and the sick.* As mentioned in chapter 7, virtually everybody agrees that these are public responsibilities. Furthermore, with the exception of the old-age pension (which was improved by 1988), people increasingly support spending for these purposes. It is the only area where a majority demand higher public expenditure.
* *Services and transfers to children (families) and the young.* Few people want to save on education and day-care institutions, nearly one-half want to spend more, and most people think that child allowances and parental leave spendings are appropriate. Parental leave (introduced in 1992/93) has the lowest priority, and a quite large minority want to save on this issue.
* *Unemployment benefits and social assistance.* The level of these transfers is typically regarded as appropriate unlike in the 1970s when they were frequently considered too generous. This change probably reflects the downward adjustment of average compensation rates for the unemployed from some 75 per cent in the mid-1970s to some 65 per cent in the mid-1990s (figures for the insured only).

Table 8.4. Attitudes toward public spending for various welfare purposes. Percentages and PDI's. (N=2021)

	The Government spends ...				PDI: too little — too much			
	too much	appro-priate	too little	don't know	1979	1985	1990	1994
1. The Health System	1	23	74	2	28	61	61	73
2. Rest homes	0	16	79	5	.	68	.	79
3. Home aid	1	21	74	4	.	.	.	73
4. Old-age pension	0	43	51	6	56	64	57	51
Index: publ.expend.: old & sick (1-4)								70
5. Education	2	48	44	6	22	44	45	42
6. Kindergardens and nursery homes	6	48	38	8	20	24	29	32
7. Child allowances	13	65	13	9	.	.	.	0
8. Leave arrangements	30	50	10	10	.	.	.	-20
Index: publ.expend: children & young (5-8)								25
9. Unemployment benefits (level)	12	69	12	7	-42	17	2	0
10. Social assistance (level)	22	54	11	13	.	30	-11	-11
Index: publ.expend: unemployed (9-10)								-06

Wording: "Now, I'd like to ask about your view on public expenditure for various purposes. For each purpose, please tell me if you think the public sector spends too much money, an appropriate amount, or too little for this purpose."

Like the above, we have constructed three additive indices for these attitudes. On most other budgets except the environment and the police, however, large proportions of the electorate want to save: 40 per cent want to save on culture, 42 per cent on aid to developing countries, and 41 per cent on support for refugees. Only 6-7 per cent want to spend more.[9] Finally, it is no great surprise that 55 per cent demand savings on public administration.

f. A Comment on Fiscal Illusions

In line with other recent studies (Sorensen 1992; Confalonieri & Newton 1995), the results above add some qualifications to the idea of fiscal illusions, i.e. the assumption that voters want lower taxes but at the same time demand more services from government:

* The premise that people want lower taxes is wrong. It is hardly on the voters' agenda, and 67 per cent agreed that "In the present economic situation, we cannot afford to lower taxes".[10]

* Among welfare issues, we only find absolute majorities for higher public spending on the basic issues of health care and care for the elderly.

* The finding that there is more support for increased spending than for budget cuts has been over-interpreted. In the first place, there is widespread support for budget cuts in quite a large number of areas. Secondly, although most of these budgets are small, demand for budget cuts include at least one very large area: public administration (this is a large area if we include sector administration in service institutions which is not counted as administration in public expenditure statistics). Finally, even though people may generally favour higher spending on such issues as health, this does not exclude the possibility that they may simultaneously want to save (or introduce user charges) on a number of concrete health programmes which are regarded as a sort of 'luxury'.

* If people still tend to demand more without being willing to pay for it, this need not be illusory if productivity increases are possible — and most people believe that they are.

To sum up, voters undoubtedly do have fiscal illusions but the conventional picture is highly exaggerated and it would be at least as accurate to say that voters have

---

9. The figures on culture and aid to developing countries may to some degree reflect the fact that Denmark spends unusually high amounts on these purposes (as per cent of GDP), see Ministry of Finance (1996a).

10. The figures reflect a strong persuasion effect but on an equivalent item concerning wage increases, there has been large fluctuations, including a majority expressing disagreement (Goul Andersen 1994).

illusions as to the possibilities of increasing productivity and of reducing administration costs. Even so, it seems not more illusory than the implicit assumption in the fiscal illusion literature that it is *not* possible to have more 'value for money' in the public sector.

g. Conclusions

We may also draw quite a few general conclusions from the marginals above:

* Basic welfare consensus. Virtually everybody believes that health care and pensions are definitely government responsibilities, and in the present Danish context, a large majority want to spend more on health care and care for the elderly.
* Policies matter. Time series on health care and unemployment benefits indicate that people do not simply demand more but adjust their demands to changing provisions.
* Governability. The data lend little support to theories of ungovernability as far as voters are concerned. Fiscal illusions and spending demands appear moderate, and surveys of political-psychological reactions to economic crises indicate that it is possible to mobilise a crisis awareness and acceptance of 'necessary' retrenchment policies.
* Satisfaction. Most people are sceptical about public sector efficiency and abuse, but they are basically satisfied with the present balance between taxes and welfare, and they disagree that the welfare state imposes guardianship upon its citizens.
* Threats to legitimacy. Potential legitimacy problems do not appear so much to lie in a lack of solidarity. Rather, abuse, inefficiency, and — not the least — financial problems are more serious threats.[11]

These findings by themselves indicate that welfare state legitimacy is not threatened by lack of solidarity. However, to test this assumption further, we turn to group variations, beginning with some of the 'conventional' divisions and subsequently proceeding to potential new divisions related to the public sector and to labour market position.

---

11. Apart from these problems, we have a few indications (not presented above) that people may be somewhat ambivalent in their attitude as to a choice between residualism and universalism. Most people do support the idea of universal, flat-rate pensions. But in other respects, people appear to be cross-pressured by the value that those who can provide for themselves should not be supported by the public. For instance, two-thirds of the respondents agree that 'child allowances should be abolished for people with good incomes'. This ambiguity deserves further analysis as it is a potentially dynamic one. However, we are not able to explore this issue further here.

8.3. Who Supports the Welfare State: The 'Middle' Groups

a. Age: The Middle Aged

As the main beneficiaries of public welfare are the young and the elderly, an interest perspective would lead to the prediction that these groups were the most favourably inclined towards the welfare state. Indeed, some findings in the literature do confirm this prediction (Huseby 1995; Pettersen 1995). However, from a cultural perspective and a perspective of social learning (which in this context is roughly the same as a socialisation perspective), we would expect the various generations to be affected by their experiences with the welfare system in their formative years, by their subsequent way of life experiences, and by the public debates and the general ideological climate, in particular at the early stage in life. Briefly, rather than a life-cycle explanation we are offered a generational explanation with different predictions about age variations: the generations socialised before the fully fledged welfare state in the 1960s should be critical about a too generous welfare state. Besides, the young generation is likely to be affected by the critical debates over welfare in recent years.

This is confirmed by the age patterns in Table 8.5. The middle-aged are the most likely to favour social reforms whereas the young and in particular the elderly are more inclined to believe that social reforms have gone too far. Even on the index of welfare vs. taxes, the taxpaying middle-aged groups assign highest priority to welfare. Similar variations are observed on concern for the economic problems ('can't afford welfare') and on social abuse. Attitudes to guardianship follow another pattern: a majority among the elderly think that the welfare state imposes guardianship upon its citizens whereas the young do not seem to experience this as a problem. All these age-related differences in attitude are hard to explain from an interest perspective.

Table 8.5. Welfare attitudes, by age. 1994. Index values and PDI's in favour of welfare (percentage points)

	18-24 years	25-29 years	30-44 years	45-59 years	60+ years	All	eta
Social reforms too far	32	44	46	42	15	35	.14
Welfare or tax relief	03	13	13	07	−05	06	.10
Can't afford welfare	−16	−20	−22	−26	−43	−27	.14
Paternalism	33	41	38	18	−14	20	.24
Efficiency	−55	−53	−45	−44	−54	−49	.08
Abuse	−39	−28	−16	−27	−58	−33	.23
Expenditure: old & sick	65	67	70	70	71	70	.06
Expenditure: children & young	41	34	33	22	08	25	.29
Expenditure: unemployed	−17	−08	01	01	−15	−06	.16
(N)	219	222	585	462	533	2021	

When it comes to concrete budgets, age patterns are more consistent with an interest perspective. Thus we find a strong negative association between age and the children/youth expenditure index. This might be interpreted also in terms of generational differences but a closer inspection of attitudes towards child care and education expenditures confirms an interest interpretation (see Table 8.6). From an interest perspective, one would predict that support for pre-school child care would decline sharply between the age of 35-39 and the age of 45-49 years. This is exactly what we find. And contradicting a generational interpretation, we have observed a similar (yet somewhat larger) break-off within the same age interval in 1985 (Goul Andersen 1992b). When it comes to public expenditures on education, we should expect the strongest support among those who attend some sort of education, and among their parents (with a peak around 40-44 years). Again, the prediction is confirmed. However, there remain some age differences among people aged more than 50 years which probably require a generational explanation.

Voting and Political Attitudes in Denmark

Table 8.6. Attitudes to child care and education budgets, by age. 1994. PDI's. Per cent favouring more minus per cent favouring less government expenditures

	Child Care	Education	(N)
18-19 years	48	75	52
20-24 years	47	64	167
25-29 years	45	51	222
30-34 years	46	45	194
35-39 years	46	47	202
40-44 years	35	54	189
45-49 years	28	47	195
50-54 years	24	37	138
55-59 years	19	38	129
60 years or more	15	23	533

Age differences in attitudes to spending on the old and the sick, on the other hand, are negligible; but as the elderly in Denmark were previously the *least* demanding even on the issue of pensions (Goul Andersen 1992b), at least the change since 1985 may be attributed to increasing awareness of interests. Finally, attitudes towards expenditures for the unemployed do not conform with an interest perspective which would predict negative attitudes among people above pension age but positive attitudes among the young (Pettersen 1995). However, only the former prediction is confirmed. The young are the most inclined to think that benefits are too high. This probably requires a generational explanation although the life cycle experience of relatively low or moderate wages among the young may also make unemployment benefits appear higher than among the middle-aged.

To sum up, attitudes to expenditures for children and the young was the only instance where we found empirical support for the interest perspective. Otherwise the differences between age groups (which are rather small but significant) are more readily explained as generational differences not related to immediate interests. And somewhat paradoxically, even the exception to the rule confirmed the general pattern that the welfare state is most popular among the middle aged, least popular among the elderly and the young.

b. Social Class: The 'Middle Mass'
As far as effects of social class are concerned, the predictions from an interest perspective and a culture perspective diverge only marginally, both perspectives predict a clear dividing line between employees and self-employed. Even though social rights such as unemployment benefits have been extended to the self-employed,

and even though employers' social contributions are very small in Denmark, self-employed have less interest in welfare state regulation than employees. However, whereas an interest perspective would predict a consistent relationship with social status, a cultural perspective would stress the difference between three ways of life (Højrup 1983), i.e. the way of life of the self-employed, the career-oriented way of life of the higher salariat and the wage earners' way of life of the majority. The way of life perspective implies that the differences between unskilled workers, skilled workers and lower-level salariat is unimportant.

The last-mentioned prediction is largely confirmed by our data (Table 8.7): the main dividing line is between 'ordinary employees' and the self-employed, with the higher salariat falling in between. This pattern is encountered in general attitudes to welfare as well as in the index on the costs of welfare. Even on the children/youth expenditure index (which includes education), and on the unemployment expenditure index, we find no significant differences between unskilled workers, skilled workers and lower salariat.

The only association which comes close to a status pattern is found with attitudes to spending for the old and the sick where one would not expect large status differences from an interest perspective as everybody can get old, sick or disabled. It may be argued, though, that the Danish system of flat-rate pensions based on citizenship rather than contributions, is advantageous for low-status groups and that lower-status groups have no alternative to public provision of health and care. At any rate, this provision of basic welfare is especially important to workers, and exactly at this point (health and care), people are very dissatisfied with insufficient welfare in the 1990s (Ministry of Finance 1995a, 1996c) a view/an attitude which is also reflected in the wish to increase expenditures. Clearly, workers have other welfare priorities than the better-educated middle class, and this may even contribute to an explanation of the turn to the right in 1994 (see chapter 5).

Otherwise the exceptions typically place manual workers among the more sceptical: manual workers tend to be more suspicious of abuse and inefficiency than lower-level non-manuals, and they are a bit more inclined to accuse the welfare state of guardianship. The suspicion of abuse is in accordance with earlier observations (Goul Andersen 1982; Svallfors 1989), and it is to some degree an effect of education.

Even though aggregate middle class support for the welfare state is a little below working class support — this becomes particularly clear if we focus on the private sector only — there is little or no class difference among the 75 per cent of the economically active who belong to the working class or to the lower salariat. What Wilensky labelled 'the middle mass' is the very core of the social basis of the welfare state in Denmark.

Table 8.7. Welfare attitudes by class, 1994. Index values and PDI's in favour of welfare among the economically active

	Unskilled worker	Skilled worker	Lower-level non-man. empl.	Higher-level non-man. empl.	Self-empl./ assist. spouse	eta
Social reforms too far	52	53	50	26	03	.19
Welfare or tax relief	19	17	15	−11	−44	.29
Can't afford welfare	−19	−15	−25	−31	−44	.12
Paternalism	22	32	41	36	−06	.22
Efficiency	−50	−57	−36	−54	−75	.21
Abuse	−17	−23	−01	−08	−42	.17
Expenditure: old & sick	78	74	72	54	61	.25
children & young	35	32	34	21	08	.24
unemployed	06	00	01	−09	−24	.19
(N)	263	180	560	174	147	
Per cent of econ.active pop.	21	14	40	14	11	

c. Income: Middle Incomes

Danish income taxes are among the most progressive in Europe (even after tax deductions for interests etc, see Ministry of Taxation 1990; Ministry of Finance 1996a; Goul Andersen 1997), and in particular transfers are highly redistributive (e.g. flat-rate pensions based on citizenship; nearly flat-rate unemployment benefits (in practice) with high compensation rates for low-income groups and long-term unemployed etc., see Goul Andersen 1992b, p. 232 for an overview). Thus, from a narrow interest perspective, there is every reason to believe that income would be a strong determinant of attitudes towards the welfare state.

But from the associations with age and class described above, it comes as no surprise that the association with income is a different one to that predicted by a narrow interest perspective (from this perspective, it is the uncontrolled rather than the controlled associations that are interesting). The associations are typically bell-shaped, that is, strictly contrary to Wilensky's predictions (1975), we find the most positive attitudes in the 'middle mass' and somewhat more negative attitudes among the lowest and (in particular) the highest income groups. Besides, the associations are weak, and we have to use a quite detailed income scale in order to catch the variations which are found only at the two extremes of the income scale (Table 8.8). A conventional trichotimisation into low, medium and high incomes would not show much variation.[12]

Even controls for third variables do not remove the bell-shaped association but only weaken it. Perhaps this may be related to the emphasis on service provisions. In particular, public child care means that medium-income families are often among the big consumers of public services. Although they may have quite a large deficit in their transactions with the public sector over the life cycle, the subjective balance may be positive: at least people are aware that they get something in return.[13] And above all, the public sector supports the way of life of modern, two-income families.

Table 8.8. Welfare attitudes by family income (in 1000 Dkk), 1994. Index values and PDI's in favour of welfare. Percentage points. Married or cohabiting only

	70-119	120-199	200-299	300-399	400-499	500-599	600+	total	eta
Social reforms too far	35	31	39	46	47	20	11	37	.12
Welfare or tax relief	08	10	13	15	09	−14	−31	05	.18
Can't afford welfare	−47	−26	−26	−24	−19	−31	−57	−28	.13
Paternalism	−33	17	13	25	38	27	39	21	.16
Efficiency	−39	−51	−48	−48	−43	−47	−58	−48	.08
Abuse	−61	−42	−41	−23	−18	−41	−36	−33	.16
Expenditure:									
old & sick	81	74	71	75	70	59	56	70	.19
children & young	20	17	23	28	28	23	22	24	.10
unemployed	−10	−11	−02	01	−02	−14	−14	−06	.13
(N)	40	161	232	315	252	111	70	1322	

There are a few issue variations in the general pattern described above. The efficiency index and the children and youth expenditure index are unrelated to income, and attitudes to guardianship are related in a way that is impossible to interpret. Finally, we do observe a straightforward, linear relation in one instance: attitudes towards

12. The results are basically the same, regardless of income concept (household income for all people, household income for cohabiting or married people, personal income for all respondents, or personal income for men).
13. In public debates, it is sometimes claimed that people paying high taxes are extremely eager to get something in return. However, no evidence or plausible arguments have been put forward to support this assumption, and in a universal welfare system, the opportunities for well-to-do people to exploit the system consciously are typically rather small (Rothstein 1993).

         Voting and Political Attitudes in Denmark

expenditure for the old and the sick — by tradition the core of welfare provision — are negatively related to income.

d. Gender

The Scandinavian welfare model has obviously been conducive to the improvement of the position of women on the labour market, and in society at large (Jensen 1996). Therefore it comes as no surprise that women are particularly favourable in their attitude to the welfare state (Table 8.9). The differences are mainly concentrated around four indices: tax relief versus welfare, public sector efficiency, children/youth expenditure, and spending for the old and the sick. The two first-mentioned gender effects are explainable in terms of interests (lower incomes, high frequency of public employment), and the preference for spending on child care, education and child allowances may be explained both in terms of interests and values. However, the most significant gender effect is found on spending for the old and the sick, i.e. for health care, care for disabled old people, and old-age pensions. Although some subtle interest arguments might be put forward to account for such variations, it seems more obvious to point at gender differences in values as a more likely explanation.

Table 8.9. *Welfare attitudes by gender, 1994. Index values and PDI's. Percentage points*

	Men	Women	eta
Social reforms too far	32	38	.03
Welfare or tax relief	−03	15	.13
Can't afford welfare	−26	−29	.02
Guardianship	21	18	.02
Efficiency	−56	−42	.12
Abuse	−21	−15	.04
Expenditure: old and sick	64	75	.18
children and young	21	31	.13
unemployed	−10	−2	.08
(N)	1017	1004	

Our data so far confirm the conventional finding that gender differences in attitudes to welfare are quite modest, perhaps even surprisingly modest. However, this may be an effect of question technique. When turning to priorities in economic policies (chapter 9), far more radical gender differences emerge.

e. Not only the Poor

Even though the Danish welfare state is among the most redistributive in the world (Ministry of Finance 1995b, 1996c), the social base of support is very broad. In particular, the majority of the middle class, the middle-aged, and the middle income groups support the welfare state at least as much as the working class, the young and the old, and the lower income groups. This does not mean that interests are entirely irrelevant (as witnessed by attitudes towards expenditure for children and youth) but it does mean that this sort of reasoning is not very important with regard to differences in attitudes towards the welfare state. Rather, it is culturally determined values and orientations that seem to be important. And overall, the social variations are relatively small.

Thus the conventional view of the welfare state as resting on a public consensus is confirmed. But is this consensus able to withstand new challenges of labour market marginalisation rooted in technological change, a new international division of labour, and perhaps even (as some economists would have it) in the disincentives and inflexibility of the welfare state itself? In the following we portray another view of the social structure, based on the relationship to the labour market and to the public sector, in order to test the proposition that we face an increasing polarisation between insiders or outsiders, that is, between privately employed insiders and people dependent on the public sector for their incomes.

8.4. A New Social Structure?

Since the mid-1970s, most European welfare states have experienced quite dramatic changes at the labour market. Because of technological change and a new international division of labour, structural unemployment has increased, concentrating particularly on the unskilled, the elderly, and other low-productive workers. Accordingly, there has been an increasing marginalisation on the labour market. Furthermore, some economists argue that this marginalisation is reinforced by welfare arrangements securing high minimum wages which makes it more difficult for low-productive workers to find a job at all. At any rate, unemployment and early retirement mean that an increasing proportion of the population are outside the labour market. In the 21st century, ageing populations will contribute further to increasing the part of the population that is supported by the public sector.

Roughly speaking, this is the background of speculations, both among public choice theorists and others inspired by economic actor models, as well as among sociologists, that we are facing a new social structure where the most important cleavages are no longer between classes but between groups with different positions *vis-à-vis* the labour market and the public sector. Not least among public choice theorists, divisions between public employees and the privately employed are frequently added to the list. In this and the following section, we describe the composition of the adult population according to their relationship to the labour market and the public sector and examine whether such new divisions are about to replace conventional political divisions according to social class.

As mentioned, not least the public choice theorists have argued that such divisions are increasingly important. However, public choice theories are based on a purely economic conception of social groups stressing their myopic self-interests *vis-à-vis* the public sector. From a sociological point of view, however, such a conception would seem highly inadequate and misleading as it ignores entirely the life trajectories of individuals, the effects of early and adult socialisation, the conditions of group structuring, etc. Briefly, from a sociological point of view the conception of actors in public choice theory is naïve and irrelevant to understanding political behaviour.

Still, even from a sociological point of view, such new divisions may be relevant. This holds not only for divisions between private and public employees but also for new divisions on the labour market to the extent that a new sort of class structuring is taking place (enabling the marginalised groups to form common identities), and to the extent that solidarity declines among the insiders, not only because of the economic burdens of transfers but mainly because of a loss of citizenship among the marginalised which places them more or less outside the community, subject to stigmatisation. In this and the following section, we examine to which degree such new divisions are taking place. In this section, we concentrate on the formal economic categories which in public choice theories are frequently believed to determine the interests of actors.

According to our survey estimates in Table 8.10, housewives and employed in the private sector encompass less than 35 per cent of the adult population; about one-fifth are public employees; and the remaining 45 per cent are publicly supported.[14] This means that public employees and the publically supported outnumber the gainfully employed in the private sector by about 1:2 whereas the ratio between publically supported and gainfully employed is about 4:5. It also emerges, however, that the majority of the publically supported are students, old-age

---

14. The survey-based figures are not exact measures of the size of the various categories but calculations on official statistics suggest that they are good estimates. Even though methods are increasingly developed to avoid double-counting in social and labour market statistics, these figures are not perfect either as they are based on the counting of recipients or contributors whereas our survey data are based upon (self reported) main employment status. Standard survey weighting does not affect the figures but it does seem that disablement pensioners and privately employed are a bit under-represented whereas most of the remaining categories, in particular public employees, are a bit over-represented in our survey.

pensiers and recipients of early retirement allowance; even if we include persons on leave arrangements, 'only' one sixth of the adult population are publically supported for *social* reasons.[15]

Table 8.10.   Categories of public employees, welfare recipients and state non-dependents. Election Survey 1994

		Percentage of adult population in survey+)
State non-dependents, total		**33.7**
Employees		25.3
	Manual workers	12.2	
	Non-manuals	12.3	
	Not classified	.8	
Self-employed, assisting spouse		7.1
Housewives		1.4
Public employees, total		**21.1**
	Manual workers	4.4	
	Non-manuals	16.4	
	Not classified	.3	
Publicly supported/Welfare Recipients, total		**45.2**
Students, pupils (largely supported by the state)		7.4
Unemployed (unemployment benefits or social assistance)*)		7.7
Parental, maternity, educational or sabbatical leave		2.8
Disabled/ Early retirement pensioners		5.1
Early retirement or transitional allowance		4.2
Old-age pensioners, state pensioners		17.4
Others		.6

+)   The sample is not perfectly representative. Privately employed, disablement pensioners and to some degree old-age pensioners are a little under-represented. But the deviations are relatively small.

*)   Including unemployed on parental leave.

---

15. Unlike much research in Scandinavia, we do not regard early retirement as much as a social problem but more as an extension of welfare (see also Zeuner & Nørregaard 1991).

Actually, the small proportion of gainfully employed in the private sector is not so extreme from a historical or comparative viewpoint. What *has* changed, and what *is* different in Denmark, is the fact that nearly all adults are entitled to some sort of transfer income if they are not gainfully employed. This *might* put a strong pressure on the solidarity of the employed. The polarisation hypothesis is based on the premise that welfare state attitudes are determined by self-interest. It may be formulated in two versions:

(1) As polarisation between the employed majority and the publically supported minority. With transfer expenditures increased, solidarity declines among the employed. Correspondingly, political trust declines among the publicly supported.

(2) As polarisation between people receiving their income from government and the non-dependent minority. Solidarity declines among the last-mentioned minority but they furthermore become increasingly distrustful as they have less and less political influence.

Our alternative hypothesis is that such a polarisation is not likely to occur because of shared values and little class structuration, i.e. because the 'outsiders' are very much part of ordinary social life — or because they are not really 'outsiders' but only retired persons or persons on their way to becoming 'insiders'.

Table 8.11 provides a general overview of basic welfare attitudes among the various groups. The results may be summarised as follows:

* There is almost no attitudinal difference between the gainfully employed and the publically supported. Only one eta coefficient is significant, and it is as low as .07. Besides, the publically supported do not have less confidence in politicians than the employed. Thus version 1 of the polarisation hypothesis is not confirmed.

* The second version is partly confirmed as employed in the private sector assign higher priority to tax relief than the two other groups (eta=.19). But the effect is small on the other two measures, and there is no difference in political trust.

* Group variations are moderate. No subgroup majority think that social reforms have gone too far, and all subgroups fear that welfare arrangements will become too expensive.

* Intra-group variations are much larger than variations between groups. This holds for class effects among privately employed and (except in one case) for group variations among the publically supported. The important divisions cut across the formal relationship to the public sector: workers, public employees and some publically supported groups are the most positive towards the welfare state; self-employed, higher non-manual employees in the private sector, and old-age pensioners are the most negative.

From this we may conclude that the *publically supported sector is mainly a formal umbrella category, not a group in any sociological sense.* In particular, three sub-groups diverge: students, old-age pensioners, and people on early retirement allowance.

Table 8.11.   *Basic welfare state attitudes, by labour market position. 1994. Indexes and PDI's in favour of the welfare state*

	Maintain social reforms		More welfare or lower taxes		Can afford welfare state		Political trust		(N)
	PDI	eta	Index	eta	Index	eta	PDI	eta	
1. Non-dependents[1]	29		−12		−32		06		682
2. Public employees	50		25		−23		18		427
3. Publically supported	32	.09***	11	.20***	−26	.05**	05	.05	912
Employed (1+2)	37		02		−29		10		1109
Publically supported (3)	32	.03	11	.07**	−26	.02	05	.02	912
Private income (1)	29		−12		−32		06		682
Public income (2+3)	38	.05*	16	.19**	−25	.05*	09	.02	1339
Publically supported:									
Students	28		16		−11		39		149
Unemployed	63		21		−13		−15		155
Parental & other leave	66		40		−04		−04		56
Disabled	49		18		−19		−04		104
Early Retirem. Allowance	19		08		−30		06		84
Old-age pensioner	12	.24***	−02	.18***	−44	.22***	06	.17***	351
Privately employed[1]									
Unskilled worker	42		08		−20		−09		127
Skilled worker	57		08		−15		02		121
Lower non-manual	37		−08		−38		11		166
Higher non-manual	04		−32		−42		30		84
Self-employed[2]	01		−46		−44		03		141
Housewives	43	.25***	14	.32***	−46	.18***	00	.11	28
Public employees:									
Manual worker	49		41		−24		02		85
Lower non-manual	52		25		−23		21		254
Higher non-manual	44	.04	05	.17*	−21	.01	24	.09	71

1)   Including housewives (and a few apprentices not presented in the table).
2)   Including wives working in husband's firm.
*   sig < .05
**   sig < .01
*** sig < .001.

To conclude, *the hypothesis which claims a polarisation between the employed and the publically supported, receives no data support at all.* As this is the version most frequently discussed, this is perhaps the most remarkable finding. Furthermore, even the second version which claims a division between people who receive their main income from the public sector and the privately employed (or privately supported) minority is confirmed only in one instance: privately employed are more inclined to prefer tax relief before improvements of welfare whereas the majority among public employees and, to a lesser degree, among the publically supported, have the opposite preference. But there is little effect on the other welfare variables and on political trust.

Whereas this might seem odd and surprising from an economic point of view, considering the immediate interests in welfare and taxes, the results are pretty self-evident from a sociological point of view. Old-age pensioners, people on early retirement allowance, and students are not publically supported for any *social* reasons but only as a stage in the *life-cycle*.[16] Receiving public support as a life cycle phenomenon cannot be expected to generate common outlooks or common identities in any broader sense. From a political-sociological point of view, only those who are publically supported for social reasons are relevant.

8.5. Labour Market Position and Welfare Attitudes among the 18-59 Years Old

Having established that there are no important attitudinal differences between the employed and the publically supported at the aggregate level, we now turn to the *sociologically* relevant categories. In the following, we examine if there is any polarisation in welfare attitudes between the employed and the publically supported among the 18-59 years old. Students are excluded from the analysis, and leave is treated as equivalent to unemployment, mainly because this classification is the most favourable to the polarisation hypothesis which we want to disprove. Further, we have distinguished between employed in the public and the private sector, and among the last-mentioned, we have sorted out those who have had some unemployment experience in the family within the last two years as a separate category.

---

16. The formal pension age in Denmark is 67 years, and persons on early retirement allowance are frequently referred to as a group which is publically supported for social reasons. However, this habit rests on an ideological bias without much connection to realities. Changing values concerning self-actualisation and leisure means that more and more people want to exploit the opportunities to leave the labour market at an early age, and the *de facto* pension age in Denmark is approaching 60 years as more than two-thirds expect to retire at the age of 60 or even earlier. That people retire because of rising expectations rather than for social reasons is confirmed also by the fact that the young expect to retire earlier than the older (Nørregaard 1996).

This leaves us with quite another description of the social structure (Table 8.12). From a perspective of political sociology, the relevant group of publically supported include only 20 per cent of the 18-59 years old (14 per cent of the adult population), even by the broadest possible definition that includes all unemployed, disablement pensioners and persons on leave.

Table 8.12. *Distribution of 18-59 years old (excluding students), according to labour market position. (A) As percentage of age group, and (B) As percentage of adult population*

	Percentage of age group	Percentage of adult population
1. Privately employed[1] without any unemployment or leave experience in family	30	20
2. Privately employed[1] with some unemployment or leave experience in family	19	13
3. Public employees	31	21
4. Publically supported	20	14
Total	100	68
(N)	1365	2021

1) Including housewives. Unemployment experience is defined as having been unemployed for at least one month within the last two years (or equivalent experience for spouse, children or parents). Publically supported include the unemployed, the disabled, and persons on leave.

Public employees constitute a larger group that includes 31 per cent of the age group. Another 49 per cent (33 per cent of the adult population) are privately employed or privately supported. However, quite a large proportion of this group has some sort of unemployment experience in the family within the last two years. There is no reason to believe that this group should feel no solidarity with the marginalised; thus we are in fact left with a small group of only 30 per cent (20 per cent of the adult population) who have no immediate interests in public services (*qua* public employees) or public transfers.

This illustrates that the premises even of the sociological discussion about an emerging two-thirds society are wrong: the discussion ignores the existence of a public sector, and it fails to recognise that people live in families. If there is any tendency towards polarisation, it is not between *economically* defined groups of insiders and outsiders. But there *may* be a polarisation between a small group of super-insiders and a small group of outsiders, with various groups in between who cannot be expected to support either pole. Even if there is a polarisation along an axis of marginalisation, the sheer size of the relevant groups thus makes the consequences less dramatic. This association is described below. Unfortunately, we are not at present able to control for (former) social class. But as a standard of comparison of the strength of the (uncontrolled) effects, we have chosen the effect of social class among the privately employed.

To begin with *general welfare state attitudes*, we should expect a strong increase in welfare state support as we move from the entirely state independents to public employees and publically supported. And we should expect to find negative welfare state attitudes among the first-mentioned group. Our data in Table 8.13 give some support to the first-mentioned but not to the last-mentioned prediction. On the question on social reforms, the PDI's increase from 25 among the entirely state independents to 62 among the publically supported. But in all groups, a majority deny that social reforms have gone too far. A similar pattern is found on the index concerning the financial problems of the welfare state: there are significant group differences but even the publically supported are worried about the financing of welfare. The strongest effect is found on the index measuring trade-off between tax relief and more welfare, with a range from −19 to +27. This is reflected in an eta coefficient as high as .28. Still, it is difficult to read any sort of welfare *hostility* into these answers. Furthermore, it turns out that class effects among the employed in the private sector are *stronger* on all three indices than the effects of labour market position.[17]

From an interest perspective, one should expect a sharp division between public employees and the other groups in attitudes to welfare state guardianship. The association runs in the predicted direction but it is very weak. Next, one might expect that the unemployed felt that they were clientilised. Again, the prediction is partly confirmed but differences are quite small. When it comes to *efficiency*, we should expect an even more clear division between public employees and others — and little difference between privately employed and publically supported. The first expectation is confirmed, and we observe a very strong association (eta=.35). But surprisingly, public employees receive quite a lot of support from the publically supported on this question. Finally it emerges that even the majority of public employees concede that productivity in the public sector is relatively low.

On the question of *abuse*, we should expect strong differences between publically supported and the employed but no difference between private and public employees. However, the last-mentioned prediction is not confirmed: public employees are

---

17. To control for possible spurious effects of unemployment experience (which is more widespread among workers), we have also performed an analysis of class effects among the entirely state independents but the coefficients were almost the same and remained higher than the effects of labour market position.

even less suspicious of abuse than the publically supported. Furthermore, we observe the same sign in all groups. On the other hand, there is a strong difference between publically supported and the 'super-insiders' on this issue, and at this point, labour market/sector divisions are stronger than class divisions.

Table 8.13.   *Welfare attitudes among 18-59 years old, by labour market position, 1994. Index values and PDI's in favour of welfare*

	Privately employed, no unem-ployment experience	Privately employed, some unem-ployment experience	Public em-ployees	Publically supported	Population average	Effect of labour market position[1] eta	Effect of social class[2] eta
Social reforms too far	25	37	52	62	35	.17	.23
Welfare or tax relief	−19	01	26	27	06	.28	.31
Can't Afford Welfare	−37	−24	−22	−09	−27	.14	.17
Guardianship	21	32	39	25	20	.08*	.14
Efficiency	−69	−61	−21	−43	−49	.35	.18
Abuse	−48	−30	−08	−17	−33	.22	.14
Expenditure: old & sick	67	68	70	78	70	.13	.29
children & young	21	29	33	34	25	.15	.29
unemployed	−15	−05	02	14	−06	.22	.19
Political trust[3]	15	−06	18	−11	08	.13	.11
(N)	406	263	417	279	2021		

1)   Based on the four categories in the table.
2)   Class division among the 18-59 years old; no sector division but same class division as among privately employed in Table 8.11.
3)   "How much trust do you have in Danish politicians in general?" ('great' or 'some' minus 'not much' or 'very little').

This is also encountered on the index on unemployment expenditures but the effect is surprisingly low and only marginally exceeds the effect of social class. On the other expenditure items, we find only marginal differences. As far as the publically supported is concerned, this is in accordance with an interest hypothesis. But from an interest perspective, it is highly surprising that *public employees do not deviate from the population average as far as attitudes to spending for the most important public services is concerned.*

The conventional wisdom is that political distrust is nourished by labour market marginalisation but as the private labour force with stable employment becomes a small minority of the population, these 'super-insiders' might well feel exploited and lose solidarity as well as political trust. However, our data confirm the conventional wisdom — with the addition that the association is weak.

To sum up, the conventional polarisation hypothesis is falsified but the modified hypothesis stating that there is a polarisation between the minority of 'super-insiders' and the outsiders aged less than 60 is partly confirmed. Still, it seems more appropriate to speak of interest-determined differences than about polarisation. Typically, the sign of the PDI's or indices are the same among the super-insiders and the outsiders; there are no signs of a breakdown of solidarity. Typically, deviations between the super-insiders and the population average are small. Maximum deviations are found on the questions of tax relief versus more welfare (25 index points), efficiency (20 index points), and abuse (15 index points). The remaining deviations do not exceed 10 index points. All these figures refer to uncontrolled effects: if we take account of the fact that manual workers predominate among the unemployed and disablement pensioners, the causal effects become even smaller. In other words, 18-59 years old who benefit from the welfare system are very positive towards maintaining the welfare system but by and large, they are joined by those who pay the bill. And besides, even the uncontrolled effects of labour market position are not stronger than the effects of social class. Finally, even conventional class polarisation is not very strong, and this is perhaps the most important point: overall, there is a large degree of consensus over the welfare state.

8.6. Conclusions

As we have seen, welfare attitudes tend to be overwhelmingly positive and quite homogeneous across social classes and groups except among the self-employed. The legitimacy of the Danish welfare state appears to be safely ensured unless the government loses control over the economy, over public expenditure, or both. Fear of future costs, fear of inefficiency, and fear of social abuse are among the potential threats to legitimacy whereas taxes seem to play an insignificant role. Most hypotheses concerning decline of legitimacy or decline of solidarity receive little or no support in our material. Typically, this is not very surprising either as the hypotheses were frequently formulated within the context of other welfare state models with less integrative capacities.

Despite severe problems for a minority of the unemployed, stigmatisation, social deroute, loss of citizenship and political polarisation between the employed and the unemployed have largely been avoided (Goul Andersen and Hoff 1995). It may be argued that Denmark more than other countries has pursued a sort of 'citizens' wage' policy which is exactly what is advocated by those liberal political theorists who believe that mass unemployment is more or less unavoidable (e.g. Dahrendorf

1988; Offe 1996; Loftager 1996). Whether this is an economically feasible course is questioned by most economists, and at least few would disagree that there may be serious side-effects in the long run if adjustments are not made regularly.

Thus, even if there are signs of a somewhat larger polarisation among the younger generations than among the middle-aged and older generations, the general conclusion is that Denmark has been successful in preventing excessive marginalisation and polarisation in society. Most of the long-term unemployed remain socially and politically integrated; welfare state support has largely been maintained by those who are entirely independent on public income; and if solidarity declines, its impact is bound to be limited as a huge majority of the population are *more or less* dependent on public income from time to time.

This does not mean that welfare state legitimacy is secured forever. But the future of welfare state legitimacy does not hinge upon any polarisation of attitudes or decline of solidarity associated with changes in the social structure. If the welfare state is perceived to suffer from inefficiency, abuse, or problems of financing, welfare state support may decline in the future; but in that case, support for the welfare state is likely to decline among *all* groups, even the 'outsiders'.

9

ATTITUDES TOWARDS UNEMPLOYMENT POLICIES

9.1. Introduction

Unemployment or marginalisation is generally recognised both as the most serious social problem and as the most serious economic threat to west European welfare states. Since 1975, unemployment has also invariably been among the most salient issues among Danish voters, typically the most salient issue. Nevertheless, since the mid-1970s, we find few signs that governments are punished or rewarded for their performance in terms of unemployment (Nannestad 1991; Paldam and Schneider 1980) — unlike in the 1960s when the issue was probably far less salient, at least if we may extrapolate from the first election survey in 1971.

The 1994 election confirms the absence of any association between government popularity and government performance in this field. The government was not very successful in lowering unemployment before the election but already from December 1993, *expectations* were greatly enhanced, and from June 1994, shortly before the election, a majority was convinced that unemployment would decline (see Figure 9.1). Nevertheless, the government was not rewarded in the election, and since 1994, government popularity has continued to decline in spite of a decline in unemployment by almost one third from 1994 to 1996.

There are several possible explanations for this paradox: voters may be less concerned about unemployment than indicated by their answers; or they may have little confidence in available policy options.

Figure 9.1. *Expectations about unemployment twelve months ahead, 1993-94.*
Per cent expecting unemployment will rise minus per cent expecting
it will fall

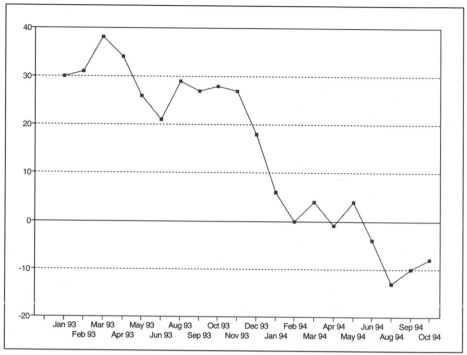

This chapter is only concerned with the last question, i.e. with analysing perceptions and attitudes towards unemployment policies. To which degree are such policies considered efficient, and to which degree are they considered acceptable? Do people at all hold firm convictions on these matters? To which degree do perceptions and opinions at the mass level conform with the policy proposals of the 'policy elites', i.e. with the proposals of public officials and other policy experts? This chapter begins with a typology of various policy strategies which are examined mainly on the basis of the 1994 election survey but supplemented by various other surveys to validate and complete the picture.

A typology of policies that have been pursued or suggested by governments, political parties, experts and others is presented in Figure 9.2. We have distinguished between five main strategies which encompass several concrete sub-strategies. As unemployment is a matter of imbalance between demand and supply in the labour market, we may begin with strategies aiming at increasing demand or reducing supply of labour power, respectively.

Voting and Political Attitudes in Denmark

(1) Strategies aiming at increasing demand for labour power encompass at least four different types of *growth strategies*:

— the consumption strategy: stimulating private consumption.
— the welfare strategy: expanding public consumption and jobs in public services
— the export strategy: enhancing the country's competitive powers
— the service strategy: subsidising low-productive household services

To some degree, this also represents a historical ordering. The consumption strategy was applied in the mid-1970s to combat unemployment after the first oil crisis but it only worsened the country's chronic balance of payment problems. Later in the 1970s, the welfare strategy was applied as a conscious 'switch policy' from private to public consumption as private consumption contained more imports.[1] But taxation and public deficits limited further exploitation of this instrument, and this left the export strategy as the only strategy that was considered feasible.[2] Later on, as the export strategy generated too few jobs, however, a service strategy subsidising labour-intensive household services was proposed. Although a household service programme was implemented in 1993, it has enjoyed half-hearted support from the government, and its impact has until now been small. Consequently, growth strategies in Denmark are, first and foremost, associated with export strategies.

(2) Strategies aiming at a reduction of labour supply have perhaps been the most exploited unemployment policies in Denmark as in most other European welfare states. This includes:

— shorter working hours (from 42½ hours a week in 1973 to 37 hours in the mid-1990s)
— longer holidays (from 4 to 5 weeks a year in 1979)
— early exit (early retirement allowance at the age of 60 from 1979; experiments with a transitional allowance from the age of 50 in 1992-95; and a steady, though unintended, increase in disablement pensions throughout the entire period)

---

1. With the (partial) exception of the period 1982-92 when bourgeois governments were in office, the welfare strategy has always been applied in the sense that there has been a constant but not always intended growth in the public service sector.
2. Besides, there was a significant change in policy measures. Until 1982, devaluation combined with incomes policy was the dominant export strategy but from 1982/83, the devaluation instrument was buried once and for all, along with indexation of wages. Later on, incomes policies were dropped as a means of achieving low wage increases in favour of labour market policies aimed to achieve greater flexibility in the labour market (Damsgaard Hansen et al. 1990).

Figure 9.2.   A Typology of Anti-Unemployment Policies, 1974-95

	Main strategy	Substrategies	Examples	
Demand/ supply strategies	**1. DEMAND STRATEGIES**			
		1.1. Export strategies	— Low wage increases — Low corporate taxes — Industrial policies	
		1.2. Consumption strategy	— Fiscal policies — Monetary policies	'Soft' strategies
		1.3. Welfare strategy: increasing public consumption		
		1.4. Service strategy: subsidising household services		
	2. REDUCTION OF LABOUR SUPPLY/JOB SHARING			
		2.1. Shorter working hours		
		2.2. Prohibition against overtime and side jobs		
		2.3. Early exit programmes		
		2.4. Leave programmes (e.g. parental and educational leave)		
		2.5. Share jobs by taking leave in turn ('garbage collectors' model')		
		2.6. Citizens' wage		
Structural strategies	**3. QUALIFICATION STRATEGIES**			
	3.1. Education programmes			
	3.2. Job training programmes			
	3.3. Individual plans of action			
	4. MARKET/INCENTIVE STRATEGIES			
		4.1. Subsidised employment of long-term unemployed		
		4.2. Lowering minimum wages	— in general — introduction wage for the young	'Hard' strategies
		4.3. Stronger incentives	— lower unemployment benefits — shorter periods of benefits — restricted access to benefits — rights according to seniority	
	5. STRONGER CONTROLS/STRONGER REQUIREMENTS			
	5.1. Stronger requirements as to mobility across trade borders			
	5.2. Stronger requirements as to geographical mobility			
	5.3. Workfare: duty to work in return for benefits			

— leave arrangements from 1992/93: parental leave, educational leave and sabbatical leave (to this comes significant improvements in maternity leave which were not designed, however, as a measure against unemployment).

Regulations of overtime and jobs on the side have only been adopted sporadically, and although the welfare state has been accused of 'introducing a citizens' wage through the back door', the idea of a citizens' wage has been strongly opposed among nearly all policy elites. The same holds for the idea of taking leave in turn so as to share jobs which was suggested by a union of garbage collectors (and subsequently labelled the 'garbage collectors' model'). This idea aroused much public discussion in 1993/1994.

Basically, the above-mentioned strategies are rooted in a perception of unemployment as a temporary phenomenon — or at least they may be considered most adequate under this assumption. Around 1988/89, however, there was a change in policy paradigm concerning unemployment. Now unemployment was basically conceived as a structural phenomenon (Ministry of Labour et al. 1989; Udredningsudvalget 1992). Among economists, structural unemployment is most frequently defined as the lowest possible unemployment compatible with a non-accelerating inflation rate (NAIRU). Structural unemployment derives from several sources, but in particular, the mismatch between high minimum wages and low productivity for the lower-educated segments of the labour force has been stressed as a major obstacle to an increase in employment.

(3) Within this paradigm, the third main strategy, supported by the Labour Movement, is the *qualification strategy* aiming to enhance productivity and increase flexibility. Denmark has for many years pursued a strategy of active labour market policies (although not to the same extent as in Sweden), offering education and job training etc. to the unemployed. Under the Labour Market Reform of 1993, this strategy was intensified, in particular by individual action plans for the unemployed.

(4) The fourth cluster of strategies could be called *market or incentive strategies*. In a free market, demand and supply of labour power are more likely to match but only at the expense of larger wage differentials and much lower minimum wages. The same effect may be obtained by subsidising the employment of the long-term unemployed. Another possibility is the lowering of minimum wages, either generally, or especially for young workers. This has often been suggested by economists but has never been implemented.[3] Finally, there are a large number of possibilities to *strengthen the incentives* of the unemployed to seek a job and to accept less favourable jobs: lower compensation rates for the unemployed (from 1975 to 1995, average compensation rates were lowered from 75 per cent to about 65 per cent),[4]

---

3.   Denmark has no legally decided minimum wage. Rather, a *de facto* minimum wage is agreed upon in collective negotiations between employers the unions. Indirectly, it is also supported by the level of welfare benefits.

4.   The Danish system of unemployment insurance follows the Ghent model, i.e. it is based upon voluntary membership of unemployment insurance funds which are largely controlled by the trade unions but mainly financed by the state (contributions constitute only a minor

shorter periods of full unemployment benefits, restrictions in access to obtain unemployment benefits (e.g. by demanding a longer period of contributions), or seniority rules relating the period of unemployment benefits to previous contributions as is common in many other countries.

(5) The fifth set of strategies comprises a strengthening of controls and requirements. This includes stronger requirements that people should accept jobs outside their trade or further away from where they live. In the 1990s, governments have also increasingly adhered to the idea of 'workfare' requiring the unemployed should work in return for their benefits rather than be 'passively supported', in order to avoid a 'dependency culture'.[5]

The list is not complete but encompasses most programmes and most proposals for reforms. Questions about attitudes towards most of these strategies have been included in the 1994 election survey, or in other surveys from the 1990s. As mentioned, one may distinguish between demand/supply strategies (1 and 2) and strategies based on a perception of unemployment as a structural phenomenon (3, 4 and 5). However, one may also distinguish between 'soft' strategies (1.2, 1.3, 1.4, 2, 3, and 4.1) and 'hard' strategies (all other strategies). Until the mid-1990s, 'hard' strategies were applied only to a limited extent whereas nearly all possible types of 'soft' strategies (except job sharing programmes) have been applied, although with rather limited success (Damsgaard Hansen et al. 1990; Mærkedahl et al. 1992). Below, we examine voters' attitudes towards these strategies. Although the aim of the analysis is basically explorative, we may formulate a number of hypotheses (not always mutually exclusive) as our point of departure.

In the first place, we may hypothesise that people in general have *little confidence in the programmes that have been adopted or suggested by public policy elites*. After twenty years of anti-unemployment policies it is likely that people are disillusioned not only about existing programmes but also by the alternatives that are suggested by the same elites.

Secondly, one could imagine that *people generally tend to prefer the 'soft' strategies*, or at least that the unemployed unambiguously prefer such strategies. Alternatively, one could suggest that the fight against unemployment *is a process*

---

part).

5.   This is not the place to discuss social policy problems but it may be mentioned that there are different conceptions of what contributes mostly to a 'dependency culture'. Some would argue that a right-based social security system with adequate support is a basic element of the Scandinavian welfare system which contributes much more to a strengthening of the autonomy of the individual whereas 'workfare' policies tend to be paternalistic and turn the unemployed into clients (Loftager 1996; see also Dean and Taylor-Gooby 1992).

of social learning (both at the mass level and at the elite level). This third hypothesis which overlaps with the first hypothesis implies that people may support 'hard' programmes if they are efficient, and gradually lose confidence in 'soft' programmes if they fail to fulfil the intentions.

Whereas the hypotheses above are concerned with differences between programmes, other hypotheses relates to the social variations in attitudes. Thus a fourth hypothesis is an *interest hypothesis* which suggests that people's attitudes depend on their employment status and on their risk of becoming unemployed. There may be two variants: in the first place, the unemployed may be more opposed to all sorts of unpleasant strategies than the unemployed; alternatively, following the insider/outsider theory (Lindbeck & Snower 1988), one might expect that the unemployed would be more favourable than the 'insiders' towards policy proposals such as lowering the minimum wages in order to provide more employment opportunities for the 'outsiders'.

However, we do not expect any of these interest hypotheses to be confirmed. On the contrary, we suppose that attitudinal divisions between the unemployed and the employed are small. Insider/outsider divisions tend to be weak in Denmark. In the first place, due to the Ghent system of unemployment insurance, the unemployed are typically trade union members. Secondly, insider/outsider divisions are strongly modified by the fact that Danish wage earners enjoy less security in employment than wage earners in most other countries: rather, social security is obtained by providing generous support for people who have become unemployed (Jensen 1989; Goul Andersen and Munk Christiansen 1991; Esping-Andersen 1996). This means that the trade unions have to consider the interests of the unemployed, and that the insiders are less protected against unemployment if they seek to take too much advantage of their insider position.

Our alternative hypothesis is that people do not follow such simple, rational calculations of immediate self-interests. Rather, we shall suggest that *social divisions tend to be small because of shared values* — be it shared values in the entire population, or values related to the way of life of different generations and different classes; at any rate, we hypothesise that it is values and perceptions rather than calculations of self-interests that count. This also means, however, that policy elites may persuade voters to change attitudes by changing their perceptions, changing their values or changing their perception of which values are involved.

9.2. Attitudes towards Various Unemployment Strategies

Growth Strategies

As mentioned, growth strategies based on a conscious stimulation of private consumption were largely dismissed in the 1970s because of the negative balance of payment-effects. In the mid-1980s, a similar lesson was drawn from a largely unintended expansion of private consumption, and in 1987-89, the balance of payment-problem had top priority on the voters' political agenda (Goul Andersen 1994, pp. 46-53). Therefore it comes as no surprise that voters tend to have little confidence in this strategy. According to a 'crisis survey' in 1994,[6] most people acknowledged that it might have *some* impact but only 9 per cent believed that it would have a *large* effect. This was the lowest proportion among all seven strategies mentioned in the survey (Table 9.1). Unfortunately, we have no measurement of the *attitudes to* this strategy but it is obvious that people have learned from experience. And it is likely that this has influenced the evaluations of the government's policies in 1993/94 which were to a large degree based on exactly this strategy (Regeringen 1993).

---

6. Conducted as the last survey in a series of 'Crisis Surveys' in 1982, 1986, 1988, 1990 and 1994. The 'crisis project' was directed by Prof. Eggert Petersen, Dep. of Psychology, University of Aarhus (see Petersen et al. 1996 for a description of the project).

Table 9.1. Evaluations of the efficiency of various strategies against unemployment. Crisis survey 1994. Percentages (N=1803)

Strategy (see Figure 9.2)	Large effect	Some effect	No effect	Adverse effect	Don't know	PDI: great effect minus no or adverse effect
1.2. Stimulate private consumption	9	54	31	3	3	−25
2.4. Parental leave programme	25	40	31	2	2	−8
2.5. Share jobs by taking leave in turn	38	43	15	2	2	+21
3.2. Job Training	18	43	35	2	2	−19
4.2.a. Introduction Wage for the young	15	42	37	3	3	−25
4.3.b. Lower Unemployment Benefits[1]	14	31	49	4	2	−39
5.2. Stronger duty to move for a job	15	35	42	5	3	−32

Wordings: "There is much disagreement among politicians, economists, and 'ordinary people' as to what should be done in order to fight unemployment. I shall mention some of the policies that have been applied already as well as some policies that are recently discussed. In each case, I should like to hear whether you think that this policy will be efficient in fighting unemployment. In your opinion, how much effect would it have to ...

1.2.   Stimulate larger private consumption.
2.4.   Provide parental leave (according to leave programme).
2.5.   To introduce the so-called 'garbage colletors' model', i.e. sharing jobs by working three weeks for normal wage and taking leave in the fourth week but with unemployment benefits.
3.2.   To provide job training for the unemployed.
4.2.a. To implement a lower 'introduction wage' for the young.
4.3.b. To lower unemployment benefits after a certain period, in order to enhance the incentives of the unemployed to seek a job.
5.2.   To tighten demands that the unemployed should be willing to move for a job."

In the 1994 election survey, the consumption strategy was not even included but respondents were asked to assign priorities between the three remaining growth strategies: the export strategy, the welfare strategy, and the service strategy. The results are presented in Table 9.2.

Table 9.2.   Preferred strategy to increase demand for labour power. Election survey 1994. Percentages (N=2021)

	Best strategy	Second best	Worst
1. Welfare strategy	42	31	17
2. Export strategy	46	30	14
3. Service strategy	5	27	57
None of these	1	3	3
Don't know/or no answer	6	9	9
Total	100	100	100

Wording: "During the past 20 years we have had three main strategies for creating more jobs. Which do you think it the best, and the second best:
1.   The welfare strategy: expanding the welfare state with more public employment to care for the old, for health care, and for other unsatisfied needs?
2.   The export strategy: we should give priority to manufacturing and exports by means of strong competitiveness and the service jobs this will generate?
3.   The service strategy: we should give priority to private services, e.g. by giving subsidies or tax deduction for home services?"

As expected, only a few respondents prefer the service strategy.[7] More surprisingly, a large proportion of the voters are attracted by the welfare strategy. 42 per cent think that this strategy should be preferred. Only a few more — 46 per cent — prefer the export strategy. As the welfare strategy is hardly even discussed among policy elites as a relevant option,[8] this is a very significant finding. It may indicate an absence of learning — or a disbelief in the economic philosophy of most policy elites. As revealed by the following sections, the last-mentioned interpretation is the most plausible.

Strategies Reducing Labour Supply
Like other west European welfare states, Denmark has applied various strategies to reduce labour supply, in particular early retirement allowance and leave programmes, and as in other welfare states, such programmes have almost been too successful. They are also popular among the population at large. From Table 9.1 it emerges that parental leave is regarded as one of the more efficient measures against unemployment. About two out of three want to maintain the leave programmes

---

7.   This does not mean that voters are *against* the service strategy. On another question, 60 per cent indicate that they are in favour of the home service programme, only 19 pct. are against, and 21 per cent have no opinion. People simply do not seem to believe that it will make much of a difference.
8.   At least not as a *conscious* measure. Unintentionally there has been a rapid increase in public employment since 1992/93.

(the weekly *Mandag Morgen* 31/1994), and an overwhelming majority want to maintain the early retirement allowance (the weekly *Mandag Morgen* 37/1995).

Table 9.3. *Voters' attitudes to early retirement and leave arrangements in general. Election survey 1994. Percentages*

	Leave and retirement arrangements
Should go much further	10
Should go a little further	19
Suitable as it is	43
Has gone a bit too far	17
Has gone much too far	6
Don't know	5
Total	100

Wording: "In the last years we have got programmes making it possible to take leave from the labour market permanently or temporarily. Some think we should go further in this direction while others think it has gone much too far. What do you think? Should we go much further, a little further, are present programmes appropriate, have present programmes gone a bit too far, or have we gone much too far?"

This is also confirmed by the election survey 1994. As revealed by Table 9.3, a majority support the general philosophy behind the retirement and leave programmes; but at the same time it is noteworthy that only 29 per cent think that these policies should proceed any further. 23 per cent believe that these policies have already gone too far. Thus it is not, therefore, a support entirely without qualifications. People are worried about the increasing costs of income transfers (see chapter 8), and the leave arrangements have been much criticised for having exactly this effect. Thus a learning process seems to be involved here.[9]

---

9. It might be argued that people's concern about the costs of income transfers is a mechanical reflection of what they are told. But it is more than that. From 1994 to 1996 when the debate was intensified, there has not only been a marked increase in people's concern about the costs of income transfers but also corresponding signs of a weaker support for the welfare state which seems to be rooted in this concern (the weekly *Mandag Morgen* 34/1996; Goul Andersen forthcoming).

Correspondingly, as shown in Table 9.4, a majority of 52 per cent prefer a strategy of economic growth over a strategy of sharing jobs (37 per cent).[10] These figures allow us to conclude that *generally speaking*, economic growth, in particular export-oriented growth, is the type of unemployment policies that enjoys the largest support.

Table 9.4. Priorities between growth strategies and job sharing strategies. Election survey 1994. Percentages

(A) Prefers job sharing	37
(B) Prefers growth strategy	52
Neither	6
Don't know	5
Total	100

Wording: "Then we have a question about economic growth and the fight against unemployment.

A says: We cannot count on a decline of unemployment. Therefore we must try to share the work that can be found.

B says: The best way to fight unemployment is by economic growth. Otherwise there will be no work to share."

The main battery of questions on unemployment strategies in the 1994 election survey allows us to explore the attitudes towards reduction of labour supply further. The battery included 11 different strategies and was designed to measure both perceptions of efficiency and approval/disapproval of policies. Economic growth strategies were not included in this battery.

If social learning is important, voters should be critical of plans to lower working hours. In the 1970s and 1980s, people appeared to view this strategy as one of the most adequate means against unemployment. But as working hours were lowered from 40 to 37 hours a week in 1987, that is, at the beginning of the longest recession in recent Danish history, it is likely that the subsequent increase in unemployment has been interpreted as counter-evidence against previous optimism. This is confirmed by Table 9.5. Shortening/reducing working hours is considered quite inefficient, and this strategy is rejected by a relative majority of the respondents.

This holds also for prohibition against overtime or side jobs which is considered more efficient but probably rejected on the grounds that it would interfere with individual freedom. A majority also reject the idea of a citizens' wage even though

---

10. The distribution of answers of course reflect question wordings, and the argument for growth may have been presented a bit too rethorically. Still, there is little doubt that a growth strategy is preferred.

Voting and Political Attitudes in Denmark

it is considered efficient; while 39 per cent believe that it would have a great effect on unemployment, nevertheless it is rejected, probably because it runs against the work ethic of many respondents.

A citizens' wage strategy is also rejected by most policy elites on the grounds that it would undermine economic incentives and work morals and lead to a permanent increase in the burden of supporting people on transfer incomes. The same arguments have been launched almost unanimously against the strategy of job sharing by taking leaves in turn — a strategy suggested by a local union of garbage collectors. On this point, ordinary people do not share the perceptions of policy elites at all, indeed quite the contrary as this proposal is considered by far the most efficient among all proposals in the question battery (the same result was found in the crisis survey in Table 9.1), and it is supported by a huge majority of 83 per cent of the respondents whereas only 10 per cent are against. No other proposals enjoy such a widespread support at the mass level.

This may also help to explain why the level of unemployment has no measurable effect on support for the various political parties: ordinary people seem to believe mostly in unemployment strategies that are rejected by government and opposition parties alike.[11] By the same token, with the exception of the export strategy, most solutions proposed by the political parties, by the government, and by other policy elites are considered inefficient, unacceptable, or both, among the population at large.

---

11. The preference for this sort of job sharing might reflect a simple preference for 'pleasant' programmes. However, even though one should not be too naïve about real motives it does seem that solidarity with fellow workers is among them: thus a large number of surveys confirm that people (verbally, at least) are willing to make sacrifices in order to maintain employment in their company or provide more jobs for the unemployed (by Sonar in *Morgenavisen Jyllands-Posten* 5.5.1991 and 13.12.1993; by Greens in *Børsen* 16.9.1991 and 13.12.1993; by IFKA in *Arbejdsgiveren*, quoted in *Berlingske Tidende* 25.3.1993).

Table 9.5. Perceptions of efficiency and attitudes towards various unemployment strategies. Election survey 1994. Proportions (in percentages) and PDI (percentage points)

Strategy (Figure 9.2)	Expected effects					Good/bad proposal			
	great effect	small effect	no effect	don't know	PDI	good	bad	don't know	PDI
2. Job sharing strategies									
2.1. Reducing working hours	24	40	32	4	−8	43	48	9	−5
2.2. Prohibiting overtime/side jobs	33	33	29	5	+4	40	53	7	−13
2.5. Sharing jobs taking leave in turn	62	27	6	5	+56	83	10	7	+73
2.6. Citizens' wage	39	22	27	12	+12	40	46	14	−6
3. Qualification strategies									
3.1. Education	30	33	29	8	+1	57	32	11	+25
3.3. Individual action plans	8	26	26	40	−18	23	33	44	−10
4. Market-/incentive strategies									
4.2.a. Introduction wage	29	32	28	11	+2	39	47	14	−8
4.3.b. Reducing benefits	19	31	40	10	−21	24	64	12	−40
4.3.c. Restricting access	17	30	38	15	−21	23	59	18	−36
5. Control strategies									
5.1. Work outside trade	35	34	23	8	+12	47	42	11	+5
5.2. Work far from residence	18	37	36	9	−18	16	74	10	−58

Wordings: "There is much disagreement over the ways to fight unemployment, and there are many proposals. People disagree both as to whether these proposals will work, and whether they are good or bad because they may also have side effects. I shall now read some proposals to you and ask (a) whether you think the proposal will have a great or small effect, and (b) whether you think it is a good or bad proposal, taking everything into account.
2.1.   Reducing the working hours.
2.2.   Prohibiting overtime works and second jobs.
2.5.   Taking leave in turn so as to share jobs.
2.6.   Introducing a citizen's income for everyone who do not want to have a job.
3.1.   Education and courses for the unemployed.
3.3.   Setting up individual plans of action for the unemployed.
4.2.a. Introducing lower starting wages for the young.
4.3.b. Limiting young people's access to unemployment benefits.
5.1.   Forcing the unemployed to take work outside their trade.
5.2.   Forcing the unemployed to take work far from where they live."

Qualification Strategies

A case in point is the various qualification strategies: to a larger degree than most other EU countries except Sweden, Denmark has assigned priority to active labour market policies in the fight against unemployment. Thus education, courses and job training have been offered to the young and the long-term unemployed. In 1993, this was supplemented by individual plans of action for the long-term unemployed. Such policies are generally recommended by OECD and others as an alternative to passive support; viewed in this light, the perceptions and attitudes of Danish voters are much of a disappointment. A large majority of 57 per cent do support the idea that the unemployed should be offered more courses and education but only about one third believe that it will have much effect. A similar proportion think that it has no effect at all. Roughly the same results are found for job training programmes in Table 9.1.[12] The individual action plans of the 1993 labour market reform seem to have gone almost unnoticed by the voters as 40 per cent answer don't know.

Apart from sheer ignorance, the answers reflect a general lack of confidence in the active labour market policies that have been conducted in Denmark. When asked if it was better to cancel all such arrangements and leave the problems to the market, a relative majority in fact agree (see Table 9.6). Although these figures should not be taken too literally, it is obvious that confidence in qualification strategies is low.

---

12. Because of different response categories, the crisis survey produces lower PDI's. But as three items — taking leave in turn, introduction wage, and reduction of benefits — were included in both surveys, with slightly different wordings, the response categories seem to have caused a difference in PDI's of some 20-30 percentage points. This means that confidence in job training is almost the same as confidence in education programmes for the unemployed.

Table 9.6. Priority between market and qualification strategies. Crisis survey 1988 and election survey 1994. Percentages

	1988	1994
(A) Prefers qualification strategy	41	40
(B) Prefers market strategy	50	44
Neither	.	8
Don't know	9	8
Total	100	100

Wording: "Then a question about how best to fight unemployment.

A says: Government should make extra efforts to secure jobs to the unemployed, e.g. through education or public works.
B says: Public efforts to fight unemployment are largely a waste of money. It would be better to lower taxes and improve conditions for business, then the problems of unemployment would solve themselves."

Stronger Incentives

If qualification strategies are the preferred policies of the labour movement, incentive strategies have increasingly become the preferred strategies of the Conservatives and the Liberals. Many economic experts take a similar stand as structural unemployment is increasingly interpreted as a sign of 'system failures' rather than 'market failures', that is, as a side-effect of welfare arrangements and minimum wages.

However, as it emerges from Tables 9.1 and 9.5 above, most of the incentive strategies that follow from this diagnosis are not considered efficient or desirable among ordinary people. The only exception is an introduction wage for the young which was accepted by 39 per cent of the respondents even though people were not very optimistic about its effects. Another survey reveals, however, that more than 80 per cent support an introduction wage if it is ensured that the young 'receive some education and job training' (Goul Andersen 1996a, p. 214). A majority also accepted an introduction wage 'for groups who have been outside the labour market for a long time'. But most other proposals for strengthening incentives are rejected. Thus it emerges from Table 9.5 that the proposals for lowering unemployment benefits after one year of unemployment and restricting entitlements to unemployment benefits for the young are considered quite inefficient and even less desirable by most voters.

Of course, this does not mean that all concrete proposals are rejected. According to a survey conducted in 1995, a majority supported the idea that the period of entitlements to unemployment benefits (at that time seven years) should be reduced to five years (median value of the answers), see Goul Andersen 1996c, p. 5), and in a 1994 survey, only small majorities rejected the proposals that young people should have employment for a longer period in order to be entitled to unemployment benefits, or that maximum benefits should be reduced from 90 to 80 per cent of previous earnings (Goul Andersen 1996a, p. 214).[13]

Nevertheless, attitudes are overwhelmingly negative towards policies aiming at strengthening incentives — obviously because they at the same time involve a decline of social security. And this holds in particular for one of the preferred strategies among many policy experts; a lowering of minimum wages. As revealed by Table 9.6, only 17 per cent would accept this strategy in the fight against unemployment.[14]

Table 9.7. Attitudes towards a lowering of minimum wages as a means against unemployment. Election survey 1994. Percentages

(A) In favour of lowering minimum wage	17
(B) Against lowering minimum wage	74
Neither	4
Don't know	5
Total	100

Wording: "Then we have a question about the minimum wage and unemployment.

A says: The minimum wage should be lowered so that it does not prevent the unemployed from getting a job. Otherwise unemployment will continue to increase.

B says: Unemployment must be fought by other means. In any the case, the minimum wage should be at least as high as it is today."

Stronger Controls and Requirements

From the answers above it is obvious that even though the demand for more equality is generally declining, most people are not ready to accept increasing *in*equality, and they do not want to give up social *rights*. But this does not exclude the possibility that people are willing to accept stronger *duties* for the unemployed, and stronger controls.

In particular, a relative majority of 47 per cent support the view that the unemployed should be forced to take work outside their trade (Table 9.5), and this is also seen as one of the most efficient strategies/measures against unemployment. A number of surveys have revealed even higher support for various

---

13. Two out of three voters also answer affirmatively when asked if there is too little difference between wages and unemployment benefits (survey by Sonar in *Morgenavisen Jyllands-Posten* 14.9.1991) but in the 1994 election survey, only a minority of 12 per cent answered that benefits should be lowered when presented with a battery of public expenditure questions.

14. For similar figures on an equivalent question, see the newspaper *B.T.*, 22.1.1992.

concrete proposals, also if it is made clear that unemployed professionals could be forced to take a job as an unskilled worker (Goul Andersen 1996a, pp. 219-20).

From a number of surveys it also appears that people to a large extent support the 'workfare' line, i.e. the idea that the unemployed should work in return for benefits. Thus in 1989, 89 per cent agreed that young social assistance clients should work in return for social assistance. Only three per cent disagreed (Observa in *B.T.* 17.9.1989). When asking a similar question referring to social assistance clients in general, 80 per cent agreed and only 13 per cent disagreed (Gallup in *Berlingske Tidende* 19.2.1995). However, these answers need not only reflect a wish to strengthen control of the unemployed; they may also reflect a wish that the labour power of the unemployed could be used to satisfy social and other needs (Goul Andersen 1996a, pp. 220-21).[15]

When it comes to geographical mobility, however, the attitudes are entirely different. Whereas policy elites have been quite supportive of strengthening the requirements that the unemployed should move or at least accept jobs far from their residence, this is not supported by the general public. According to Table 9.4 above, 74 per cent reject this proposal; only 16 per cent accept it. And when asked about proper requirements as to the relocation time, most voters suggest figures far below the present formal requirements (Goul Andersen 1996c, p. 35). At this point it also turns out that there are entirely different orientations among professionals and other people. Most professionals are willing to move for a job, or for a better job; most ordinary people, except young people without children, are not (Goul Andersen 1995). This also means that the orientations of policy elites in this respect are entirely different from those of most ordinary people.

Conclusions

Several conclusions follow from this survey of perceptions and attitudes concerning unemployment policies. In the first place, it emerges that ordinary people do hold quite firm and relatively stable attitudes towards most unemployment policies: across all surveys and over time, the basic patterns are roughly the same, with the possible exception of strategies where social learning seems to have taken place (e.g. working hours or consumption strategy). This means that people are not only concerned with policy effects; they also have strong attitudes about proper means. This is confirmed also by the political divisions below, and this may help to explain why voters do not simply react to policy effects as suggested in the literature on vote and popularity functions.

---

15. As 'workfare' questions were not included in the 1994 survey, we are unable to test the associations with perceptions of abuse and preference for the welfare strategy, respectively.

Next, we observe that the perceptions and attitudes at the mass level diverge very much from the predominant perceptions and attitudes among policy elites. To some degree, these perceptions and attitudes may converge as far as export-driven economic growth strategies are concerned (even though ordinary people assign relatively higher priority to welfare strategies). But next to economic growth, job sharing strategies are clearly considered the most efficient and the most desirable, in particular the model of sharing jobs by taking leave in turn which was suggested by a union of garbage collectors.

Qualification strategies are generally accepted by the voters but not because people have much confidence in their effects; rather, most people seem to think that they are inefficient but harmless and worth supporting as long as no more convincing alternatives are available. The same scepticism is encountered when it comes to incentive strategies; with the exception of an introduction wage, they are generally considered even less efficient, and they are quite forcefully rejected, probably on the grounds that they would undermine social rights.

Finally, there seems to be quite widespread support for strengthening the requirements as to mobility across trade borders and work in return for benefits. It is tempting to suggest that this is related to fears of abuse, and this is confirmed by the correlations in the last column in Table 9.9: attitudes towards this strategy are more strongly correlated with attitudes towards abuse — than are attitudes towards any other strategies.

Strengthening the requirements as to geographical mobility, on the other hand, is rejected by large majorities even though quite a few respondents acknowledge that it might have an effect on unemployment. At this point, the discrepancy between mass and elite level orientations is probably a reflection of the career-oriented way of life of the last-mentioned; also among the unemployed, there are dramatic differences between people with higher education and others at this point.

This is not the place to discuss whether the difference in mass-elite perceptions of unemployment is simply a matter of ignorance among the general public[16] but at least it emerges that there is a marked lack of confidence both in the solutions put forward by the labour movement and in those suggested by the right.

---

16. It is not likely that ordinary people are able to understand mechanisms such as the negative dynamic effects of job sharing strategies but on the other hand it must be acknowledged that evaluations of the effects of qualification programmes are overwhelmingly pessimistic (Mærkedahl et al. 1992) and that effects of (dis-)incentives (e.g. on the behaviour of the unemployed) have been proved to be surprisingly small or at least difficult to measure (see e.g. Goul Andersen 1995; Pedersen and Smith 1995).

To some degree, this may of course reflect wishful thinking, and there is little doubt that people's perceptions about efficiency are to a very large degree determined by their attitudes (rather than the other way around). Still, as it emerges from Table 9.8, there is also some independent variation. In particular, attitudes towards geographical mobility and a citizens' wage are not as strongly related to perceptions of efficiency as the other attitudes; nearly one-half of those who think it would be efficient nevertheless reject proposals to strengthen requirements as to geographical mobility.

This also means that a multiplicity of factors are involved in determining attitudes to unemployment policies. The assumption that people uncritically prefer the 'soft' policies is rejected, e.g. by the relatively negative attitudes to citizens' wage strategies and by the relatively positive attitudes to workfare or forced mobility across trade borders. Like the lack of a perfect association between attitudes and perceptions of efficiency above, these data rather suggest that side effects on such values as work ethics and distributional equity, probably also personal freedom, plays an important role. This also implies that self-interest is likely to be insufficient in explaining attitudes; side effects on values are also likely to play an important role. This value interpretation is also touched upon in the following section 9.3.

Table 9.8. *Attitude towards various unemployment strategies, by perceptions of efficiency (PDI), 1994. Per cent good minus per cent bad proposal*

	Great effect	Little effect	No effect
Introduction wage for young	+82	−23	−86
Restrictions in access for young	+57	−39	−86
Lower benefits after one year	+50	−38	−91
Mobility across trade borders	+76	−11	−78
Geographical mobility	+11	−66	−94
Lower working hours	+88	−8	−70
Prohibition against overtime/side jobs	+69	−33	−85
Citizens' wage	+52	−18	−82
Taking leave in turn	+96	+58	−55
Education and courses	+98	+32	−57
Individual plans of action	+93	−1	−68

Note: For wording of items, see note of Table 9.5.

9.3. Social and Political Divisions

Composite Indices

To describe the social and political divisions, we have combined the items in the election survey battery above into four indices. A factor analysis of the 11 items produces a three-factor solution where the first factor combines the incentive and control strategies (see Table 9.9). The second factor measures attitudes towards job sharing strategies, and the third factor consists of attitudes towards qualification strategies.

Table 9.9. *Factor analysis of attitudes towards unemployment policies. Factor loadings. Varimax rotation[1]*

	Factor 1: incentive and control strategy	Factor 2: job sharing strategy	Factor 3: qualifica- tion strategy	Correlation with attitudes to abuse[2]
Introduction wage for young	.54	−.12	−.02	.15
Limited access for young	.69	.02	.07	.27
Lower benefits after one year	.70	−.12	−.04	.27
Mobility across trade borders	.59	−.12	−.05	.30
Geographical mobility	.61	−.02	−.12	.21
Lower working hours	−.08	.64	.23	−.20
Prohibition against overtime/side jobs	−.01	.66	−.06	−.10
Citizens' wage	−.15	.61	−.12	−.19
Taking leave in turn	−.10	.40	.29	−.09
Education and courses	−.15	.04	.76	−.17
Individual plans of action	.06	.03	.77	−.13
Eigenvalue	2.31	1.35	1.13	
Per cent of variance	21.0	12.3	10.3	

Note: For wording of items, see Table 9.5.
1)   Missing values treated as neutral/centre.
2)   Correlation with the item "Too many get social welfare without needing it".

It not surprising that the strategies of control and incentives constitute one common factor. But they are conceptually distinct: unless one accepts the idea of a citizens' wage, weak incentives must necessarily be accompanied by strong controls. On the other hand, controls are less necessary if incentives are strong. Therefore use of incentives is a less bureaucratic and more flexible instrument but also entails less social security. In Denmark, the combination of weak incentives and weak controls pushed the unemployment system quite far towards a citizens' wage system in the 1980s and early 1990s. In the active labour market policy tradition of Social

Democratic Sweden, the control strategy was pushed very far by a strong workfare ideology and by strong mobility requirements (Jensen 1989). We hypothesise that social and political determinants are also different in Denmark, i.e. that Social Democrats and workers are more ready to accept control strategies than incentive strategies.

This leaves us with four indices, measuring attitudes towards the strategies 2-5 in Figure 9.2. The indices are constructed as simple additive indices which are transformed so that the index values may be interpreted almost as average proportions in favour of each set of strategies.[17] However, the growth strategy (strategy 1) was not covered by the battery. Therefore we have included the proportion preferring the export strategy (rather than the welfare or service strategy) in the following analyses. Table 9.10 presents the main results.

Gender

The gender variations are highly remarkable as they show a fundamental disagreement between men and women as to which economic strategy should be pursued. 67 per cent of the male voters assign highest priority to the export strategy whereas only 36 per cent of the female voters prefer this strategy.[18] This is one of the most significant findings in the 1994 election study which indicates that gender differences in political attitudes have been underestimated because they have not been adequately measured. In Denmark as elsewhere, a large number of studies have demonstrated gender differences in attitudes towards welfare, equality, the environment and other issues. But in the first place, such differences have typically been small, and secondly, they have mainly been located in less important issues outside the field of economic politics. But the question above is not only about economic politics; it is about the most fundamental issue of economic strategy. This indicates that gender differences are much more fundamental than formerly assumed. Furthermore, as revealed by the multivariate analysis in Table 9.11, gender

---

17. The indices are constructed as simple additive indices where 'good proposal' is assigned the value one and 'bad proposal' the value zero. 'Don't know' is coded as .5. Respondents with two-thirds or more 'don't know' answers (for each index) are treated as missing. Finally, the additive indices are divided by the number of items, that is, they may range from zero (total rejection) to one (total approval). Thus the index values are almost equivalent to average proportions accepting the policy proposals. Figures above .50 indicate a majority in favour of these proposals, figures below .50 indicate a majority against.

18. Don't know answers are treated as missing. As there are virtually no social and political variations in preference for the service strategy, the social differences in preference for the export strategy correspond with equivalent differences in preference for the welfare strategy.

is by far the most important social determinant of such attitudes — even more important than social class.

Table 9.10. *Social and political divisions in attitudes towards unemployment policies, 1994. Index values*

	Export strategy best (per cent)[1]	Job sharing/ reduced labour supply	Qualification strategies	Incentive strategies	Control strategies	(N) min.[2]
Total sample	50	.56	.54	.35	.36	1808
Men	67	.51	.53	.36	.39	934
Women	36	.61	.55	.34	.33	874
18-24 years old	54	.52	.66	.30	.34	199
25-29 years	54	.60	.60	.28	.27	205
30-44 years	52	.61	.55	.29	.30	538
45-59 years	50	.57	.49	.34	.36	414
60 years or more	44	.51	.49	.46	.48	493
Basic educ. 7-9 y.	42	.55	.50	.37	.39	783
10 years	54	.58	.54	.33	.35	664
12-13 years	60	.56	.61	.33	.31	394
Unskilled worker	43	.61	.55	.23	.33	234
Skilled worker	53	.57	.51	.24	.28	169
Lower salariat	45	.63	.56	.29	.28	462
Higher salariat	67	.54	.53	.38	.36	160
Self-employed	69	.45	.45	.54	.47	134
Under education	58	.54	.66	.33	.30	169
Retired	44	.52	.51	.44	.47	458
Housewife	43	.55	.53	.28	.38	26
Private employee	59	.54	.52	.32	.35	461
Public employee	43	.64	.58	.28	.29	413
Unemployed	40	.68	.51	.18	.20	122
Left-wing party	28	.72	.62	.13	.16	192
Social Dem.	38	.64	.58	.26	.31	547
Centre party	46	.57	.60	.38	.40	138
Liberals, Cons.	68	.45	.49	.48	.46	622
Progr.party	54	.49	.35	.42	.44	83

1) Wording, see Table 9.2. Entries are proportions preferring the export strategy among those who have a first preference.
2) N varies a little from one index to another because of missing values. N's indicate the lowest figures.

There is also a significant gender difference in attitudes towards job sharing strategies. This is less surprising, however, as women have always expressed a preference for shorter working hours, job leave, etc. A more interesting question is what explains such differences. Even though the welfare strategy and job sharing strategies may be especially beneficial to women, simple self-interests are insufficient to explain the gender differences. From an interest perspective we should also expect considerable gender differences in attitudes towards other strategies: as unemployment, in particular long-term unemployment, is higher among women than among men, women are much more likely to fall victim to strategies that strengthen incentives and controls. Conversely, women probably have more interest in qualification strategies than men. But at these points, gender differences are absent or negligible. This indicates that simple self-interest is not very important and that gender differences in attitudes are much more rooted in values.

Table 9.11.   Attitudes towards unemployment strategies, by gender, age, education and occupation. MCA analysis. Beta coefficients

(A) All respondents	Export strategy	Job sharing	Qualification	Incentives	Controls
Gender	.27	.18	$.01^{ns}$	$.00^{ns}$	.08
Age	$.04^{ns}$	.14	.13	.15	.17
Education	.17	$.03^{ns}$	.07	$.01^{ns}$	$.04^{ns}$
Occupation	.12	.18	$.09^{ns}$	.23	.14
R^2	11.5 %	9.5 %	3.5 %	8.9 %	7.7 %

(B) Employees only	Export strategy	Job sharing	Qualification	Incentives	Controls
Gender	.21	.15	$.02^{ns}$	.09	.08
Age	$.03^{ns}$	.15	.12	.11	$.10^{ns}$
Education	.13	$.05^{ns}$	.11	$.04^{ns}$	$.03^{ns}$
Occupation	$.08^{ns}$	.13	$.06^{ns}$	.19	.10
Sector	.12	.17	.11	.16	.16
R^2	9.7 %	10.6 %	4.1 %	6.7 %	7.7 %

(C) Including party choice	Export strategy	Job sharing	Qualification	Incentives	Controls
gender	.20	.17	$.00^{ns}$	$.02^{ns}$	.07
Age	$.04^{ns}$	.09	.13	$.11^{ns}$	.14
Education	.13	$.02^{ns}$	$.06^{ns}$	$.00^{ns}$	$.03^{ns}$
Occupation	$.05^{ns}$	$.12^{ns}$	$.08^{ns}$	.18	$.13^{ns}$
Sector	$.05^{ns}$	.07	.13	.08	.09
Party choice	.30	.31	.19	.34	.24
R^2	17.8 %	20.9 %	7.2 %	19.8 %	15.0 %

Age and Education

Value differences also seem more important than immediate self-interests in explaining age variations. In particular, we find a significant division between people below and above 60 years. Among respondents aged more than 60 years, 'hard' incentive and control strategies are very popular; they enjoy the same support as job sharing and qualification strategies; among the other age groups, job sharing and qualification strategies enjoy about twice the support of incentives and controls. This may of course reflect the fact that most people above 60 years have left the labour market but typically, people do not change attitudes simply because of retirement. Thus a generational interpretation is more plausible, and probably the answers reflect the fact that the age groups above 60 years were socialised before the expansion of the welfare state in the 1960s. Therefore, they tend to have lower expectations as to social rights and, conversely, a stronger ethic of self-reliance.

Another age division is between the youngest cohort(s) and the 30-59 years old. This is particularly obvious when it comes to job sharing and qualification strategies. Job sharing is the preferred strategy among the 30-44 years old whereas the young are very much in favour of the qualification strategy (which they also regard as relatively efficient) and, to a lesser degree, the export strategy. The preference for the qualification strategy among the young is easy to explain in terms of self-interests. But it is less obvious why the young should be so unfavourably disposed towards job sharing strategies. It turns out, however, that in this case, age variations run in different directions on the individual strategies. As revealed by Table 9.12, support for prohibition against overtime and second jobs *increase* almost linearly with age whereas support for shorter working hours follows almost the opposite pattern. The attitudes towards a citizens' wage reveals yet another pattern as it is opposed *both* by the elderly and by the young but receives a positive judgement among the 30-44 years old.

Table 9.12   Attitudes towards unemployment strategies, by age. 1994. PDI (good minus bad proposal). Percentage points

	Age				
	18-24	25-29	30-44	45-59	60+
2. Job sharing					
a. Lower working hours	+2	+11	+10	−12	−23
b. Taking leave in turn	+72	+79	+75	+72	+66
c. Prohibition overtime/second jobs	−37	−18	−12	−8	−4
d. Citizens' wage	−23	+5	+15	−2	−29
3. Qualification					
a. Education and courses	+57	+36	+29	+15	+11
b. Individual plans of action	+4	+2	−12	−17	−14
4. Incentives					
a. Introduction wage	−40	−41	−12	−1	+17
b. Lower unempl.benefits after one year	−29	−39	−49	−35	−15
c. Restricted access for young	−37	−43	−52	−41	−15
5. Controls					
a. Mobility across trade borders	−7	−21	−4	+10	+27
b. Geographical mobility	−57	−69	−75	−64	−33

Note: For wording of items, see Table 9.5.

As young people have far the most overtime work and second jobs, self-interest may explain the age variations on this issue; however, a value interpretation in terms of individual freedom is equally plausible. The age pattern of attitudes towards a citizens' wage, however, can only be explained in terms of generation-specific values. Although it is impossible to specify the effects of self-interests and values, it is obvious that values play an important role and that a simple interest interpretation would be misleading.

Educational variations are, generally speaking, small and insignificant. The differences are significant only at two points: the support for an export strategy and for a qualification strategy increases with higher education.[19]

---

19. Sympathy for the idea of increasing geographical mobility among people with university or equivalent education is also observable in the election survey but in the first place, this group constitute only a minor part of the better-educated group, and secondly, the better-educated are less favourable towards increasing mobility over trade borders which is also included in the index in Tables 9.10-11.

Class and Sector

When it comes to class differences, the most significant division is between the self-employed on the one hand and employees on the other. Self-employed are strong adherents of an export strategy, and of incentives and controls. To a large degree, however, these strategies are also supported by the higher salariat. Even though workers voted further to the right in 1994 than in any other election since 1973, they are to a large degree 'fundamentalists' as far as unemployment policies are concerned. Thus they are strongly opposed to incentive strategies, in particular the idea of an introduction wage for the young where PDI for unskilled and skilled workers is –41 and –45, respectively, as compared to –17 among the lower salariat and +10 among the higher salariat.

As predicted, control strategies reveal less class variations. For instance, the PDI for higher mobility across trade borders is +9 among unskilled workers, –15 among skilled workers, and +5 among higher salariat. Obviously, self-interests are at stake here: better-educated groups have more to lose than unskilled workers. But as pointed out above, support for the idea of higher mobility is also strongly related to suspicion of abuse, and workers are more suspicious of abuse than non-manuals. Thus on the question "Many among the unemployed are not really interested in getting a job", we found a PDI of +11 among manual workers but –6 among non-manual employees. Workers are very much against a weakening of social rights of the unemployed but less opposed to the idea of strengthening the duties, e.g. via stronger controls.

When it comes to sector differences, there are two dividing lines. Private employees are much more in favour of an export strategy than are public employees and the unemployed. This is in accordance with immediate self-interests but perhaps this is not a sufficient explanation as we observe the same division in attitudes to job sharing strategies. Not surprisingly, job sharing strategies are strongly favoured by the unemployed but we find almost the same figures among public employees. When it comes to incentive and control strategies, however, the main dividing line is between the employed on the one hand and the unemployed on the other (although in the multivariate analysis in Table 9.11, public employees come out more in an intermediate position even on these dimensions).

Party Choice

Finally, it is not very surprising that we also find very significant political divisions in attitudes to unemployment policies which — with the partial exception of qualification strategies — follow a clear left-right pattern. This is a rather trivial fact but it has a less trivial corollary: people are not only concerned about the level of unemployment; they are also hold strong attitudes towards the *means* of fighting unemployment. This implies that the implicit assumption in political business cycle theories that all that matters are the results is not very plausible. For instance, if people do not believe in job sharing as a means of lowering unemployment, they are unlikely to be impressed and to reward a government which obtains a decline in unemployment this way.

Our data in Table 9.11 also indicate that there is more political disagreement over incentive strategies (beta=.34) than over control strategies (beta=.24). Again, this is as predicted but a closer inspection reveals that this is caused mainly by a rejection of increasing geographical mobility in all party groups; on the item of mobility across trade borders, party differences between left and right are even larger than on the incentive questions. We cannot exclude the possibility that this conclusion hinges upon the selected issues but it is also imaginable that the Social Democrats in Denmark have been far less associated with an ideology of workfare than in Sweden. Another finding is also interesting, however. Even though the Liberals and in particular the Conservatives have gone quite far with ideas about stronger incentives and controls, there is relatively little support for these strategies among their own voters.

9.4. Employed and Unemployed

It is of course particularly interesting to examine the attitudes among the unemployed. On the one hand, having personal experiences with the effects of unemployment policies, they are perhaps the most qualified to judge on the effects. On the other hand, they are also likely to be concerned about their own interests. But then comes the question about how the unemployed themselves conceive of their interests. They may be oriented towards protecting their own immediate interests as unemployed whilst, at the same time, they may be more concerned about returning to employment and consequently less inclined to support those rights that may generate insider/outsider divisions, including a fixed minimum wage. In fact this is what is assumed in economic insider/outsider theories. Therefore we are not only interested in indices as above but also to a large degree in concrete questions. Furthermore, we are not only interested in attitudes but also in evaluations as to the efficiency of various proposals and programmes. The main results are presented in Table 9.13.

Table 9.13. *Evaluations of unemployment strategies, by employment status. Election survey 1994. Percentages and PDI*

Strategy (Figure 9.2)	Expected effects						Support PDI: good/bad proposal	
	Unemployed (N=155)					Employed (N=1128)	Unemployed	Employed
	Great effect	Small effect	No effect	Don't know	PDI: great minus no effect	PDI	PDI	PDI
2. Job sharing strategies								
2.1. Shorter working hours	39	31	26	4	+12	−8	+19	−2
2.2. Prohibition overtime/second jobs	41	33	22	4	+19	+1	+6	−18
2.5. Taking leave in turn	70	20	6	4	+66	+56	+77	+73
2.6. Citizens' wage	52	24	16	8	+36	+22	+31	0
3. Qualification strategies								
3.1. Education and courses	27	29	34	10	−7	+2	+25	+26
3.3. Individual action plans	11	28	34	27	−23	−19	−20	−11
4. Market-/incentive strategies								
4.2.a. Introduction wage	17	36	38	9	−21	−1	−36	−11
4.3.b. Reduce benefits after one year	9	29	59	3	−50	−21	−78	−22
4.3.c. Restricted access for young	12	24	55	9	−43	−23	−62	39
5. Control Strategies								
a. Work outside trade	19	32	38	11	−19	+12	−39	+5
b. Work far from residence	9	32	52	7	−43	−21	−82	−67

Note: For wording of items, see Table 9.5.

Beginning with the experiences of the unemployed; these people are certainly in a better position to judge the efficiency of qualification strategies than the employed. The results are quite negative, however. Only 27 per cent believe that education and courses have 'a great effect', and the individual plans of action which were launched as a new, efficient strategy by the Social Democratic government in 1993, are evaluated even worse — only 11 per cent believe they can have a great effect and 34 per cent think that they will have no effect at all. This means that the unemployed are even more pessimistic about the efficiency of these strategies than the employed. And when it comes to attitudes, a relative majority among the unemployed indicate that individual action plans are bad strategy.

Turning to the other strategies, we find that a relative majority among the unemployed express confidence in job sharing programmes and lack of confidence in all other proposals. This may be a rationalisation of attitudes which follow the same pattern: a relative majority among the unemployed approve of any job sharing programme, and of any 'soft' proposal or programme, except individual plans of action (which are perhaps not so 'soft' at all in the eyes of many among the unemployed), and they disapprove of all the 'hard' policies. Thus there is no sympathy among the unemployed for an introduction wage which might improve the competitiveness of 'outsiders' against the 'insiders'.

The same pattern is encountered when asking directly about lowering minimum wages as a means of fighting unemployment. As mentioned, only a few voters support this idea. But among the unemployed, adherents of a lower minimum wage are almost totally absent. As shown in Table 9.14, only 5 per cent of the unemployed approve of the idea of lower minimum wages. When insider/outsider theorists sometimes speak of the 'interests' of the unemployed or 'outsiders', this may rely on an 'objective' rather than 'subjective' conception of interests — or simply on the ideology of the researcher.

Table 9.14. Attitudes towards lower minimum wages and job sharing, by employment status. Per cent and PDI

	Unemployed				Employed
	For	Against	Other	PDI	PDI
Lower minimum wages	5	89	6	−84	−64
Job sharing rather than economic growth	51	41	8	+10	−14

Question wordings: see Tables 9.7 and 9.4, respectively.

Attitudinal differences between employed and unemployed are particularly large on the strategies of lowering benefits after one year, mobility across trade borders, and citizens' wage. These figures may indicate that some of the unemployed are not so interested in having a job *at any price* — a conclusion that is also confirmed in other studies among the unemployed (Goul Andersen 1996b). At any rate, it is the immediate interests of the unemployed *as* unemployed, more than their interests as potentially employed, that structure their attitudes. Nevertheless, an interpretation in terms of polarisation would be misleading as we also find negative evaluations and attitudes among the employed majority on most incentive and control strategies. Besides, a control for social class would reduce the effects of employment status.

In other to obtain a less interest-biased picture of the *evaluations* among the unemployed, we may choose to look at the previously unemployed rather than the presently unemployed; being out of unemployment now, the formerly unemployed are more in a position to give a 'neutral' evaluation. The relevant figures are presented in Table 9.15.

Surprisingly, the picture is almost the same as in the above: the attitudes and perceptions among the formerly unemployed resemble the attitudes and perceptions among the unemployed, or they are in an intermediate position between the employed and the unemployed. But there is one very significant exception: the formerly unemployed hold quite positive evaluations about the qualification strategies — even more than the employed — both as to the efficiency and desirability of these strategies. This may be interpreted as a sign that these programmes after all do have *some* effects.

Table 9.15. *Evaluations of unemployment strategies, by employment status.*[1] *Election survey 1994. PDI*

	Expected effect (PDI=great minus none)			Support (or attitude) PDI: good/bad proposal		
	Unem-ployed	Former unempl.	Em-ployed	Unem-ployed	Former unempl.	Employed
2. Job sharing strategies						
2.1. Shorter working hours	11	0	–9	25	21	–5
2.2. Prohibition overtime/second jobs	14	10	1	2	–9	–18
2.5. Taking leave in turn	64	64	55	81	74	73
2.6. Citizens' wage	39	22	21	34	22	–1
3. Qualification strategies						
3.1. Education and courses	–9	22	1	25	42	25
3.3. Individual action plans	–27	–9	–19	–19	–6	–10
4. Market/incentive strategies						
4.2.a. Introduction wage	–22	–23	1	–36	–37	–9
4.3.b. Reduce benefits after one y.	–54	–46	–18	–81	–54	–43
4.3.c. Restricted access for young	–49	–37	–21	–68	–43	–39
5. Control Strategies						
5.1. Work outside trade	–19	1	14	–42	–20	8
5.2. Work far from residence	–46	–27	–20	–84	–65	–67

Note: For wording of items, see Table 9.5.
1. Employed include persons on leave and former unemployed with less than three months of unemployment experience.

However, it is also worth noting that the formerly unemployed do not think that an introduction wage or other incentive strategies would help much in the fight against unemployment; if anything, one may note a somewhat more positive evaluation of control strategies even though the formerly unemployed are also quite negative here.

9.5. Conclusions

Considering the attitudes towards unemployment policies among ordinary people, it is not very surprising that no relationship is found between government performance in terms of unemployment and aggregate voter support. In the first place, people are not only concerned with policy effects but also have quite strong convictions as to the proper strategies. And secondly, these convictions to a large degree run counter to available policy options suggested by the political parties. The strategy which is believed to be most efficient is the strategy of taking leaves in turn in order to share jobs which is rejected by most experts as well as by most political parties. Conversely, with the exception of the export strategy, voters tend to have little confidence in those options that *are* available. In particular, there is not much confidence that the labour market policies implemented by the government in 1993/94 will have any effect, and the same holds for the strategy of stimulating private consumption.

The difference between mass and elite evaluations of unemployment policies seems to be rooted in very different understandings of the problem of unemployment. Among ordinary people, the problem mainly seems to be conceived as a problem of generating as many jobs as possible by export-oriented growth, allocating available jobs between the employed and the unemployed, assigning idle resources of the unemployed into socially useful purposes, and securing against too widespread abuse of the system — that is, exports, job sharing, workfare and control. Most people do not seem to acknowledge the dynamics of the functioning of labour markets which are presently at the core of most policy elites' thinking about structural unemployment problems.

This is not the place to consider the rationality of ordinary people's understanding of unemployment problems. But we may consider to which degree the answers reflect a self-interested rationality — as this is usually specified, i.e. as a myopic self-interested orientation. Clearly, this does influence some of the answers, and in particular some of the social variations in attitudes. But on the other hand, several observations speak to the contrary. This holds for the negative evaluations of the consumption strategy and the strategy of shorter working hours, as well as for the social variations between age groups and between men and women, just to mention a few.

In the first place, social learning seems to play an important role. Strategies which have been applied without significant effects are rejected (as in the case of lower working hours) or at least accepted only in the absence of more convincing solutions (as in the case of qualification strategies). Secondly, acceptance of policies depends on side effects in relation to other values such as individual freedom (as in the case of prohibition of overtime or second jobs), work ethics (as in the case of the rejection of a citizens' wage), or, last but not least, equity (as in the case of lower minimum wages or incentive strategies). To a great degree, one may speak of shared values (as in the case of rejection of strong requirements as to the geographical mobility of the unemployed). But clearly, value differences also to a large degree lie behind age and gender variations. The preference for welfare strategies among women, and the relatively high preference for incentive and control strategies among people socialised before the development of the modern welfare state in the 1960s and 1970s, are both remarkable. Even the harsh resistance among workers to an introduction wage is not rooted in *narrow* considerations of self-interests.

The fact that people do not simply take a self-interested stand is also important for the expectations as to the long-term political effects of unemployment. As in the previous chapter, only to a larger extent, we did find quite significant differences in attitudes between the employed and the unemployed. But as in the previous chapter, the unemployed are generally supported by the majority of the employed in their resistance to too hard measures towards the unemployed. This does not mean that the employed will necessarily react. But it does mean that retrenchment policies *vis-à-vis* the unemployed will not be a result of decline of solidarity and pressures 'from below' but is more likely to emerge 'from above', i.e. from political elites seeking possible saving objects. And that is an entirely different situation.

10

DANISH ATTITUDES TOWARD EUROPE

10.1. Introduction

From looking at the series of referenda on the European Community or European Union (Table 10.1) one may get the impression that Danish attitudes toward European integration have changed very little over the years.

Table 10.1.   Results of Danish referenda on EU. Per cent

| | Valid Votes | | Voting |
	yes	no	turnout
2 Oct 1972	63.4	36.6	90.4
27 Feb 1986	56.2	43.8	75.4
2 June 1992	49.3	50.7	83.1
18 May 1993	56.7	43.3	86.5

Source: Siune, Svensson, and Tonsgaard 1994, p. 33.

In October 1972, when the issue was largely one of participating in an association guaranteeing Danish agriculture, the acceptance was an overwhelming 63 per cent Yes against 37 per cent No. In February 1986, when the issue was further economic integration in the form of free internal market, acceptance had dropped to 56 per cent Yes against 44 per cent No. Six years later, in June 1992, when European integration had been pushed toward the goal of a political union, the Danish voters narrowly rejected the Maastricht Treaty for a European Union with a vote of 49 per cent Yes against 51 per cent No. Finally, after the treaty had been softened with reservations, added at the Edinburgh summit meeting in December 1992, it was accepted by the voters in a new referendum in May 1993, the vote dividing 57 per cent Yes against 43 per cent No. Hence Danish public opinion seems to stand as a solid rock in the stream of European integration. The rate of acceptance declines in rough proportion to how much sovereignty would be handed over to EU institutions. But this does not mean that attitudes toward the individual policies and agencies of EU are unaffected by events. For example it has been found that goals such as a common European currency and a common European foreign policy declined in popularity between 1992 and 1993 (Nielsen 1993; Goul Andersen 1994).

    The politicians of the major parties have been ahead of the population in arguing the positive sides of EU. Of the major parties the leaders of the Liberals and the

Conservatives have moved along with the current of European integration, with the Liberals clearly in the lead. Social Democratic representatives have moved behind them, dividing almost evenly between supporters and opponents of Danish membership of the EC. The Socialist People's party has been against the EC membership right until its reservations were incorporated in the so-called national compromise, which became the Danish stand at the Edinburgh meeting in December 1992. The Progressives have gone the other way, dropping from the position of the Conservatives to last place as the only party advocating a No in the 1993 referendum. But in the aggregate, the parliamentarians had by 1992 run far ahead of the great mass of voters, and only by back-pedalling with regard to their position on the Maastricht Treaty in 1993 did they resume contact with the field of voters. This was especially important for the Social Democratic party because of the resistance to EU among its voters; and it probably contributed greatly to the outcome of the 1993 referendum that the Social Democrats had come to power in January 1993.

The Danish attitudes to EU continue to be dominated by the division into supporters and opponents or 'Eurosceptics'. However, there has for some time been evidence showing that this is a too simplistic view: the 'European attitude' is not one-dimensional but affected by at least three psychological factors (Goul Andersen 1994, p. 161). The decision to join the Maastricht Treaty and the EU now having been made, it is plausible to expect these attitudes to be increasingly differentiated into stands on various issues for EU policy. In the following analysis we therefore seek to describe Danish attitudes to EU policy in different fields in much the same way as we have done in previous chapters. The contribution of Danish voters to EU policy, we submit, is influenced by values, ideological and social positions similar to those guiding their demands and voting choices in domestic politics. Our main objective will be to describe the pattern in these positions and the predispositions for choosing these positions in various voter groups, i.e. the Danish voter bases of EU policy.

10.2. Opinions about EU Policies

The 1994 election survey included six items concerning EU policy which can be used for the analysis of Danish voter positions.[1] The distribution of the sample on these six items is shown in Table 10.2.

---

1. Some of these items have appeared also in the 1990 election study and in a separate survey in Sweden and Norway (cf. Goul Andersen and Hoff 1992).

Table 10.2.   Attitudes to EU policy. Percentages

	Agree	Neu-tral	Dis-agree	Total	N (100 per cent)
1. Rich pay to poor countries	46	12	42	100	(1782)
2. EU parliament more power	38	17	45	100	(1432)
3. Common currency	27	6	67	100	(1865)
4. EU to play military role	35	12	53	100	(1618)
5. Extend EU to east Europe	62	11	27	100	(1733)
6. EU to fight unemployment	78	8	14	100	(1855)

Note: The 'agree' and 'disagree' responses were graded into 'quite' and 'partially' agree or disagree.

In the Danish electorate as a whole, by far the strongest support is given on item 6, "Fighting unemployment should have the highest priority on the agenda of EU". Almost four out of five respondents agreed with this statement. Second comes item 5, "Over time the EU should be extended to some of the east European countries", on which more than three out of five agreed. Third in place is item 1, "Within EU there should be a comprehensive economic levelling such that the rich countries pay for pulling the poor countries along", but already here the opinion is almost evenly divided between supporters and opponents. Item 2, "The EU parliament should have more power relative to the Council of Ministers and the Commission"" is characterised by a lower response rate than the others, probably because not everyone is able to distinguish these components of the EU structure from one another; besides, the item measured the attitude toward the EU in addition to the attitude toward democratisation, thereby inviting some respondents to pass over it. The remaining two items definitely have fewer supporters than opponents. Slightly more than one third endorse item 4, "EU should play a larger global and military role which corresponds to the economic importance of the EU countries", and only a little more than a quarter endorse item 3, "Over time the EU cooperation should lead to a common currency".

Thus the two items that most clearly imply a closer integration, namely the common currency and the military role, are the ones that receive the least support. The strongest support goes to those measures which have to do with solidarity either with the unemployed, with the poor countries within EU, or with the former east European countries. It seems clear which functions of the EU receive the most sympathy. If the majority of the Danish population were to decide, the EU would develop into a sort of weak European welfare state, bordering on a humanitarian organisation.

As we shall later discuss in more detail, there is a tendency for some of these attitudes to go together and merge into the general attitude of support for v. opposition to the EU. For the moment, we may utilise the aggregated responses in Table 10.2 to classify our respondents into three groups. Since every respondent may score between 1 (quite agree) and 5 (quite disagree) on each item, we choose the combined responses to items 3 and 4 to select to select a group of 'unionists' with scores 2-5, that is, people who more or less agree that the EU should work toward a common currency and toward playing a global and military role. From among the rest we select a group who adhere to a 'welfare' model of the EU by adding the scores on items 1 and 6, selecting those scoring 2-5 on these items, that is, people who more or less agree that the rich countries should help the poor countries and that fighting unemployment should have first priority in EU policy. Those rejecting even these policies can be classified as having no conceptualisation of the content of EU politics. The fact that they may have agreed that the European Parliament should have more power, and that the EU should be extended to east European countries is not relevant here because we are dealing exclusively with the structure of the EU. Thus we may sort out three groups of respondents:

I. Those with a unionist attitude, favouring the goals of a common currency and a global military role for EU. They constitute 28 per cent of the respondents.

II. Those favouring a welfare model of the EU, rejecting a common currency and a global role of EU but favouring the tasks of fighting unemployment and redistributing EU means from the richer to the poorer countries in EU. This group includes 41 per cent.

III. Those having no EC policy, rejecting all of these four tasks for the EU; they constitute 31 per cent of the sample.

These groups differ of course in their ideological, partisan and social composition. For a closer study we turn to a study of the individual positions on EU policy and their implications for the Danish support for EU. Our analysis will be guided by the political agenda and the policy distance models that were set forth in chapters 4 and 3, respectively.

10.3. The Impact of Ideology on EC Policy Positions

As a first step in the analysis we expect respondents' positions on EU policy to be at least in part derived from their political values. Knowing little about what the EU can do or is actually doing, their demands will be an extension of their demands for domestic policy. They typically want the EU to do the same things as they want their own government to do — not taking much account of the idea that the EU might do something that their own government cannot do. If, for example, they want their own government to protect the Danish environment more efficiently they also want the EU to protect the European environment more efficiently.

However, in addition to the six relatively specific demands listed in Table 10.2 we must also include a more general orientation toward EU integration among the 'demands' raised by respondents. Actually, by far the most of the analysis of the EC or EU issue conducted in Denmark, Norway and Sweden has concentrated on the simple support v. opposition dimension; this has been seen as the EC issue *par excellence* (see, however, Goul Andersen and Hoff 1992; Goul Andersen 1993, 1994; Büchner 1993; cf. also the theoretical perspective in Habermas 1994). Now, in David Easton's much-used terminology (Easton 1965) the opinion that Denmark should join the EU and participate in the process of European integration is readily identified as a policy demand. But it may also be viewed as support for a political system, namely, the EU. Actually the association between these two orientations is so close that whether one asks the respondents whether Denmark should join the EU, or whether they fell positively about the EU, the answer will probably be the same. The idea that anybody can be in favour of the EU but against Danish membership appears so strange that nobody thinks of it.

Therefore, the respondent's orientation to EU has the double role of demand and system support in Easton's framework. For our analysis in the present section this orientation should therefore stand as a policy demand for general integration of EU along with the more specific demands listed in Table 10.2. However, as an indicator of 'covert' support it should stand as the dependent variable in the analysis, and this is how it will be treated in the following section. The item in the Danish 1994 questionnaire had the form, "What is your general attitude to EU — very positive, rather positive, rather negative, or very negative?" The coding, however, included a middle category and thus five response categories.

The general attitude to EU may, furthermore, be expected to have a dominant standing in the voters' minds, possibly affecting other EU policy positions. At four hotly contested referenda, joining or not joining the various versions of EC/EU has been the issue, colouring all other thinking about the EU among the lay public. The repeated exposure to this issue may have had curious consequences. A Danish socialist will normally be in favour of keeping up and extending welfare. However, since that person believes the EU to be an instrument of capitalistic interests, he or she may well be opposed to handing over any authority to the EU, even for such a sympathetic purpose. The reverse may happen to a conservative who is opposed to extending welfare. Being anxious not to accept anything negative about the EU, that person may nonetheless argue in favour of extending the so-called 'social dimension' in the EU. So, the idea of conducting welfare policy with the aid of EU may generate dissonance among both supporters and opponents of the EU. The probable result is that its correlation with the left-right ideology is weakened.

In testing these hypotheses we look at the impact of ideology on respondent's stand on the six issues listed in Table 10.2. In accordance with the new politics theory set forth in chapter 2 we expect the issues to divide into old politics and new politics issues. Economic issues are supposed to belong to the old politics agenda whereas issues of democratisation and equal treatment are supposed to belong to the new politics agenda.

Table 10.3 shows the correlations of issue positions and support for the EU with respondents' positions on the old politics and new politics index.

Table 10.3. *Correlations between positions on EU policy and scores on old and new politics indices. Pearson r*

	Old politics	New politics
1. Rich pay to poor countries	−.12**	−.13**
2. EU parliament more power	.08*	−.07*
3. Common currency	.32**	.01
4. EU to play military role	.27**	.15**
5. Extend EU to east Europe	.06	−.29**
6. EU to fight unemployment	−.15**	−.04
7. Support for EU	.31**	.05

Note: For the definition of these indices, see Table 2.2.

Positive coefficients indicate that agreement with the policy statement is highest in the conservative end of the index. From the first column it turns out that the issues of a common currency or monetary unit and a greater political and military role of EU are associated with the old politics dimension. As we guessed from Figure 10.1 the 'unionists' are the voters of the old right. The bottom figure indicates that support for the EU is also associated with the old right. Negative and somewhat weaker relations are found for the issues of redistribution between countries and of giving highest priority to the fight against unemployment. These lines of policy therefore tend to be associated with the old left. But the relationship is weaker, consistent with the dissonance discussed above.

The second column shows that even though support for the EU is not related to new politics, some of the policy issues are. The idea of extending EU eastward appeals very much to the new left which also, to some extent, finds the redistributive policy of EC attractive. More surprisingly the idea of giving more power to the EU Parliament gets a lukewarm reception among the new left; but then, the Socialist People's party claims that Danish interests are best defended in the Council of Ministers. Among the new right the idea of turning EU into a global military power seems to be the main argument for supporting the EU, at least so far as these six issues are concerned.

The correlations of the seven items with old and new politics position is illustrated in Figure 10.1.

Figure 10.1. Correlations of seven attitudes about EU policy with old politics position (X) and new politics position (Y)

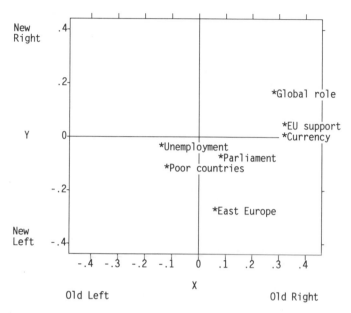

The diagram shows the demand for a common currency in EU to be located directly on the X axis as an old right position. Above that point, the demand for a greater global and military role of the EU appears as a position of the old right as well as the new right. The demand for more power to the Parliament relative to the Commission and the Council of Ministers is fairly unaffected by the ideological dimensions. The demand for extension of the EU to east European countries is promoted by the new left, whereas the demand that EU should fight unemployment is promoted by especially the old left. Between these two, the demand for redistribution from rich to poor countries is supported by both the old left and the new left.

Finally the general attitude toward the EU is located among the old right. This is probably the result of the way the EC has been presented to the Danish population right back to the original campaign in 1972. The EC was seen as a free trade association including guarantees for the prices on agricultural products. The idea of European political unity was kept in the background when the proponents discovered that it had little charismatic value on the pragmatic Danish population. As late as in the campaign for the inner market in February 1986, the Danish Prime Minister declared that the issue was the inner market, whereas the European Union was a 'dead issue'. Thus it is in no little degree the proponents of Denmark's membership of EC who have contributed to placing that issue just where it appears in Figure 10.1.

The character of the support for EU as fairly well integrated with the right side of the old politics dimension means that this attitude also correlates with the respondents' self-placement on a left-right scale. On closer investigation, however, it is not the rightmost position which is associated with the strongest support. Support as measured by the PDI value increases from −76 per cent at the leftmost position 1 to +57 per cent at position 8, then declines slightly to +44 per cent at the rightmost position 10. There is thus a tiny tendency toward an opposition on the right in addition to the much more prominent opposition on the left on the EU issue; but it is indeed slight in comparison with for example the Conservative 'Thatcherite' opposition in England.

Danish membership of the EU, as we suggested, is the 'master issue' among the seven issues. The result of its dominance is that most of the other points in the diagram are drawn toward the right; for example none of the points are located in the upper left quadrant. However, we know from chapter 2 that the voting population is spread over all four quadrants fairly evenly, although with fewer in the lower right quadrant (the Green Bourgeois, as we called them) than in the other three quadrants. What does this imbalance of the EU policy positions mean?

One can assume that the pattern of the map in Figure 10.1 would be approximately the same if, instead of the correlations, we had plotted the 'Agree' group on the old politics/new politics map. The 'Disagree' groups would then be diametrically opposite them on the map. For example those *disagreeing* that the EU should play a global role would be found in the lower left quadrant, among those whom in chapter 2 we called the Left Wing.

The emptiness of the upper left quadrant therefore means that the Old Socialists are left without any constructive EC policy. They may be sceptical of extending the EU eastward and of giving the European Parliament more power, but there is nothing dynamic in these policy positions. This foot-dragging attitude also becomes a problem for Social Democratic EU policy because, as we know from chapter 2, the Social Democratic voters come disproportionately from the ranks of the Old Socialists.

10.4. EU Policy and Support for the EU

We shall now shift our analysis to a study of EU support as a function of attitudes to specific EU policies. This will be done by applying the policy distance model that has served as our framework for analysis in chapter 3. According to that model, support for (Danish membership of) the EU should rise with proximity between the respondent's demands and actual EU policy. If that policy is believed to be the promotion of free markets, economic growth, and a larger role in global politics, then conservatives and economic liberals clearly are the more proximate and should display more support than socialists. *Generally speaking* such an hypothesis easily gets support in Denmark, as well as in Norway and Sweden, for in all three countries the political right is more sympathetic than the left toward the EC (Siune, Svensson, and Tonsgaard 1992, p. 71, 1994, p. 101; Gilljam and Holmberg 1993, pp. 162-165; Aardal and Valen 1995, p. 121). But we want to explain *why* this is so. The policy distance model should give us a clue because it starts out from *specific policy demands* that may be the causes of support or opposition to EU in general, an approach having much in common with the Fishbein/Ajzen theory of attitudes (cf. Tonsgaard 1992). It should be noted, however, that the causality suggested by the proximity model may work in the reverse direction, from the general attitude toward more specific policy attitudes, as we suggested in the foregoing section. Having no clear idea of what policy is or should be pursued by the EU, respondents may be influenced by their general feeling of nearness to, or distance from, EU policy. That is, supporters would tend to take policy positions which are near to the mainstream of EU policy whereas opponents take positions far from what they believe to be EU policy. In that case the degree of support for the Danish EU membership (associated, in Easton's framework, with support for the regime and the political community) gives rise to specific policy demands rather than the other way round. But, whatever the direction of the causality the proximity model at least predicts a negative *correlation* between EU policy positions and support for the EU.

To begin with, we take a look at the simple correlations between the six specific attitudes to EU policy and the general attitude to EU in Table 10.4 and the regression effects of the impact of the specific attitudes on the general one.

Table 10.4.   Regression effects of EU policy attitudes on support for EU

	Beta	r
1. Rich pay to poor countries	.04	.16**
2. EU parliament more power	.08**	.26**
3. Common currency	.33**	.50**
4. EU to play military role	.25**	.46**
5. Extend EU to east Europe	.11**	.27**
6. EU to fight unemployment	−.02	.00

The main effect stems from the attitude toward a common European currency and the global role of EU. Lesser effects are due to the attitude toward extending the EU eastward and enhancing the power of the European Parliament. The two remaining attitudes have no effect when the others have been controlled. The multiple correlation in the regression function is .58, which seems a fair result.

Are we entitled to see this result as a confirmation of the policy distance hypothesis? The answer is yes only if we assume that the 'real' policy of EU can be characterised as working toward (1) an economic-monetary union including a common European currency, (2) a stronger foreign-policy cooperation involving a European army, (3) extending EU with east European countries, and (4) democratising the EU decision process by giving the European Parliament more power.

Unfortunately we have no survey questions regarding the Danish voters' perceptions of real EU policy. We will argue that some of the above assumptions are unrealistic and should be altered. Whereas we agree with the first three, we believe there is a fair amount of opposition within the EU to the other three policy statements that we have used as items. We therefore assume (4) that EU policy is divided on the question of giving more power to the EP, (5) that it is only with some reservations ready to transfer more resources from the richer to the poorer countries, and (6) that in practice it is divided on the issue of giving highest priority to the fight against unemployment. Therefore, on items 3, 4 and 5 we shall compute the policy distances from the 'quite agree' position; on item 1 we compute them from the 'agree partly' position; and on items 2 and 6 we compute them from the middle position, 'neither agree nor disagree'.

Under these assumptions the policy distance hypothesis is tested in Table 10.5, which shows the regression effects of policy distance on the six specific issues upon the general attitude, or support for EU.

Table 10.5. *Regression effects of distances from EU policy upon support for EU*

	Beta	T value
1. Rich pay to poor countries	−.05*	−1.98
2. EU parliament more power	−.17**	−4.36
3. Common currency	−.25**	−12.67
4. EU to play military role	−.19**	−9.16
5. Extend EU to east Europe	−.10**	−4.84
6. EU to fight unemployment	−.10*	−2.34

Danish Attitudes toward Europe

In accordance with the hypothesis, distance on all six issues have significant negative effects; after we have altered the assumptions, on items 1 and 6 also has policy distance become efficient in lowering the EU support. The difference with the foregoing regression model is, that the items on common currency and military role lose in predictive power while the item on parliamentary power and that on fighting unemployment gain. The total explanatory power is only slightly improved to R=.59, but at least we have had the satisfaction of testing a model which is more theoretically sound than the former.

We now want to compose a variable measuring respondent's distance from EU policy in general. Hypothetically, the best procedure would be to weigh distances on the six issues according to their relevance to the respondent's EU support. However, we have no way of telling how important these issues are to the respondent. We might then assume the beta effects in Table 10.5 to represent the importance of the issue to the average respondent and employ them as weights. Such a *post facto* strategy would maximise the chance of a successful test but also involve an element of circular reasoning. Therefore we simply add up the distances on the six issues as we defined them, composing an index of policy distance which runs from 0 to 19. A person with the largest distance from EU policy is one who disagrees completely that the EU should work toward a common currency, play a military role, extend the EU eastward, and transfer large sums from the rich to the poor country members; and who takes extreme positions for or against giving more power to the parliament and putting unemployment on the top of the EU agenda.

The policy distance hypothesis states that EU support will be an approximately linear function of policy distance. This is shown to be the case in Figure 10.2, except that the shape of the curve suggests that support only starts to fall at a certain amount of policy distance, about the scale point of 3 or 4. The same impression is given by the regression line fitting EU support to distance from EU policy. When EU support is measured as PDI value (that is, agree=1, neither agree nor disagree=0, and disagree=−1), and distance is defined as above, the best-fitting line is Y=1.38 — .114X. For those nearest to EU policy that line predicts a support of more than one, which is nonsense. But from the distance of 4 scale units and onward, the predicted PDI of the EU support falls from 92 per cent by 11.4 per cent with each scale unit, until it reaches −79 per cent when the distance reaches its maximum, 19 scale units. This decline seems very much like the one in Figure 10.2.

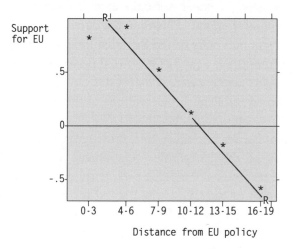

Figure 10.2. Relationship between distance from EU policy (X) and support for EU (Y). Correlation r=−.97 (N=6)

Policy distance, the X axis of Figure 10.2, is to a great extent associated with ideological leftism. Yet the two should not be regarded as the same. As mentioned in the previous section, support for the EU falls off slightly at the extreme right; and actually, policy distance rises slightly at the same end of the political spectrum: the mean distance drops from 13.2 at the leftmost position to 8.8 at the moderate right position 8, but is slightly higher at the rightmost positions 9 and 10. Thus it seems to be policy distance rather than left-right position which affects support. In the following analysis, distance from EU policy will therefore be used as a base variable to explain or sort out the impact of various other factors on EU support among the Danish respondents.

10.5. Partisanship and Support for the EU

Opinion polls over many years have meticulously followed the division of various parties' voters into EC supporters and opponents. Obviously it has been of major interest for the politicians and the media to ascertain to which extent the different parties were in agreement with their voters. The public debate has focused especially on the large number of EC opponents among Social Democrats. That group has also been made responsible for the poor performance of the Social Democratic party at EC parliamentary elections and the voter support for specific candidate lists of opponents at these elections. In the June 1994 election these lists obtained four out of the sixteen Danish seats in the European Parliament. At the Maastricht referendum in 1992 the dissent of Social Democratic voters was seen as the main cause of the defeat. 'The party was unable to control its voters' ran the accusations of the bourgeois parties (cf. Siune, Svensson, and Tonsgaard 1994, pp. 100-101). Between the 1992 and 1993 referenda the vote for EU increased from 46 to 59 per cent among Social Democratic voters (*ibid.*), the change contributing greatly to the outcome of the second referendum. This time the defection from the party line was especially notable among voters of the Socialist People's party. Though the vote for EU increased from 8 per cent in 1992 to 20 per cent in 1993 among these voters, the remaining eighty per cent were in theory defectors, since the Socialist People's party had co-authored the Danish reservations to the Maastricht Treaty and in turn recommended its voters to accept the EU.

However, the division of parties into those 'for' and 'against' the EU is much too simple for an analysis of the party/voter relationship on the EU issue. Consequently we asked the respondents to place each party on a scale from 1 to 5 where 1 stood for opting out of the EU while 5 stood for a policy promoting integration of the EU countries. Below, the first column in Table 10.6 shows the mean position of the parties on that scale whereas the second column indicates the mean position of each party's 1994 voters on the same scale

Table 10.6.   *Mean positions of the parties and the parties' voters on EU integration*

	Party position	Voter position
Liberal	4.66	3.83
Conservative	4.36	3.84
Centre Democratic	3.94	3.63
Social Democratic	3.69	2.82
Radical Liberal	3.60	2.92
Christian People's	3.28	2.75
Progress	2.23	2.68
Socialist People's	2.12	2.10
Unitary List	1.22	1.67
All		3.07

Note: Scores on both variables run from 1 (opposition to EU) to 5 (support for further integration of EU).

Studying this table and the illustration of it in Figure 10.3, we find that there is a fairly close relation between party positions and voter positions. All the same there are also noteworthy deviations. Overall the parties are located as more extreme than the parties' voters locate themselves. Whereas the parties range from 4.66 (Liberal) to 1.22 (Unitary List), the means of their voters range only from 3.84 to 1.67. This fact also shows up in the slope of the regression line in Figure 10.3, which is only .62. For all of the major parties this implies that they are viewed as being more positive to EU than their voters see themselves. The exceptions are the Progress party and the Unitary List, who are thought to be more opposed to the EU than their voters. The Socialist People's party, in spite of its support for the Maastricht Treaty after the Edinburgh amendments, is not seen as particularly positive to the EU. Actually it is seen as slightly more negative than the Progress party although the latter recommended the voters to vote down the treaty. It is worth noting that according to this table it is not the Socialist People voters who are at variance with their party; rather it is the voters of the two largest parties, the Social Democratic and the Liberal, who are more reluctantly European than their party. The average Social Democratic voter, like the average Radical Liberal and Christian People voters, is on the opposite side of the centre position (position 3) than are their parties. According to the directional theory which we discussed in chapter 3, this fact should decrease the utility of their party while increasing the utility of the Socialist People's party, the Unitary List, and the Progress party in the eyes of these voters.

Figure 10.3. Positions of the parties (X) and their voters (Y) on a scale of support for the EU

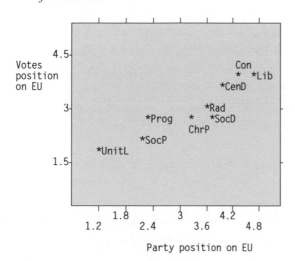

Note: Correlation = .94 (N=9), regression line Y = .92 + .62 X

These shades of EU support among the parties need not be interpreted as misperceptions on the part of the electorate. The parties had to recommend either voting yes or no in the 1993 referendum for tactical reasons so as to give the appearance of unity and resoluteness. But the electors show some subtlety and differentiate the parties according to shades of support for EU. The parties' positions on the X axis may turn out to be very good guides for the policy positions taken by Danish parliamentarians in the EP and Danish ministers in the Council. And on the whole, the voters correctly assess their parties to be more positive than themselves on the EU issue. A simple computation reveals that two thirds of the voters place themselves in a position less positive to EU than the position of their party, only one third placing themselves in a more positive position (the party positions in this computation are defined as the mean assessment of all respondents, not the individual respondent).

The deviation of voters from the party line when it comes to EU politics has naturally been the topic of much debate. It has not been shown that the results of the successive referenda on EU or of the EP elections have had any influence on the result of Danish general elections; although the 1972 referendum have been suspected of contributing to the fragmentation of the party system in 1973, the European referenda and elections tend to stand, as it were, in parentheses in Danish voting behaviour. On this point Denmark differs strongly from Norway, where the EU issue has torn severe rifts in the party system. Still, the incapacity of the political elite to pull along their constituencies is critical because the Danish constitution requires popular consent when sovereignty is surrendered. The fact that Danish parliamentarians are generally more positive toward EU than are their voters is also a permanent calamity for Danish relations with the EU. The gap between political elite and mass leads to a loss of confidence among the voters (as we shall discuss in the next chapter) and a tendency to sweep the problems of EU policy under the rug, downplaying the sliding of the EC toward a union. Symptomatically the pro-EU parties prevented the term *European Union* from appearing on the ballot of 1993 referendum, prescribing instead the term *European Community* which was supposed to have more positive connotations.

In the foregoing section we pictured the voter's support for EU as a function of his or her positions on six issues. We may now employ that function to investigate whether the voter's partisanship is capable of swaying the support given to EU one way or the other depending on where the party is itself located. For example, are Liberal voters more supportive of EU than Social Democratic voters *at the same policy distance?*

In view of the stubbornly sceptical attitude of the Danish voters compared with the attitude of most Danish parliamentarians, it might be thought that the voters took their stands according to their own impressions of EU policies, disregarding the stands of their parties. But such a thought is easily dispelled when we look at Table 10.7.

Table 10.7.   *Regression analysis of EU support as a function of respondent's policy distance and the EU support of respondent's party*

	b	beta
R's distance to EU policy	−.13**	−.45**
EU support of R's 1994 party	.44**	.35**

Note: Multiple correlation R=.66 (N=1091). Distance to EU policy measured on a scale from 0 to 19. EU support of party and of respondent measured on a scale from 1 (Denmark out of EU) to 5 (Further integration of EU). **=significant at .1 per cent level.

The result shows a clear effect of both R's policy stands and the general position of R's party on the EU issue. The magnitude of the latter effect corresponds to a difference of .44 scale points in respondent's stand for each scale point respondent's party is moved toward higher or lower support for the EU. Admittedly the two independent variables are correlated so as to produce some multicollinearity, which means that it is somewhat difficult to sort out the two effects from one another. Still, the combined effect is larger than their separate effect, as shown by the multiple correlation of coefficient of .66.

10.6. Why Women Are Against the EU — Or Why Men Are in Favour

Among the social differences in the attitude to EU or vote on EU membership, the difference between men and women appears to be the most important as well as the most general and enduring. In the Danish 1992 referendum 53 per cent of the men but only 46 per cent of the women voted 'yes' (Siune, Svensson and Tonsgaard 1992, p. 67). In the referendum one year later 62 per cent of the men but only 55 per cent of the women voted yes (Siune, Svensson and Tonsgaard 1994, p. 96). If the Maastricht Treaty had been decided by the men alone in 1992 it would have accepted, and no 'national compromise' leading to the Danish reservations in the Treaty would have been necessary.

The gender difference is at least as great in Sweden and Norway. Oskarson (1996, p. 211) reports that 59 per cent of the men but only 46 per cent of the women were in favour of Swedish membership, and Aardal and Valen (1995, p. 134) find that 28 per cent of the Norwegian men as against 20 per cent of the women were in favour of Norway joining the EU.

The policy distance model can be used in an attempt to account for the gender difference. Compared with the men, the women may be opposed to the EU either *because* they have a longer policy distance or *even though* their policy distance is the same as the men's. In the latter case we must look to other, less policy related (and some would say, less rational) factors in accounting for the gender difference.

The simplest procedure is to add gender as a variable to the relationship between policy distance and support for the EU. The result of the regression analysis is shown in Table 10.8.

Table 10.8.   *Regression analysis of EU support as a function of policy distance and gender*

	beta	r
Policy distance	−.56**	−.57**
Female gender	−.01	−.10**

Note: EU support measured on a five point scale from 1=wants us out of EU to 5=fast integration of EU.

We find that the effect of gender vanishes after control for policy distance. In other words the lower support for the EU among women than among men is determined by the larger average policy distance of women compared with men, and not by some 'intrinsic' tendency among women to be opposed to the EU. Corresponding with this finding we also find the average distance from EU policy on the 0-19 scale to be smaller among the men than among women, 9.9 as against 11.1 scale units.

We may proceed one step further, asking which issues generate the greatest difference between the men and the women. Table 10.9 answers this question at least partly by presenting the support for the six items for the two genders separately.

Table 10.9.   *Support for EU and opinion balance on six issues about EU policy among men and women. Per cent positive minus per cent negative*

	Men	Women
Support for EU	23	11
Opinion on EU Policy:		
1. Rich pay to poor countries	7	1
2. EU parliament more power	−2	−14
3. Common currency	−23	−59
4. EU to play military role	−10	−29
5. Extend EU to east Europe	45	25
6. EU to fight unemployment	65	64

The difference in PDI is about twelve percentage points on the EU support, corresponding to a difference of some six percentage points in the number who are for the EU. With respect to the separate issues the gender difference is particularly large, about 36 points on the issue of a common European currency. On the issue of EU as a global power the difference is 19 points, and on the issue of extending EU eastward the difference is 20 points. These three issues together go far toward accounting for the failure of the women to support the EU, or conversely, the great attraction for men of the EU.

10.7. Self-Images and EU Support

Apart from specific policies and institutions, the EU is associated in the minds of the voters with various identifications and self-evaluations. Among them we shall examine two attitudes which have been the topic of much public debate. The first is that support for the EU has been associated with feeling as a European rather than feeling as a Dane. Often without referring to specific policies the proponents of the European Union have sought to promote and draw on the idea of a community of Europeans as the affective basis for voting for the Danish EU membership. The opponents of EU have sometimes responded that the EU was not Europe, and sometimes that the feeling of being Danish or Nordic was more dear to them than feeling European.

The second attitude which has recurred in the public debate in relation with the EU membership seems to be an awareness of feeling powerless, of losing contact with politicians and bureaucratic officials, which goes with the membership of a political unit as large as the EU. In the debates leading up to the referenda this feeling has been politicised as an accusation that Denmark will lose independence and self-determination, a key argument of the opponents (Siune, Svensson and Tonsgaard 1992, 1994, passim).

These attitudes have been shown in a previous study (Goul Andersen and Hoff 1992, p. 6) to emerge from a factor analysis of EU-related attitudes. The first and by far the most important factor was related to economic and military integration. The second factor was termed powerlessness, and we shall have more to say about it in chapter 11. The third factor was termed European identity and was related to EU policies in favour of more economic equality among member countries and more power to the European Parliament.

Here we want to include these self-images as supplementary variables to our policy distance model in accounting for EU support.It is possible that they exert a certain effect on EU support beyond the effect of policy distance, since they do not directly refer to specific policy preferences. Thus they represent what Easton terms diffuse support as distinct from specific support (cf. chapter 7). Table 10.10 shows the result of a regression analysis which includes two survey items, "I feel just as much a European as I feel a Dane", and "I know so little about the EU that I have almost given up following what happens".

Table 10.10.   *Regression analysis of EU support as a function of policy distance,*
European identification, and the feeling of powerlessness in relation
to EU

	Effect on Support for EU	
	beta	r
Policy distance	−.51**	−.57**
European Identity	.10**	.28**
Ignorance of EU	−.10**	−.22**

Note: EU Support measured on a five point scale from 1=Wants us out of EU to 5=Wants fast
integration of EU. The feelings of European identity and ignorance of EU were both
measured on five point scales. N's around 900.

It is obvious that both attitudes have a separate effect on respondent's support for
EU. The beta effect of respondent's European identity is positive, .10, and that
of respondent's feeling of ignorance about EU is negative and of the same magnitude.
For both attitudes the crude correlation is higher as shown in the second column.
Evidently this is because the effects tend to overlap one another and also tend to
overlap the effect of policy distance. Therefore the effect of policy distance also
declines numerically from r=−.57 to beta=−.51 by control for the two identification
variables. In other words, those with a European identity have a smaller mean distance
from EU policy than the rest, whereas those declaring themselves ignorant about
EU have a larger distance than other respondents. The identification variables exert
a double effect, both directly on the EU support and indirectly through their effects
on the policy distance.

10.8. Conclusion

In this chapter we have attempted to set forth the attitude of Danish voters to the
European Union as a logical result of their policy preferences compared to the
mainstream of EU policy on a number of specific issues. Most Danes prefer an
EU that is oriented more towards welfare and the solution of social and environmental
problems than it seems to be at present. They shy away from the full implications
of a monetary economic union and a powerful political union, goals that are written
into the Maastricht Treaty. Hence they feel at distance from EU policy and react
with scepticism. That scepticism was effectively countered by the Danish reservations
which came out of the Edinburgh meeting in late 1992, and which caused a seven
per cent swing in public opinion on the EU, more than enough to bring about the
second Danish referendum on the Maastricht Treaty in May 1993.

In our analysis in this chapter the party choice has a different function than
to that in previous chapters. To treat EU support as analogous with policy voting

means that the parties can be treated as agents or sources of influence rather than end-points in the voter's decision process. Combining the 1994 vote and the perceived stands of the parties on the EU issue, we generated an indicator of the effect of the party on the attitude to EU, and demonstrated that besides their own stands on EU policies, the respondents are quite strongly influenced by their partisanship. Thus the positive stand taken by most Danish parliamentarians on the EU issue certainly has an effect on public opinion on EU matters. In the next chapter we show, however, that there is a price to be paid for such an influence.

11

ISSUES AND POLITICAL TRUST

11.1. Introduction

Democracy is a way to resolve conflicts over issues, and gets support in proportion to how well it performs this general function. Hence, regime support must be assumed somehow to be related to issues, but the relation needs to be specified. In David Easton's framework (Easton 1965) political support is suggested as an input category along with demand input. A simple relation is then established between the key categories of policy output, demand input, and political support: an agreement or consonant relation between demand input and policy output generates political support, whereas a discrepancy between the first two reduces support. Easton, however, distinguishes specific support which is policy-related from diffuse support which is not, and hypothesises that support for the incumbent government is specific whereas support for the regime is diffuse (p. 457). The empirical question to which research has addressed itself is therefore to specify if and how dissent over various issues affects attitudes to basic democratic institutions such as the parliament, elections, and the authority of the government. For research on the micro level, the political support given by the individual voter is hypothesised to attain a maximum when actual policies coincide with the individual's preferred policies. Remaining support not explained by such policy distances may then conveniently be discussed under the heading of diffuse support.

In applying this simple model we may turn to some of the perceptions and attitudes that have been analysed in previous chapters. For example, distance between the voter's position on an issue and the position representing actual government policy can be hypothesised to contribute to low political support. On this topic we are equipped with information on respondent's own position as well as his or her perception of the parties' positions on seven issues that were thought important for the 1994 vote. This data was used in chapter 3 for a study of issue voting. For the present purpose, because of the dominance of the Social Democratic party in the present government we may tentatively equate the Social Democratic position with actual government policy.

As another example, suggestions for government spending are readily interpreted as an excess of demand input over perceived policy output, or a deficit if the suggestion is less spending rather than more spending. This data was used in chapter 7 for a study of budget demands. We may assume that the going budget represents actual policy and that suggestions for changing the budget signal a lack of coincidence between the individual's preferred policy and actual policy. That is, suggestions for either more or less spending on any budget item should contribute negatively to the amount of political support given by the individual voter. Such a relationship has been found in a comparative study of British, German and Italian data (Borre 1995a).

In both of these examples the sources of political support are sought in the sphere of rational calculation. It is the discrepancy between what the individual wants his/her government to do and what it is actually doing which is hypothesised to reduce support. The type of support stemming from such reasoning is what Easton terms specific support and distinguishes from diffuse support, a concept which seems hard to measure. However, we can imagine that low political support is given not only by people who disagree with actual policy but also by people who are unable to specify what they want from government or who have quite vague or irrational ideas about what government is doing or can do. Hence they are voters to whom the notion of policy distance does not apply. The concept of diffuse support may serve to remind us that certainly not all voters are policy voters.

But even the simple policy distance model of political support raises a number of research questions. Are policy distances on some issues more critical for reducing support than distances on other issues or budget items? Are people who vote for opposition parties less supportive of the regime than those who vote for the government parties, once their policy distances are controlled for? Is the 'policy component' of political support larger for politically interested voters than for the uninterested? Does policy distance lead to undemocratic attitudes and demands for changes in basic regime norms? And does aggregated political trust for the whole electorate show changes over time that can be understood as the outcome of aggregated changes in policy distances?

Our strategy in the following sections will be first to establish the validity of the policy distance model under fairly narrow and clear-cut assumptions, and later explore the model under circumstances that are somewhat analogous but less easy to interpret. In general research has concentrated on indicators of trust in government, or political trust, and this is what we shall also do. Thus, in all sections except the last political support will be exemplified by the attitude of political trust. Political trust, our main dependent variable, will be defined as an additive index of responses to three items in the Danish 1994 survey:

1. The politicians generally care too little about what the voters think (5 response categories)

2. In general one may trust our political leaders to make the right decisions for the country (5 response categories)
3. How much trust in Danish politicians do you have in general? Do you have great trust, some trust, not much trust, or very little trust? (4 response categories)

One notices that while the first of these items deals with the question of representativity, the second deals with the question of the politicians' competence. There is logically nothing wrong with responding differently to these two items. Politicians may constitute a closed elite but still be trusted to make good decisions; on the other hand they may faithfully reflect public opinion but lack vision. The third item sums up these and other aspects of trust in the political leadership. These speculations also fit with the correlation between the three items: items 1 and 2 are only moderately correlated ($r=.25$) whereas item 3 shows higher correlations with item 1 ($r=.33$) and especially item 2 ($r=.45$) in the 1994 survey.

Adding these responses yielded an index that ranged from 3 (low trust) to 14 (high trust). This index will be used for simpler analysis in a collapsed form where the scores 3-5 stand for low trust and 9-14, high trust. In its crude form the index also lends itself to regression analysis, but since the high scores of 12 to 14 were rare, they were combined, resulting in a fairly balanced index with ten positions suitable for regression analysis.

Three other attitudes related to political support will be explored towards the end of this chapter. One is the item on satisfaction with democracy, which appears in the Eurobarometer data and therefore can be compared with other countries. Another is the support for popular referenda, which is drawn into the analysis because it throws light on the set of beliefs underlying the acceptance of democratic regimes in their representative form. The third is sympathy with a rule by means of a 'strong man', a survey item obviously related to authoritarian attitudes. However, we refrain in this chapter from discussing democratic attitudes in a broader context.

11.2. The Development of Political Trust

Political trust in Denmark has developed as shown in Figure 11.1. The emergence of the new party system in 1973 was accompanied by a wave of political distrust, from a PDI value about –11 per cent in 1971 to almost –30 in 1975. The subsequent elections in 1977-84 entailed a partial recovery of political trust to the level of –20 per cent. For the 1987 and 1988 elections our data on political trust is incomplete. Only the item about the politicians' decisions was asked, and the responses to it suggests that the level of trust was comparatively high during the period 1985-88 but dropped to its lowest level in 1989 (Goul Andersen 1992, pp. 22-23). The last two elections in 1990 and 1994 have confirmed the return to the low trust level which characterised 1973-75, in spite of the recovery of the large parties which was discussed in chapter 1 (Figure 1.1). The new decline may be due to the so-called Tamil affair and other political scandals, but it may also reflect public fatigue in debating great economic plans which were never carried out. For the period 1986 to 1990 it has been shown (Goul Andersen 1992, pp. 138-139) that time series of responses to the item about the politicians' decisions were correlated with evaluations of the government's ability to solve the country's economic problems. In any case, if we make an exception for the unusual political situation in the 1973-75 period, the trend in political trust seems to have been downward over these twenty-four years.[1]

Figure 11.1. The development of political trust, 1971-1994

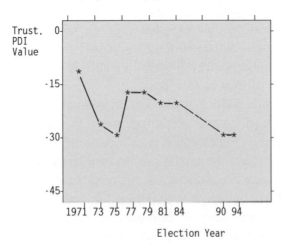

Note: Y values are computed as an average of two percentage differences, from the item, 'The politicians generally care too little about what the voters think' (disagree minus agree), and the item 'In general one may trust our political leaders to make the right decisions for the country' (agree minus disagree). Don't know responses are regarded as neutral. The first of these items was not asked in the 1987-88 survey.

11.3. Policy Distance and Political Trust

The policy distance hypothesis of political trust goes back more than twenty years. Miller (1974), examining the relation between issue positions and political distrust (or political cynicism), showed that voters on either the left or right who disagreed

---

1. These data points are constructed from the election surveys. Time series which include data points between election are much more fluctuating (cf. Goul Andersen 1992).

with official American policies on the Vietnam issue or the civil rights issue showed a high amount of distrust. Later, Miller and Listhaug (1990) studied the same relationships for Norway and Sweden and discussed explanations for the different development of political distrust in the three countries. Whereas in the United States distrust reigned for an extended period of the 1970s, in Norway it was mainly focused on the EC issue and quickly vanished after the 1972 referendum, until a new wave of distrust set in after the mid-eighties (Aardal and Valen 1995, p. 201). In Sweden distrust began to rise later than in the United States, but the rise has continued up to the present time (Gilljam and Holmberg 1993, p. 170).

The Danish decline in trust as shown in Figure 11.1 is not as consistent as the Swedish one, but it is large enough to warrant closer analysis. However, not until the 1994 election have the Danish surveys included the items necessary for a full-scale analysis of policy distance. The Danish 1994 survey included seven issue scales on which the respondent was asked to locate himself or herself. Six of these scales were used in chapter 3 to test the policy distance and directional hypotheses of issue voting, and the seventh in chapter 10 for a study of Danish attitudes toward the EU. For the present purpose the seven scales are shown in Figure 11.2 with figures indicating the level of trust at each position.

On every scale except one political trust takes on an unmistakeable inverted U-shape, the level of trust reaching its maximum at one of the moderate positions and falling off toward both ends. The exception is issue scale no. 1 about free market v. state regulation, where those at the neutral position are less trustful than those at the adjacent positions. Regarding scale no. 2, the most trustful are those with a preference for a moderately tight economic policy. On scale no. 3 those at the centre position and those with preference for moderate budget increases are the most trustful. Turning to the non-economic issues, on scale no. 4 those with a slightly liberal stance on immigration are the most trustful, and on scale no. 5 those with a moderate inclination toward a greener politics lead the field. On scale no. 6 those at the centre and those with a moderately liberal position on crime policy are the most trustful. Finally, on the EU issue the highest level of trust is found among those with a moderate pro-EU stance.

Figure 11.2. Political trust at various issue positions. Per cent trustful minus distrustful

1. Free market versus state intervention to control market forces

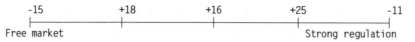

2. Tight economic policy, even in face of rising unemployment – versus increasing consumption and employment, even in the face of rising public debt.

3. Cut public expenditures and revenues versus face rising public income and expenses in the future

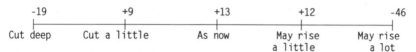

4. Take fewer or more refugees than now

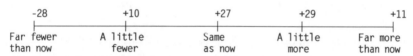

5. Putting more or less weight on environmental protection ('green dimension')

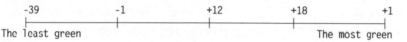

6. Maintain law-and-order with more severe punishment versus prevent crime and treat criminals in a human way.

7. Getting us out of EU versus the fastest possible build-up of EU.

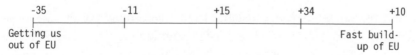

The hypothesis contends that distance from actual government policy distance generates political distrust. Actual government policy can be approximated with the position of the Social Democratic party in view of the dominance of that party in the government which resulted from the 1994 election. There may be cases in which another measure, for example a weighted mean of positions of the parties according to their parliamentary strength, might be a better indicator of actual policy, but we assume the difference to be too negligible to investigate further.

If we compare the variations in political trust in Figure 11.1 with the positions of the parties in Table 3.6 (Table 10.5 in the case of the EU issue), we observe that in accordance with our hypothesis political trust peaks near the Social Democratic position on most scales. For example, on scale 3 dealing with the issue of cutting or raising the public budgets, the Social Democratic party is located at position 3.65, between 'As now' and 'May rise slightly' — and quite in line with this position, political trust is highest at these two positions. The same is true for scale 4 on the issue of taking fewer or more refugees, where the party is located at position 3.51, midway between 'Same as now' and 'A little more'. On scale 5 the Social Democratic party is located at position 3.68 as a relatively 'green' party, and the trust is highest at position 4 followed by position 3. On scale 6, the law-and-order issue, the party is located at 2.52, midway between the second and third stands, indicating a fairly liberal policy; and consequently political trust peaks with a PDI value of 19.6 at both these positions. On scale 7, maximum trust is registered at the fairly but not totally pro-European position. This coincides with the Social Democratic stand at position 3.69.

There are, however, a minor and a major deviation from this pattern. The minor deviation occurs on scale 1, free market versus state regulation. Here the Social Democratic party is perceived by the average respondents as being moderately in favour of regulation of market forces, located at position 3.47. Political trust peaks at position 4 with 24.6 percentage points, but it would be more in accordance with our expectation if it were higher at position 3 than it actually is. The major deviation occurs on scale 2, the economic policy issue. The Social Democratic party is located at position 3.81, which means that it is perceived as quite expansionist. However, political trust peaks at position 2, among those who are moderately contractive. Thus on this important issue those near the position of the large bourgeois parties are more trustful than those sharing the position of the leading government party.

The overall agreement between distance from government policy and political distrust is anyhow so close that we feel justified in claiming success for our hypothesis about a negative relation between distance from government policy and political trust. For the illustration in Figure 11.3, respondent's absolute distances from the Social Democratic positions were aggregated over the seven issue scales. The Y values indicate the PDI value of political trust, that is, per cent trusting minus per cent distrusting. As we observe, the PDI value falls off from about +60 among those near to government to about –30 among those far from government. The

Voting and Political Attitudes in Denmark

negative relationship on this aggregate level (N=6 observations) is indicated by a correlation of r=-.98.

Figure 11.3. The relation between policy distance and political trust

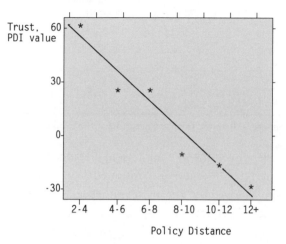

Note: Policy distance is the sum of respondent's distance from the position of the Social Democratic party, summed across all seven issues in Figure 11.2.

From the beginning, then, the evidence in favour of our policy distance hypothesis is overwhelming. Distance from the Social Democratic position not only leads to a decline in support for that party, as we saw in chapter 3, it also leads to a decline of trust in government. It is important to remember that we are here, as in chapter 3, speaking of 'true' distances not perceived distances where the perceptions may themselves be affected by partisanship.

Thus encouraged we may proceed to answer the questions which of these seven issues are most critical for generating low and high support, and whether there is a duplication of the effects of policy distance from one of these seven issues to the next issue. These questions may be settled by means of the regression analysis presented in Table 11.1.

Table 11.1.　*Regression analysis of political trust as a function of policy distance on seven issues*

Issue	Beta	T value	Sign.
European Union	−.28	−7.6	**
Immigration	−.20	−5.0	**
Free market/regulation	−.11	−2.4	*
Law-and-order	−.06	−1.4	
Environment	−.04	−1.0	
Economic policy	−.03	−.7	
Budget size	−.01	−.1	
Multiple correlation	.42		**

Note:　Policy distance is respondent's distance from the position of the Social Democratic party.

The independent variables were respondent's numerical distance from the position of the Social Democratic party on the above-mentioned seven issue scales. We find that the sign is negative as expected for all seven issues. However, it is also clear that these issues are not all equally important for generating distrust. The multiple correlation coefficient of .42 is mainly brought about by policy distance on three issues: the EU issue, the refugee issue, and the free market v. state regulation issue. It is interesting that a similar finding was made in a survey conducted in March-April 1991, when the bourgeois government was still in power. For the three items on political trust which we have used to compose the index of trust, the beta values for the impact of the attitude toward the EC ranged between .10 and .14, and for the impact of the attitude towards 'strangers', between .12 and .22 (Goul Andersen 1992, p. 122). No other issues attained a level comparable with these two. In the meantime the Danish electorate twice have been called to give their opinions on the EC or EU issue, so it is natural that this issue has advanced to first place. The change of government has changed very little in regard to the sources of political distrust — but then, the change of government has not changed government policy appreciably on these two issues. The homeless voters continue to be those who are sceptical of the immigration policy and European policy of the political establishment.

The issues which are shown here to have the strongest impact on political distrust on the level of the individual voter do not manifest any influence on the aggregate distrust in Figure 11.1. The opposition to the EU has changed little over the years, as we saw in the beginning of chapter 10, whereas the opposition to immigration rose sharply in the mid-1980s (Gaasholt and Togeby 1995, p. 113 and p. 122). None of these curves therefore fit with the rather steady decline of political trust from 1977 onward. Nor do they fit with fluctuations in trust between elections. In 1992 when the voters rejected the Maastricht Treaty, trust was at a high level;

the year after when they accepted the treaty, trust was low (Goul Andersen 1993, pp. 160-61). This fact supports our impression of a structural relationship between the experience of political 'homelessness' and the attitude of political distrust. Hence we seem to be observing a rather permanent relation between political 'homelessness' and the attitude of political distrust.

11.4. Spending Attitudes

The rising public budgets have been widely accused of causing legitimacy problems in economically advanced societies, a problem which we discussed in chapter 7. The theory of demand overload seems to suggest a mechanism whereby the citizens pose steadily increasing demands for public expenditures, threatening to withdraw support from the political system if their demands are not met. In order to maintain a high level of support, the politicians vying for power then enter into a policy of taxing or underbudgeting which is untenable in the long run.

In accord with this theory one would expect political distrust to thrive both among those respondents who, because they have unsatisfied demands, press for higher public expenditures, and among those who, because they resent the tax burden, pressure for general budget cuts. Compared with these expectations issue scale 3 in Table 11.1 performs poorly. Even though it is observed that those pressing for more government spending have the lowest political trust of all groups in Figure 11.2 (a PDI value of –46.2), the position on scale 3 ends up at the bottom among the independent variables in Table 11.1.

But arguably this is not the right way to represent the issue of demand overload. In dividing up the budget into various item groups we might still find distrust associated with unsatisfied demands in some policy fields. People setting forth these demands would argue that they do not favour rising public budgets in general as they would cut down on other budget items. Therefore it would be useful to look closer at the relation between political trust and attitudes to government spending on individual budget items. Referring to any particular item, the spending attitude may be defined as positive for those respondents who want the government to spend more than now, neutral for those wanting the same spending as now, and negative for those wanting less government spending. The overload theory predicts a positive relation between spending attitudes and political distrust on at least some items, notably the cost-heavy welfare items.

It will be noted that the overload theory is inconsistent with the policy distance hypothesis of political distrust, since the latter may be formulated as predicting a positive relationship between distrust and any deviation from government policy, whether it results in more or less government spending. Strictly speaking the notion of policy distance seems to require information on the respondent's position as well as on that of the government's, so as to allow for the calculation we employed in the foregoing section. In the case of the spending items we do not know which amount the respondents want to spend nor which amount they believe the government is actually spending. None the less it is tempting to extend the hypothesis to spending attitudes since these may also be conceived as issue positions. People demanding that the government spend more and people demanding that it spend less in a policy field can be seen as standing on opposite sides of the government's own position. Both groups therefore signal a distance from government policy. It may not be relevant for their feelings towards the political system whether the respondents have any clear idea of which amounts of money or proportions of the national income they are juggling with. Surveys of voter's knowledge often reveal a very low level of information on even the simplest budget figures. Nonetheless a voter may still have a definite opinion on whether the amount is suitable; in the same way a person may not know what the temperature is in a room but still have a definite opinion on whether it should be higher or lower. Actually, spending attitudes may work better than issue positions for the reason advanced by proponents of directional theory, namely that voters think in terms of opposites rather than positions (see chapter 3).

At the empirical level the policy distance hypothesis as applied to such data has received some support. Items on government spending have appeared in comparative surveys, and a relation between spending attitudes and political trust has indeed been shown to exist in several countries (Borre 1995a).

The policy distance hypothesis contends that both 'spenders' and 'cutters' express political distrust whereas the overload hypothesis contends that only 'spenders' do so. The implications of the two hypotheses should be clear, at least in theory. If political distrust is found particularly among the 'spenders', the political system may be pressed into an expansionist budgetary policy which is untenable in the long run. If it is found among 'spenders' and 'cutters' alike, such a development is not likely. Rather, the political problem will be to avoid a too pointed conflict between these two groups.

As shown in chapter 7, spending attitudes are measured in the Danish 1994 survey by means of a list of twenty budget items or policy fields on which the respondents were asked to indicate whether the government was spending too much, too little, or the right amount. Our first analysis deals with a crude index of all the spending items mentioned in chapter 7. Across all twenty budget items a 'policy distance' variable was scored 1 for each item on which the government was considered as using either too much or too little, 0 for items on which it was thought to use a suitable amount. In this way we obtained a distance score between 0 and

20 for each respondent. According to the policy distance hypothesis we expect the number of budget items on which the respondent disagrees with the present policy to be directly related to distrust in politics.

The distance score indeed turned out to be negatively related to political trust, r=–.29. Thus the first evidence was encouraging for the policy distance hypothesis. Table 11.2 gives an impression of the relation, trust being measured as PDI scores.

Table 11.2.   *Political trust, by number of budget items on which the government spends either too much or too little*

	Trust, PDI value	No. of cases
Government spends too much or too little on:		
0-7 items	33	(457)
8-12 items	8	(948)
13-20 items	–17	(309)

Note: Trust measured as per cent trustful minus per cent distrustful.

From the column of figures we observe that the balance of trustful to distrustful changes from +33 to –17 percentage points as we move from the group with few demands to those with many demands for change in the budgetary policy. Hence the hypothesis is supported.

Compared with positional distance as defined in the way of Table 11.1, how important is 'budget' distance in generating political distrust? To get a rough answer to that question we bring these two distance variables together in a regression analysis (Table 11.3).

Table 11.3.   *Regression analysis of political trust as a function of policy distance and budget demands*

Independent variable	r	Beta	T value
Policy distance	–.31	–.25	–6.5**
Budget demands	–.29	–.19	–6.6**
Multiple correlation	.36		

Note: Policy distance measured as distance from the Social Democratic position summed across the seven issues in Figure 11.2. Budget demands measured as the no. out of 20 items on which the respondent wants the government to spend either more or less than now.

Positional distance seems to be the slightly stronger variable as measured by correlation or regression coefficients. But both measures of distance to government clearly have a net negative impact upon political trust.

11.5. Demand Overload and Distrust

How does the 'demand overload' hypothesis fare? This of course cannot be seen in Table 11.2 because it merges respondents who think government spends too much (the 'cutters') with those who think it spends too little (the 'spenders'). The policy distance hypothesis predicts a decline in political trust in both directions, whereas the demand overload hypothesis predicts a decline in trust particularly among those who think the government spends too little. Table 11.4 tests the latter hypothesis by computing an index of net spending, defined as the number of items on which the respondent wanted the government to spend more, minus the no. on which he or she wanted it to spend less than now.

Table 11.4.   Political trust by spending attitude

	Trust, PDI value	No of cases
Government should:		
Save on 2 or more items	−1	412
Save or spend on 0-1 item	12	515
Spend on 2-3 items	11	419
Spend on 4-6 items	11	428
Spend on 7 or more items	11	247

Note: Trust measured as per cent trusting minus per cent distrusting. Spending attitude measured as difference between no. of items on which respondent wants government to spend more and no. on which he or she wants government to spend less.

In contrast to what is expected from the overload hypothesis, political trust is no lower among those who want to spend on many budget items than among those wanting to spend on a few. Indeed the only tendency we observe is the comparatively low trust among those who mention a balance of two or more items as objects for cutting the public budgets.

So far, the data favours the policy distance hypothesis over the demand overload hypothesis. However, an objection to the crude analysis in Table 11.4 is that all twenty budget items are counted equally even though of course some naturally weigh more heavily than others, both in real economic terms and in the eyes of the voters. The welfare items of spending on old age pensions, unemployment benefits, and health care especially loom large in Danish public budgets. As we know from chapter 8, these items are also of great public concern. It is therefore too early to dismiss the overload hypothesis. It may still be true that 'spenders' on these big welfare fields constitute an important part of the distrustful electorate.

We therefore want to know whether overspending or underspending in particular policy fields are important factors in causing distrust in government. Previously, demands concerning budget items were found to cluster in a few dimensions, associated with political agendas which constitute political cleavage lines (see chapter 7). Spending on welfare items constitute one such group of issues that have been a long-standing topic of controversy. Spending on cultural activities and environmental protection constituted another group of issues, probably of more recent origin. Spending on police and the military was a third cluster of issues, and one which have been a source of grievance with high ideological charge. In addition to these item clusters, which by and large have been found to exist in several west European electorates (Borre 1995a), we investigate the attitude toward aid to refugees and to developing countries since these issues have divided the new left and the new right during the 1980s (cf. chapter 2).

Our findings may be recapitulated as follows. First, an index of attitudes toward welfare spending was formed by adding the responses concerning old age pensions, health, and unemployment benefits. A clear negative relation between welfare spending and political trust was found. In terms of PDI value (per cent trusting minus per cent distrusting), political trust was highest (+31 per cent), among those who thought the government was spending too much on at least two of these three items, and it was lowest (−12 per cent) among those who thought the government was spending too little on all three items. This relation is the one predicted by the demand overload hypothesis.

Second, an index of attitudes toward spending on culture, education, and the environment was formed in the same way. Here the relation between the index value and political trust was the reverse, the PDI value for political trust reaching its maximum (+25 per cent) among those who wanted the government to spend more on all three items, and its minimum (−12 per cent) among those wanting it to spend less on at least two of these items.

Third, adding responses about expenses to the police and military forces, we found trust reaching a maximum in the middle categories and dropping off towards both ends, as predicted from the policy distance hypothesis.

Finally, adding responses concerning expenses to refugees and to developing countries, we found political trust to be particularly high among those who thought the government should spend the same as now (+31 percentage points), or spend more on one but not both of these items (+29 per cent), while the trust was lowest (−16 per cent) among those who thought the government should spend less than now on both items.

Thus the demand overload hypothesis applies to the welfare items, but on the attitude toward spending on refugees and third world aid, as well as spending on culture, education, and the environment, the distrustful seem to compensate by asking for less government activity.

What is the relative importance of these spending attitudes for respondent's trust in government? In Table 11.5 we attempt to answer this question by means of regression analysis. Preference for more spending in these four budgetary fields are entered as independent variables as determinants of political trust. Consistent with the foregoing table we expect negative effects of spending on the welfare items and positive effects of spending on refugees/third world aid and on culture/-environmental items. With regard to spending on police and the military, the linear effect is expected to vanish because of the non-linear shape of the relationship.

Table 11.5.   *Regression analysis of political trust as a function of spending attitudes in four policy fields*

	Beta	T value	Sign.
Government should spend more on:			
Welfare	−.15	−5.8	**
Culture & environment	.02	.7	
Police & defence	.01	.3	
Immigrants & third world	.24	8.6	**
Multiple correlation	.29		**

Note: The index of attitude to spending on welfare and on culture and environment were scored from +3 to –3; those on police and defence and on immigrants and third world were scored from +2 to –2.

These expectations largely are fulfilled in Table 11.5. However, the effect of spending on culture and environment vanishes into insignificance when the other budget demands are used as control variables. It is also somewhat surprising that the effect of spending on refugees and third world countries comes out as the most important source of political trust — although perhaps we should expect this result from our previous findings in Figure 11.2 and Table 11.1. That effect combines with the negative effect of welfare demands to produce a multiple correlation coefficient of R=.29.

We may conclude that in addition to the simple policy distance hypothesis we have investigated, there are also grounds for investigating the effects of more specific demands for high or low spending as sources of distrust. People who demand a *higher* level of welfare on the 'heavy' items are definitely less trustful than other voters. People who demand a *lower* level of spending on refugees and third world aid are also less trusting.

Combining these tendencies we may speak of 'welfare chauvinism' as an important source of political distrust. Welfare chauvinists want the government to spend its money on domestic welfare recipients rather than foreign or foreign-born recipients, the latter being seen as having no right to be treated on a par with citizens of the nation. It is to be noted, however, that the attitude of welfare chauvinism may well have been nourished by the concrete policies executed by the Danish political establishment. Over the years Denmark has consistently been among the leading nations in third-world aid whereas she has slid downward in expenses for the health sector.

11.6. Ideology, Education, and Political Trust

In the two last sections we have shown that distrust is systematically related to distance from actual (Social Democratic) government policy and to a preference for spending more on welfare budget items and less on items concerned with immigrations and third world aid. Such issues stands are popular among people who feel that they have little influence, that they are more or less permanently being overruled by elite decisions, etc. Resistance to Danish EU policy and Danish policy on immigration, refugees, third world countries, and probably many others that have a flavour of ethnocentrism, provincialism, and populism, seem to generate distrust in politics. We may now try to look at these findings in the old *versus* new politics framework that was introduced in chapter 2. From that chapter we should have a fairly good bird's-eye view of where the distrustful voters are located ideologically, namely to the right on the new politics dimension.

This view is confirmed by applying the distinctions in chapter 2 to our indicator of political trust. The result is shown in Tables 11.6 and 11.7.

Table 11.6.   *Political trust, by old and new politics position*

Scale Position	Old politics scale			New politics scale		
	Trust PDI		N	Trust PDI		N
Left	9		(424)	32		(440)
Centre-Left	5		(438)	18		(305)
Centre	9		(311)	14		(345)
Centre-Right	9		(426)	−1		(375)
Right	12		(276)	−18		(412)

Note: Trust measured as per cent trusting minus per cent distrusting. For the definition of
ideological position, see chapter 2. Old politics position was coded so that Left=4-8, Centre-Left=9-
11, Centre=12-13, Centre-Right=14-16, and Right=17-20. New politics position was coded
so that Left=4-10, Centre-Left=11-12, Centre=13-14, Centre-Right=15-16, and Right=17-20.

Table 11.7.   *Political trust by ideological type*

Ideological type	Trust PDI	N
Left Wing	23	(479)
Old Socialists	−5	(564)
Green Bourgeois	32	(266)
Right Wing	−1	(568)

Note: Trust measured as per cent trusting minus per cent distrusting. For the definition of the
ideological types, see chapter 2.

Table 11.6, the left-hand columns, shows that there is no relationship between old
politics position and political trust, at last on these items. The tendency toward
'cynicism of the left' and 'cynicism of the right', which has been found in American
data (Miller 1974), does not exist in the Danish electorate of the nineties, although
earlier studies suggest that it did so in the seventies (Goul Andersen 1984c). The
second column shows that by contrast there is a distinct relationship between distrust
and new right position. Political trust as measured by the PDI index moves steadily
downward from +32 to −18 percentage points as we go from left to right.

Table 11.7 combines the old and new politics dimensions into four ideological
types of voters in the way we defined in chapter 2. The result is that the Left Wing
and the Green Bourgeois are found to have a predominance of trustful voters, whereas
the Old Socialists and the Right Wing are almost equally divided between trustful
and distrustful voters.

The association between distrust and new right position has not been reported
for other countries in a form that is as unambiguous as in the Danish electorate.
And it differs in an important way from the more usual findings that voters on
the wings of the political system are less trusting than voters near the centre. It

is evidently also a more specific mechanism than the policy distance relationship we have studied in this chapter. That mechanism might explain why new right extremists are distrustful but not why new left extremists are among the most trustful.

The new right, from its inception in the Progress party and Centre Democratic party in the early 1970s, was an uprising against the new left, which was accused of exerting a left-intellectual hegemony on Danish political thinking and policy. This view was confirmed in chapter 2 where we found a distinct relation between the new politics dimension and the level of school education: the new dimension separated the well-educated on the left from the poorly educated on the right. Much like the class cleavage became politicised in the old politics dimension of industrial society, the educational cleavage has become politicised in the new politics dimension of the post-industrial society. Therefore we also should expect the problem of political support to be shifted away from the working class and toward the un-educated strata of society.

Table 11.8 is consistent with our expectations at this point. It shows a fair relationship between political trust and the level of school education, with a PDI value rising from –3 percentage points among those with seven years of schooling to 26 per cent among those with twelve years schooling.

Table 11.8. *Political trust by level of school education*

School education	Trust, PDI value	No. of cases
Primary, 7 years	–3	(545)
Primary, 8-9 years	1	(281)
Secondary, 10 years	10	(638)
Higher, 12 years	26	(413)

Note: Entries are per cent trusting minus per cent distrusting.

Now, in theory it is possible that the effect of low education on distrust and the effect of policy distance are two aspects of the same relationship. This could happen if those with low education tended strongly to exhibit a long policy distance. But there is nothing to indicate that voters with low school education are at odds with their government, especially when the government is a Social Democratic one. Rather, we assume that low education constitutes a separate source of distrust in the modern Danish political system. The diagram in Figure 11.4 supports that assumption by showing those with low education (L) lying consistently below those with higher education (H) at each level of policy distance.

Figure 11.4. Policy distance and political trust for voters at different levels of school education (L=lower, H=higher)

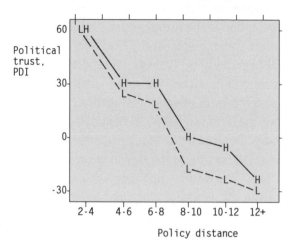

Policy distance

Note: Policy distance is the sum of respondent's distance from the position of the Social Democratic party, summed across all seven issues in Figure 11.2.

A similar tendency can be observed in regressing political trust on the level of education, controlling for policy distance (Table 11.9). The raw correlation between level of education and political trust, identical with the beta effect, is r=.16. If one controls for both policy distance on seven issues and budget demands on twenty budget items, the effect of educational level is reduced to a beta=.11. This magnitude still represents a significant effect of educational level.

Table 11.9. Regression analysis of political trust as a function of school education, positional distance, and spending attitudes

Independent variable	Pearson r	Beta
School education	.16**	.11**
Policy distance	−.31**	−.24**
Spending attitudes	−.29**	−.19**
Multiple correlation	.38**	

Note: Policy distance measured as distance from the Social Democratic position summed across the seven issues in Figure 11.2. Spending attitudes measured as no. of items on which the respondent wants the government to spend either more or less than now.

These findings, along with those of the two previous tables, indicate that policy distance is the main source of political distrust, though not the only one. Policy-related distrust may be viewed as a rather technical, matter-of-fact expression of criticism of the line of policy pursued by the present government. But the sources of distrust

318   Voting and Political Attitudes in Denmark

we have disclosed in the last sections may be described as more deep-seated problems of compatibility between voters' everyday experience and the terms of modern government. Political distrust in this sense is probably a price to be paid for a development of society which is spearheaded by an intellectually and technologically advanced elite with an international orientation.

11.7. Government and Opposition

In chapter 3 policy distance was shown to be negatively related to support for the party from whose position the distance was measured. Such findings are generally heralded in electoral research as signs of voter rationality. They imply that people who disagree with the policy of the governing party or parties normally will be closer to one of the opposition parties, and if there are enough of such people, the government as well as the government policy will change.

In the present chapter we find a different version of the inverse distance/support relationship. People whose distance from actual government policy is large respond by reducing their support for the political system, not only for the governing party or parties. In one sense this response may also be construed as rational. Government policy is in practice what the political system has to offer, the alternative policy of opposition parties being temporarily overruled. Thus the political system is identified with the government policy and as such evaluated as a vehicle for implementing the goals of the voter. Falling short of fulfilling the voter's goals, it is evaluated negatively; thus the concept of political support represents the voter's chance of implementing his own goals successfully.

However, responding with political distrust to disagreement with the government over the line of policy or the public budget may nevertheless seem ill-judged in a multiparty democracy like the Danish, which offers all sorts of parties with a variety of policy positions. The question is therefore, why withhold support for the political system when the system offers seemingly good facilities for influence? An important corollary of party democracy is that opposition parties protect the political system from losing the support of its citizens.

We may contrast three possible relationships. One possibility is that there is no appreciable difference between the voters of the government and those of the opposition with respect to political trust, once we control for policy distance. The lower level of trust among opposition voters is then produced by their longer distance from government policy. The second possibility is that opposition voters display a deficit of political support beyond the effect of their longer policy distance. Such a deficit might be due to their lack of representation in government. Because most of the important politicians belong to the enemy, the opposition voters react with negative attitudes to politicians. The third possibility is the reverse of the first. If political trust is solely generated by being in government, distrust by being in opposition, the relationship between policy distance and political distrust will vanish after control for party. This possibility is of course contrary to our hypothesis, which holds that policy distance is a genuine variable.

Table 11.10 reports the regression effect of voting for the government or opposition on political trust, when controlling for the two policy variables.

Table 11.10. *Regression analysis of political trust as a function of voting choice (government or opposition), policy distance, and budget demands*

Independent variable	r	Beta
Opposition vote	−.09**	−.02
Policy distance	−.31**	−.24**
Budget demands	−.29**	−.19**
Multiple correlation	.34**	

Note: Policy distance measured as distance from the Social Democratic position summed across the seven issues in Figure 11.2. Budget demands measured as no. of items on which the respondent wants the government to spend either more or less than now.

The main point to note is that there is no significant relationship between voting for the opposition party and political trust once controls for the policy variables are introduced. The original correlation of r=.09 is produced by a tendency for opposition voters to be at a longer distance than government voters from the Social Democratic position. Thus the first possibility is shown in our data.

11.8. Policy Distance and Support for Representative Democracy

Throughout the chapter we have used an index of three attitudinal items of political trust as an operational indicator of political support. This procedure may raise doubt as to the generality of our findings, even within the context of the Danish surveys. Is political support adequately expressed in our measure of distrust in government? That measure, as defined in the introductory section, contained one item on whether politicians were making the right decisions, and one on whether politicians cared about voter opinions. Now, one can argue that of course those who are near to government policy will agree that politicians make the right decisions, and that politicians care about voter opinions; for the typical respondent will identify his own position with the 'right' decision and with 'voter opinions'. Distrust on these counts may not go deep into the problem of the alienated voter. To mention an obvious example, a person who believes that it would be the right decision to keep Denmark out of EU, will find it difficult to agree that our political leaders make the right decisions for the country. Hence, according to our definition this person shows low political support. But it does not follow that the person thinks parliamentary decisions should not be respected. There is no reason to think that the person is chronically alienated from the political system.

According to such an argument, policy distance may have only a limited and temporary effect on political support. The 'deeper' levels of support for the democratic rules of the game and for the political community are not supposed to be affected. In testing the argument we should therefore turn to items that take as their object those national political norms which are as far as possible invariant to the change of government and indeed the turnover of the teams of leading politicians. Does the policy distance hypothesis hold also for such attitudes?

Below, we have explored two attitudinal indicators of this type, namely the degree of satisfaction with the way democracy is working, and the demands for more public referenda. For most practical purposes, 'democracy' is identified with parliaments and elections, at least in the Danish political vocabulary (Svensson 1995). Grave doubts about the functioning of democracy are invariably expressed, in parliamentary speeches or the media, when the parliament as a whole is unable to make critical decisions, to produce adequate solutions, to assume responsibility for some societal malady, or the like. The usual remedy is to recommend either a popular referendum to settle the matter or a 'strong man' equipped with power to supersede the parliamentary majority.

Table 11.11 shows the relation between on one hand the average distance from the Social Democratic position on seven issues and on the other, satisfaction with democracy and demands for more popular referenda.

It is clear that the greater the distance, the less the satisfaction with democracy and the stronger the demands for referenda. From those nearest to government policy to those most removed from it, the per cent who are satisfied with the way democracy is working drops from 98 to 66 per cent, and the support for more referenda grows from 28 to 69 per cent. Thus the argument that our findings hinge on the wording of the political distrust items can be rejected. Policy distance leads to negative feelings about the outcome of the process of indirect democracy and sympathy with more direct methods.

Table 11.11.   *Satisfaction with democracy and demands for more referenda as functions of distance from government policy on seven issues*

	Satisfied with democracy per cent	Want more referenda per cent	N (100 per cent)
Distance from Government:			
2-3.99 positions	98	28	(40)
4-5.99 positions	95	35	(205)
6-7.99 positions	92	37	(188)
8-9.99 positions	88	49	(125)
10-11.99 positions	74	68	(68)
12 or more	66	69	(38)
All	89	43	(665)

Note: Distance from government policy is the sum of respondent's distance from the position of the Social Democratic party, summed across all seven issues in Figure 11.2.

Now, according to the Eurobarometer, the Danish electorate ranks high in regard to its satisfaction with the way democracy is working (Inglehart 1990, p. 435; Goul Andersen 1994). We also observe in Table 11.11 that even among those furthest removed from government policy, two thirds are satisfied with the functioning of Danish democracy. Thus many respondents who exhibit low support on the trust items still think positively about the way the system functions. Nonetheless it cannot be denied that satisfaction with the way democracy is working has a clear policy component. About one-third of the Danish population make their support for the way democracy is working contingent on a government policy that meets their demands.

Even more make their attitude towards popular referenda contingent upon such a policy. The relationship between policy distance and attitude toward referenda suggests that popular referenda appeal to some of the 'distant' voters as one way of pulling government policy nearer toward their own position. The declining support for 'the way democracy is working' which goes with increasing policy distance, therefore, does not necessarily mean a decline in support for democratic methods.

Rather, we suggest that policy distance leads to a search for alternative channels of influence, one of which is a more direct form of democracy. It would take us beyond the scope of this chapter to investigate such an hypothesis systematically, but we cite a piece of evidence in support of it. The opinion that "It would be quite sensible to have a strong man seize power in a situation of economic crisis," obviously expresses scepticism about parliamentary methods. However, it seems to suggest the opposite solution than does response to the item about more public referenda. Nonetheless the responses to these two items are positively correlated (r=.16), and

Voting and Political Attitudes in Denmark

both are negatively related to the trust items. Thus the tendency is that policy distance breeds not only distrust in politicians but also a certain sympathy with *any* method of circumventing parliamentary methods in favour of more direct forms of decision-making.

11.9. Conclusions

The point of departure for this chapter was the idea that political support is a negative function of the agreement between demand input and policy output. That idea was to be developed into hypotheses to be tested on the micro level using the Danish 1994 election as our main source of data. In the case of the tests being successful this would speak for a theory of political support which laid its emphasis on comparatively rational notions such as political goals and interest, strategies, and rewards, rather than seeing support as expressions of emotional undercurrents, reactions to symbols, and the like.

The analysis has indeed shown policy distance to constitute an important source of political (dis)trust. In particular two issues stand out as having a sizeable proportion of distrustful voters at some distance from official Danish policy. One is the EU issue, on which the trust index varies from a high PDI value of +34 points among the moderate 'Europeans' to a low value of −35 among the ardent opponents of Danish membership. The other is the issue of refugees, where the index varies from +29 points among the supporters of a moderately liberal policy to −28 percentage points among the stubborn restrictionists.

In addition to policy distances, the inclination of a respondent to disagree with the public budget in a general way has also been shown to be associated with political distrust. According to Table 11.2, those who wanted to depart from the budget on less than one third of the items had a trust index value of +33 percentage points, whereas those who departed on two thirds of the items had a value of −17 points. Whatever the psychological mechanism involved, it seems clear that an inclination for quarrelling with the distribution of the public expenditures goes along with a low opinion of politicians. Distrust in politics implies a low acceptance of politicians' budget decisions.

But in applying the policy distance model we also noted some anomalies. People who thought the government should spend more on welfare than it currently does, were distrustful while their opposite numbers, who wanted to cut welfare expenses, were trustful. On aid to immigrants and developing countries the situation was the reverse. Thus the claim that political distrust feeds on 'welfare chauvinism' was supported. That claim anyway seems more correct than the claim that distrust feeds on demands for higher public expenses, for the distrustful also have their pet items on which they propose a cut in government expenditure. When continuing our analysis along these lines we found that political trust was related to the new left, distrust to the new right. That is, political distrust fits into a populist ideology which seems to have taken hold during the decline of both the classical left and the classical right.

Though our measure of political trust may seem too narrow to represent the entire concept of political support, we showed in the final section that it matters little if we exchange it with other indicators of attachment to the institutions of representative government. Thus our findings may well have a broader validity than is implied in the indicators we have used in this chapter.

12

CAUSES OF THE 1994 ELECTION: A SUMMARY

The Danish 1994 election was a defeat for the centre-left government led by Social Democrat Poul Nyrup Rasmussen, and a victory for its opposition on the right. In the preceding chapters we have investigated a number of factors that may have contributed to the outcome of the election. Here we review these factors and evaluate their significance for Danish voting behaviour more generally.

The election occurred while the national economy was moving into a growth phase. This had not yet materialised *e.g.* in declining budget deficits, nor in declining unemployment in spite of almost desperate attempts to 'crack the unemployment curve' by means of new leave arrangements, transitory allowances, public investments etc. But economic *expectations* had improved dramatically around the beginning of 1994. And the private economy had been improved significantly by means of lower taxes for the population and lower interest payments for house owners. In 1994, private consumption exploded. Moreover, issues related to the economy were high on the campaign agenda of both the government and the opposition. Elementary public choice theory would predict that a government should be rewarded in such a case, but it was not. The Social Democratic party went back by three per cent of the vote cast, and together the four parties constituting the government went back from 48 to 44 per cent; one of them, the Christian People's party, lost its seats in the parliament. And the following years of 1995-1996, which have brought further economic growth, have not improved the government's standing in the polls, quite the contrary. Through most of 1996, the Centre Democratic party has been around the two per cent threshold of parliamentary representation according to the polls, and by the end of the year it withdrew from the government, thereby reducing the government coalition to two parties, the Social Democratic and the Radical Liberal.

However, it is important to see the 1994 election in a longer time perspective. In chapter 1 we started by pointing out that the foregoing 1990 election was exceptionally good for the Social Democratic party, raising its share of the vote to over 37 per cent of the vote in contrast to the 30 per cent which had become the standard during the four general elections held during the eighties. Actually the Social Democratic party had almost returned to that level before its first year in government had ended, probably because of widespread scepticism about its economic policy. With the backdrop of this history it is an open question whether it was a poor performance to obtain 34-35 per cent in the 1994 election. Even the fact that the Social Democratic party had by 1996 come down to around thirty per cent, according to the polls, suggests no more than a return to the party's normal vote, thereby signifying an absence of those forces which operated in its favour in 1990, when bourgeois coalition governments had been in power for over eight years. Obviously the evaluation of the election depends on what baseline is used for comparison.

If, however, thirty per cent is to be reckoned as the future standard of the Social Democratic vote, this leads to a reassessment of the long-term partisan balance in Danish politics. Until 1980 Social Democratic government was thought to be the normal state of affairs: for the period of two generations that had elapsed since 1920, Social Democrats had been prime minsters for almost three quarters of the time.

This period roughly corresponds to the era during which the welfare state, though still growing, was built up and extended to its present standard. After 1980 the Danish welfare state seems to have become replaced by international competition as the main *dynamic* force in Danish politics. This may have broken the Social Democratic hegemony permanently.

As we noted in chapter 1, since 1987 the ideological trend has been clearly rightward, an attitudinal trend that is obscured by the result of the 1990 election. Its relevance for voting behaviour shows up better in the strength of the left-wing parties, which has declined from twenty per cent in 1987 to ten in 1994, its lowest point since 1977. This means that the total social-democratic/socialist vote has reached its lowest point since the 'earthquake' election in 1973, which separates the old from the new party system.

Under these circumstances it is hard to believe in a reinstatement of the social democratic dominance in Danish politics. An argument that points in the same direction is that the vote for the small centre parties, whose balancing position traditionally has decided Danish government formation, has been gradually decreasing toward a point at which these parties will lose their commanding position. They used their power to replace a Conservative-Liberal government with the present one in early 1993. In the 1994 election they obtained nine per cent of the vote between them, enough to secure the continuation of the government (as long as the left-wing could be counted on not to vote together with the bourgeois opposition). But this 9 per cent, the lowest level since the early 1960s, is a far cry from the 26 per cent with which the centre parties started out in the new party system of 1973. Over the years the centre parties have steadily lost voter support. It seems that there is a price to be paid for holding the key to the formation of governments.

Voting and Political Attitudes in Denmark

Hence, if the ideological drift toward the right continues, the Social Democratic hegemony is likely to be broken by a bourgeois hegemony, the beginning of which we have seen in the eighties. During that decade the dominant bourgeois party was the Conservative party; but in the nineties the initiative has been taken over by the Liberal party. This was originally the farmers' party and represented a more moderate right than the Conservative party. Lately it has launched a more consistent neo-liberal policy, sharply opposed to the Social Democratic insistence on maintaining the welfare state, and somewhat distinguished from a more communitarian ideology which is represented by the Conservative party. The Liberal party scored a great victory among the voters in the 1994 and in the polls of 1995-96 has proceeded to garner almost the same share of the vote as the Social Democratic party.

The ideological trend to the right on a number of attitudes, especially those in favour of individualism and opposed to further egalitarian politics, fits with the present strength of the Liberal party and the weakness of the Social Democratic party. Therefore, a simple explanation of the 1994 election which was suggested in chapter 1, is that it manifested this current.

However, this view was qualified on many points in subsequent chapters as our analysis was elaborated. First, setting up a framework of old *vs.* new politics in chapter 2, we cited the theoretical arguments that even though attitudes might turn toward the right on old politics matters dealing especially with economic issues, they might turn toward the left on new politics issues dealing with quality-of-life issues. And as suggested by the labels 'old' and 'new', the latter type of issues are growing in importance, the driving force being a general rise in income and educational level. In order to study the election in a two-dimensional perspective we proceeded to divide our 1990 and 1994 samples of respondents into four ideological types by combining the old and new politics dimension. As predicted we found a change toward the right (of a magnitude of 5 percentage points, cf. Table 2.2) on old politics attitudes. On new politics attitudes, no significant change either toward left or right took place between 1990 and 1994. The rightward shift in economic attitudes in spite of the favourable economic conditions suggests that the electorate reacted against traditional Social-Democratic economic policies *in spite of their apparent success*. Such a reaction would not be entirely irrational granted that these policies had run into disrepute during the former Social-Democratic government at the end of the seventies.

In order to pursue this idea it was necessary first to develop a policy-oriented framework of analysis. The question about the effects of specific economic policies was therefore not taken up until chapters 8 and 9. In chapter 3 our theoretical model was extended to include the notion of respondents' policy distances from various parties on different issues. We wanted to establish that to a great extent voters choose the 'nearest' party. Consequently, according to that model, electoral change is seen as resulting from changing policies on the part of the parties or changing issue positions on the part of the voters on pertinent issues. One explanation of the electoral defeat of a government is therefore that a group of voters discover that they are nearer to some opposition party than to the policy of their government. Actually, such is the case with major shares of the traditional Social Democratic voters on the issues of EU membership, law-and-order, and refugee policy. While the EU opposition among Social Democratic voters has been recognised for over twenty years, the resistance to the party's fairly liberal stance on law-and-order and refugee policy has mostly led a shadowy existence. It is possible that in the 1994 election it became activated and contributed to vote switching toward the Liberal and Progressive parties, whose stands were perceived by these voters to be closer to their own.

This explanation presupposes that the economic issues were not as relevant for the voters as were a number of social issues. In chapter 4 we find support for this view. The social-democratically led government was seen by the majority to be superior to a bourgeois government in handling such problems as protecting the environment and the welfare state; but in spite of its economic results, it was seen as inferior to a bourgeois government in solving the country's economic problems, in fighting the public budget deficit, and in securing the country a modern industry.

The entire four-year period of Social Democratic leadership, from the beginning of 1993 to the end of 1996, conveys the impression of good performance in economics and poor performance in politics. Yet if we ignore the previous election for a moment, as it is clearly a deviant election, the picture of the 1994 election is not nearly as bleak for the government. The estimates we can make from the tables in chapter 4 indicate that the Social Democratic party had 36 per cent of the party identifiers in our sample and received 31 per cent of the non-identifiers' votes; the government as a whole had 44 per cent of the party identifiers and received 39 per cent of the votes of those respondents who did not identify with any party. These differences of only five percentage points suggest that the uncommitted voters divided almost like the parties' core voters: there were short-term forces directed against the government, but also some indication that they may be overrated.

One component of these short-term forces might be the differential popularity of the party leaders among the electorate. The media, being preoccupied with the observable loss of voters for the government, have naturally focused their searchlight on Prime Minister Nyrup Rasmussen, pointing to an unfortunate handling of a number of decisions and appearances. We investigated this explanation in chapter 4 and concluded that even though the ratings of the leading politicians exerted a significant impact on the vote, and even after controlling for party identification and policy preferences, the difference in ratings between Nyrup Rasmussen and the two leading opposition leaders was too small to explain more than a fraction of the election result. Hence, the point is not that personal popularity does not count but that the opposition leaders were not much more popular than the Prime Minister.

To postulate that issue positions and policy voting have come to play a dominant role in Danish voting behaviour implies a perspective in which social classes either have lost their relevance or have changed so as to acquire a new relevance for the party choice. In chapter 5 the hypothesis of declining class voting was revisited. It was shown that the class division between workers and non-workers was significantly weakened in 1994 but that this did not derive from a long-term 'embourgeoisement' effect of increasing wealth among workers. At the same time, it was shown that occupational divisions in party choice have far from disappeared. New divisions have emerged, in particular between non-manual employees in the private and the public sector. To some degree, these sector changes reveal self-reinforcing processes of political mobilisation. But they also reveal different values linked to the boundaries of the welfare state strategy and to new strategies of international competition. Next, we found a most significant class-specific move to the right among manual workers in the 1994 election which is intimately linked to the conflict over 'new politics' issues where education plays an important role. Thus, our two-dimensional model of political attitudes in chapter 2 can be traced back to social change in what is somewhat loosely labelled 'post-modern society'.

These types of social change are manifested in generational and age differences, which are observed in chapter 5 to be especially significant in the case of Denmark compared with most other countries. The rather sharply bounded 'red' cohorts of voters born during the 1950s pioneered the new left, and until the end of the eighties they exerted a considerable impact on the aggregated vote for the socialist parties. The new generations born during the sixties and seventies are predominantly neo-liberal in outlook and, on the whole, less interested than their predecessors in politics.

By coupling the analysis of class and generation with our two-dimensional left-right perspective we obtain a different view of the 1994 election. Part of the explanation remains with the declining acceptance of classical socialist ideas and policies. However, the government suffered its major losses among those on the new right and within working-class group that were formerly among the core supporters of the Social Democratic party. The bourgeois parties, especially the Liberal party, made their greatest gains among those demanding a more restrictive policy on issues like law-and-order and refugees. Thus it seems that between the 1990 and 1994 elections a rather unnoticed battle between the government and the bourgeois opposition had been fought out on the new right. That battle was lost by the government, which went from a clear lead of ten per cent in the 1990 election on this ideological wing to an even clearer deficit of fourteen per cent in 1994. It seems that the government had been anxious to get in through the voters' front door with its good economic news but failed to notice that the voters were on their way out to leave by the back door.

The new politics dimension is an potentially important ideological perspective for Danish voting behaviour as social and partisan blocks of voters are clearly aligned along it, some on the right and others on the left. But the large parties tend to wage their campaigns on economic and social issues. Our analysis in chapter 7 demonstrates that the agenda of the 1994 election was focused on unemployment problems and problems related with the welfare state. More purely economic issues of wages and prices, production and foreign trade, taxes and public budgets, did not catch the attention of the electorate. What remained in the economic sphere were issues having an important social and human side, such as problems encountered during the attempts to cut welfare expenditures and reduce unemployment. Superficially it might be thought that such problem areas would more or less automatically favour a socialist government over a bourgeois one. However, chapter 7 revealed a deep cleavage between the two largest partisan blocks, the Social Democrats on one side and the Liberal-Conservative on the other, on these issues: a 'social' position favoured by the former was opposed to an 'economic' position favoured by the latter. The call for social protection was countered by liberal calls for market solutions in the welfare system.

Our explanation of the 1994 election therefore leads into a discussion of the strategies of welfare and employment policies, which we conducted in chapters 8 and 9. First, concerning welfare policies, one might expect the costly Danish welfare state to become a central topic of debate in recent elections including the 1994 one: and it is true that when asked which concerns were most important for the vote, our respondents pointed to health care, unemployment, and old age care as the three most important among ten concerns. From this one might deduce that the Social-Democratically dominated government was fighting a two-front battle, against a bourgeois opposition bent on cutting the welfare state, and against a left-wing opposition bent on expanding it. But surprising, such a squeeze was not a major factor in the election outcome. The reason is a consensus in the Danish population that the general *level* of welfare is the right one. Therefore, the partisan disagreement deals mostly with *strategies* for attaining that level, especially whether and where privatisation would work, how abuse can be checked, and how demographic changes will affect the welfare state in the future. These topics are not likely to evoke a major conflict between the haves and the have-nots; rather, they lead to skirmishes in which one side may score a point or two over the other.

Chapter 8 argues that the more basic reason for the consensus is that the Danish welfare state is integrative rather than divisive. Almost every major sector of the society has a stake in it which they do not want to lose; its benefits do not therefore stigmatise or marginalise the receivers.

Next, concerning unemployment policies, Danish public opinion appears gradually to have gravitated toward the view that there is too little work for everybody to be full-time employed. But while the public thus concurs with the economists that unemployment is structural rather than transitional, it disagrees with them about the way to face such a situation. Local arrangements for work-sharing are highly popular. Much less popular are reductions in the minimum wage or in unemployment benefits. Also unpopular are some measures that seem to have aroused the suspicion of the Danish public. This is the case with the 'growth' or 'consumption' strategy and the efforts to improve the competitiveness of Danish workers through education and incentives to social mobility. Somewhere in-between are those arrangements for parental leave or educational leave from work which have been executed by the present government.

In chapter 9 the attitudes toward these strategies are examined. In respect to partisan differences it is found that whereas job sharing and qualification strategies are especially popular among left-wing voters, market-incentive and control strategies are more popular on the right wing. But, as was the case with welfare strategies in chapter 8, the partisan conflict does not seem to crystallise into two opposing issue positions which could have affected the outcome of the 1994 election in any decisive way.

Chapter 10 analyses the Danish support for EU. We show that the attitude toward EU as a whole can be divided into positions on various policies that are associated with the European Union, such as its common currency, its attempt to centralise the foreign policy of its member states, and its failure to assign top priority to the struggle against unemployment and environmental pollution. The more the voter disagrees with such policies, the less he or she will support Danish membership; thus the attitude follows the policy distance model introduced in chapter 3.

The aggregated result is that Danish voters feel more reluctant about the EU than are the Danish party elites. The gap between parties and their respective voters leads to strains in several parties, notable the Social Democratic party and the Socialist People's party but also in the Liberal party. It might be expected that voters would shift to more congenial parties in order to reduce that strain. However, unlike in Norway, the EU issue in Denmark appears to have little impact on the vote at parliamentary elections. It was not on the agenda of the 1994 election; and that election was won by the Liberal party in spite of the fact that in its stand on EU, the Liberal party is further removed than any other party from the stand of the median Danish voter.

It is also hard to discern any parallel between Danish EU policy and domestic politics. In two referenda that attracted international attention, the Danish voters first rejected the Maastricht Treaty in the summer of 1992 and then accepted it with some modifications a year later. These referenda caused heated debates for eighteen months. Yet the change in government that took place in the middle of that debate occurred quite independently of the EU debate, and did not affect the outcome of the second referendum in May 1993. That outcome was determined by the concessions to Danish demands made at the EU summit meeting in December 1992.

In conclusion, what is the lesson to draw from these findings concerning the causality of electoral behaviour?

The three chapters in which we attempt to trace backward the source of the voter's positions (i.e. chapters 8-10) lead to the same conclusion: voters do not seem motivated by objective self-interest to any great extent. Rather, their positions are consistent with ideologies or values with which they sympathise. In almost all cases where self-interest dictates one policy position and ideology, a different one, we find the latter to prevail over the former.

If self-interest seems a poor guide to voting behaviour, this also explains why the government was not able, for all its success in the economic field, to turn the 1994 election into a success for its parties. The failure to relate stands on welfare and unemployment policies to the election outcome is precisely what we might expect under such circumstances.

If ideology and values are a better guide to the voter's policy position, it remains to be shown how they cause short-term fluctuations in party support. On this account we have pointed to several instances where the political discourse has favoured or (more often) disfavoured the government. We have also indicated which issues or issue positions were largely neglected in that discourse but played an important role as an undercurrent, so that the government seemed to be swimming against a tide. A more detailed analysis, outside the scope of this volume, might uncover these electoral forces and evaluate their role in the 1994 election and in contemporary voting behaviour in general.

REFERENCES

Alford, Robert A. (1963). *Party and Society. The Anglo-American Democracies*. Chicago: Rand McNally.

Aardal, Bernt, and Henry Valen (1989). *Velgere, partier og politisk avstand* [Voters, parties, and political distance]. Oslo: Central Bureau of Statistics in Norway.

Aardal, Bernt, and Henry Valen (1995). *Konflikt og opinion* [Conflict and opinion]. Oslo: NKS Forlaget.

Baker, Kendall L., Russell J. Dalton, and Kai Hildebrandt (1981). *Germany Transformed. Political Culture and the New Politics*. Cambridge, Mass., and London: Harvard University Press.

Bartolini, Stefano, and Peter Mair (1991). *Identity, Competition and Electoral Availability*. Cambridge: Cambridge University Press.

Bean, Clive, and Anthony Mughan (1989). 'Leadership Effects in Parliamentary Elections in Australia and Britain', *American Political Science Review*, vol. 83, pp. 1165-1179.

Bell, Daniel (1960). *The End of Ideology*. Glencoe, Ill.: The Free Press.

Bell, Daniel (1973). *The Coming of Post-Industrial Society*. New York: Basic Books.

Berelson, Bernard R., Paul F. Lazarsfeld, and William N. McPhee (1954). *Voting. A Study of Opinion Formation in a Presidential Campaign*. Chicago and London: The University of Chicago Press.

Betz, Hans-Georg (1994). *Right Wing Extremism in Western Europe*. New York: St. Martin's Press.

Bille, Lars, Hans Jørgen Nielsen and Steen Sauerberg (1992). *De uregerlige vælgere* [The Ungovernable Voters]. Copenhagen: Columbus.

Birch, Anthony H. (1984). 'Overload, Ungovernability and Delegitimation: The Theories and the British Case', *British Journal of Political Science*, vol. 14, pp. 135-60.

Borre, Ole (1974). 'Denmark's Protest Election of December 1973', *Scandinavian Political Studies*, vol. 9, pp. 197-204.

Borre, Ole (1975). 'The General Election in Denmark, January 1975: Toward a New Structure of the Party System?' *Scandinavian Political Studies*, vol. 10, pp. 211-216.

Borre, Ole (1984). 'Træk af den danske vælgeradfærd 1971-84', pp. 148-166 in Jørgen Elklit and Ole Tonsgaard (eds.), *Valg og vælgeradfærd* [Elections and Voting Behaviour]. Aarhus: Politica.

Borre, Ole (1989). 'Politiske generationer', pp. 208-304 in Jørgen Elklit and Ole Tonsgaard (eds.), *To folketingsvalg. Vælgerholdninger og vælgeradfærd i 1987 og 1988* [Two General Elections. Voter Attitudes and Voting Behaviour in 1987 and 1988]. Aarhus: Politica.

Borre, Ole (1991). 'The Danish General Election of 1990', *Electoral Studies*, vol. 10, no. 2.

Borre, Ole (1995a). 'Scope-of-Government Beliefs and Political Support', chapter 12 in Ole Borre and Elinor Scarbrough (eds.), *The Scope of Government*. Oxford: Oxford University Press.

Borre, Ole (1995b). 'Old and New Politics in Denmark', *Scandinavian Political Studies*, vol. 18, no. 3, pp. 187-205.

Borre, Ole (1996). 'Voting and Issues Stands in Recent Danish, Norwegian and Swedish Elections', paper presented at the ECPR Joint Sessions, Oslo, April 1996.

Borre, Ole, and Daniel Katz (1973). 'Party Identification and Its Motivational Base in a Multiparty System: A Study of the Danish General Election of 1971', *Scandinavian Political Studies*, vol. 8, pp. 69-111.

Borre, Ole, and Elinor Scarbrough (eds.) (1995). *The Scope of Government*. Oxford: Oxford University Press.

Borre, Ole and José Emanuel Viegas (1995). 'Government Intervention in the Economy', chapter 9 in Ole Borre and Elinor Scarbrough (eds.), *The Scope of Government*. Oxford: Oxford University Press.

Boyd, Richard W. (1972). 'Popular Control of Public Policy: A Normal Vote Analysis of the 1968 Election', *American Political Science Review*, vol. 66, pp. 429-449. Comments by Richard A. Brody and Benjamin I. Page, pp. 450-458, and by John H. Kessel, pp. 459-465. Rejoinder pp. 468-470.

Brody, Richard, and Benjamin Page (1972). 'Comment: The Assessment of Policy Voting', *American Political Science Review*, vol. 66, pp. 450-457.

Brooks, Joel E. (1985). 'Democratic Frustration in the Anglo-American Polities', *Western Political Quarterly*, vol. 38, pp. 250-261.

Brooks, Joel E. (1987). 'The Opinion-Policy Nexus in France', *Journal of Politics*, vol. 49, pp. 465-480.

Brooks, Joel E. (1990). 'The Opinion-Policy Nexus in Germany', *Public Opinion Quarterly*, vol. 54, pp. 508-529.

Brym, Robert J. (1980). *Intellectuals and Politics*. London: Allen & Unwin.

Budge, Ian, and Dennis Farlie (1983). *Explaining and Predicting Elections: Issue Effects and Party Strategies in Twenty-Three Democracies.* London: George Allen and Unwin.

Büchner, Bernd (1993). *Die Europäische Gemeinschaften in der Öffentlichen Meinung. Dänemark, Grossbritanien, Italien und die Bundesrepublik Deutschland im Ländervergleich.* Ph.D. Diss., Florence: European University Institute.

Campbell, Angus (1960). 'Surge and Decline: A Study of Electoral Change', *Public Opinion Quarterly*, vol. 24, pp. 397-418.

Campbell, Angus, Philip E. Converse, Warren E. Miller, and Donald E. Stokes (1960). *The American Voter.* New York: Wiley.

Christensen, Ann-Dorthe (1994). 'Køn, ungdom og værdiopbrud', pp. 175-210 i Johannes Andersen and Lars Torpe (eds.), *Demokrati og politisk kultur. Rids af et demokratisk medborgerskab.* Herning: Systime.

Commission (1995). *Employment in Europe* (Danish ed. 1995). Bruxelles: European Commission.

Confalonieri, Maria A., and Kenneth Newton (1995). 'Taxing and Spending: Tax Revolt or Tax Protest?', pp. 121-148 in Ole Borre and Elinor Scarbrough (eds.), *The Scope of Government. Beliefs in Government Volume Three.* Oxford: Oxford University Press.

Converse, Philip (1962). 'The Nature of Belief Systems in Mass Public', in David Apter (ed.), *Ideology and Discontent.*

Converse, Philip E. (1966). 'The Concept of a Normal Vote'. Chapter 3 in Angus Campbell, Philip E. Converse, Warren E. Miller and Donald E. Stokes, *Elections and the Political Order.* New York: Wiley.

Crozier, Michel L., Samuel P. Huntington and Joji Watanuki (1975). *The Crisis of Democracy.* New York: New York University Press.

Dahrendorf, Ralph (1988). *The Modern Social Conflict.* London: Weidenfeld & Nicolson.

Dalton, Russell J., Scott C. Flanagan, and Paul Beck (eds.) (1984). *Electoral Change in Advanced Industrial Democracies.* Princeton, N.J.: Princeton University Press.

Damsgaard Hansen, E., Kaj Kjærsgaard, and Jørgen Rosted (1990). *Dansk økonomisk politik. Teorier og erfaringer.* Copenhagen: Handelshøjskolens Forlag.

Dean, Hartley, and Peter Taylor-Gooby (1992). *Dependency Culture. The Explosion of a Myth.* London: Harvester Wheatsheaf.

Debray, Regis (1980). *Teachers, Writers, Celebrities. The Intellectuals of Modern France*. London: Verso.

Downs, Anthony (1957). *An Economic Theory of Democracy*. New York: Harper and Row.

Dunleavy, Patrick (1980). 'The Political Implications of Sectorial Cleavages and the Growth of State Employment', *Political Studies*, vol. 28, pp. 364-83.

Duverger, Maurice (1964). *Political Parties*. London: Methuen.

Easton, David (1965). *A Framework for Political Analysis*. Englewood Cliffs, N.J.: Prentice-Hall.

Elklit, Jørgen (1984). 'Det klassiske danske partisystem bliver til' [The classical Danish party system emerges], pp. 21-38 in Jørgen Elklit and Ole Tonsgaard (eds.), *Valg og vælgeradfærd. Studier i dansk politik* [Elections and voting behaviour. Studies in Danish politics]. Aarhus: Politica.

Esping-Andersen, Gösta (1980). *Social Class, Social Democracy and State Policy: Party Policy and Party Decomposition in Denmark and Sweden*. København: Nyt fra Samfundsvidenskaberne.

Esping-Andersen, Gösta (1990). *The Three Worlds of Welfare Capitalism*. Princeton, NJ: Princeton University Press.

Esping-Andersen, Gösta (1996). 'After the Golden Age? Welfare State Dilemmas in a Global Economy', pp. 1-31 in Gösta Esping-Andersen (ed.), *Welfare States in Transition*. London: Sage.

Festinger, Leon (1957). *A Theory of Cognitive Dissonance*. New York: Harper and Row.

Flanagan, Scott F. (1987). 'Values in Industrial Society', *American Political Science Review*, vol. 81, pp. 1303-1319.

Fuchs, Dieter, and Hans-Dieter Klingemann (1990). 'The Left-Right Schema', pp. 203-234 in M. Kent Jennings and Jan van Deth (eds.), *Continuities in Political Action*. Berlin and New York: Walter de Gruyter.

Gaasholt, Øystein, and Lise Togeby (1995). *I syv sind. Danskernes holdninger til flygtninge og indvandrere* [In two minds. Danish attitudes to refugees and immigrants]. Aarhus: Politica.

Gilljam, Michael, and Sören Holmberg (1993). *Väljarna inför 90-talet* [The voters during the nineties]. Stockholm: Norstedts Juridik.

Gilljam, Michael, and Sören Holmberg (1995). *Väljarnas val* [The Voters' Choice]. Stockholm: Fritzes.

Glans, Ingemar (1977). 'Socialdemokratiets väljarutveckling i Danmark i Skandinavisk perspektiv', pp. 99-124 in Erik Damgaard, Carsten Jarlov, Curt Sørensen (eds.), *Festskrift til Erik Rasmussen* [Essays in Honour of Erik Rasmussen]. Aarhus: Politica.

Glans, Ingemar (1984). 'Fremskridtspartiet — småborgerlig revolt, högerreaktion eller generell protest?' [The Progress Party — petty bourgeois revolt, rightwing reaction, or general protest?], pp. 195-228 in Jørgen Elklit and Ole Tonsgaard (eds.), *Valg og Vælgeradfærd. Studier i dansk politik* [Elections and Voting Behaviour. Studies in Danish Politics]. Aarhus: Politica.

Glans, Ingemar (1989). 'Langtidsudviklingen i dansk vælgeradfærd', pp. 52-83 i Jørgen Elklit and Ole Tonsgaard (eds.), *To Folketingsvalg. Vælgerholdninger og vælgeradfærd i 1987 og 1988* [Two General Elections. Voter Attitudes and Voting Behaviour in 1987 and 1988]. Aarhus: Politica.

Glans, Ingemar (1993). 'Det stabila klassröstandet. Utvecklingen i Danmark och Sverige'. Dep. of Political Science, University of Aarhus.

Goldthorpe, J.H., and David Lockwood et al. (1968-9). *The Affluent Worker*. Cambridge: Cambridge University Press.

Gorz, André (1981). *Økologi og frihed* [Translation of Ecologie et liberté]. Copenhagen: Politisk Revy.

Goul Andersen, Jørgen (1979). *Mellemlagene i Danmark*. Aarhus: Politica.

Goul Andersen, Jørgen (1982). 'Den folkelige tilslutning til socialpolitikken - en krise for velfærdsstaten?', pp. 175-209 in Dag Anckar, Erik Damgaard, Henry Valen (red.), *Partier, ideologier, väljare*. Åbo: Åbo Academy Press.

Goul Andersen, Jørgen (1984a). 'Udviklingen i sociale modsætningsforhold frem mod år 2000', pp. 13-89 i J. Goul Andersen, Finn Kenneth Hansen og Ole Borre, *Konflikt og tilpasning*. Egmont Fondens Fremtidsstudie no. 3. Copenhagen: Aschehoug.

Goul Andersen, Jørgen (1984b). *Kvinder og politik* [Women and Politics]. Aarhus: Politica.

Goul Andersen, Jørgen (1984c). 'Aspekter af den politiske kultur i Danmark efter 1970', pp. 17-49 i E. Damgaard (red.), *Dansk demokrati under forandring* [The Changing Danish Democracy]. Kbh.: Schultz.

Goul Andersen, Jørgen (1984d). 'Decline of Class Voting or Change in Class Voting? Social Class and Party Choice in Denmark in the 1970's', *European Journal of Political Research*, vol. 12 (1984), pp. 243-59.

Goul Andersen, Jørgen (1988). 'Arbejderklassen i det postindustrielle (?) samfund - Nogle empiriske pejlinger', *Politica*, vol. 20, no. 2, 1988, pp. 146-66.

References   337

Goul Andersen, Jørgen (1989). 'Social klasse og parti', pp. 176-207 in Jørgen Elklit and Ole Tonsgaard (eds.), *To Folketingsvalg. Vælgerholdninger og vælgeradfærd i 1987 og 1988* [Two General Elections. Voter Attitudes and Voting Behaviour in 1987 and 1988]. . Aarhus: Politica.

Goul Andersen, Jørgen (1990). 'Denmark: Environment Conflict and the 'Greening' of the Labour Movement', *Scandinavian Political Studies*, vol. 13, no. 2, pp. 185-209.

Goul Andersen, Jørgen (1990a). ''Environmentalism, 'New Politics' and Postindustrialism: Some Theoretical Perspectives', *Scandinavian Political Studies* vol. 13, pp. 101-18.

Goul Andersen, Jørgen (1991a). *Class Theory in Transition*. Aarhus: Dep. of Political Science, Aarhus University.

Goul Andersen, Jørgen (1991b). 'Vælgernes vurderinger af kriseårsager', pp. 61-80 in Eggert Petersen et al., *De trivsomme og arbejdsomme danskere*. Krisen og den politisk-psykologiske udvikling 1982-90. Aarhus: Dep. of Psychology/Aarhus University Press.

Goul Andersen, Jørgen (1992). *Politisk mistillid i Danmark* [Political distrust in Denmark]. Aarhus: Institute of Political Science.

Goul Andersen, Jørgen (1992a). 'The Decline of Class Voting Revisited', pp. 91-107 in Peter Gundelach and Karen Siune (eds.), *From Voters to Participants*. Aarhus: Politica.

Goul Andersen, Jørgen (1992b). 'Sources of Welfare-State Support in Denmark: Self-Interest or Way of Life?', *International Journal of Sociology*, vol. 22(4), pp. 25-48.

Goul Andersen, Jørgen (1993). *Politik og Samfund i forandring*. Copenhagen: Columbus.

Goul Andersen, Jørgen (1994). 'Samfundsøkonomi, interesser og politisk adfærd' [National economy, interests, and political behaviour], pp. 15-136 in Eggert Petersen (ed.), *Livskvalitet og holdninger i det variable nichesamfund* [Life Quality and Attitudes in the Variable Niche Society]. Aarhus: Institute of Psychology.

Goul Andersen, Jørgen (1995). *De ledige ressourcer*. Copenhagen: Ugebrevet Mandag Morgen.

Goul Andersen, Jørgen (1995b). 'Valgkampen og valget 1994. Valgkampens meningsmålinger'. *Working Paper from the Danish Electoral Programme*, no. 3.

Goul Andersen, Jørgen (1996a). 'Hvordan skal arbejdsløsheden bekæmpes?', pp. 169-258 in Eggert Petersen et al. (1996), *Danskernes trivsel, holdninger og selvansvarlighed under 'opsvinget'. Træk af den politisk-psykologiske udvikling 1982-86-88-90-94*. Aarhus: Dep. of Psychology/Aarhus University Press.

Goul Andersen, Jørgen (1996b). 'Marginalisation, Citizenship and the Economy: The Capacity of the Universalist Welfare State in Denmark', pp. 155-202 in Erik Oddvar Eriksen and Jørn Loftager (eds.), *The Rationality of the Welfare State*. Oslo: Scandinavian University Press.

Goul Andersen, Jørgen (1996c). *Marginalisering, Medborgerskap og generøse velferdsydelser*. Bergen: LOS-Senter notat 9604.

Goul Andersen, Jørgen (1996d). *Membership and Participation in Voluntary Associations in Scandinavia, in a Comparative Perspective*. Department of Economics, Politics and Public Administration, Aalborg University.

Goul Andersen, Jørgen (1997). 'The Scandinavian Welfare Model in Crisis? Achievements and Problems of the Danish Welfare State in an Age of Unemployment and Low Growth', *Scandinavian Political Studies*, vol. 20, pp. 1-31.

Goul Andersen, Jørgen (forthcoming). 'Krisebevidsthed og velfærdsholdninger i en højkonjunktur', i *Festskrift til Eggert Petersen*.

Goul Andersen, Jørgen, and Tor Bjørklund (1990). 'Structural Changes and New Cleavages: The Progress Parties in Denmark and Norway', *Acta Sociologica*, vol. 33 (3), pp. 195-217.

Goul Andersen, Jørgen, and Tor Bjørklund (1997). 'Radical Right-Wing Populism in Scandinavia: From Tax Revolt to Neo-Liberalism and Xenophobia', forthcoming in Paul Hainsworth (ed.), *The Extreme Right in Europe and the USA*, 2.ed. London: Pinter Publishers.

Goul Andersen, Jørgen, and Peter Munk Christiansen (1991). *Skatter uden velfærd. De offentlige udgifter i international belysning* [Taxes without Welfare]. Copenhagen: Jurist- og Økonomforbundets Forlag.

Goul Andersen, Jørgen, and Jens Hoff (1992). *Reluctant Europeans and the European Union: Citizenship and Democratic Deficit*. Copenhagen: Institute of Political Science.

Goul Andersen, Jørgen, and Jens Hoff (1995). 'Lighed i den politiske deltagelse', pp. 30-76 in Morten Madsen, Hans Jørgen Nielsen and Gunnar Sjöblom (red.), *Demokratiets mangfoldighed: Tendenser i dansk politik*. Copenhagen: Forlaget Politiske Studier.

Goul Andersen, Jørgen, and Jens Hoff (forthcoming 1997). *Democratic Citizenship in the Scandinavian Welfare States*. London: Macmillan

Gundelach, Peter, and Ole Riis (1992). *Danskernes værdier*. [The Values of the Danes]. Copenhagen: Forlaget Sociologi.

Habermas, Jürgen (1973). *Legitimationsprobleme im Spätkapitalismus*. Frankfurt: Suhrkamp.

Habermas, Jürgen (1981). *Theorie des Kommunikativen Handelns, I-II*. Frankfurt: Suhrkamp.

Habermas, Jürgen (1994). 'Citizenship and National Identity', pp. 20-35 in Bart van Steenbergen (ed.), *The Condition of Citizenship*. London: Sage.

Heider, Fritz (1958). *The Psychology of Interpersonal Relations*. New York: Wiley.

Hibbs, Douglas (1987). *The American Political Economy: Macro-economic and Electoral Politics*. Harvard: Harvard University Press.

Hibbs, Douglas (1993). *Solidarity or Egoism*. Aarhus: Aarhus University Press.

Hildebrandt, Kai, and Russell J. Dalton (1978). 'The New Politics: Political Change or Sunshine Politics?', in Max Kaase and Klaus von Beyme (eds.), *Elections and Parties*.

Hoff, Jens (1989). *Klasseanalysens problemområder. Teoretisk og empirisk klasseanalyse i Danmark*. Ph.D. Thesis, Dep. of Political Science, University of Copenhagen.

Hoff, Jens (1993). 'Medborgerskab, brugerrolle og magt', pp. 75-106 in Johannes Andersen et al., *Medborgerskab. Demokrati og politisk deltagelse*. Herning: Systime.

Hoff, Jens (1995). 'Micropower. The Politics of Welfare State Roles. User Participation in Scandinavia'. Dep. of Political Science, University of Copenhagen. Working Paper 1995/17.

Hoff, Jens, and Jørgen Goul Andersen (1986). 'Reformismens krise og Socialdemokratiets diskursive potens'. Dep. of Political Science, Copenhagen University.

Holmberg, Sören (1981). *Svenska väljare* [Swedish voters]. Stockholm: LiberFörlag.

Holmberg, Sören (1992). 'The Undermining of a Stable Party System', pp. 61-107 in Peter Gundelach and Karen Siune (eds.), *From Voters to Participants*. Aarhus: Politica,

Holmberg, Sören, and Mikael Gilljam (1987). *Väljare och val i Sverige* [Voters and Elections in Sweden]. Stockholm: Bonnier Fakta.

Huntington, Samuel P. (1975). 'The United States', in Michel J. Grozier, Samuel P. Huntington and J. Watanuki, *The Crisis of Democracy*. New York: New York University Press.

Huseby, Beate (1995). 'Attitudes toward the Size of Government', chapter 4 in Ole Borre and Elinor Scarbrough (eds.), *The Scope of Government. Beliefs in Government. Volume Three*. London: Oxford University Press.

Hviid Nielsen, Torben (1994). 'Velfærdsstatens attituder: Ambivalens og dilemmaer', pp. 93-124 in Johannes Andersen and Lars Torpe (eds.), *Demokrati og politisk kultur. Rids af et demokratisk medborgerskab*. Herning: Systime.

Højrup, Thomas (1983). *Det glemte folk* [The forgotten people]. Copenhagen: Institut for europæisk folkelivsforskning.

Inglehart, Ronald (1971). 'The Silent Revolution in Europe: Intergenerational Change in Post-Industrial Societies', *American Political Science Review*, vol. 65, pp. 991-1007.

Inglehart, Ronald (1977). *The Silent Revolution. Changing Values and Political Styles Among the Western Publics*. Princeton, N.J.: Princeton University Press.

Inglehart, Ronald (1990). *Culture Shift in Advanced Industrial Society*. Princeton, N.J.: Princeton University Press.

Inglehart, Ronald, and Hans-Dieter Klingemann (1976). 'Party Identification, Ideological Preference and the Left-Right Dimension among Western Publics', in Ian Budge, Ivor Crewe, and Dennis Farlie (eds.), *Party Identification and Beyond*. London and New York: Wiley.

Inglehart, Ronald, and Jacques-René Rabier (1986). 'Political Realignment in Advanced Industrial Society: From Class-Based Politics to Quality-of-Life Politics', *Government and Opposition*, vol. 21, pp. 456-79.

ISSP 1985. Role of Government (1985). Köln: Zentralarchiv für empirische Sozialforschung der Universität zu Köln.

ISSP 1990. Role of Government II (1990). Köln: Zentralarchiv für empirische Sozialforschung der Universität zu Köln.

Janda, Kenneth (1980). *Political Parties. A Cross-National Survey*. New York: Free Press.

Jensen, Per (1989). *Den svenske model — forudsætninger, funktionsmåde og fremtidsudsigter*, vol. 1-2. København: Sociologisk Institut.

Jensen, Per (1996). *Komparative velfærdssystemer*. København: Samfundslitteratur.

Jenssen, Anders Todal (1993). *Verdival. Ny massepolitikk i Norge* [Value choice. New mass politics in Norway]. Oslo: Ad Notam Gyldendal.

King, Anthony (1975). 'Overload: Problems of Governing in the 1970s', *Political Studies*, vol. 23, pp. 284-296.

Knutsen, Oddbjørn (1988). 'The Impact of Structural and Ideological Party Cleavages in West European Democracies: A Comparative Empirical Analysis', *British Journal of Political Science*, vol. 18, pp. 323-52.

Knutsen, Oddbjørn (1995). 'Left-Right Materialist value Orientations', in Jan W. van Deth and Elinor Scarbrough, *The Impact of Values*. Oxford: Oxford University Press.

Kolberg, Jon Eivind and Esping-Andersen, Gösta (1991). 'Welfare States and Employment Regimes', *International Journal of Sociology*, vol. 21(3), pp. 3-35.

Kristensen, Ole P. (1980). 'The Logic of Political-Bureaucratic Decision-Making as a Cause of Governmental Growth', *European Journal of Political Research*, vol. 8, pp. 249-264.

Kristensen, Ole P. (1982). 'Voter Attitudes and Public Spending: Is There a Relationship?', *European Journal of Political Research*, vol. 10, pp. 35-52.

Kristensen, Ole P. (1984). 'On the Futility of the 'Demand Approach' to Public-Sector Growth', *European Journal of Political Research*, vol. 12, pp. 309-324.

Kristensen, Ole P. (1987). *Væksten i den offentlige sektor. Institutioner og Politik*. Copenhagen: Jurist- og Økonomforbundets Forlag.

Lazarsfeld, Paul F., Bernard Berelson, and Hazel Gaudet (1944). *The People's Choice*. Chicago: University of Chicago Press.

Lindbeck, Asser and Snower, Dennis (1988). *Involuntary Unemployment as an Insider-Outsider Dilemma*. Stockholm: Institute for International Economic Studies.

Lipset, Seymour Martin (1960). *Political Man*. London: Heinemann.

Lipset, Seymour Martin (1964). 'The Modernisation of Contemporary European Politics', in S.M. Lipset, *Revolution and Counterrevolution*. London: Heinemann.

Lipset, Seymour Martin (1981). *Political Man. Expanded and Updated Edition*. Baltimore: Johns Hopkins University Press.

Lipset, Seymour M., and Stein Rokkan (1967). 'Cleavage Structures, Party Systems, and Voter Alignment: An Introduction', pp. 1-64 in Seymour M. Lipset and Stein Rokkan (eds.), *Party Systems and Voter Alignments*. New York: The Free Press.

Listhaug, Ola (1989). *Citizens, Parties and Norwegian Electoral Politics 1957-1985. An Empirical Study*. Trondheim: Tapir.

Loftager, Jørn (1996). 'Citizens' Income - a New Welfare State Strategy?', pp. 134-154 in Erik Oddvar Eriksen and Jørn Loftager (eds.), *The Rationality of the Welfare State*. Oslo: Scandinavian University Press.

Logue, John (1982). *Socialism and Abundance*. Copenhagen: Akademisk Forlag.

Luttbeg, Norman R. (ed.) (1981). *Public Opinion and Public Policy*. Ithaca, Ill.: F.E. Peacock Publishers.

Maddens, Bart (1996). 'Directional Theory of Issue Voting: The Case of the 1991 Parliamentary Elections in Flanders', *Electoral Studies*, vol. 15, pp. 53-70.

Marshall, T.H. (1949). *Class, Citizenship and Social Development.* Cambridge: Cambridge University Press.

Merrill, Samuel (1995). 'Discriminating between the Directional and Proximity Spatial Models of Electoral Competition', *Electoral Studies*, vol. 14, pp. 273-287.

Middendorp, C.P. (1978). *Progressiveness and Conservatism.* Hague: Mouton.

Miller, Arthur M. (1974). 'Political Issues and Trust in Government 1964-1970', *American Political Science Review*, vol. 68, pp. 951-972.

Miller, Arthur M., and Ola Listhaug (1990). 'Political Parties and Confidence in Government: A Comparison of Norway, Sweden and the United States', *British Journal of Political Science*, vol. 20, pp. 357-386.

Miller, Warren E., and Teresa E. Levitin (1976). *Leadership and Change: Presidential Elections from 1952 to 1976.* Cambridge, Mass.: Winthrop Publishers, Inc.

Ministry of Finance (1988). *Moderniseringsredegørelse 1988.* Copenhagen: Ministry of Finance.

Ministry of Finance (1993). *Borgernes syn på den offentlige sektor*, December 1993. Copenhagen: Ministry of Finance.

Ministry of Finance (1995a). *Borgernes syn på den offentlige sektor* [The Citizens' Views on the Public Sector], April 1995. Copenhagen: Ministry of Finance.

Ministry of Finance (1995b). *Finansredegørelse 1995.* Copenhagen: Ministry of Finance.

Ministry of Finance (1996a). *Budgetredegørelse 1996.* Copenhagen: Ministry of Finance.

Ministry of Finance (1996c). *Borgernes syn på den offentlige sektor*, December 1996. Copenhagen: Ministry of Finance.

Ministry of Labour et al. (1989). *Hvidbog om arbejdsmarkedets strukturproblemer.* Copenhagen: Ministry of Labour.

Ministry of Taxation (1990). *Skattepolitisk redegørelse 1990.* Copenhagen: Ministry of Taxation.

Mærkedahl, Inge, Anders Rosdahl, and Ivan Thaulow (1992). *Genvej til beskæftigelse? En sammenfatning af evalueringer af aktiveringsindsatsen for langtidsledige.* Copenhagen: Socialforskningsinstituttet.

Nannestad, Peter (1991). *Danish Design or British Disease?.* Aarhus: Aarhus University Press.

Nannestad, Peter, and Martin Paldam (1990). The Demand for the Public Sector in the Rich Welfare State of Denmark. Memo 1990:30. Dep. of Economics, Aarhus University.

Nannestad, Peter, and Martin Paldam (1995). 'It's the Government's Fault. A Cross-Section Study of Voting in Denmark, 1990-93', *European Journal of Political Research*, vol. 28, pp. 33-62.

Nannestad, Peter, and Martin Paldam (1997). 'From the Pocketbook of the Welfare Man. A Pooled Cross-Section Study of Economic Voting in Denmark 1986-92', *British Journal of Political Science*, vol. 27, pp. 119-136.

Nie, Norman H., with Kristi Andersen (1974). 'Mass Belief Systems Revisited: Political Change and Attitude Structure', *Journal of Politics*, vol. 36, pp. 540-587.

Nielsen, Hans Jørgen (1976). 'Politiske meninger og vælgeradfærd', i Ole Borre et al., *Vælgere i 70'erne*. Copenhagen: Akademisk Forlag.

Nielsen, Hans Jørgen (1993). *EF på valg*. Copenhagen: Columbus.

Nørregaard, Carl (1996). *Arbejde og tilbagetrækning i 90'erne — og fremtidens pensionister*. Working Paper. Copenhagen: Socialforskningsinstituttet.

Offe, Claus (1984). *Contradictions of the Welfare State* (ed. John Keane). London: Hutchinson.

Offe, Claus (1996). 'Full Employment: Asking the Wrong Question?', pp. 120-33 in Erik Oddvar Eriksen and Jørn Loftager (eds.), *The Rationality of the Welfare State*. Oslo: Scandinavian University Press.

Oskarson, Maria (1994). *Klassröstning i Sverige. Rationalitet, lojalitet eller bara slentrian*. Stockholm: Nerenius and Santérus Förlag.

Oskarson, Maria (1996). 'Skeptiska kvinnor - entusiatiska män' [Sceptical women — enthusiastic men]. In M. Gilljam and Sören Holmberg, *Ett knappt ja til EU* [A bare yes to EU]. Stockholm: Norstedt.

Paldam, Martin, and Friedrich Schneider (1980). 'The Macroeconomic Aspects of Government and Opposition Popularity in Denmark, 1957-78', *Nationaløkonomisk Tidsskrift*, vol. 118, pp. 149-70.

Pedersen, Peder, and Nina Smith (1995). 'Unemployment and Incentives', pp. 193-226 in Viby G. Mogensen (ed.), *Work Incentives in the Danish Welfare State. New Empirical Evidence*. Aarhus: Aarhus University Press.

Petersen, Eggert et al. (1987). *Danskernes tilværelse under krisen, I-II*. Aarhus: Aarhus University Press.

Petersen, Eggert et al. (1996). *Danskernes trivsel, holdninger og selvansvarlighed under 'opsvinget'. Træk af den politisk-psykologiske udvikling 1982-86-88-90-94.* Aarhus: Dep. of Psychology/Aarhus University Press.

Pettersen, Per Arnt (1995). 'The Welfare State: The Security Dimension', pp. 198-233 in Ole Borre and Elinor Scarbrough (eds.), *The Scope of Government. Beliefs in Government volume three.* Oxford: Oxford University Press.

Pomper, Gerald M. (1972). 'From Confusion to Clarity: Issues and American Voters, 1956-1968', *American Political Science Review*, vol. 66, pp. 415-428. Comments by Richard A. Brody and Benjamin I. Page, pp. 450-458, and by John H. Kessel, pp. 459-465. Rejoinder pp. 466-467.

Poulantzas, Nicos (1978). *Classes in Contemporary Capitalism.* London: Verso.

Przeworski, Adam (1977). 'Proletariat into Class: The Process of Class Formation from Karl Kautsky's 'The Class Struggle' to Recent Controversies', *Politics & Society*, vol. 7, no. 4.

Pöntinen, S., and Hannu Uusitalo (1986). *The Legitimacy of the Welfare State: Social Security Opinions in Finland 1975-1985.* Report no. 15., The Finnish Gallup Co.

Rabinowitz, George, Stuart E. Macdonald, and Ola Listhaug (1991). 'New Players in an Old Game: Party Strategy in Multiparty Systems', *Comparative Political Studies*, vol. 24, no. 2, pp. 147-185.

Rabinowitz, George, and Stuart E. Macdonald (1989). 'A Directional Theory of Issue Voting', *American Political Science Review*, vol. 83, pp. 93-121.

Regeringen (1993). *Ny kurs mod bedre tider.* Copenhagen: Regeringen.

Rogowski, Ronald (1974). *Rational Legitimacy: A Theory of Political Support.* Princeton: Princeton University Press.

Rokkan, Stein (1970). *Citizens, Elections, Parties.* Oslo: Universitetsforlaget.

Rold Andersen, Bent (1984). *Kan vi bevare velfærdsstaten?* Copenhagen: AKF.

Roller, Edeltraud (1995). 'Political Agendas and Beliefs about the Scope of government', chapter 4 in Ole Borre and Elinor Scarbrough (eds.), *The Scope of Government.* London: Oxford University Press.

Roller, Edeltraud (1995b). 'The Welfare State: The Equality Dimension', chapter 7 in Ole Borre and Elinor Scarbrough (eds.), *The Scope of Government.* London: Oxford University Press.

Rose, Richard, and Guy Peters (1978). *Can Governments Go Bankrupt?*, New York: Basic Books.

Rothstein, Bo (ed.) (1993). *Politik som organisation.* Stockholm: SNS Förlag.

Rusk, Jerrold M., and Ole Borre (1974). 'The Changing Party Space in Danish Voter Perceptions', *European Journal of Political Science*, vol. 2, no. 4, pp. 329-361.

Sainsbury, Diana (1987). 'Class Voting and Left Voting in Scandinavia: The Impact of Different Operationalizations of the Working Class', *European Journal of Political Research*, vol. 15, pp. 507-26.

Sandmo, Agnar (1991). 'Presidential Address: Economists and the Welfare State', *European Economic Review*, vol. 35 (2-3), pp. 213-39.

Siune, Karen, and Ole Borre (1975). 'Setting the Agenda for a Danish Election', *Journal of Communication*, vol. 25, pp. 65-73.

Siune, Karen, Palle Svensson, and Ole Tonsgaard (1992). — *det blev et nej* [It was a no]. Aarhus: Politica.

Siune, Karen, Palle Svensson, and Ole Tonsgaard (1994). *Fra et nej til et ja* [From a no to a yes]. Aarhus: Politica.

Sorensen, R. (1992). 'Fiscal Illusion: Nothing but Illusion?', *European Journal of Political Research*, vol. 22, pp. 279-305.

Stewart, Marianne C., and Harold D. Clarke (1992). 'The (Un)Importance of Party Leaders: Leader Images and Party Choice in the 1987 British Election', *The Journal of Politics*, vol. 54, no. 2, pp. 447-470.

Stokes, Donald E. (1963). 'Spatial Models of Party Competition', *American Political Science Review*, vol. 57, pp. 368-377.

Svallfors, Stefan (1989). *Vem älskar välfärdsstaten?* Lund: Arkiv Avhandlingsserie.

Svensson, Palle (1995). *Demokratiets krise?* [The crisis of democracy?]. Aarhus: Politica.

Svensson, Palle, and Lise Togeby (1986). *Politisk opbrud. De nye mellemlags græsrodsdeltagelse*. Aarhus: Politica.

Svensson, Palle, and Lise Togeby (1991). *Højrebølge?* [Right Wave?]. Aarhus: Forlaget Politica.

Svensson, Palle, and Lise Togeby (1992). 'Post-Industrialism and New Social and Political Classes', pp. 108-131 in Peter Gundelach and Karen Siune (eds.), *From Voters to Participants*. Aarhus: Politica.

Thomsen, Søren Risbjerg (1995). 'The 1994 Parliamentary Election in Denmark', *Electoral Studies*, vol. 14, no. 3.

Togeby, Lise (1994). *Fra tilskuere til deltagere. Den kollektive politiske mobilisering af kvinder i Danmark i 1970'erne og 1980'erne*. Aarhus: Forlaget Politica.

Tonsgaard, Ole (1992). 'A Theoretical Model of Referendum Behaviour', in Peter Gundelach and Karen Siune (eds.), *From Voters to Participants*. Aarhus: Politica.

Udredningsudvalget (1992). *Rapport fra udredningsudvalget om arbejdsmarkedets strukturproblemer*. Copenhagen: Udredningsudvalget.

Valen, Henry, Bernt Aardal, and Gunnar Vogt (1990). *Endring og kontinuitet. Stortingsvalget 1989* [Change and continuity. The general election 1989]. Oslo: Central Bureau of Statistics in Norway.

Visser, Jelle (1991). 'Trends in Trade Union Membership', chapter 4 (pp. 97-134) in *OECD Employment Outlook*, July 1991. Paris: OECD.

Wilensky, Harold (1975). *The Welfare State and Equality*. Berkeley, Cal.: University of California Press.

Worre, Torben (1980). 'Class parties and class voting in the Scandinavian Countries', *Scandinavian Political Studies*, vol. 3, pp. 299-320.

Wright, Erik Olin (1978). *Class, Crisis and the State*. London: New Left Books.

Wright, Erik Olin (1985). *Classes*. London: Verso.

Wright, Erik Olin, and K.-Y. Shin (1988). 'Temporality and Class Analysis', *Sociological Theory*, vol. 6, pp. 58-84.

Zeuner, Lili, and Carl Nørregaard (1991). *Fortjent otium. En sociologisk belysning af ældres arbejdsophør*. Rapport 1991:10. Copenhagen: Socialforskningsinstituttet.

INDEX

Australia 96, 200
Authoritarian attitudes or values 53, 63, 64, 154, 159, 175, 302
Authoritarianism 150, 153

Balance of payment 88, 95, 249, 254
Balance of trade 20
Beauty-seeking 14, 204-206, 213-214
Belief systems 191
Birth cohorts 169-173, 177, 187, 188
Britain 11, 33, 96, 192, 200, 201, 204, 301

Child care 206, 207, 230, 231, 234, 235
Class conflict 48, 142
Class consciousness 116, 117, 140, 142, 150, 153
Class identification 116-118, 139-150, 154, 159, 215
Class interests 48, 116, 117, 154, 162, 174, 182-184
Class polarisation 136-139, 150, 245
Class voting 12, 13, 114-118, 120-125, 127-130, 132, 136, 138, 139, 144, 146, 154, 158, 159, 189, 329
Cohort analysis 168
Collectivism 63, 139
Columbia school 37
Communist parties 39, 181, 192
Competitiveness 256, 276, 331
Conservatism 46, 190, 210
Contagion effect 178
Crisis awareness 218, 228
Culture 14, 15, 43, 53, 88-91, 192, 197, 202-205, 207, 210-213, 225, 227, 231, 252, 313, 314

Day care for children 200
Dealignment 25
Defence 30, 200, 203-205, 207, 208, 210-214, 314
Demands:
- input, or policy demands 191-196, 288, 300, 301,
- for spending, see spending attitudes

- budget demands 200-203, 208, 211, 300, 311, 314, 318, 320
- for welfare 225-228, 231
- demand/supply strategy 252
- for EU policy 283-287
- for referenda, see referenda
- demand overload 194, 196, 202, 217, 218, 309, 310, 312-314
Development aid, developing nations 41, 42, 44, 200
Directional model 27, 69, 73-75, 79, 80
Directional score 73, 74, 78
Discourse 12, 71, 332
Discussion 50, 58, 97, 135, 189, 218, 224, 242, 251, 330
Division of labour 193, 218, 236
Dutch 201

East Europe 21, 36, 39, 282, 285, 286, 288, 289, 296
EC 11, 281, 283-288, 291, 294, 304, 308
Economic agenda 89, 91, 107
Economic equality 11, 29, 30, 42, 46, 136-139, 181, 210, 297
Economic growth 21, 40, 42, 43, 67, 68, 95, 113, 195, 217, 258, 265, 276, 288, 325
Economic policy 11, 70, 71, 79, 82, 87, 94, 156, 157, 159, 184, 194, 198, 304-306, 308, 325
Education:
- and new politics 13, 40, 61-64, 329
- expansion of 14, 40, 160
- issue 88-91
- better-educated 174-180
- spending on 200, 203-205, 207, 210-212, 225-226, 230-232, 235
- programmes 250-251, 260-262, 265-267, 275, 277, 331
- effect on unemployment policy 270-272
- sector 216
- policy 204-205
- and political trust 315-318

Issue voting 13, 34, 35, 65, 68-69, 75, 85, 112, 117, 136, 139, 140, 145, 146, 148, 300, 304
Italy, Italian 181, 200, 204, 301

Job creation 206, 207
Job leave 21, 270

Kindergardens 226

Large family support 207
Law enforcement 203-205, 210-212
Leadership 12, 36, 86, 96, 98, 100, 106, 107, 109, 112, 113, 151, 154, 158, 222, 302, 328
Legitimacy crisis 194
Lego toy firm 60
Liberalism 14, 20, 21, 30, 190, 194, 199, 201, 211, 215
Local community 60

Maastricht Treaty 11, 280, 281, 292, 293, 295, 298, 308, 332
Marginal utility 53, 194
Marginal voter 37
Marginalisation 219, 220, 236, 242, 244, 246, 247
Market liberalism 14, 20, 30
Median voter 193
Middle mass 136, 217, 231-233
Mortality 170
MPM dimension 50, 51, 199, 204

NATO 11, 16, 36, 146, 147, 184
Netherlands 192
New middle class 13, 115, 116, 118, 120, 121, 125, 127, 128, 131, 155, 156, 189
New politics agenda 70, 71, 89-90, 285
New politics attitudes 58, 71, 327
New politics dimension 40, 41, 43, 45, 46, 48, 49, 51, 52, 55-58, 61, 64, 207, 208, 211, 315, 317, 327, 330
New politics hypothesis 82
New politics index 46, 47, 62, 63, 285
New politics issues 46, 48, 56, 58, 59, 68-70, 150, 153-155, 157, 285, 327
New politics parties 56
New politics position 48-50, 57, 58, 61-63, 70, 147, 158, 209, 212-213, 286, 316
New politics scale 209, 316

New politics theory 47, 48, 50, 52, 64, 70, 158, 194, 202, 284-285
New politics thesis 40, 41, 46, 56, 197, 201
Nonvoters 166
Normal vote 326
Norway, Norwegian 23, 26, 33, 41, 43, 63, 83, 114, 121-124, 128, 152, 195, 196, 201, 204, 281, 284, 288, 294, 295, 304, 331
Nursery homes 226

Oil crisis 20, 249
Old age pensions 89, 200, 201, 203, 204, 207, 208, 210, 211, 312, 313
Old middle class 13, 115, 116, 120, 122, 189
Old politics dimension 40, 41, 43, 46, 49, 51, 55, 56, 61, 64, 68, 70, 207, 285, 287, 317
Old politics index 46, 47
Old politics issues 46, 58, 70, 71, 150, 153, 154
Old politics position 47, 48, 50, 52, 57, 61, 158, 209, 212, 286, 316
Old politics scale 209, 316
Opinion polls 19, 86, 291
Order-seeking 14, 204-206, 213-214
Outsiders 218-220, 236, 239, 242, 245, 246, 253, 276

Parental leave 226, 238, 250, 255, 256, 331
Paternalism 218, 219, 222, 230, 233, 234
Pensioners 27, 121, 122, 212, 218, 237-242, 245
Performance of governments 94, 100
Performance ratings 13, 87, 92, 99, 102, 107, 109, 110
Period effects 46, 52
Personal economy 111
Physical security 203, 211
Police 14, 200, 203, 207, 208, 213, 214, 227, 313, 314
Policy demands 191-195
Policy distance 13, 15, 65, 67, 68, 74, 76, 79, 81, 82, 283, 287-291, 294-298, 301, 303, 304, 305, 307-314, 317-323, 331
Policy output 191, 192, 216, 300, 323

350

Voting and Political Attitudes in Denmark